CU00747252

THE COMÉDIE-FRANÇAISE

BY THE SAME AUTHOR

Rameau

A Royal Shakespeare Company Book

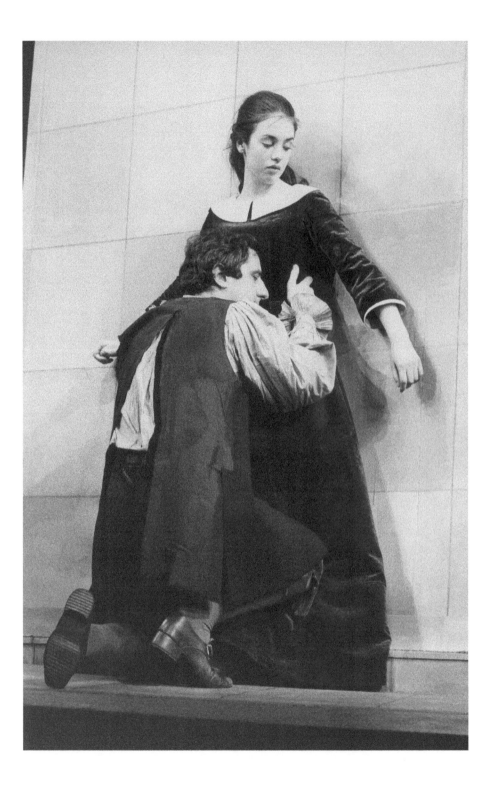

THE COMÉDIE-FRANÇAISE

from Molière to Éric Ruf

SIMON TROWBRIDGE

ENGLANCE *PRESS*

First published by
Englance Press, Oxford, in 2020

ISBN 978-1-9997305-5-0

Frontispiece:

1. *L'École des femmes* by Molière, Richelieu, 1973. Jean-Paul Roussillon (mise
en scène), Jacques Le Marquet (décor and costumes). Michel Aumont
(Arnolphe), Isabelle Adjani (Agnès). Photograph by Patrice Picot.

To Claire

Contents

Preface   15
Introduction   17

1 MOLIÈRE   23
1   Jean-Baptiste and Madeleine   25
2   On the Road   28
3   Paris and Fame   29
4   Final Years   38
5   Racine   42

2 THE TROUPE   43
1   The Creation of the Comédie-Française   45
2   The Age of Voltaire   49
3   Shakespeare Enters the Repertoire   66
4   The Saint-Val Affair   71
5   Figaro   75

3 REVOLUTION AND WAR   85
1   Talma   87
2   Olympe des Gouges   92
3   Terror   96
4   Napoléon   104

4 LE DRAME ROMANTIQUE   109
1   The Shakespeare Effect   111
2   Dumas   117
3   Hugo and the Battle of Hernani   120
4   Le Roi s'amuse and Lucrèce Borgia   124
5   Aftermath   127

5 FROM THE SECOND EMPIRE TO THE COMMUNE		129
1	Alfred de Musset	131
2	Theatre Under the Second Empire	135
3	The Siege	138
4	The First Voyage to England	145
6 THE BELLE ÉPOQUE		155
1	Mounet-Sully and the Return of Sarah	157
2	The Second Voyage to England	160
3	'Organise the theatre!'	170
4	Thermidor	174
5	Hamlet	176
6	Tragedy	180
7 THE GREAT WAR		185
1	In Paris	187
2	At the Front	191
8 THE INTERWAR YEARS		199
1	Changes to the Repertoire	201
2	Internal Disputes	203
3	Jacques Copeau and the Vieux-Colombier	207
4	The 1930s	211
9 THE OCCUPATION		223
1	Copeau as Administrator	225
2	Jean-Louis Vaudoyer	230
3	Montherlant's La Reine morte	233
4	Claudel's Le Soulier de satin	236
5	The Liberation	240
6	The Old Vic and the Comédie	246
10 THE FOURTH REPUBLIC		249
1	The Post-War Years	251
2	The Era of Jean Weber	255
11 THE RETURN OF PIERRE DUX		261
1	Maurice Escande	264
2	May 1968	269
3	Pierre Dux	272
4	Jacques Toja	283

12 THE TURN OF THE MILLENNIUM   285
1   Vitez and Lassalle   288
2   Jean-Pierre Miquel   294

13 TOWARDS THE PRESENT   305
1   Marcel Bozonnet   307
2   Muriel Mayette   312

14 ÉRIC RUF   329
1   A Clear Vision   331
2   On the Stage   334
3   La Cité du Théâtre   347

15 LA MAISON DE SHAKESPEARE?   353

NOTEBOOK   361
I The Troupe in 2019/20   363
II General Administrators since 1859   365
III Seasons 2002/03 to 2019/20   368
IV Authors and Plays 2000/01 to 2019/20   402
V Prominent Directors 2000/01 to 2019/20   412
VI Shakespeare at the Comédie-Française   418
VII Performances in Great Britain   422
VIII Sociétaires 1680 to 2020   425

Works Cited   431

List of Illustrations   438

Index   440

Le Théâtre-Français n'est pas un théâtre comme less autres. Quand on y apporte un manuscript, il y a les bustes qui vous regardent.

ALEXANDRE DUMAS *fils*

Preface

What follows is a narrative history of the Comédie-Française, from the troupe's creation in Paris in the late 17th century to the current year. One of the pleasures of writing the book was to discover that the narrative branched out in ways that were unexpected, for the Comédie-Française has been impacted by many of the great events in its country's history.

More often than not, I refer to the Comédie-Française as 'the Comédie'. I sometimes use the term 'Comédiens-français' (the French-actors) when discussing the actors collectively. In some of the quoted sources, the troupe is referred to as the Théâtre-Français, its alternative name.

Translations are my own unless otherwise attributed, or unless a corresponding footnote begins 'Quoted in' as opposed to 'Quoted (in French) in'. Also in the footnotes, when a member of the troupe is first mentioned in the text in a significant way, I provide brief biographical information – name, date and place of birth (if known), followed by: year joined the Comédie-Française, year made a sociétaire, year departed, in the form: CF j1970 s1976 d2010.

I'd like to mention here four essential websites. The Comédie-Française's official site is very well designed and contains a wealth of archival material. A sister site, the *Comédie-Française Registers Project*, managed by the Bibliothèque-Musée de la Comédie-Française, covers the troupe's first hundred years and contains vital data for researchers. The Bibliothèque nationale de France's *Gallica* site provides many relevant documents and images. *Les Archives du*

Spectacle is a searchable database of French theatre and opera productions.

My thanks go to Claire Pérotin, for her encouragement and suggestions; to Alice Bachman; to my sister Dinah; to Brigitte Enguérand, Christophe Raynaud de Lage and Alain Richard for allowing me to include a number of their photographs; and to Sian Phillips of Bridgeman Images for her help in sourcing photographs by Pascal Victor. The photographs by Raphael Gaillarde were sourced via Getty Images. Full credits are given in the list of illustrations at the end of the book.

Terry Hands graciously spoke to me about his time working as a director at the Comédie-Française during the 1970s.

My father died during the writing of this book. A pioneer in the field of Computational Electromagnetics, he was as passionate about the arts as he was about physics. Although poor eyesight and the onset of dementia meant that he was unable to read the manuscript, our many conversations on the topic helped me to clarify my ideas and encouraged me to keep going.

Introduction

2. *La Nuit des rois* by Shakespeare, Richelieu, 1980. Terry Hands (mise en scène), John Napier (design). Left: Jacques Eyser (Sir Toby), Francis Huster (Sébastien), Geneviève Casile (Olivia). Centre: Dominique Rozan (Feste), Michel Aumont (Malvolio). Right: François Beaulieu (Orsino), Ludmila Mikaël (Viola). Photograph by Manuel Litran.

France's national theatre company, the Comédie-Française, was established by Louis XIV in 1680. Over three hundred years later, the company still operates under the aegis of the French state and is still governed by set rules that ensure that it remains true to the ensemble principle, with its permanent members sharing in the decision-making and entitled to a pension. During its long history, the Comédie-Française has survived the vanity of kings and the trauma of revolutions and wars.

Because of its official status as the state theatre, in the 20th century the Comédie was regularly dismissed by the avant-garde as a venerable institution paralysed by tradition. Its work was often overshadowed by the innovative creations of Jean Vilar and Roger Planchon's Théâtre national populaire, Peter Brook's Bouffes du Nord, Patrice Chéreau's Théâtre des Amandiers at Nanterre, and Ariane Mnouchkine's Théâtre du Soleil. Since the turn of the century, though, the Comédie has been revitalised and revalued.

Both the strengths and the weaknesses of the Comédie-Française – as an institution – are inseparable from its governing principles. Three key ideas underpin the Comédie-Française. First, the troupe. The Comédie is a society of actors, a co-operative. In all of the long history of the troupe, there have only been 535 sociétaires, a continuous chain of actors stretching back to Molière. Although the power of the actors has fluctuated over the years, and has sometimes been restricted by either the government or by an autocratic General Administrator, it has never been dismantled.

Second, the repertoire. Only the plays selected for the troupe's main house, the Salle Richelieu, enter the official repertoire. Although the repertoire consists, currently, of close to three hundred plays, it is a work in progress, carefully managed to ensure range and quality, and to create a dialogue between plays of different eras.

Third, the principle of *alternance* (the repertory system). The public is offered a number of works, performed in repertory, during every week of the season. The actors often play two or more parts concurrently, in very different plays. This demands a high level of skill and commitment. In June 2018, for example, the repertory consisted of Goldoni's *La Locandiera*, Lars Norén's *Poussière*, Wedekind's *L'Éveil du printemps* (*Spring Awakening*), Racine's *Britannicus*, David Lescot's *Les Ondes magnétiques*, and Strindberg's *Les Créanciers* (*Creditors*): two new plays, and four classics from different countries and times.

The General Administrator is appointed by the President of the Republic on the recommendation of the Minister of Culture. Decisions can be politically motivated, at least in part. An Administrator is likely to be replaced if there is a change of government and his or her term is up for renewal. This fate befell Jacques Lassalle in 1993 and Marcel Bozonnet in 2006, to name just two. A system that allows the political control of national theatres is outdated but there are no signs that it will be reformed. Éric Ruf, in post since 2014, survived the transition from François Hollande to Emmanuel Macron. He runs the Comédie as both artistic director and administrator: he programmes the three theatres, casts the productions, chooses the directors, and hires new actors (known as *pensionnaires*). However, because of the co-operative model, he collaborates with the sociétaires when it comes to the promotion of a pensionnaire to become a sociétaire; and, before adding a new play to the repertoire, he consults the members of the reading committee. Since 1960, the government has often appointed the General Administrator from within the troupe – eight of the last twelve appointees, including Ruf and his two predecessors, have been sociétaires who also direct. The General Administrator appoints a Managing Director to help with the burden of administration.

The Comédie-Française offers its public a shared style, based on togetherness and intimacy, along with strength in depth, consistency and the chance to get to know a troupe of actors over a long period of time. Performing traditions are no longer handed down like theatrical costumes. However, for young people who choose an acting career, the Comédie-Française can seem unattainable. For over two centuries there was a direct link between the Comédie and the *Conservatoire national supérieur d'art dramatique*

(CNSAD), France's premiere drama school established as the Conservatoire de Paris in 1795. Senior members of the Comédie taught at the Conservatoire, and the top graduates (winners of the annual prizes) were automatically admitted into the troupe. There was effectively no other route for a new actor to become a member. There is no longer a direct link between the two institutions, but the Comédie still recruits many of its members from the Conservatoire. Just over fifty per cent of the current sociétaires (March 2020) graduated from CNSAD. For a young person aspiring to act at the Comédie, a place at the Conservatoire is no longer essential but still offers the best chance: the acceptance rate is less than three per cent.

Because the modern Comédie-Française's empire consists of three theatres – the historic main house, the Salle Richelieu, at the Palais-Royal on the Right Bank, in which the company has performed since 1791 (862 seats); Jacques Copeau's old theatre in Saint-Germain on the Left Bank, the mid-sized Vieux-Colombier, given to the Comédie-Française in 1993 (300 seats); and the modern Studio-Théâtre in the Carrousel du Louvre – the troupe has been able to extend the programming to include experimental and new plays as well as a wider range of classical work.

The company model gives all of the advantages outlined above but also contains some inevitable flaws. The number of sociétaires is set, so young actors can't progress to full membership unless older sociétaires retire from the troupe. This can lead to senior actors being retired in a manner that can seem brutal (some stay connected to the troupe as sociétaires honoraires). Even then, there are few opportunities for pensionnaires to progress and many are not chosen. At the end of every year, the work (and conduct) of each member of the troupe is reviewed by a committee consisting of the Administrator, the *doyen* (the most senior actor) and eight of the sociétaires. The committee has the power to eject an actor from the troupe. To be judged by your peers in this way must be difficult, divisive and traumatic. However, many members feel that it is better to be judged by ten people than by an artistic director with the power to follow his or her own prejudices.

Tensions within the troupe over opportunities, equality and poor remuneration have, at times, been a cause of conflict. These disputes normally remain private, but when, in 1927, Madeleine Renaud and Marie Bell, the two young stars of the time, threatened to resign if they weren't promoted, the dispute reached the news columns of *The Times*. Another flaw is that actors who want to work outside of the troupe, while remaining in the troupe, are unable to do so to any great degree. The rigid structure of the Comédie-Française means that the Administrator cannot be as flexible as he or she would like to grant members of the troupe the best of both worlds. Actors who choose to devote their careers to the Comédie have to make sacrifices.

Unlike England's Royal Shakespeare Company, which abandoned its founding principles and unique status (it used to function in a similar way to the Comédie-Française as a permanent company committed to the repertory principle), the Comédie-Française's written constitution saves it from the whims of fashion and the pursuit of change for change's sake. In modern times, the Comédie's most successful administrators have shown that it is possible to be innovative and outward-looking without compromising the ensemble, the repertoire or the concept of *alternance*.

1

Molière

3. *Le Misanthrope* by Molière, Richelieu, 2014. Clément Hervieu-Léger (mise en scène), Éric Ruf (décor), Caroline de Vivaise (costumes), Bertrand Couderc (lighting). Yves Gasc (Basque), Georgia Scalliet (Célimène). Photograph by Alain Richard.

1   Jean-Baptiste and Madeleine

The history of the Comédie-Française begins with Molière and the troupe he led as both actor and playwright. For this reason, the Comédie is also known as the Maison de Molière.

Molière was born Jean-Baptiste Poquelin in Paris in 1622, the son of a master *tapissier* who rose to become *tapissier ordinaire de la maison du roi*. The family business, located in Les Halles at the corner of the rue Saint-Honoré and the rue des Vieilles-Étuves, made bed furnishings. The house was known as the Pavillon des singes (pavilion of monkeys). Molière was educated at one of the best schools in the kingdom, the Jesuit Collège de Clermont (Louis-le-Grand) in the Latin Quarter. The Jesuits' rigidly organised method of learning, founded on discipline, hard work and competition, and consisting of classes on classical languages and literature, grammar, the Humanities and Rhetoric, produced many of the great figures of the *ancien régime*. For boys at the Collège de Clermont who, like Molière, became writers for the theatre, their schooldays were both formative and vocational, for every year the students took part in performances of tragedies and comedies in Latin. Molière's father wanted his son to follow a career in the law and at court and purchased for him the position of *valet de chambre ordinaire et tapissier du roi*. Molière took up the position in 1641, and for a short time studied law, probably in Orléans.

However, Molière was about to disobey his father. At twenty-one, in 1643, he gave up the financial security and social status of the life he was born into and joined the actress Madeleine Béjart, who was probably already his mistress, in the creation of a new theatre company – the Illustre Théâtre. Actors were considered to be outsiders and had no status in society. In the public mind, they were associated with vagabonds and mountebanks; while actresses were associated with prostitutes. This was true even in the big cities, where some actors become famous, admired by the king for their art and the pleasure they gave. Actresses, in particular, were celebrated and desired, but also abused and despised. The common use, in the 17th century and early 18th century, of an article before an actress's name in place of the polite title Mademoiselle – 'La Lecouvreur' – began as a scornful means of belittling the woman, of denying her status, of talking about her as though she was an object. It was a time when titles were used very precisely to denote social status. Some actresses, though, would not be ashamed to be referred to in a way that confirmed that they were special. The use of the article faded from use, at least in respectable society, as the 18th century progressed. 'We are no longer of an age, you and I,' Voltaire wrote to his friend Thiériot in 1735, 'where terms that are careless and without respect are agreeable to us. [...] This mark of politeness distinguishes those who use it. The fops of the rue Saint-Denis said la Lecouvreur, and Cardinal Fleury said Mademoiselle Lecouvreur.'[1]

The Church ensured that actors would never truly belong by keeping them in a state of excommunication. If an actor didn't renounce his profession before dying he would not be buried in holy ground. This would remain the case until the Revolution. Some of the most intellectually enlightened men of the 18th century, men who were essentially anti-clerical in their thinking, considered actors and actresses to be, by definition, morally corrupt and dissolute: Diderot (who wrote stage works and loved the company of actresses in his youth) and Rousseau went so far as to make this case in their writings.[2] Voltaire, in contrast, railed against the hypocrisy of a nation that loved and honoured the great works of

[1] Quoted in Virginia Scott, *Women on the Stage in Early Modern France, 1540-1750* (Cambridge: Cambridge University Press, 2010), p.7.
[2] See Diderot, *Paradoxe sur le comédien* (ca.1778) and Rousseau, *Lettre à M. d'Alembert sur les spectacles* (1758).

dramatic literature but despised and condemned the artists who brought them to life.[1]

Molière spent the considerable sum of 600 livres on the new venture, while Madeleine's mother provided financial support, even mortgaging her house. Madeleine's brother Joseph and younger sister also joined the company. If most members of the troupe were at best semi-professionals, they set about the practical and business aspects with reckless intent, leasing a *jeu de paume* (tennis court) with living quarters in Saint-Germain, hiring musicians and making an agreement with Nicolas Desfontaines to perform his tragedies. Molière adopted his alias, choosing, as was the norm, the name of a place. At this time, he was a physically awkward actor, his style unsuited to tragedy. One contemporary compared him to an 'overloaded mule'. He fared better, though, than Madeleine's brother Joseph, who acted with a pronounced stutter. The new company was heavily in debt from the start. Was Madeleine, previously on the brink of real success in the established theatres, indulging her younger lover by aligning herself to a band of unintentionally comical novices? Or did she sense the genuine talent that lay beneath the enthusiasm?

It was difficult to break into Paris's restricted and limited theatrical scene. There were only two theatre companies performing plays in French, the long-established Comédiens du roi led by Valleran le Conte at the Hôtel de Bourgogne, and the troupe of the Théâtre du Marais, a converted *jeu de paume* opened in 1634 by a former member of Valleran le Conte's company. The Hôtel de Bourgogne's repertoire was dominated by the tragedies and tragicomedies of Alexandre Hardy, while the Théâtre du Marais quickly became known for the farces of Jodelet and the innovative tragedies of Pierre Corneille. In 1647, the Théâtre du Marais's leading actor, Floridor, defected to the Hôtel de Bourgogne, taking Corneille with him. Unable to compete with these theatres on any level, the Illustre Théâtre failed to attract a loyal following and ran up huge debts. The company folded after less than two years in 1645. As

[1] See Voltaire (trans. Leonard Tancock), *Letters on England* (Penguin, 1980), p.112-14.

the leader, Molière was imprisoned until the creditors were paid –
by a friend who was reimbursed by Molière's father.

2   On the Road

Molière and Madeleine left Paris and became travelling players.
They would spend thirteen long years on the road. They joined the
accomplished troupe of Charles Dufresne, under the patronage of
the duc d'Épernon, governor of Guyenne and Gascogne (Aquitaine). Dufresne wanted Madeleine, but with Madeleine came
Molière and her siblings. Molière, though, would soon become the
troupe's most important member after its leader.

The troupe entertained Épernon at his homes in Bordeaux and
Agan and accompanied him on his official travels in the southwest.
Because of the rebellions provoked by Cardinal Mazarin's tax policies (the Fronde), the late 1640s and early 1650s were years of
political turmoil in many of the French provinces, including Guyenne. Épernon, who supported the crown, faced rebellion in
Bordeaux; he resigned as governor and the troupe, cut free, travelled to the more stable region of Languedoc, finding work in noble
houses from Nîmes to Toulouse. Performing in town squares and
courtyards was not an option because the local people didn't speak
French and the actors didn't speak Occitan. For some months, Molière and company entertained the representatives of the États
Généraux de Languedoc in Pézenas. During the winter season of
1752/53, they were resident in Lyon, where they acquired a new
member, the actress Marquise-Thérèse de Gorle. Around this time,
Molière succeeded Dufresne as leader of the troupe.

Later in 1653, back in Pézenas, the troupe secured the patronage
of the prince de Conti. Conti had led the failed rebellion in Bordeaux. Living in self-exile in Pézenas, where his family owned an
estate, he engaged Molière's troupe to relieve the boredom of country life. He kept the actors on retainer in his household and paid
them handsomely. By this time, Molière was writing comedies for

the troupe to perform. The earliest to come down to us, *L'Étourdi ou les contretemps* (*The Bungler*), freely adapted from Niccolò Barbieri's *L'Inavvertito*, was premiered in November 1752. The play is dominated by a scheming servant, Mascarille, the role that Molière played himself. Molière's acting and writing style, initially based on the stock characters and improvisational style of commedia dell'arte, developed during the next few years until he was ready to target contemporary mores with the mocking wit and irreverence that made his name.

In 1656, the prince de Conti suddenly discharged Molière's troupe. Riddled with syphilis, he had decided to live a devout life. After performing during the États Généraux in Béziers, the troupe headed north up the Rhone valley and spent most of 1657 in Lyon and Dijon. Molière and Madeleine were now thinking about Paris. To prepare for their return, they spent the summer of 1658 in Rouen, close enough to the capital to make their presence felt. The troupe had acquired a significant reputation and also benefited from some connections at court. Molière travelled to Paris and secured the patronage of the king's brother, Philippe I, duc d'Orléans, just eighteen-years-old and looking to impress his brother.

3   Paris and Fame

Molière and his fellow actors arrived in Paris in October 1658 and made their debut performing Corneille's *Nicomède* before the king and his courtiers at the Louvre. The pressure could not have been greater. The performance was effectively an audition that would decide the troupe's future. The Comédiens du roi at the Hôtel de Bourgogne, and their influential backers, determined to prevent the establishment of a rival troupe in Paris, were petitioning against Molière. Molière was acutely aware that his company was stronger performing farces than tragedies, which was why, at the conclusion of the Corneille, he stepped forward to the footlights and appealed to the king to excuse his 'country manners' and the 'defects' of his troupe by allowing the performance of one of the *petits divertissements* that had made his name in the provinces. *Le Docteur amoureux*, in which Molière played the title role, greatly pleased the king.[1] Molière was granted permission to share – with the commedia dell'arte actors of Tiberio Fiorillo, famous as Scaramouche – the theatre in the Hôtel du Petit-Bourbon, on the Right Bank adjacent to the Louvre.

During his first season at the Petit-Bourbon, 1658/59, Molière presented the only full-length plays that he had written up until this point, *L'Étourdi* and *Le Dépit amoureux*. The public lapped up these farces, but stayed away from the troupe's productions of Corneille. The troupe did not initially receive any money from either their patron or his brother and needed excellent box-office returns throughout each season to survive. Unfortunately, Molière's productions of tragedies continued to misfire even after a new actor – La Grange[2] – joined the company in 1659. La Grange took on the young male leads in both tragedies and comedies. Molière had not been able to engage a great tragic actor of the stature of the three actresses who were his troupe's chief asset as well as a constant cause of professional and personal grief. Keeping Madeleine, Catherine de Brie and Mlle du Parc all happy meant casting them equally, which was near impossible. The fact that Molière had a complex (and spent-out) sexual history with at least two of them, made the task even harder. Mlle du Parc decided to defect to La Roque's Théâtre du Marais, about to reopen after a closure of two years. Molière got his own back on La Roque by luring his leading farceur, Jodelet, to the Petit-Bourbon. Within a year, though, Jodelet had died and Mlle du Parc had returned to Molière's company.

Molière and the Béjarts leased a house on the quai de l'École. Molière realised that, if his company was going to survive, he would need to write new plays for the actors to perform. A new comedy,

[1] From an account of the performance written by La Grange and Vivot in 1682. See Virginia Scott, *Molière: a Theatrical Life* (Cambridge University Press, 2000), p.91-92.

[2] Charles Varlet, dit La Grange (1635-92, b. Montpellier). La Grange kept a register of performances and receipts.

Les Précieuses ridicules, was written in time for the troupe's second season. The names of the characters reveal the actors for whom they were written: Cathos (Catherine de Brie), Magdelon (Madeleine Béjart), La Grange, Du Croisy and Jodelet. *Les précieuses* was the term given to witty and refined women who engaged in intellectual conversations. In his play, Molière satirises the *précieuses* as vain, affected and ridiculous. Two young women from the provinces refuse to marry the men chosen by their father because they consider them to be unrefined. They fall instead for the valets of these men, who, in disguise, pretend to be gentlemen.

The play opened in November 1659, performed, as was the custom for one-act farces, after a full-length tragedy – Corneille's *Cinna*. The talk in the cafés and salons after the show was all about Molière's little play when it should have been about *Cinna*. One commentator recorded that *Les Précieuses ridicules* provoked 'endless laughter'. Corneille's brother Thomas complained in a letter to the abbé de Pure that was made public that Molière's success confirmed that his troupe was only 'fit to sustain trifles'.[1] *Les Précieuses ridicules* had the visual exaggerations that people expected from a farce – Molière, playing the role of Mascarille, wore a wig that was so long it touched the floor – but it was more than a trifle. The fashionable people in the audience laughing at Molière's two girls from the provinces were actually being mocked themselves.[2]

Molière's next one-act farce, *Sganarelle*, was written under the influence of Fiorillo. Despite its reliance on commedia dell'arte, it had its own bitter flavour. It introduced one of Molière's favourite themes, the fear of female betrayal. The king, back in Paris following his wedding to Maria Theresa of Spain, asked Molière to perform both *Sganarelle* and *Les Précieuses ridicules* for his pleasure at the Château de Vincennes. Louis's liking for both Molière and his work brought the playwright both prestige and 500 *livres*.

Soon after the premiere of *Sganarelle*, in October 1660, the Petit-Bourbon was demolished to allow for an extension to the Louvre. The king's Superintendent of Buildings, Ratabon, took pleasure in

---

[1] Quoted in Scott, *Molière: a Theatrical Life*, p.101.
[2] Most recent production at the CF: 2007, by Dan Jemmett.

not telling Molière in advance. When challenged, he remarked that he hadn't thought it necessary to consider the Comédie when improving the Louvre. 'Ratabon's malicious intention was clear,' La Grange wrote in his register.[1] The king agreed with his brother that Molière should be given the theatre at the Palais-Royal. By now the company was called the Troupe de Monsieur in Orléans's honour. The Palais-Royal's theatre, designed for Cardinal Richelieu by the architect Lemercier, was situated in the east wing of the palace, on the other side of the courtyard from where the Comédie-Française's present home, the Salle Richelieu, would be built just over a hundred years later. After years of non-use the theatre was in a poor state of repair and needed to be converted into a venue suitable for public performances. Ratabon was instructed to repair the roof, but only attached a large blue cloth over the hole. Once it was restored, it gave Molière more than he could ever have wished for during his long years of exile. The troupe began its first season at the Palais-Royal, in January 1661, with a performance of *Le Dépit amoureux*.

Following the failure of his tragi-comedy *Dom Garcie de Navarre*, Molière finally accepted that his particular talent lay in comedy, although, as he started to write full-length plays for the troupe, he could not have predicted either the sudden flowering of creativity or the profundity of which he was capable. During the next ten years, Molière wrote thirty works, among them the plays that contributed to his lasting fame.

L'École des maris, the first of Molière's full-length plays,[2] was premiered at the Palais-Royal in the summer of 1661, and then performed for the king at Fontainebleau. Sganarelle, the role played by Molière, is so possessive of his ward (and intended wife) Isabella that he keeps her locked away. In contrast, Sganarelle's older brother, Ariste, treats his ward Léonor well, trusting her to be faithful. Sganarelle is cuckolded; Ariste is not. The play is a debate in verse between two points of view, and its creation stemmed directly

---

[1] La Grange, *Registre de La Grange (1658-1685): précédé d'une notice biographique*. Publié par les soins de la Comédie-Française. (Paris: J. Claye, 1876), p.26.

[2] Most recent production at the CF: 1999, by Thierry Hancisse.

from Molière's own life. The ageing playwright had fallen for seventeen-year-old Armande Béjart, a fledgeling actress in his troupe who was either Madeleine's illegitimate daughter or her sister (the truth is debated). Molière had known Armande all her life, and had acted as her guardian. His seduction of Armande troubled the members of his circle, and it's hard to comprehend how Madeleine coped in these circumstances. No-one could dissuade Molière from marrying Armande. La Grange records this profound moment in one plain sentence: 'Mr de Molière espousa Armande Claire Élisabeth Grésinde Béjart, le Mardi Gras de 1662.'[1] By the end of the year, Molière had written another play that related to his infatuation with Armande and the sexual jealousy that was already tormenting him: *L'École des femmes*, which opened at the Palais-Royal on the 26 December, was a new style of play, impossible to categorise as either a farce or a tragi-comedy. Molière's first big success, it was performed over thirty times during the rest of the winter season. 'The play,' wrote Jean Donneau de Visé, 'produced some quite unprecedented effects. Everyone said it was wicked – and everyone flocked to see it. The ladies complained about it, but didn't miss it. Nobody liked it – yet is was successful.'[2]

In the play, a middle-aged man, Arnolphe, played by Molière, schemes to keep his young ward, Agnès, ignorant and innocent so that he can marry her. The plan fails the moment a young man looks at Agnès and she looks back. After which, Agnès is a quick learner, easily able to outwit her enraged guardian. Arnolphe shows his real colours and makes a play for Agnès that is explicitly sexual – 'Sans cesse nuit et jour je te caresserai, Je te bouchonnerai, baiserai, mangerai' – and which the girl coldly rejects. This scene can still provoke a feeling of discomfort, and was especially powerful when played by sixty-five-year-old Pierre Dux and seventeen-year-old Isabelle Adjani at the Comédie-Française in 1973. More recently, Jacques Lassalle directed Thierry Hancisse and Julie-Marie Parmentier (2011).

[1] La Grange, *Registre de La Grange*, p.31.
[2] Jean Donneau de Visé, *Les Nouvelles nouvelles*, t.2 (February 1663), p.210. Quoted in William D. Howarth (ed.), *French Theatre in the Neo-classical Era, 1550-1789* (Cambridge: Cambridge University Press, 2008) p.271.

It looked as if Molière was using the play not only to express his desire for Armande and his fear of being betrayed by her, but also to provoke his moral critics. *L'École des femmes* provoked the 'War of Comedy', a public quarrel that saw Molière opposed by conservative writers – led by the Corneille brothers – and their supporters as well as by the Comédiens du roi. Armande Béjart wasn't cast as Agnès, but made her debut in June 1663 as the mischievous Élise in the *Critique de l'École des femmes*, Molière's loaded response to his critics.[1] Molière played le Marquis, with Brécourt as Dorante. The cast was completed by Catherine de Brie, Mlle du Parc and Du Croisy.

L'École des femmes was revived at the same time. The many sexual puns and illusions in the text partly explained why it was a *succès de scandale*, and Molière, via the character played by his wife, takes pleasure in the *Critique* in mocking the prudes and the pedants who had published pamphlets against the play. His enemies, including Corneille's friend Edmé Boursault in *Le Portrait de peintre*, performed by the Comédiens du roi at the Hôtel de Bourgogne in October 1663, insinuated that he had married his own child. Molière took his revenge by lampooning the leading actors of the Hôtel de Bourgogne, including the fat tragedian Montfleury, in *L'Impromptu de Versailles*, presented at Versailles a couple of weeks later.

In 1665, the king formally took over the patronage of Molière's actors from his brother – the Troupe de Monsieur became the Troupe du roi au Palais-Royal. At court, Molière created a series of comédie-ballets, a new genre of his own invention combining a play with music and dance. The first of these works, *Les Fâcheux*, was written with the composer Pierre Beauchamps for a *fête* organised by Nicolas Fouquet, Surintendant des Finances, at Vaux-le-Vicomte in 1661. The comédie-ballet genre particularly appealed to the king. During the next ten years, Molière wrote eleven comédie-ballets, most of them with the king's Surintendant de la Musique, Jean-Baptiste Lully. Molière's partnership with Lully

---

[1] *La Critique de l'École des femmes* is rarely staged today. Jean Weber's production of 1957 stayed in the repertoire for more than a decade. Clément Hervieu-Léger directed a new production in 2011, with Loïc Corbery as Dorante, Georgia Scalliet as Élise and Serge Bagdassarian as the Marquis.

produced a major work – *Le Bourgeois gentilhomme* – but it was fraught from the start and would end badly. Molière believed that the text was paramount; but for Lully, these works were ballets with plays attached. The king tended to agree with his court composer. Lully had risen from a humble beginning. Born in Florence, he began his career at court as a violinist in the orchestra and caught Louis's eye as a dancer. Hugely ambitious, and hugely gifted at self-promotion, Lully could not be trusted by his fellow artists.

Molière was treated with disdain at court because he was an actor. The contempt was mutual. Molière was intent on exposing folly and hypocrisy in elegant alexandrine couplets and by so doing he challenged the establishment and made some powerful enemies. In 1664, his play *Le Tartuffe, ou l'Imposteur*, a major departure, was performed at Versailles. In this biting satire, Orgon, the head of a wealthy household, falls under the spell of a man he believes to be pious and wise, a conduit of divine authority. He invites Tartuffe into his home and takes spiritual instruction from him. Tartuffe, though, is an imposter, a rogue, who through his ability as an actor sets out to exploit Orgon and to seduce his wife Elmire. Elmire and Orgon's son Damis are not taken in by Tartuffe, and work to expose his treachery.

The play pleased the king but outraged church leaders at court, who believed that Molière was making a point about religious hypocrisy and that his real target was the Church. The archbishop of Paris, Hardouin de Péréfixe, had been Louis's tutor. He urged the king to ban the play and Louis reluctantly agreed. His pragmatic view was that the public could mistakenly believe that the play was impugning the clergy. In issuing the order to ban the play he made it known that he did not doubt the good intentions of its author. The 'bataille du Tartuffe' would continue for five years. The Compagnie du Saint-Sacrement, a secret body of powerful members of the devout party, believed that *Tartuffe* was an 'evil play'. Molière's former patron the prince de Conti, who had dismissed his troupe back in 1656, was a member of the Compagnie du Saint-Sacrement (satirising Conti's conversion to piety may have been one of the Molière's motivations). Molière must have had some knowledge of this secret society for Tartuffe quotes the society's dictum 'Pour la gloire du Ciel et le bien du prochain' as his own: an astonishing provocation. Because Molière retained the support of the king, he was able to survive demands for his imprisonment and prosecution. With the influence of the *dévots* in decline, the king finally allowed the play to be staged in Paris in February 1669. *Tartuffe*'s long ban meant that the Paris public was curious about Molière's scandalous play, and swarmed to the Palais-Royal. Molière took the role of Orgon, with Du Croisy as Tartuffe, Armande as Elmire, Catherine de Brie as Mariane, La Grange as Valère, Madeleine Béjart as Dorine, Hubert as Damis, and La Thorillière as Cléante.

Molière had the final word. He ended his preface to the published edition of *Tartuffe* with an anecdote that concerned a conversation between the king and one of his courtiers following the performance of a play called *Scaramouche*. The king asked: 'I would like to know why those people who are so scandalised by Molière's comedy have nothing to say about *Scaramouche*?' To which the courtier replied: 'It is because *Scaramouche* mocks heaven and religion, and these gentlemen don't care about that; but Molière's play mocks them, and they care very much about that.'[1] Molière was taking a huge liberty in putting words into the mouth of the king. It was around this time that Louis's attitude towards the playwright started to cool.

Tartuffe was played more often, and earned more money, than any of Molière's other plays, and it would remain pre-eminent for three centuries. After the creation of the Comédie-Française in 1680, *Tartuffe* was performed every year until 1976.[2]

Between *Tartuffe*'s first performance at court and its triumph at the Palais-Royal, Molière wrote a companion piece, another study

[1] Molière, *Le Tartuffe, ou L'imposteur* (Paris: Imprimé aux despens de l'autheur, 1669), 'Préface'.

[2] Most recent production at the CF: 2014, by Galin Stoev – starring Michel Vuillermoz (Tartuffe), Elsa Lepoivre (Elmire), Didier Sandre (Organ), Serge Bagdassarian (Cléante), Nâzim Boudjenah (Valère), Anna Cervinka (Mariane) and Christophe Montenez (Damis). Earlier productions: 1980, by Jean-Paul Roussillon – starring Jean-Luc Boutté, Catherine Ferran and Jean Le Poulain; 1997, by Dominique Pitoiset – starring Philippe Torreton, Jean Dautremay and Cécile Brune; 2005, by Marcel Bozonnet – starring Éric Génovèse, Florence Viala and Bakary Sangaré.

in hypocrisy, *Dom Juan, ou le Festin de pierre*, premiered at the Palais-Royal in February 1665. The story was well known from earlier plays, but Molière's Dom Juan was his own creation – an atheist and free-thinker as well as a cold-hearted seducer. This was a further provocation, not just of the devout party, but also of more moderate thinking, for Molière's atheist pretends to have found God so that he can dupe his father and deceive society. Dom Juan's servant, Sganarelle, the character played by Molière, is a man of faith, but his faith, based on superstition, is satirised. Molière was accused of defending immorality and of mocking faith. The censor demanded cuts but the play wasn't banned. It only ran for fifteen performances and wasn't revived. La Grange created the role of Dom Juan, with Mlle du Parc, Catherine de Brie and Armande as the women he seduces.[1]

Molière's marriage was already under strain. Armande had many admirers. Attacks on her character were to be expected, particularly as they were a means of attempting to humiliate Molière.[2] Many believed that Célimène in Molière's *Le Misanthrope*, premiered at the Palais-Royal in 1666, was Molière's portrait his wife: Armande was playing Molière's view of her, but was she playing herself? The public adored the piquancy of this situation. It was around the time of *Le Misanthrope* that Molière started to live apart from his wife, although they continued to act together.[3]

The play was only a moderate success, perhaps because it was a

---

[1] Most recent production at the CF: 2011, by Jean-Pierre Vincent – starring Loïc Corbery, Serge Bagdassarian, Suliane Brahim and Jennifer Decker. Earlier productions: 1952, by Jean Meyer – starring Jean Debucourt; 1967, by Antoine Bourseiller – starring Georges Descrières; 1979, by Jean-Luc Boutté – starring Francis Huster; 1993, by Jacques Lassalle – starring Andrzej Seweryn.

[2] Armande would later be the victim of a *libelle* entitled *La Fameuse comédienne, ou histoire de la Guérin* (1688).

[3] Most recent production at the CF: 2014, by Clément Hervieu-Léger – starring Loïc Corbery and Georgia Scalliet or Adeline d'Hermy. Earlier productions: 1936, by Jacques Copeau – starring Marie Bell and Aimé Clariond; 1947, by Pierre Dux; 1963, by Jacques Charon; 1975, by Jean-Luc Boutté and Catherine Hiegel; 1977, by Pierre Dux; 1984, by Jean-Pierre Vincent; 1989, by Simon Eine; 2000, by Jean-Pierre Miquel; 2007, by Lukas Hemleb.

darker and more ambiguous depiction of men and women than Molière had previously attempted. Alceste, the misanthrope, calls out hypocrisy and other vices and always tells the truth about his fellow men, with zero concern for social niceties, but is he truthful about himself? The philosophes of the *Encyclopédie* would debate the meaning of the play. For Jean-Jacques Rousseau, writing in his *Lettre à M. d'Alembert sur les spectacles* of 1758, the play was weakened by Molière's decision, as he saw it, to generate laughter by making Alceste angry, petulant and somewhat ridiculous. For Jean-François Marmontel, responding to Rousseau in the *Mercure de France*, Alceste's contradictions made him human, and his virtues were not negated because he was a flawed being.

Molière's bitterness over Armande surely influenced the text of his opéra-ballet *George Dandin, ou Le Mari confondu*, created with Lully and presented during the festival that celebrated the treaty of Aix-la-Chapelle in July 1668. In the play, the hapless Dandin, a rich peasant who has married above his station, is betrayed by his wife Angélique. The roles were played by Molière and Armande. La Grange played Angélique's lover Clitandre. This social drama about betrayal and class was an unusual entertainment to dress up in Lully's pastoral music and perform before the king in an idyllic outdoor setting.[1]

4　Final Years

The most important of the comédie-ballets produced by Molière and Lully was *Le Bourgeois gentilhomme*, premiered before the king at the Château de Chambord in the Loire Valley in October 1670. In this work, a satire targeting both middle-class social climbing and aristocratic contempt, Molière's achievement was to fully integrate the dance sequences into the action of the play. The play ends with a long ceremony in which M. Jourdain is duped into believing

[1] Most recent production at the CF: 2016, by Hervé Pierre – starring Jérôme Pouly, Claire de La Rüe du Can, Pierre Hancisse and Rebecca Marder.

that he is being ennobled by the Sultan of Turkey. This ceremony was entirely presented in music and dance: no fewer than six *entrées* of dance provided Lully with the opportunity to proclaim his dominance over Molière. Today, *Le Bourgeois gentilhomme* is usually performed without Lully's music.[1]

Molière's friendship with Lully was in the process of disintegrating, and their rift would cloud the last few years of his life. There was the personal issue of the precocious boy actor Michel Baron, an orphan, who was Molière's protégé and who lived with him in the house he kept for his own use at Auteuil. Molière may have been infatuated with the boy. According to Molière's first biographer, Grimarest,[2] the playwright was unable to prevent Lully, notorious within private circles as a predatory homosexual, from including Baron in his debauched suppers. Professionally, Molière was out-manoeuvred by Lully in the serious matter of obtaining control over the use of music and dance in the public theatre. The trend of the 1660s was for stage works that united all of the arts and used elaborate stage machinery to achieve magnificent *coups de théâtre*. In January 1671, Molière and Lully produced a work that went much further than their earlier collaborations in the delivery of spectacle. *Psyché*, mounted in the Salle des Machines at the palais des Tuileries (a grand space, constructed in 1662 for the production of an Italian opera by Cavalli, but unused since because of its size), was the most lavishly produced theatre work ordered by the king to that date: along with *Le Bourgeois gentilhomme*, it pointed the way towards Lully and Quinault's creation of a French form of opera. Molière wrote the outline of the story and acted as producer, but because of limited time he only wrote some of the spoken text; the rest was written by Corneille, while Quinault wrote the verses that Lully set to music. *Psyché*, then, was created by men who were at best reluctant collaborators. The original production at the Tuileries was the theatrical equivalent of Versailles, a proclamation of

---

[1] The CF's most recent production of the play was created, by Jean-Louis Benoit, in 2000. A new production will be mounted in 2020 with music and dance. Éric Ruf has commissioned a new score.

[2] Author of *La Vie de M. de Molière*, published in 1705.

grandeur and wealth and the realisation of the seemingly impossible in the name of the France of Louis XIV. The production employed hundreds of performers (marshalled, it was said, by seventy dancing masters) and took five hours to perform. 'As for the last scene,' wrote the marquis de Saint-Maurice, 'it is quite the most astonishing thing that can be seen, for one sees all at once three hundred people appear suspended either in clouds or in a glory, and that makes the finest symphony in the world.'[1]

So that he could revive *Psyché* at the Palais-Royal, Molière raised money to modernise the theatre and to install the necessary machinery. At the same time, the roof was finally repaired. Even a chamber-sized production of *Psyché* required fifteen musicians, sixteen dancers and eight singers. *Psyché* was hugely popular with the public, and made a decent profit. During the next two years, *Psyché* was performed over eighty times.[2]

It may have been Molière's idea to buy the *privilège* to stage operas from Pierre Perrin. Perrin had been granted the privilège by the king in 1669, but had failed to make significant progress and was drowning in debt. Lully, closer to the king than Molière, jumped first and was granted the privilège in March 1672. He immediately moved against Molière and other theatre managers. Only Lully's Académie Royale de Musique (under construction in the rue de Vaugirard) would be allowed to mount productions dominated by music and dance. All other theatres would only be allowed to employ two singers. This went too far for the king, who decided that theatres would be allowed to employ up to six singers and twelve musicians. Despite the new rules, and the poor availability of leading singers and dancers after Lully had made his choices, Molière premiered a new comédie-ballet at the Palais-Royal, *Le Malade imaginaire*, with music by Charpentier. This satire on the medical profession was closely related to *L'Amour médecin* (1665) and *Le Médecin malgré lui* (1666).

At some point in the early 1670s, Molière and Armande were reconciled. Molière's final years were sombre. Madeleine died in

---

[1] The marquis de Saint-Maurice to the duc de Savoy: January 1671, quoted in Howarth (ed.), *French Theatre in the Neo-classical Era, 1550-1789*, p.218.

[2] Most recent production at the CF: 2014, by Véronique Vella.

1672. Molière was suffering from tuberculosis, but continued to work, managing the company, writing and performing on the stage. His death, in February 1673, could have been written as an exercise in dramatic irony. Desperately ill, he nevertheless insisted on going on stage to play Argan, the hypochondriac, in *Le Malade imaginaire*. Baron would later recall that Molière had told him that night, poignantly: 'I can no longer stand these pains and griefs, that give me not a moment of relief. A man must suffer before he dies. However, I feel that I am done for.'[1] He managed to complete the performance, and was taken to his home in the rue Richelieu; but during the night he started to haemorrhage. He asked Baron to fetch Armande, but he had very little time left and died before she arrived. Molière asked for a priest, but the priest also arrived too late.

Armande pleaded with the archbishop to allow her husband a Christian burial. Because Molière had not recanted his profession, the archbishop refused. The king intervened. The archbishop instructed the curé of Molière's parish, Saint-Eustache, to bury his body in the parish's cemetery of Saint-Joseph,[2] but at night and without a service. Molière's wife and daughter, his friends and all the members of his company, walked from the rue Richelieu to the cemetery with torches in their hands.

Not long after Molière's death, Jean Donneau de Visé seemed to predict his undying appeal for the French theatre and especially for French actors when he wrote of him:

> He was all actor, from his feet to his head; it seemed that he had many voices, everyone spoke in him, and, with a step, a smile, a wink of the eye and a shake of the head, he conveyed more meaning than the greatest speaker could have done in an hour.[3]

---

[1] Quoted in Scott, *Molière: a Life in the Theatre*, p.257.

[2] Molière's remains were disinterred from Saint-Joseph during the Revolution and eventually ended up in Père Lachaise; however, it is unlikely that these are Molière's bones since the location of his grave in Saint-Joseph wasn't known.

[3] In *Mercure galant*, 14 June 1673. Quoted in Scott, *Molière: a Life in the Theatre*, p.256.

5   Racine

Jean Racine was born in Picardy in 1739. Educated by the Jansenists, he came to Paris to study law at the collège d'Harcourt. He probably met Molière before his long stay in the southern town of Uzès, where he was seeking a benefice. In Uzès, Racine was a devout man; in Paris, a lover of pleasure and worldly success. On his return to the capital, still only in his early twenties, ambition motivated his ascendency in the theatre. He wrote his first two major plays, *La Thébaïde ou les frères ennemis* (1664) and *Alexandre le Grand* (1665), for Molière's troupe at the Palais-Royal. Molière felt betrayed when, soon after his theatre's premiere of *Alexandre*, Racine gave the play to the Comédiens du roi at the Hôtel de Bourgogne. Racine made matters worse by seducing Molière's leading actress, Mlle du Parc, and persuading her to join the Hôtel de Bourgogne (1667). Mlle du Parc died less than two years later. It was said that she died either in childbirth or from a botched abortion. The poisoner La Voisin would later claim that Racine poisoned the actress. There is no evidence to substantiate the claim.

Racine's austere, unadorned, poetic explorations of human psychology in plays such as *Andromaque* (1667), *Britannicus* (1669), *Bajazet* (1672), *Mithridate* (1673), *Iphigénie* (1674) and *Phèdre* (1677), all of them written for the Hôtel de Bourgogne, would influence the French theatre long into the next century. Admired as much for his ability to build dramatic tension as for the beauty of his verses, Racine, though, was inimitable. After *Phèdre*, he stopped writing secular dramas and returned to the Jansenist fold. He turned his back on the public stage and accepted the position of royal historiographer at court.

2

The Troupe

1673 to 1788

4. *L'Heureux stratagème* by Marivaux, Vieux-Colombier, 2018. Emmanuel Daumas (mise en scène), Katrijn Baeten and Saskia Louwaard (décor and costumes), Bruno Marsol (lighting). L-R: Claire de La Rüe du Can (La Comtesse), Nicolas Lormeau (Blaise), Jennifer Decker (Lisette). Photograph by Christophe Raynaud de Lage.

1   The Creation of the Comédie-Française

After Molière's death, his troupe's theatre at the Palais-Royal was re-assigned to Lully's Académie Royale de Musique. Lully lobbied the king to make this happen. Molière's actors were evicted from their home while they were still grieving the loss of their leader. Armande was instrumental in ensuring the survival of the company. She used 11,000 *livres* of her inheritance as a down payment to secure a new home on the Left Bank in Saint-Germain – the Théâtre de Guénégaud, located in a former *jeu de paume* in the rue des Fossés de Nesle (today's rue Mazarine). Then, endorsed by royal decree, the actors came together with some of their rivals from the Théâtre du Marais to form a new troupe at the Théâtre de Guénégaud.

Louis XIV, who had ensured that the lyric arts were state-controlled by giving the exclusive licence to produce operas to Lully and establishing the Académie Royale de Musique, now turned his attention to the spoken theatre. In 1680, following the death of La Thorillière, leader of the Comédiens du roi at the Hôtel de Bourgogne, Louis established a state-controlled national company by ordering the merger of the troupe of the Théâtre de Guénégaud (led by La Grange) and the Comédiens du roi. This new company, the Troupe française des comediens du roi, soon to be called the Comédie-Française or Théâtre-Français, was awarded the sole right to perform plays in the French language. The *lettre de cachet* signed by Louis at Versailles on 21 October, stated that the troupe would consist of twenty-seven players, chosen by the king on merit so as to 'make the performances of plays more perfect' ('rendre les représentations des comédies plus parfaites'):

> His Majesty having judged it fitting to unite the two troupes of
> actors established at the Hôtel de Bourgogne and in the rue de
> Guénégaud in Paris to make of them in future a single troupe, so
> as to render performances of plays more perfect by means of the
> actors and actresses to whom he will have given places in this
> troupe. His Majesty has ordered and orders that in future these
> two troupes of French actors be united so as to compose a single
> troupe. And this will be composed of actors and actresses on the
> list to be drawn up by His Majesty, and so as to give them the
> means ever to improve themselves. His Majesty wishes that this
> troupe perform plays in Paris, forbidding all other French actors
> to establish themselves in the town and faubourgs, without ex-
> press permission of His Majesty. His Majesty enjoins the sieur de
> La Reynie, Lieutenant général de police, to ensure the execution
> of the present order.[1]

An important task of the new troupe was, in line with the work
of the Académie Française, to uphold the purity of the French language. The merger meant that the plays of Molière and Racine
(fifteen years after the rupture of their authors' friendship) would
be performed by the same group of actors on the same stage. Two
styles of acting were present in the new troupe. The static, declamatory style of the tragedians of the Hôtel de Bourgogne and the
seemingly spontaneous style of verbal fencing, of actors sharing a
scene, developed by Molière and his actors from the improvisational method of the Italian exponents of commedia dell'arte. This
latter style still informs French acting today.

The Comédiens-français followed tradition by signing a binding
act of association based on the sharing of box office receipts. Their
motto was 'être ensemble et être soi-même'. However, independence was illusionary. With the privileges given to them by the
crown, including the subsidy that secured their future, came the
scrutiny of officials, for the troupe came under the authority of the
Premiers gentilshommes de la chambre du roi (First Gentlemen of the

---

[1] Quoted in Howarth (ed.), *French Theatre in the Neo-classical Era, 1550-
1789*, p.289-90.

King's Chamber). At any one time, there were four First Gentlemen, serving in rotation. In 1680, the duc d'Aumont was in charge.
As employees of the king, the actors had to be mindful of notions
of decorum, church conservatism and national pride.

The merger inevitably resulted in unhappiness and conflict
among the actors, for some were forced to retire and others faced a
reduction in their share of income. Former rivals had to work together and compromise over roles. To mitigate disputes over
casting, the crown decided that the duc d'Aumont would allocate
the parts in Molière's plays and that Corneille, Racine and
Quinault would cast their own plays. Of the chosen twenty-seven
players, twelve were women. Members of Molière's troupe who
were founding members of the Comédie-Française, included Armande Béjart (Mme Guérin), Michel Baron, La Grange, Du
Croisy, Catherine de Brie, and Marie Claveau (Mlle du Croisy).
Founding members who originally came from either the Theatre
du Marais or the Hôtel de Bourgogne, included Charles Chevillet
(Champmeslé), Claude de La Rose (Rosimond), Noël Lebreton
(Hauteroche), and Racine's favourite actress Marie Champmeslé.

For its debut performance, on 25 August 1680, the troupe performed Racine's *Phèdre*, still only three years old, and a one-act
farce by La Chapelle. The king's interest in the theatre was waning.
This would be regretted by the actors, for, in 1684, control was
handed to the king's daughter-in-law, the sickly and usually disregarded Mme la Dauphine (Maria Anna Victoria of Bavaria). Mme
la Dauphine latched onto her new power. She immediately dismissed four actors and took charge of the distribution of roles. The
actors were forbidden from making any decision without seeking
the consent of Mme la Dauphine via the Premiers gentilshommes
de la chambre. For example, under a royal decree of 3 April 1685,
recorded by La Grange in his register, it was stated that Mme la
Dauphine 'wishes and intends that whenever one of the actors or
actresses dies, or others desire to retire from the troupe and no
longer perform plays, Messieurs the current Premiers gentilshommes de la chambre will report to her so that she may order the

vacant shares and portions of shares as it pleases her'.[1] Mme la Dauphine attempted to head off internal disputes over the repertoire by declaring that 'no play will be performed without the consent of the entire company assembled together'.

La Grange and his fellow actors quickly learned to tread carefully in their dealings with Mme la Dauphine. At Easter 1685 (19 April), the troupe travelled to Versailles to present a new member, Jean-Baptiste de Rochemore. La Grange left an account of what happened next:

> People with evil intentions took this opportunity to say such bad things about Baron and Raisin the younger that they were excluded from the troupe by order of the king, apparently for having shown insufficient respect for Mme la Dauphine. The troupe was very much concerned to defend them, and employed all possible credit and solicitations. Finally, on 2 May, they obtained their pardon, and the following day they went to thank Mme la Dauphine, and performed in public on Friday, 4 May.[2]

Mme la Dauphine died in 1690, but rules issued in her name would remain in place until the Revolution.

The actors performed at the Théâtre de Guénégaud until 1687, when they were forced to find a new home. The theatre was located a stone's throw from the newly completed Collège des Quatre-Nations, and the clerics of the university demanded the eviction of the sinful actors. The troupe moved further up the road to a theatre built especially for them at the site of a former *jeu de paume* in the rue des Fossés-Saint-Germain-des-Prés (the site today is at 14 rue de l'Ancienne-Comédie). This theatre, designed by the architect François d'Orbay, would remain the Comédie-Française's home until 1770. Italian in style, it was, for the time, a grand space, with elaborate decoration in green and gold and three galleries. The

---

[1] 'Règlement de la Dauphine', 3 April 1685. See La Grange, *Registre de La Grange (1658-1685): précédé d'une notice biographique*, p.350. Quoted in Howarth (ed.), *French Theatre in the Neo-classical Era, 1550-1789*, p.291.

[2] La Grange, *Registre de La Grange (1658-1685): précédé d'une notice biographique*, p.349-50. Quoted in Howarth (ed.), *French Theatre in the Neo-classical Era, 1550-1789*, p.297.

troupe performed Molière's *Le Médecin malgré lui* and Racine's *Phèdre* to open the theatre in 1689. The turn of the century was a time of loss and renewal. La Grange died in 1692, Marie Champmeslé in 1698 and Armande Béjart in 1700. Mlle Duclos took over the leading roles in Racine's tragedies, but was soon usurped by the emergence of Marie Champmeslé's niece Charlotte Desmares,[1] who made her debut in 1699. The following year, the Premier gentilhomme de la chamber, La Trémoille, accorded to Mlle Desmares six roles previously played by Mlle Duclos, so that she would have the opportunity of 'appearing more often on stage to perfect her declamation'. La Trémoille was acting on behalf of Philippe d'Orléans, the son of the king's brother and the future Regent of France, who had taken the young actress as his mistress.

2   The Age of Voltaire

During its first hundred years, from 1689 to 1789, the Comédie-Française retained its exclusive right to perform the plays of the great established writers of French drama. The Théâtre-Italien offered the public an alternative. The Italians, under Fiorillo, had shared the theatre of the Palais-Royal and then the Théâtre de Guénégaud with Molière's troupe. On the formation of the Comédie-Française, the Italians became officially known as the Comédiens-Italiens and returned to the theatre they had used before 1645, the Hôtel de Bourgogne. Their popularity and semi-independence concerned the crown. In 1697, they overreached themselves by planning to stage a play – *La Fausse prude* – that ridiculed the king's wife Mme de Maintenon. Louis ordered their banishment. After Louis's death, the regent, Philippe d'Orléans, eager to enliven the Paris stage, re-established the Théâtre-Italien by inviting Luigi Riccoboni to bring a troupe of Italian actors to the capital. The

---

[1] Charlotte Desmares (1682-1753, b. Copenhagen). CF j1690 s99 d1721. It is believed that the woman holding a mask in Watteau's painting *Les Acteurs de la Comédie-Française* is Mlle Desmares.

reformed Comédiens-Italiens, once more at the Bourgogne, continued the practice, established by their predecessors, of performing new plays in French. The Comédie jealously guarded its rights and took legal action to try and prevent the actors of the Saint-Germain and Saint-Laurent fairs from performing works with dialogue in French, but the Italians were given a certain leeway. (The directors of the fair theatres nearly always found a way of circumventing the regulations. When the authorities, on behalf of the Comédie, dismantled their stages they simply rebuilt them overnight.)

A new generation of players, including the actresses Mlle Dangeville, Mlle Clairon, Mlle Gaussin and Mme Vestris, and the actors Le Kain, Préville and Molé, emerged during the early and middle decades of the century. Like their predecessors, they needed to be resilient to overcome the stresses and challenges of performing on the Paris stage. The Comédie-Française's theatre in the rue des Fossés-Saint-Germain-des-Prés, so admired at the time of its unveiling, was, in truth, like all converted tennis courts, a demanding space for the actor. Spectators seated in the boxes that lined both sides of the rectangular auditorium faced each other rather than the stage. People went to the Comédie to interact with other people. The men who stood in the long pit (the *parterre*) were often boisterous and aggressive in the heckling of the actors, and they came and went during performances. Experienced players often gave as good as they got. During the first performance of Houdar de La Motte's *Inès de Castro*, in April 1723, men in the pit started to laugh. Mlle Duclos,[1] playing Inès, looked down into the pit and said: 'This is the play's finest moment, but go ahead and laugh, you blockheads.'[2] The pit fell silent.

Drunkenness, arguments and fistfights were common. Benches on the small stage, reserved for the most privileged audience members, took up a lot of the space: from this vantage point, aristocrats could watch the riffraff in the pit as if they, and not the actors, were providing the night's entertainment. Riffraff is a relative term, for

[1] Marie-Anne de Chateauneuf, dite Mlle Duclos (1670-1748). CF j1693 s93 d1736.

[2] Denis Diderot, *Paradoxe sur le comédien* (Paris: Société française d'imprimerie et de librairie, 1902), p.47.

the ticket prices tended to exclude most members of the lower orders (even entry to the pit cost the equivalent of a day's wages for a tradesman). These restrictions and distractions clashed with the refined presentation of the tragedies that formed such an important part of the repertoire. In the *Persian Letters* (1721), Montesquieu satirises the behaviour of spectators at the Comédie by having one of his Persian travellers fail to understand the relationship of the stage to the auditorium. He believes that the spectators are actors too.

Complaints about the indiscipline of actors were common. Some players would argue with the prompter, or talk to people they knew in the audience from the stage. Others would walk across the foyer in full costume. For Voltaire and, later in the century, Diderot and Grimm, the tyranny of the *parterre* was detrimental to good acting for it meant that actors were always conscious of the audience and forced to play in an artificial manner as a result: to be truthful, actors needed to be able to perform as if the audience wasn't there.

Aristocrats enjoyed easy access to the performers. It was the aspect of the Comédie that Casanova chose to record in his memoirs. We need to acknowledge an anecdote of this type, while being sceptical of its complete reliability:

> My great pleasure was to go there on the days when something old was being given and there were not two hundred spectators. I saw *Le Misanthrope*, *L'Avare*, *Le Joueur*, and pretended I was seeing their first performances. I arrived in time to see Sarrazin, his wife Grandval, La Dangeville, La Dumesnil, La Gaussin, La Clairon, as well as several actresses who had retired from the stage and were living on their pensions, among them La Levasseur. I talked with them with pleasure, for they told me the most savoury anecdotes. A tragedy was being performed in which a pretty actress played the mute role of a priestess. 'How pretty she is!' I said to one of these matrons. 'Yes delicious. She's the daughter of the actor who played the confidant. She is very agreeable in company and shows a great deal of promise.' 'I should very much like to make her acquaintance.' 'Lord! That's not difficult. Her father and mother are civility itself, and I am sure they will be delighted if you ask them to invite you to supper, and they will not be in

your way; they will go off to bed and leave you at table with the girl for as long as you please.'[1]

In the second half of the 18th century, women starting out at the Comédie were very young. Virginia Scott calculates that the average age of *débutantes* between 1750 and 1790 was seventeen, and it wasn't uncommon for a girl to go on the stage at the age of thirteen.[2] Girls this young were acutely vulnerable, often too immature and too unprotected to fend off unwanted male attention, as well as in need of money since their share of the theatre's revenue was small and they needed to pay for their lodgings and to buy their own costumes. The extract from Casanova's memoirs implies that some older members of the company were prepared to facilitate access to novices.

The Comédiens-français premiered the work of many dramatists during the 18th century, among them Gresset, Piron, Fagan, Pellegrin, Destouches, Crébillon, Marmontel and Voltaire. Voltaire believed in the superiority of tragedy over other genres of drama. At the age of twenty-three, he wrote his first tragedy, *Œdipe*, daring to place himself in direct comparison with both Sophocles and Corneille. The actors of the Comédie-Française, knowing their audience, initially turned the play down because there was no love interest. Voltaire reluctantly revised his play. Premiered in November 1718, with Quinault-Dufresne[3] and Charlotte Desmares in the roles of Œdipe and Jocaste, it was an extravagant success. Adrienne Lecouvreur[4] took over the role of Jocaste during the 1720s. Voltaire, like so many others, was deeply enamoured of this young actress whose natural style of acting was ahead of its time, although there is no evidence that their relationship was sexual. Voltaire's close friend d'Argental's love for the actress is better documented, for she wrote frequently to him. An anonymous commentator in

---

[1] Giacomo Casanova (trans. Willard R. Trask), *History of My Life*, vol.3 (Baltimore: Johns Hopkins University Press, 1997), p.144.

[2] See Scott, *Women on the Stage in Early Modern France*, p.263.

[3] Abraham-Alexis Quinault, dit Quinault-Dufresne (1693-1767, b. Verdun).

[4] Adrienne Lecouvreur (1692-1730, b. Damery, Marne). CF j1717 s17 d30.

the *Mercure de France* wrote of her: 'Perhaps no one has ever understood so well the art of silent acting, that is to say, has known how to listen, and to register the meaning of the words spoken by the actor on stage with her.'[1] No other actor of the 18th century provoked a printed comment of this kind, a comment that might have been written about a player of today. Born in Champagne, she had acted in the provinces from the age of fourteen; seduced and supported by some powerful men, she made her debut at the Comédie in 1717 in Crébillon's *Électre* and Molière's *George Dandin* (as Angélique). In 1726, she created the role of the Marquise in Pierre de Marivaux's *La Seconde surprise de l'amour*. The mystery that surrounded her early death in 1730 – it was said that she had been poisoned at the instigation of the duchesse de Bouillon, her love-rival for the affections of the maréchal de Saxe – ensured that she would be remembered long into the future. In fact, it is likely that the cause of death was dysentery. An autopsy, demanded by Voltaire, revealed no evidence of foul play. Voltaire was enraged by the Church's refusal to allow a Christian burial:

> The English have been criticised for burying in Westminster Abbey the famous actress Mrs Oldfield with nearly the same honours that were paid to Newton. It has been suggested by some that they had affected to honour the memory of an actress to this extent in order to make us appreciate still more the barbarous injustice they reproach us with, namely of having thrown the body of Mlle Lecouvreur on to the garbage heap.[2]

Marivaux was the great playwright of the 1720s and 1730s. Born Pierre Carlet in Paris in 1688, his formative years were spent in the Auvergne, where his father worked as *Contrôleur de la Monnaie* at Riom and then Limoges. Marivaux was meant to follow in his father's footsteps, so in 1710 he returned to Paris to study law. Marivaux wrote his first play, the one-act comedy *Le Père prudent et équitable ou Crispin l'heureux fourbe*, while still living in the Auvergne, and in Paris he neglected his studies while he wrote a novel

[1] *Mercure de France* (March 1730), p.580.
[2] Voltaire (trans. Leonard Tancock), *Letters on England*, p.112.

– *Les Effets surprenants de la sympathie* (1712). Marivaux came under the influence of the distinguished writer, and member of the Académie Française, Fontenelle, who participated in the great intellectual debate of the time – the 'Querelle des Anciens et des Modernes' – on the side of the moderns. Like Fontenelle, Marivaux attended the salon of Mme de Lambert in the rue de Richelieu. Mme Lambert supported Montesquieu and Antoine Houdar de la Motte, a leading proponent of the moderns, and was a champion of young writers. It was at Mme Lambert's salon that Marivaux met actors from the Comédie, including Adrienne Lecouvreur.

Marivaux wrote articles for the *Mercure de France*, admired for their wit and elegance, and several parodies, including a re-telling of Homer's *Iliade* (1716). In the early 1720s, Marivaux suffered a double blow – the death of his wife and the loss of his inheritance, invested in John Law's Mississippi Company. His first major play was a verse tragedy, *Annibal*, accepted by the Comédie-Française in 1720. The play failed and was withdrawn after three performances. Later that year, Marivaux wrote a one-act comedy for the Théâtre-Italien called *Arlequin poli par l'amour*. Such was Marivaux's liking for Riccoboni and his actors, their style of playing and their bonhomie, that he aligned himself with the troupe. He would create most of his leading female characters for Riccoboni's star actress, Silvia Balletti (b. 1701). *La Surprise de l'amour*, a comedy in which a man and a woman, who have both renounced love, are manoeuvred by their servants into falling in love, was premiered at the Théâtre-Italien in 1722. It was the first of a string of hits that included *La Double inconstance* (1723), *La Fausse suivante* (1724), *Le Jeu de l'amour et du hasard* (1730) and *Les Fausses confidences* (1737).

Marivaux's style of play, although influenced to a certain extent by Molière and commedia dell'arte, was recognised as being new. It divided opinion. The aspects of Marivaux's art that make his work seem modern today – his preoccupation with feelings, language, irony and dramatic illusion in plays that explore the complexities and the contradictions of the human heart – made his work seem frivolous and lightweight to many of his contemporaries. Voltaire repeatedly dismissed Marivaux's work because he found it slight as well as overly concerned with the metaphysics of love. Marivaux was sensitive to criticism and sought the recognition that a hit at the Comédie-Française would bring. He had supporters in the troupe. Eleven of his plays were accepted by the Comédie. The best received of them was *La Seconde surprise de l'amour*, premiered in 1727, and performed fourteen times in its initial run. The play was regularly revived up until the Revolution. The others were: *Le Dénouement imprévu*, 1724, six performances; *L'Île de la raison*, 1727, four performances; *La Réunion des amours*, 1731, nine performances; *Les Serments indiscrets*, 1732, nine performances; *Le Petit-maître corrigé*, 1734, two performances (rediscovered by the Comédie in 2016); *L'Épreuve*, 1736, four performances; *Le Legs*, 1736, ten performances, regularly revived; *La Dispute*, 1744, one performance; and *Le Préjugé vaincu*, 1746, seven performances, regularly revived.[1]

Les Serments indiscrets, a major work in five acts, was Marivaux's best hope at the Comédie. Voltaire wrote to a friend: 'This summer a new prose comedy by M. Marivaux, entitled *Les Serments indiscrets*, will be presented [at the Comédie]. There will be a great deal of metaphysics but little naturalness. The cafés will applaud but honest people will find nothing of interest.'[2] In fact, the cafés were not convinced. The Comédie's patrons, wedded to the conventions of the classics and the pre-eminence of verse, were harder to crack than those of the Théâtre-Italien. Simon-Henri Dubuisson was just one of Marivaux's contemporaries who wanted to understand why his work mostly succeeded at the Théâtre-Italien but mostly failed at the Comédie:

> I have tried to fathom the reasons, and believe I have discovered two: the first, that with the Italians one does not look for the same perfection that one expects of the French. With the former a self-indulgent excess of wit is tolerated, but it will be hissed in the

---

[1] See *The Comédie-Française Registers Project*, online at https://www.cfregisters.org (accessed 7/4/2020).
[2] Voltaire to Jean Baptiste Nicolas Formont: Friday, 18 April 1732, in *Electronic Enlightenment Scholarly Edition of Correspondence*, ed. Robert McNamee et al. Vers. 3.0. University of Oxford. 2018. Web. 7 Aug. 2019.

case of the latter. The second reason is that Mlle Silvia has a manner of speaking which seems ideally designed to give expression to M. Marivaux's dialogue: her clipped pronunciation and her foreign accent make a perfect match with this author's terseness and bizarre turns of phrase.[1]

Marivaux achieved great popularity during the 1720s, but Voltaire's view took hold, a cabal formed, and younger writers such as Crébillon *fils*, Grimm and Marmontel perpetuated the view that Marivaux's work lacked depth. However, a much greater figure of the younger generation, d'Alembert, saw things more clearly, as he so often did. While believing that Marivaux's greatest work was his unfinished novel *La Vie de Marianne*, and finding, as many contemporaries did, that Marivaux's plays were too unvaried in their themes, d'Alembert, writing in 1763, recognised that the theme of the 'éternelle surprise de l'amour' was unique to Marivaux and delivered with a rare subtlety. In summation, he wrote:

> The works of Marivaux are so numerous, and the nuances which distinguish them are so delicate, that it is difficult to know either the man or the author without conducting a subtle and detailed analysis, which would require more words than is possible in a concise portrait.[2]

While Marivaux's reputation as a writer for the theatre went into decline, Voltaire's remained high. *Œdipe* was the first of over thirty plays written for the Comédie-Française, many of them constantly revived during the 18th century and more present in the repertoire than the works of both Corneille and Racine. In fact, we could easily think of the Comédie-Française of this period as the maison de Voltaire. A full-sized statue of Voltaire by Houdon (1781) still stands in the foyer of the Salle Richelieu alongside a bust of Molière.

Zaïre, presented in August 1732 after Voltaire's return to Paris

[1] Dubuisson to the marquis de Caumont: 21 May 1735. Quoted in Howarth, *French Theatre in the Neo-classical Era, 1550-1789*, p.566-67.
[2] Jean le Rond d'Alembert, *Éloge de Marivaux* (Paris: Seuil, 1967), p.17.

following his years of exile in England, equalled *Œdipe*'s popularity. Here, Voltaire departed from tradition by writing a tragedy about French characters, and by tapping into the public's fascination with the Muslim world, especially the scenario of a young French girl seduced by a Muslim ruler. Voltaire's *Zaïre*, though, had none of the dark eroticism suggested by the plot and was surprisingly sentimental in tone. There are superficial similarities with *Othello*.

Jeanne-Catherine Gaussin,[1] who had only joined the Comédie-Française the previous year, played Zaïre, alongside Quinault-Dufresne (Orosmane), Grandval (Nérestan) and Sarrazin (Lusignan). She had grown up in the milieu of the Comédie, but in the servants' quarter, for her father was a coachman who worked for the actor Baron. She won many hearts. Voltaire expressed his admiration in verse: 'Young Gaussin, receive my tender homage. […] *Zaïre* is your work; […] it is your eyes, so full of charm, your touching voice and your enchanting sounds.'[2] For the young men of literary Paris, making their way as writers and thinkers, the generation of the *Encyclopédie*, the appeal of the theatre was inseparable from the appeal of its young women, and Gaussin's desirability made her an overnight star. Denis Diderot was eighteen, and a student at the university, when Mlle Gaussin played *Zaïre*. Looking back, he wrote:

> When I was young, my life was balanced between the Sorbonne and the Comédie. In the depth of the winter season, I would go to the solitary alleys of the Luxembourg, where I would recite

---

[1] Jeanne-Catherine Gaussem, dite Mlle Gaussin (1711-1767, b. Paris). CF j1731 s31 d63.

[2] Voltaire, *Épître 38* (1732):
Jeune Gaussin, reçois mon tendre hommage,
Reçois mes vers au théâtre applaudis;
Protège-les: Zaïre est ton ouvrage;
Il est à toi, puisque tu l'embellis.
Ce sont tes yeux, ces yeux si pleins de charmes,
Ta voix touchante, et tes sons enchanteurs,
Qui du critique ont fait tomber les armes;
Ta seule vue adoucit les censeurs.

aloud the roles of Molière and Corneille. What was my plan? To
be applauded? Perhaps. To make myself known to the women of
the theatre whom I found infinitely lovely and whom I knew to
be very easy? Certainly. I don't know what I would have done to
please Mlle Gaussin, who had just made her debut and who was
beauty itself.[1]

Years later, Mlle Clairon praised her older rival, but not without
a little dig: 'She had the loveliest face, the most touching voice. She
had a noble presence and all her movements had a child-like grace
which was irresistible; but she was Mlle Gaussin in everything.'

Zaïre was performed thirty-one times in 1732 alone. Translated
into English under the title *Zara*, the play was a hit at the Drury
Lane Theatre in 1736 with Susannah Maria Cibber in the title role
and was thereafter frequently revived. David Garrick played the
part of Lusignan in 1774, opposite Elizabeth Younge as Zara.

Voltaire's *Le Fanatisme, ou Mahomet le prophète*, a five-act tragedy that attacked religious fanaticism and the Islamic faith, and by
extension the other great organised religion, was staged by the Comédie in 1742. The play, banned after only three performances, is
an example of how Voltaire's plays reflected his philosophy and his
political and social ideas. However, Voltaire's originality was more
apparent in his reforming ideas on stagecraft and theatrical presentation than in his plays. Voltaire took an interest in all aspects of
theatrical production. It was Voltaire who removed the on-stage
seating so that the stage could be used to create the world of the
play. In achieving reform, Voltaire was aided by the tragic actor Le
Kain.[2] Le Kain first appeared at the Comédie-Française at the age
of twenty-one in 1750, cast by Voltaire as Titus in his play *Brutus*.
He had previously acted as an amateur in the *théâtres de société*.
Voltaire's advocacy of Le Kain was resented by some of the troupe's
senior actors who did not initially believe that he had the talent or
the pedigree to be a member. Two years would pass before he was
made a sociétaire. Walpole summed up the paradox of Le Kain in
the following words: 'He is very ugly and ill made, and yet has a

[1] Denis Diderot, *Paradoxe sur le comédien*, p.145.
[2] Henri Cain, dit Le Kain (1729-1778, b. Paris). CF j1750 s51 d78.

heroic dignity which Garrick wants, and great fire'.[1] Le Kain remained close to Voltaire, and visited him often at Ferney. In a letter to the duc de Richelieu, dated 1755, Voltaire wrote:

> A great actor came to find me at my retreat, it is Le Kain, your protégé, Orosmane.[2] He is also the best child in the world. He played at Dijon and delighted the Burgundians. He played *chez moi* and he made the Genevans cry. I advised him to go and earn some money in Lyon for at least eight days while he waits for the orders of the duc de Gesvres. He does not earn more than two thousand *livres* a year from the Comédie of Paris. I promise you a new tragedy if you deign to protect him on his journey to Lyon.[3]

Voltaire was sometimes critical of Le Kain's mannerisms and innovations. When the actor played Ninias in Voltaire's *Sémiramis*, he decided to appear – having killed his mother – with blood on his hands and arms. 'This is a bit English,' Voltaire complained,[4] thinking, perhaps, of Shakespeare and *Macbeth*. 'We should not give in to such ornaments.'

Voltaire was well served by the two young actresses who lit up the Comédie's stage during the middle decades of the century – Mlle Dumesnil[5] and Mlle Clairon.[6] Voltaire cared for them both,

[1] Horace Walpole to M. Montague: 22 September 1765. Quoted in Fleury (ed. Theodore Hook), *The French Stage and the French People as Illustrated in the Memoirs of M. Fleury*, vol.1 (London: Henry Colburn, 1841), p.101.

[2] Le Kain enjoyed a great success playing Orosmane in *Zaïre* before the king at Versailles. The king was said to have remarked: 'He made me weep and I never weep.'

[3] Voltaire to Louis François Armand de Vignerot du Plessis, 3rd duc de Richelieu: Wednesday, 2 April 1755, in *Electronic Enlightenment Scholarly Edition of Correspondence*, ed. Robert McNamee et al. Vers. 3.0. University of Oxford. 2018. Web. 9 Jul. 2019.

[4] Voltaire to Charles Augustin Feriol, comte d'Argental: Wednesday, 4 August 1756. *Electronic Enlightenment Scholarly Edition of Correspondence*, ed. Robert McNamee et al. Vers. 3.0. University of Oxford. 2018. Web. 12 Jul. 2019.

[5] Marie-Françoise Marchand, dite Mlle Dumesnil (1713-1803, b. Paris. CF j1737 s37 d76.

[6] Clair Josèphe Hippolyte Leris, dite Mlle Clairon (1723-1803, b Condé-sur-l'Escaut, Nord). CF j1743 s43 d76.

but the two women spent their careers in a state of bitter enmity. Mlle Dumesnil acted in the provinces before joining the Comédie in 1737. For Voltaire, her playing of the title role in his tragedy *Mérope* in 1743 was a landmark moment, for it ended the chant-like monotony of declamation: 'With unseeing eyes and broken voice, [she] raised a trembling hand to sacrifice her own son. [...] Mlle Lecouvreur had grace, simplicity, truth, decorum: but for the grand pathos of action, we saw that for the first time in Mlle Dumesnil. It is only in recent years that actors have ventured to be what they ought to be, living pictures: before, they declaimed.'[1] Little is known about Mlle Dumesnil's private life. She lived with another sociétaire, the actor and playwright Granval, for many years, and owned a private theatre in Montmartre where indecent plays by Granval were performed. Mlle Gaussin performed in these plays, if a letter written many years later by the marquis de Paulmy d'Argenson is accurate.[2]

Mlle Clairon was younger than Mlle Dumesnil by ten years. The daughter of a humble soldier, she made her debut at the Théâtre-Italien at the age of thirteen. She appeared at Rouen for a number of years and was the victim of a cruel *libelle* that would haunt her for the rest of her life.[3] She initially struggled to enter the Comédie-Française. When the opportunity came, in 1743, she caused a sensation as Racine's Phèdre. Like Le Kain, she supported Voltaire in the call for reform, choosing to wear realistic costumes and playing tragedy in a measured style without an excess of emotion. In 1750, she played Electre in Voltaire's *Oreste*. On the evening of the premiere, 12 January, Voltaire sent the young actress his 'notes' on her performance. The letter is fascinating because it reveals that Voltaire was a director, guiding his actress by pinpointing small textual details in the manner of an 18th century John Barton:

---

[1] Voltaire, *Appel à toutes les nations* (1761). Quoted in Howarth, *French Theatre in the Neo-classical Era, 1550-1789*, p.546-47.

[2] See Scott, *Women on the Stage in Early Modern France*, p.258-59.

[3] *Histoire de la vie et mœurs de Mlle Cronel, dite Frétillon, écrite par elle-même, actrice de la Comédie de Rouen* (La Haye 1739).

You were admirable; you have shown in twenty passages the perfection of art and the role of Electre is certainly your triumph; but I am a father, and along with the great pleasure that I feel on hearing the compliments given to my daughter by an enchanted public, I will make a few small, pardonable observations. Press, but without declaiming, passages such as: 'Sans trouble, sans remords, Egiste renouvelle, de son hymen affreux la pompe criminelle, vous vous trompiez, ma sœur, hélas! tout nous trahit.' You cannot believe how much these lines benefit from variety in the playing. In your imprecation against the tyrant 'L'innocent doit périr, le crime est trop heureux' you do not press enough. You speak the line 'the innocent must perish' too slowly, too languidly. The impetuous Electre must have, at this moment, a furious, precipitous despair. The cry is too tame for me; it must be more intense. 'La nature en tout temps est funeste en ces lieux.' You placed the accent on *fu*, so we applauded: but you have not yet made enough of this. You cannot be too expressive in the two passages of the fourth and fifth acts. These Eumenides demand a voice that is more than human. Again, set yourself free, [...] so as not to be uniform in the painful speeches. You must give everything. There are many critics. I have been very critical to mention these nuances given the extent of my admiration and gratitude. Good evening, Melpomene; sleep well.[1]

Diderot's *Paradoxe sur le comédien*, written in the 1770s, is a key source for anyone seeking an insight into acting and the theatre during the 18th century. A philosophical study on the nature of acting, it takes for its examples the work of some of the stars of the Comédie-Française of the period. The underlying idea of Diderot's polemic is that the great actor doesn't *feel* the emotions he expresses on the stage, but presents the illusion of feeling. Emotional acting is by its nature uneven and unrepeatable night after night. The actor, therefore, must be guided by his intelligence and not by his nature or his emotions; he should be able to slip in and out of character in the blink of an eye. Diderot cited Quinault-Dufresne and Le Kain as two players who possessed this swiftness of thought and

[1] Voltaire to Claire Josèphe Hippolyte Léris de Latude: Monday, 12 January 1750. *Electronic Enlightenment Scholarly Edition of Correspondence*, ed. Robert McNamee et al. Vers. 3.0. University of Oxford. 2018. Web. 10 Jul. 2019.

who didn't need to feel an emotion to play it. When performing Sévère in Corneille's *Polyeucte*, Quinault-Dufresne spoke some of his lines softly, as the text demanded. Berated by the pit to speak louder, he replied, 'No, Messieurs, you speak less loud'. 'Only a man of self-possession,' declared Diderot, 'the exceptional actor, the player *par excellence*, can so slip in and out of character.'[1]

The anecdote chosen by Diderot for Le Kain related to that moment of innovation in his performance as Ninias in *Sémiramis* that so irritated Voltaire:

> Le Kain enters with blood-stained hands. He is horror-stricken and his terror is so visceral it is shared by the spectators. Suddenly he spots an earring that has fallen from an actress's ear onto the stage. [Without halting his performance] he kicks it into the wings. And this actor feels? Impossible. Would you call him a bad actor? Of course not. What, then, is Le Kain? A cold man, who is without feeling, but who simulates it beautifully.[2]

Le Kain and Mlle Clairon often appeared together, but not always harmoniously. 'Clarion will tell you, if you ask her, that Le Kain would maliciously cause her to play badly, and that she would get her own back by getting him hissed.'[3] Diderot especially admired Mlle Clairon for her analytical mind and dedication to her art. Not only did she take instruction well (see above), she would sometimes come up with an improvement. Voltaire was in the audience one night when he was heard to exclaim: 'Did I really write that?'[4] In contrast, Marie Dumesnil 'enters the stage without knowing what she is going to say; half the time she doesn't even know what she is saying: but she has one sublime moment'. Those aspects of Mlle Clairon's acting that Diderot praised were recognised by

---

[1] Denis Diderot, *Paradoxe sur le comédien*, p.47-48.

[2] Denis Diderot, *Paradoxe sur le comédien*, p.48. To add to Diderot's examples: an actor during the RSC's 1989 production of *Othello* scuffed up the corner of a Persian rug. Actors came and went but none of them knew how to deal with the rug. Finally, Ian McKellen entered the scene and, without missing a beat, nonchalantly kicked the corner back in place.

[3] Denis Diderot, *Paradoxe sur le comédien*, p.28.

[4] Denis Diderot, *Paradoxe sur le comédien*, p.56.

David Garrick too, but he came to a different conclusion: 'She has everything that art and a good understanding, with great natural spirit can give her – but then I fear the heart has none of those instantaneous feelings, that life blood, that keen sensibility, that bursts at once from genius. But you must not betray me my good friend; La Clairon would never forgive me…'[1] Garrick enjoyed exchanging gossip about actors in his private correspondence. The minor actress (with the Théâtre-Italien) and novelist Marie-Jeanne Riccoboni entertained Garrick by savaging some of the great names of the Comédie. Responding to Garrick's question 'Does the Clairon bear the loss of publick applause like a Philosopher?', asked after Mlle Clairon had retired from the Comédie, she wrote: 'Pale and green in the morning, the after-dinner rouge does not hide the lividity of her borrowed lilies. The pit has quite forgotten her: they applaud all the ugly monkeys who dare to aspire to take her place. The best and ugliest is Mlle Saint-Val: her face is a grimace, but when it comes alive it's a fury.'[2]

Diderot's view of actors as people was not enlightened. He agreed with polite society, and the Church, that the men of the theatre lacked honour and the women lacked virtue. But actresses didn't need to be immoral to be accused of immorality, and we should be wary of contemporary gossip about their behaviour. In old age, Mlle Clairon published her memoirs, the first actress to do so. She denied the debauchery of which she was accused: 'Envy, slander and impunity have so exaggerated the case that I find it impossible that a thinking person would believe it. […] Love is a need of nature: I have satisfied it, but not in ways that make me blush; I defy people who call me a shameful whore, and challenge them to name a single man who paid me, a wife or father to whom I caused pain.'[3] There are, in these memoirs, moments of self-revelation, eloquently expressed. Here Mlle Clairon is writing about the

---

[1] Garrick to Peter Sturz: 3 January 1769. Quoted in Howarth, *French Theatre in the Neo-classical Era, 1550-1789*, p.634.

[2] Marie-Jeanne Riccoboni to David Garrick: 29 January 1767. Electronic Enlightenment Scholarly Edition of Correspondence, ed. Robert McNamee et al. Vers. 3.0. University of Oxford. 2018. Web. 14 Oct. 2019.

[3] Mlle Clairon, *Mémoires de Mlle Clairon, actrice du Théâtre-Français, écrits*

libellous attack on her character that almost destroyed her career when she was a teenager in Le Havre:

> I was far from my protectors, ignorant of what I should do. [...] I took no steps to try and discover the motive behind this outrage; my innocence even allowed me to believe that I could count on the justice of men. But even if I had been wiser, what in truth could I have done? If I had condemned this unfortunate man to a few months in prison I would not have prevented the pamphlet from being circulated. My supposed shame would still have been believed. [...] I was nothing, and could do nothing. Alas! what does it matter to society that there is one more unhappy creature? I know now that certain people like to see others suffer, that their malignity and egotism feeds on the tears and despair of my sex; however incredible the scandalous story might be, their own perversity makes them believe it, and the impunity given to them allows them to cruelly, and with audacity, assert it. [...] The libel that was made against me is today lost in the immensity of lies told about everyone. Innocence, greatness, not even divinity, can protect us from the wickedness of others, and all that I have read about others must certainly console me for all that has been written about me.[1]

A new actor, Le Kain's protégé Fleury,[2] emerged during the 1770s. Fleury made his debut at the Comédie in 1774 playing Egisthe in Voltaire's *Mérope*. Mlle Dumesnil, at the age of seventy, played the title role. When the nervous debutant dried, Mlle Dumesnil graciously whispered the line in his ear. Later, she suggested that he follow her practice of drinking a mixture of wine and *bouillon de poulet* before every show. 'The frequency with which she partook of this nauseous mixture,' Fleury would later write in his memoirs, 'gave rise to the calumnious report that she indulged in the use of strong drinks. When in some of her most sublime flights,

par elle-même, Nouvelle ed. (Paris, 1822), p.46-47.

[1] *Mémoires de Mlle Clairon*, p.23-25.

[2] Joseph-Abraham Bénard, dit Fleury (1750-1822, b. Orléans). CF j1774 s78 d1818.

her enemies used to remark that she was not inspired but intoxicated, and that she was not *Iphigénie en Aulide* but *Iphigénie en Champagne*.'[1]

Voltaire's final play, *Irène*, was presented at the Comédie-Française in the spring of 1778. The eighty-three-year-old Voltaire travelled from Geneva to Paris. On his arrival at the home of the Marquis de Villette, on the Left Bank in the rue de Beaune, he was greeted by all the actors of the Comédie. Voltaire expected to see his protégé Le Kain, but the great actor had died suddenly a short number of days before. 'Voltaire's grief was deep and sincere,' wrote Fleury.[2] On 30 March, at the end of a performance of *Irène*, Voltaire was feted on the stage by the actors and spectators. He died two months later. *Œdipe* and *Zaïre* continued to be performed during the 19th century (Sarah Bernhardt played Zaïre in 1874), but interest rapidly declined in the 20th. *Zaïre* was last presented by the Comédie-Française in 1936, and the troupe's last performance of any play by Voltaire (discounting an adaptation of *Candide*) was of *L'Orphelin de la Chine* in 1966. The rediscovery of Voltaire's dramatic œuvre seems unlikely. The consensus view is that his plays lack originality and are dramatically inert, and it is hard to see how they could be updated to tell us something about our own time. However, the theatre is a mysterious machine. Plays that are dead on the page can come alive on the stage.

Another major figure whose plays were destined to be forgotten, was Prosper Jolyot de Crébillon. Crébillon, born in Dijon in 1674, enjoyed his biggest success at the Comédie-Française during the first decades of the century, when Voltaire was still at school: *Idoménée* (1705) and *Atrée et Thyeste* (1707) possessed a sombre power that some people found shocking. 'Crébillon,' wrote d'Alembert years later, 'showed human perversity in all its brutality.' Crébillon had many supporters, including Mme de Pompadour, and had been elected to the Académie Française. He was also the royal censor. Voltaire despised Crébillon because he

---

[1] *The French Stage and the French People as Illustrated in the Memoirs of M. Fleury*, vol.1, p.83.
[2] *The French Stage and the French People as Illustrated in the Memoirs of M. Fleury*, vol.1, p.96.

had censored some of his plays. He sought revenge by taking the subjects of Crébillon's tragedies – including *Sémiramis* and *Electre* – and writing his own (supposedly) superior versions. The Comédie-Française remained loyal to both writers, and their admiration for Crébillon was such that when he died, in 1762, they organised a service in his honour that outraged the archbishop of Paris.

A playwright who found success during the final decades of the *ancien régime* was Pierre-Laurent de Belloy. The Comédie-Française staged some of his tragedies in the 1760s and 1770s. His patriotic tragedy *Le Siège de Calais*, written in the aftermath of the Seven Years War, was accepted by the Comédie despite opposition from Le Kain (perhaps on Voltaire's behalf). The play, premiered in February 1765, was a huge success. The king instructed the actors to perform it at Versailles.

3   Shakespeare Enters the Repertoire

It was Voltaire who first made the French aware of Shakespeare, when, after his return to Paris from England, he published the *Lettres philosophiques* (1734). Voltaire's view of Shakespeare, balanced precariously between admiration and repulsion, had a lasting influence in France. David Garrick was one of the Englishmen who, knowing the reach of Voltaire's fame on the Continent, engaged with him on the issue of Shakespeare:

> Sir, [...] had it been in my power to have follow'd my inclinations, I should have paid my respects at Ferney long before this time, but a violent bilious fever most unluckily seiz'd me upon the road & confin'd me to my bed five weeks at Munich [...]. You were pleas'd to tell a Gentleman that you had a theatre ready to receive me; I should with great pleasure have exerted what little talents I have, & could I have been the means of bringing our Shakespeare into some favour with Mr Voltaire I should have been happy indeed! No enthusiastick Missionary who had converted the Emperor of China to his religion would have been

prouder than I, could I have reconcil'd the first Genius of Europe to our Dramatic faith. I am, Sr, Your most humble & most Obedient servant, David Garrick. PS. Tho I have call'd Shakespeare our dramatick faith yet I must do my countrymen ye Justice to declare, that notwithstanding their deserv'd admiration of his astonishing Powers they are not bigotted to his errors, as some French Journalists have so confidently affirm'd.[1]

Voltaire, sensitive to English criticism, defended his critique of Shakespeare in a fascinating letter to Horace Walpole, written four years later in July 1768. The letter contained little of the contempt for England and Shakespeare that Voltaire, during and after the Seven Years' War, often expressed to his compatriots:

> You have nearly succeeded in making your countrymen believe that I despise Shakespeare. I was the first writer who made Shakespeare known to the French: forty years ago I translated passages from his works, as from Milton's, Waller's, Rochester's, Dryden's, and Pope's. I can assure you that before my time no one in France knew anything about English poetry: and had hardly ever heard of Locke. [...] Fate willed that I should be the first to explain to my fellow-countrymen the discoveries of the great Newton, which many people among us still speak of as the systems. I have been your apostle and your martyr: truly, it is not fair that the English should complain of me. I said, long ago, that if Shakespeare had lived in the time of Addison he would have added to his genius the elegance and purity which makes Addison admirable. I stated that his genius was his own, and his faults the faults of his age. [...] His is a fine but untutored nature: he has neither regularity, nor propriety, nor art: in the midst of his sublimity he sometimes descends to grossness, and in the most impressive scenes to buffoonery: his tragedy is chaos, illuminated by a hundred shafts of light.[2]

---

[1] David Garrick to Voltaire: 15 October 1764. *Electronic Enlightenment Scholarly Edition of Correspondence*, ed. Robert McNamee et al. Vers. 3.0. University of Oxford. 2018. Web. 15 Oct. 2019.

[2] Voltaire to Horace Walpole: Friday, 15 July 1768, in *Electronic Enlightenment Scholarly Edition of Correspondence*, ed. Robert McNamee et al. Vers. 3.0. University of Oxford. 2017. Web. 9 Jun. 2018.

Voltaire was writing before any play by Shakespeare had been performed in French in France. This changed less than a year later, when, in 1769, Shakespeare first entered the repertoire of the Comédie-Française: the troupe performed *Hamlet* in a version by Jean-François Ducis. Ducis's *Hamlet* was a very free adaptation. Hardly anything from Shakespeare's original survived after the text had been cleansed to meet the expectations of French classical drama and the public's taste for order and refinement. Ducis, following Racine, wrote in alexandrines and respected the unity of time and place. His *Hamlet* was a play for six characters, and they were not the characters created by Shakespeare. Gertrude was a villainess; Hamlet and Ophelia were sexless; Ophelia didn't go mad (etc.). It was the start of a very long journey, for it wouldn't be until the 20th century that a truly accurate translation of the play would be staged at the Comédie. As Ducis explained himself in a letter to Garrick:

> I conceive, Sir, that you must have thought me exceedingly rash in placing such a tragedy as *Hamlet* on the French stage. Not to speak of the barbarous irregularities with which it abounds – the spectre in full armour and long speeches, the strolling actors, the fencing bout – all these appeared to me to be matters utterly inadmissible on the French stage. Nevertheless, I deeply regretted being unable to bring upon it that awful ghost who exposes crime and demands revenge. I was therefore obliged, in a certain sense, to create a new play. I simply tried to make an interesting part of a parricidal Queen, and above all to paint in the pure and melancholy soul of Hamlet a model of filial tenderness.[1]

Ducis wrote his Hamlet for Le Kain, but Le Kain turned down the role. He shared Voltaire's opinion that a public used to the sublime works of Racine and Corneille would not tolerate the 'vulgarity' of Shakespeare, as did the leading actress Mlle Clairon,

---

[1] Quoted in Paul Benchettrit, 'Hamlet at the Comédie Française: 1769-1896', in *Shakespeare Survey*, vol.9 (January 1956), p.59.

who wrote in her memoirs: 'English manners permit the most re-
pulsive realities on the stage; Richard III is represented there with
all the deformities he had from nature… The French *parterre* will
accept in tragedy only what is elegant and noble.'[1] François-René
Molé[2] played Hamlet. Molé had joined the troupe in 1760. He was,
at the age of thirty-five, the troupe's biggest star, a player whose
charismatic appeal was equalled by his ambition and versatility.
Later, when the Shakespeare enthusiast Talma came on the scene
and took over the part, Ducis's *Hamlet* would grow in popularity.

For Voltaire and his followers, the very French concept of *goût* –
taste – was necessary to 'perfect' genius. At the Comédie, especially,
conventions based on the concept of taste were demanded by audiences, self-regulated by actors and policed by the Académie
Française and the censor. A precedent had been created in 1637 by
the reaction to Corneille's early play *Le Cid*. Corneille was forced
to withdraw and revise his play because the Académie Française
judged it to be immoral and defective: Corneille had not observed
the unities. Plays were required to have a moral purpose; they
should obey the unities of time, place and action; they should not
contain coarse language; they should not depict acts of violence or
lust; and comic characters should not appear in tragedies. All things
which Shakespeare did with abundance.

Not everyone agreed with Voltaire. For some, French refinement
was cold and sterile. The abbé Provost had visited England and
wrote admiringly of Shakespeare's work, particularly *Hamlet*, in his
journal *Le Pour et contre* during the 1730s and 40s. Diderot and
d'Alembert proclaimed the essential importance of genius – daring,
insight, originality, excitement – in artistic creation. They saw in
Shakespeare the artistic equivalent of their God, Newton, and proclaimed Shakespeare's genius in the *Encyclopédie*, published
between 1751 and 1772. In the entry on 'Tragédie', written by
Louis Jaucourt, we find: 'Shakespeare never had a master or an
equal. [His was a] genius full of naturalness and strength, without
rules: we find in this great genius, an inexhaustible and sublime

---

[1] Quoted in Scott, *Women on the Stage in Early Modern France*, p.210.
[2] François-René Molé (1734-1802, b. Paris). CF j1754 s61 d1802.

imagination. [...] He surpasses all poets.' D'Alembert, in the entry 'Ecole', acknowledged Shakespeare's coarseness, but for him that wasn't the point: 'Shakespeare's plays have barbaric rudeness; but through this thick smoke shine traits of genius that only he could produce; it is according to these traits that we must judge him.' In his book *Shakespeare Goes to Paris*, John Pemble quotes from a letter written by Diderot to François Tronchin: 'Ah, Monsieur, this Shakespeare was a terrible mortal... a colossus who was gothic, but between whose legs we would all pass without our heads even touching his testicles.'[1] Diderot and d'Alembert believed that Shakespeare was the supreme master of dramatic literature, but this didn't mean that they thought his plays were suitable for the public stage.

The publication, in 1776, of the first two volumes of Pierre Letourneur's translation of Shakespeare's works, a project that had the blessing of the king, helped to make Shakespeare fashionable beyond the radical young of literary Paris. In extreme old age, Voltaire's transparent fear that Shakespeare's theatre would win out over his own grew into an obsession, and he seemed to forget that there was a side to Shakespeare – the beauty of his poetry and the profundity of his thought – that used to move him to tears. Complaining about the new translations to his friend d'Argental, he wrote: 'It is frightful that this monster has a following in France. [...] It was I who was the first to show the French some pearls that I had discovered in his enormous dung-heap. [...] Le Kain tells me that [...] the scaffolds and brothels of the English stage are taking over the theatre of Racine...'[2] Le Kain had clearly exaggerated for theatrical effect. In his *Lettre à l'Académie Française*, Voltaire set out to expose Shakespeare's appalling love of dirty words, among other sins, but d'Alembert refused to read out the letter as written to his fellow academicians and insisted on revisions.

In fact, despite further productions of Shakespeare's tragedies (in adaptations by Ducis) at the Comédie – *King Lear* and *Macbeth*

[1] John Pemble, *Shakespeare Goes to Paris: How the Bard Conquered France* (London: Hambledon and London, 2005), p.5.
[2] Quoted in Ian Davidson, *Voltaire: A Life* (London: Profile Books, 2010), p.439.

during the 1780s and *Othello*, with Talma in the title role, in 1792 – it would take a further fifty years before his work became as fashionable in the theatre as it was in the salons and libraries of radical opinion. A large body of conservative opinion would take from Voltaire the belief that Shakespeare threatened the primacy of French culture: resisting Shakespeare became a matter of national pride and cultural identity.

4   The Saint-Val Affair

Political control of the Comédie-Française, set out in the 1680s, would not change until the Revolution, and then only briefly. The *Intendant des menus plaisirs* (Superintendent of Royal Entertainments) was responsible for the daily supervision of the troupe, under the authority of the four *Premiers gentilshommes de la chambre*. However, in the 1750s and 1760s, the crown instigated the creation of a formal structure of internal management by members of the troupe, the purpose being to end anarchy and irresponsibility. New regulations established a committee of senior actors, elected by the entire company, and required them to meet regularly and to deal with all matters relating to the daily business of the troupe: the committee was instructed to report to a general assembly of all the actors, which would meet once a week. The *semainers*, chosen from among the senior male sociétaires, were responsible for the daily management of the troupe – they reported directly to the *intendant*. To enforce discipline, actors were fined if they turned up late, or not at all, to a meeting, rehearsal or performance. Excuses after the event were frequent and often charming. On missing an assembly, Mlle Dumesnil wrote to the *semainer*: 'Oh, what a cold. I cannot sleep or eat; my head is in pieces and my voice…When I speak it frightens my dogs. Think of the effect it would make on the assembly!'[1]

Decisions taken by the actors, for instance over repertoire, still

---

[1] Quoted in Scott, *Women on the Stage in Early Modern France*, p.286.

had to be referred to the troupe's political masters for authorisation, and issues relating to company politics – ever-present because of rivalries and disputes, for instance over the distribution of roles – took up much of the Superintendent's time. Actors used their connections at court to get their own way. This aspect of life within the Comédie-Française before the Revolution is illustrated by the Saint-Val (or Sainval) affair.

In 1779, a dispute between the two star actresses of the time – Mademoiselle Saint-Val aînée[1] and Mme Vestris[2] – split the troupe in two and became a *cause célèbre*. Both women were born in 1743, and both had joined the Comédie in the late 1760s – Mlle Saint-Val in 1766 and Mme Vestris in 1768. Their rivalry became bitter and deadly when Mme Vestris, supported by the great comic actor Préville,[3] took advantage of Saint-Val's absence at the moment when the new repertoire was decided. Mme Vestris's claim of ownership of a majority of the leading roles in French tragedies was endorsed by the Premier gentilhomme de la chambre, the duc de Duras,[4] who was close to the actress. Mme Vestris, in a letter published in the *Journal de Paris*, offered to share some of the parts. Mlle Saint-Val, already in a state of distress, was infuriated that Mme Vestris was trying to look generous when, in fact, she was still claiming a majority of the parts for herself. With the help of her friend Mme de Chamont, Mlle Saint-Val wrote and circulated a pamphlet in which she exposed her rival's machinations and the role played in the affair by the duc de Duras. She went so far as to include in the pamphlet private letters written by Duras, a catastrophic error, for Duras reacted by ending her career with the stroke of his pen. He dismissed her from the Comédie and exiled her to southern France. For a time, she was forbidden from playing in any theatre.

The troupe was divided, as were the patrons of the Comédie and

---

[1] Pauline Alziari de Roquefort, dite Mlle Saint-Val aînée (1743-1830). CF j1766 s67 d79.

[2] Françoise-Marie-Rosette Gourgaud, dite Mme Vestris (1743-1804). CF j1768 s69 d1803.

[3] Pierre-Louis Du Bus, dit Préville (1721-1799). CF j1753 s53 d86.

[4] Emmanuel-Félicité de Durfort, duc de Duras.

the wider public. Molé supported Mlle Saint-Val. Saint-Val's younger sister Mlle Saint-Val cadette, also a member of the troupe, had to be persuaded not to go on strike. When she made her first entrance following her sister's dismissal, the audience applauded for many minutes and shouted out 'Les deux Sainval' multiple times. To fill the gap left by Mlle Saint-Val, the Superintendent, Denis-Pierre-Jean Papillon de la Ferté, brought back into the troupe Mlle Raucourt,[1] who had caused a sensation six years before as Didon in Lefranc de Pompignan's play. Mlle Raucourt inspired Bauchaumont to write: 'She has the most beautiful, most noble, most dramatically striking face, the most enchanting voice, a prodigious intelligence.' She was only sixteen and therefore easily exploited. A society obsessed with the beauty and grace of girls sanctioned their abuse and then made them take the blame. The jealousy of Vestris and Saint-Val had been a factor in Mlle Raucourt's departure, for they complained about their young colleague's promiscuity, in particular her liaisons with women.

According to Fleury, the actress's reputation was first slandered during an intimate supper party hosted by the duc de Richelieu, whose influence as a statesman was equalled by his notoriety as a libertine. He was a former Premier gentilhomme de la chambre. Mlle Raucourt was present with her mother. A letter arrived for Richelieu from his friend Voltaire. Richelieu decided that it should be read out at the dinner table. In the letter, Voltaire, who was piqued that Mlle Raucourt had turned down the offer of a leading role in his new play *Les Lois de Minos*, causing its premiere to be postponed, repeated a rumour that she had succumbed to the advances of a Spanish nobleman. Mlle Raucourt was humiliated. As a consequence of Voltaire's letter and the rapid circulation of its content, Mlle Raucourt was besieged by men who thought she was available. This anecdote can be backed up to a certain extent by the historical record. Voltaire did write a letter to Richelieu, dated 10 January 1773, in which he expressed his regret that Mlle Raucourt

---

[1] Françoise-Marie-Antoinette Saucerotte, dite Mlle Raucourt (1756-1815). CF j1772 s79 d99.

had refused to take a role in *Les Lois de Minos* and repeated a scandalous rumour about her character.[1] In a later letter, written that August, Voltaire implored Richelieu to help reconcile him with Mlle Raucourt, reminding him that it was his decision to read the January letter to his supper guests that had wounded the young woman and caused her to resent its author.[2]

Mlle Raucourt's return to the company provoked further discontent. She was living with the opera singer Sophie Arnould, but was less vulnerable to scandal than before because she benefited from the support of the new queen, Marie-Antoinette, who believed her when she promised to live a chaste life. The queen even conceived a plan to marry Mlle Raucourt to Fleury, but Fleury resisted.[3] La Ferté finally managed to re-established order, writing in his journal:

> I managed to placate [the actors] somewhat, especially with regard to Mlle Raucourt. However, Mlle Sainval the younger has now begun to harass Mlle Raucourt by claiming the right to play queens, and I find myself in a fresh difficulty. This whole business has caused me a constant succession of meetings and discussions. However, I finally succeeded in solving the problem by means of an agreement between the ladies concerned.[4]

Arguments and rivalries were not restricted to female members of the company. Molé's defence of Mlle Saint-Val was inevitable given that Préville was supporting Mme Vestris. In 1766, Préville had been humiliated when his wife, the actress Angélique Drouin, left him for Molé. Molé soon tired of her, and Préville took her

---

[1] Voltaire to Louis François Armand de Vignerot du Plessis, 3rd duc de Richelieu: c. Sunday, 10 January 1773. *Electronic Enlightenment Scholarly Edition of Correspondence*, ed. Robert McNamee et al. Vers. 3.0. University of Oxford. 2018. Web. 10 Oct. 2019. Unfortunately, the letter is lost.

[2] Voltaire to Louis François Armand de Vignerot du Plessis, 3rd duc de Richelieu: Thursday, 26 August 1773. *Electronic Enlightenment Scholarly Edition of Correspondence*, ed. Robert McNamee et al. Vers. 3.0. University of Oxford. 2018. Web. 10 Oct. 2019.

[3] See *The French Stage and the French People as Illustrated in the Memoirs of M. Fleury*, vol.1, p.139-144.

[4] Quoted in Howarth, *French Theatre in the Neo-classical Era, 1550-1789*, p.411.

back, writing to Garrick, 'Je suis avec ma femme, mes enfants, depuis un mois, et je suis heureux'.

A longstanding dispute between Molé and Fleury came to a head when Molé sent a sick note a couple of hours before the beginning of a performance of Voltaire's *Zaïre*, knowing that Fleury would have to appear, as Nerestan, in his place and would face the anger of the pit (people had paid to see Molé). During the performance, Fleury noticed that Molé was in the wings, taking pleasure from watching his younger colleague as the audience moaned and hissed. Fleury walked to the footlights and told the pit that Molé was not ill and was standing in the wings.[1]

Disputes between actors cannot simply be dismissed as the result of petty jealousies. The actor's life was hard. Long hours, low wages (even those sociétaires entitled to a full share of the divided income struggled financially), and a constant hum of anxiety over what the future would bring, contributed to the competitive nature of company life. It was not uncommon for actresses adored when young to end their lives in obscurity and poverty.

5   Figaro

By 1770, the Comédie-Française's theatre in the rue des Fossés-Saint-Germain-des-Prés was so outdated and in such poor condition that the troupe departed and took temporary possession of the Salle des Machines in the Palais des Tuileries. It was here that Voltaire watched his final tragedy. The king ordered the building of a new theatre for the troupe, in Saint-Germain, close to the Palais du Luxembourg, on the site of the hôtel de Condé.[2] The initial idea to redevelop the Comédie's former home was dismissed on the advice of the police. Because the rue des Fossés-Saint-Germain-des-Prés

---

[1] See *The French Stage and the French People as Illustrated in the Memoirs of M. Fleury*, vol.1, p.135-36.

[2] See Louis XV, *Lettres patentes... pour la construction des bâtimens devant servir à la Comédie françoise, sur les terreins de l'ancien hôtel de Condé... Registrées en Parlement le 19 août [1773]* (Paris, 1773).

was narrow, people streaming to the theatre had been the cause of daily traffic jams, blocking the passage of vehicles 'necessary for the exchange of commerce in our good town of Paris'. Two young architects, Charles de Wailly and Marie-Joseph Peyre, were commissioned to design a grand theatre with a seated parterre. Their conception of a horseshoe-shaped auditorium (which pre-dated Louis Victor's design for the theatre in Bordeaux) resulted from a detailed consideration of how a theatre should enhance the experience of watching a play:

> We have thought ourselves all the more justified in fixing upon the shape of the circle for this project, because by virtue of its regularity it is the most attractive shape of all, because it is the most satisfying to look at, because it is not susceptible to those angles which are always detrimental to the reverberation of sound, and finally because it affords the audience the welcome advantage of both better visibility and acoustics.[1]

They placed their circular auditorium within a neoclassical building, and made it the focal point of the redeveloped quarter. The new theatre (the present-day Odéon) realised Voltaire's dream, expressed in his *Dissertation sur la tragédie ancienne et moderne* of 1749, of a modern theatre that would provide a clear view of the stage from every seat. It also diminished the disruptive power of the *parterre*. The theatre opened in 1782.[2] Arthur Young saw a performance by the Comédiens-français at their new Théâtre-Français in 1788: 'In the evening to *L'École des pères* [by Alexis Piron], at the Comédie-Française, a crying, *larmoyant* thing. This theatre, the principal one at Paris, is a fine building, with a magnificent portico. After the circular theatres of France, how can anyone relish our ill-contrived oblong holes of London?'[3]

By the time of Crébillon's death the French theatre was in need

---

[1] Quoted in Howarth, *French Theatre in the Neo-classical Era, 1550-1789*, p.489.

[2] The present-day Odéon is a reconstruction of the original, for the theatre was destroyed by fire in 1799 and 1818.

[3] Arthur Young, *Travels During the Years 1787, 1788 and 1789...* (Dublin, 1793), p.132-33.

of some new voices. The generation of the *Encyclopédie* led by Diderot took a deep look at the theatre to examine how it could be reformed and modernised. Diderot believed that the division of dramatic literature into two dominant and opposing genres, tragedy and comedy, was archaic and artificial and the enemy of the realistic representation of real life. He wanted theatre to reflect the lives of ordinary people, and advocated a genre that became known as *drame bourgeois*; but his plays, *Le Père de famille* and *Le Fils naturel*, presented by the Comédie-Française in, respectively, 1761 and 1771, were defeated by their polemical nature: as drama they were found to be both lacklustre and overly sentimental. The failure of these plays, though, may have been partly the responsibility of the actors. Diderot's friend Friedrich Melchior Grimm believed that the actors were at fault because they did not adapt their mannered declamatory style of playing. A domestic drama, performed in a domestic setting, required a naturalistic, low-key style of acting. 'The actors ought to have convinced themselves,' wrote Grimm just after the premiere of *Le Père de famille*, 'that they were in a salon, and not on a stage, in front of an audience. They have simply shown us their habitual manner, which is neither truthful nor relaxed, since it is always designed for the benefit of the *parterre*, whom a true actor should never acknowledge.'[1]

A new playwright with a distinctive voice finally broke through in the 1770s. Pierre-Augustin Caron de Beaumarchais came late to the literary scene. Beaumarchais was an extraordinary figure whose interests and achievements were too numerous and too various for any biographer to get a true sense of who he really was. He was as self-serving as he was altruistic; a man who, on the one hand, saved for posterity many of the works of Voltaire as the publisher of the first printed edition of his *œuvre*; and who, on the other, made a significant contribution to the fight for American independence as a diplomat and arms dealer.

Beaumarchais was born Pierre-Augustin Caron in Paris in 1732, the son of a watchmaker. Before finding success in the theatre, he

[1] Friedrich Melchior Grimm, *Correspondance litteraire, philosophique et critique*, vol.4 (Paris: Garnier, 1878), p.355. Quoted in Howarth (ed.), *French Theatre in the Neo-classical Era, 1550-1789*, p.570.

was best-known as a courtier (music teacher to the king's daughters) and diplomat. At the age of twenty, he invented a device that improved the accuracy of timepieces. He found himself at the centre of a scandal when the king's watchmaker, Jean-André Lepaute, attempted to take credit for the invention. The Académie des sciences found in Beaumarchais's favour and Lepaute was disgraced.

As a playwright, Beaumarchais began by writing two plays in the manner of Diderot's *Le Père de famille*. The Comédiens-français presented these plays – *Eugénie* in 1767 and *Les Deux amis* in 1770. The first was a modest success, but didn't come close to satisfying the ambitions of its author. Beaumarchais next wrote *Le Barbier de Séville*, a comic-opera, with music by Antoine-Laurent Baudron, in part inspired by his long sojourn in Spain in 1764. When the Théâtre-Italien turned down the work, Beaumarchais revised his text to create a five-act play and offered it to the Comédie-Française. The play, premiered in February 1775, needed revisions, but was subsequently much admired. At one level, Beaumarchais's play fitted neatly within the French tradition that evolved out of commedia dell'arte. Figaro, the barber of the title, helps his former master, count Almaviva, to out-manoeuvre the elderly guardian of the girl he loves, Rosine. *Le Barbier de Séville* occupies the same territory as Molière's *L'École des femmes* (performed during the 1775 season) and a large number of lesser plays; but it has its own contrary spirit, and, in Figaro, a character so intellectually superior to his social betters, and, more to the point, so knowingly and so arrogantly superior, that the play was provocatively new. Beaumarchais, very deliberately, made the guardian, Don Bartholo, an enemy of the *Encyclopédie* and of all progressive ideas and inventions. The message was clear: the future will belong to the Figaros of this world.

People enjoyed the play as an extremely well-crafted and sharply written entertainment with an exotic Spanish flavour; and the members of the Comédie-Française, led by Préville as Figaro, must have loved performing a play that stood up to comparison with Molière. Garrick called Préville 'a child of nature'. In his follow-up play, *La Folle journée, ou Le Mariage de Figaro*, Beaumarchais took Figaro into a new scenario that was more socially and politically radical, for he was intent on making a point about privilege and rank. In *Le Mariage de Figaro*, Almaviva and Rosine are married and living at Almaviva's country estate; Figaro is working as Almaviva's steward.

The plot, motored by endless misunderstandings about the characters' real feelings and with elements of pure farce, is tortuous. Almaviva is no aristocratic tyrant, except in sexual matters: he intends to claim his 'right', as master, to have sex with Figaro's beloved Suzanne on their wedding day. The comedy results from the plotting of Figaro – who, made vulnerable by his love for Suzanne, is less formidable than in *Le Barbier de Séville* – and the two much more capable women, Suzanne and Rosine, to foil the count's plans. A member of the aristocracy is outwitted by his servants. This was in itself provocative, but Beaumarchais went further in the final act. Figaro organises the estate workers and threatens rebellion unless Almaviva agrees to abolish *droit du seigneur*, and he makes a long speech in which he rails against the archaic privileges of the aristocracy, censorship and the unjust justice system and advocates advancement through merit. Beaumarchais was using Figaro as a mouthpiece for his own libertarian views. Beaumarchais believed in the established order: on the behalf of self-made middle-class men like himself, he was advocating its reform and in no sense its destruction.

Le Mariage de Figaro was accepted by the Comédie-Française in 1781, but promptly banned by the police and the censor. Three years would pass before the play reached the public. Beaumarchais made minor changes to his text, changing the setting from France to Spain, but these revisions would have counted for little without the support of Marie-Antoinette. Marie-Antoinette arranged for the king to attend a private reading of the play. The reader, Mme Campan, later revealed that the king was particularly outraged by the play's attack on state prisons. Beaumarchais's aggressive campaigning on behalf of his play – he even wrote a letter to the king – was counter-productive. However, Marie-Antoinette and her faction at court admired the play's wit and cleverness, as did many of the more enlightened members of the nobility, who decided it was good form to enjoy a play that poked fun at their own class. It seems that the king, indecisive on this matter as on so much else, relented partly because of his wife; but partly because the momentum of the play seemed unstoppable.

The premiere finally took place on 27 April 1784, at the troupe's Théâtre-Français in the Faubourg Saint-Germain (the Odéon). The play triumphed as few plays had in the history of the company. Earlier in the day, there had been a riot outside the theatre as some people pushed and even fought to gain access, resulting in three people being crushed to death: but not even tragedy could derail Figaro. Inside the golden auditorium, the normally hierarchical seating arrangement broke down as people sat wherever they could find a place – some of the ladies of the court broke protocol by sitting on benches in the parterre. The applause and bravos at the end continued for minutes on end. The nearly seventy consecutive performances given by the troupe was a record, as was the amount of money taken at the box office. A play that everyone recognised was challenging the established order, was the talk of the town. Beaumarchais celebrated his triumph by writing a letter to the *Journal de Paris* in which he wrote that, in his struggle to see his play performed, he had defeated 'lions and tigers'.[1] Louis XVI interpreted the phrase as a reference to himself and sent Beaumarchais to the Saint-Lazare prison.

Because of Beaumarchais's notes on the characters, included in the preface to the first edition, we know the casting of the leading roles:

> The part of [Almaviva] is made more difficult to play by the fact that the character is consistently the least sympathetic. But in the hands of an excellent actor (Monsieur Molé), it raised the profile of the other roles and ensured that the play was a success. [...] The Countess, torn between two conflicting emotions, should keep a tight rein on her feelings and show only muted anger [...].

[1] Beaumarchais, 'Pierre-Augustin Caron de Beaumarchais aux Auteurs du Journal', in *Journal de Paris*, n.66 (7 March 1785), p.272. 'Pourtant, Messieurs, quel est votre objet, en publiant de telles sottises quand j'ai du vaincre lions et tigres, pour faire jouer une Comédie, pensez-vous, après son succès, me réduire, ainsi qu'un Servante Hollandoise, à battre l'ozier, tous les matins, sur l'insecte vil de la nuit?'

This part, one of the more difficult to play, offered a challenge which was triumphantly met by the great talents of the younger Mlle Saint-Val. […] The actor who plays [Figaro] cannot be urged too strongly to enter into the character's mind and feelings, as Monsieur Dazincourt did. […] Suzanne [is] a shrewd, sharp-witted young woman, fond of laughter but with none of the almost brassy high spirits of the scheming maids of theatrical tradition. Her character is sketched in the preface, which actresses who did not see Mlle Contat in the part should study if they are to play the role properly. [The part of] Chérubin can only be played, as it was, by a pretty young woman. The stage currently boasts no young male actor mature enough to grasp all its subtleties.[1]

Dazincourt[2] had deserted his post as secretary to maréchal de Richelieu to become an actor. Richelieu later gave him his blessing. Dazincourt was coached in the role of Figaro by Préville. Mlle Saint-Val cadette[3] and Louise Contat[4] were admired for their elegance and sparkling wit. Mlle Contat, a friend of Marie-Antoinette, excelled playing Molière's vivacious women. The actress who scored such a success as Chérubin was twenty-year-old Mlle Olivier.[5] Mlle Olivier was the troupe's rising young actress. 'Blonde aux yeux noirs, elle charme par sa modestie et sa gentillesse. Elle ne crée pas moins de dix-sept rôles d'ingénues et de jeunes premières, en sept ans de carrière.'[6] These roles included Agnès in *L'École des femmes* and Junie in *Britannicus*. She died at the age of twenty-three in 1787.

For all his admiration for the actors of the Comédie-Française,

---

[1] Beaumarchais (trans. David Coward), *The Figaro Trilogy* (Oxford: OUP, 2003), p.80-82.

[2] Joseph Jean-Baptiste Albouy, dit Dazincourt (1747-1809, b. Marseille). CF j1776 s78 d1808.

[3] Blanche Alziari de Roquefort, dite Mlle Saint-Val cadette (1752-1836). CF j1772 s76 d92.

[4] Louise Contat (1760-1813, b. Paris). CF j1776 s77 d1809.

[5] Jeanne-Adélaïde Gérardin, dite Jeanne Olivier (1764?-1787). CF j1780 s82 d87.

[6] Entry on *Jeanne-Adélaïde Gérardin dite Jeanne Olivier*, Comédie-Française website, at https://www.comedie-francaise.fr (accessed 4/6/2018).

Beaumarchais led an author's campaign against their control of literary property, even withdrawing the third play in the Figaro trilogy, *L'Autre Tartuffe, ou La Mère coupable*.[1] Once the income generated by a play fell below 1,200 *livres* in winter and 800 *livres* in summer (fixed by the Conseil d'Etat in 1757 and 1761), the play became the property of the Comédie: its author would receive no further income. The anger of authors was increased by what they considered to be a rigged system of calculating their share even during the period when they were paid. An author's remuneration was based on the box office takings for each performance minus subscriptions and the Comédie's expenses. Playwrights accepted this biased system because of the prestige of seeing their work performed at the Comédie. It was not uncommon for a playwright to give up his rights to Préville or Molé to secure performances of his play. In 1777, though, Beaumarchais was the instigator of the Société des auteurs dramatiques, a union established over supper with Marmontel and others. It was the beginning of a campaign that would eventually result in the passing of copyright legislation. Beaumarchais was particularly vexed by the Comédie's refusal to provide him with a statement of the earnings achieved by *Le Barbier de Séville*. The actors of the Comédie resisted the demands of the authors because they could not afford to give up further income: money was tight. They were aggrieved by the dispute, and made the point that Voltaire would never have behaved in such a vulgar way.

The phenomenon of *Le Mariage de Figaro* spread rapidly to other parts of Europe. Translated into English by Thomas Holcroft as *The Follies of the Day*, it was performed at Drury Lane in December 1784. In Vienna, Lorenzo Da Ponte adapted the play into an Italian libretto for Mozart. Mozart's opera buffa, which opened at the Burgtheater in May 1786, only two years after the premiere of the play in Paris, would eventually become better known than Beaumarchais's orginal, at least outside of France. Wary of the censor,

---

[1] Shortly before Beaumarchais went into exile, in June 1792, *La Mère coupable* was premiered – unsuccessfully – at the Théâtre du Marais. The Comédie-Française revived the play in 1990, in a production by Jean-Pierre Vincent.

Da Ponte and Mozart eliminated the play's dangerous call for egalitarianism.

After the storming of the Bastille in 1789, after the execution of the king and the blood-letting of the Terror, many people living through those times believed that Beaumarchais's play had been a signpost on the road to Revolution.

Chaxles

Si l'une est ma maîtresse.

L'autre est mon serviteur.

Acte Iᵉʳ Scene IIᵐᵉ

A Paris, chez Martinet, Libraire, rue du Coq N.º 15.

5. *Le Barbier de Séville* by Beaumarchais. Dazincourt as Figaro. Print.
Martinet (Paris), 1786.

3

Revolution and War

1789 to 1815

6. *Hamlet* by Jean-François Ducis. Talma (Hamlet) and Joséphine
Duchesnois (Gertrude). Print. Martinet (Paris), 1807.

1   Talma

The outbreak of the Revolution divided the troupe. Only a minority of its members were committed revolutionaries who relished the severing of the chains that had bound the troupe to the monarchy since 1680. For the others, the future looked at best uncertain. The actors were given civil rights, but they had lost their royal pensions and privileges.

The writer and revolutionary Jean-François de La Harpe, speaking before the National Assembly in August 1790, declared: 'Il faut que la régénération de la scène française date de la même époque que celle de la France entière.' ('The regeneration of our theatre must be achieved alongside the regeneration of the whole of France.') Just as the state had been despotic and decadent, so had its theatre. La Harpe, who, in common with most playwrights active during the *ancien régime*, resented the power exercised by the Comédiens-français as gatekeepers to France's premier stage, envisaged a brave new world:

> Theatre productions must quickly assume a more masculine, bolder and more patriotic character; and poets of patriotism and liberty will not allow themselves to be the slave of actors. Our famous stage, so admired throughout the world for its master-pieces, is a creation of the last century, when despotism, supported by genius, at least had some brilliancy; it leaned towards decadence, just as despotism corrupted and debased everything; now it must be reborn under the auspices of liberty.[1]

[1] Jean-François de La Harpe, *Adresse des auteurs dramatiques à l'Assemblée nationale prononcée par M. de La Harpe, dans la séance du mardi soir 24 août*

La Harpe's younger contemporary Marie-Joseph Chénier went even further in assigning to the theatre a civic duty to instruct the public on questions of morality. The determination of the revolutionary authorities to reform and control cultural bodies, including theatres, took a while to be written into law, but this changed in January 1791 when the National Assembly passed a decree that democratised the theatre while at the same time introducing regulation. The first two articles of the act formally ended the historic privileges of the Comédie-Française, and article six handed the job of regulating theatres to the municipal authorities, but with limited powers.

> Article 1: Any citizen may establish a public theatre and mount plays in all genres, but must notify the relevant municipality. Article 2: The plays of authors who have been dead for five years or more are in the public domain and may be performed in all theatres, for the old privileges have been abolished. [...] Article 6: The directors and actors of theatres will be subject to inspections by the municipal authorities. The municipal authorities may not forbid the performance of a play without the agreement of its author and actors, and can only enforce the laws of the land, the regulations of the police and the decrees of the Committee of the Constitution.[1]

The other articles protected the rights of authors and their heirs.

The act was progressive and reasoned, especially when compared to the restrictive and sinister decrees of the years ahead. Many members of the Comédie resented the enforced change to the status of their theatre and were reluctant to accept any interference from the Municipality. Change was happening too quickly for members of the troupe who remained sympathetic to the king and who cared deeply for the company's century-old legacy.

The revolutionaries found it all too easy to condemn the Comédiens-français as propagandists for the *ancien régime*. The actors

[1790] (1795), p.10.
[1] *Archives parlementaires de 1787 à 1860*, t.22 (Paris: Paul Dupont, 1885), p.214.

changed the name of their theatre to the Théâtre de la Nation, but it was not enough. The republican group, led by the charismatic young actor Talma, had all the best lines (as well as the best threats); the royalists, led by Jean-Baptiste Naudet,[1] defended their principles with courage and refused to capitulate.

François-Joseph Talma's impact and influence in France would be comparable to that of Garrick's in England. He was born in Paris in 1763, the son of a dentist who established a business in London: he therefore spent his formative years in England. In England, Talma discovered Shakespeare. 'I had studied Corneille and Racine, but recognised that Shakespeare was the greatest master,' he wrote in his memoirs.

> Shakespeare seemed so real to me that after reading one of his plays I could draw and dress the principal characters; this was not the case after I read a French tragedy. [...] Shakespeare was the god of my youth, my master, my guide in the study of human passions.[2]

The English political system, more liberal and tolerant than the French, also left a profound mark. Talma returned to Paris to work as a dentist, but, already an amateur actor, abandoned this trade for the stage. In 1786, he entered the newly-established *École royale dramatique* to study under Dugazon,[3] Molé and Fleury. This led naturally to his entry into the Comédie-Française in November 1787. He made his debut playing Séide in Voltaire's *Mahomet*. Around this time, a young woman joined the company who would share the stage with Talma regularly during the next decade – Louise Desgarcins.[4] Her success was immediate: during her first year with the troupe she played Atalide in Racine's *Bajazet*, the title

---

[1] Jean-Baptiste Naudet (1743-1830, b. Champlitte, Haute-Saône). CF j1784 s85 d1806.

[2] François-Joseph Talma (ed. Alexandre Dumas), *Mémoires de J.-F. Talma: écrits par lui-même*, t.1 (Paris: H. Souverain, 1850), p.166-67; t.3, p.234.

[3] Jean-Henri Gourgaud, dit Dugazon (1746-1809, b. Marseille). CF j1771 s72 d1809.

[4] Magdelaine-Marie Des Garcins, dite Louise Desgarcins (1769-1797, b. Mont-Dauphin, Hautes-Alpes). CF j1788 s89 d91.

role in Voltaire's *Zaïre* and Chimène in Corneille's *Le Cid*. Within the formal rules of French acting, the actresses who received particular acclaim almost always possessed a quality of naturalness. 'Louise n'était pas jolie,' recalled Talma, 'mais elle avait une extrême distinction: tous ses mouvements étaient pleins de naturel et de noblesse.'[1] Both actors became sociétaires in 1789. It is unclear whether they were romantically involved. Talma's mistress, later his wife, was Julie Carreau, a former dancer at the Opéra who had performed in works by Rameau and others when she was very young. Her salon, in the rue Chantereine, was one of the most fashionable in Paris. Her wealth and connections brought Talma a comfortable lifestyle.

During the months that followed the storming of the Bastille, Talma, despite having only just become a full member of the troupe, broke the code of company solidarity in the most public way possible, from the stage of the Théâtre de la Nation. Talma addressed the audience from the footlights, utilising the weapons of the great tragic actor – voice, physical presence and empathy – in a speech, written by Chénier, that railed against aristocratic tyranny. The phrase 'As my enemies, I have all those who owe their lives to prejudice and who regret the passing of servitude' was surely directed at unreformed members of the troupe.

In November 1789, the Comédie-Française staged Chénier's play *Charles IX*, a work previously banned by the censor. While other actors, wary of the sensitive political implications and implied parallels of a drama about an unstable monarch who, encouraged by representatives of the church, committed genocide (the Saint Bartholomew's Day massacre), declined to play the title role, Talma welcomed the opportunity and made the part his own: it was the first great success of his career. Talma, in Simon Schama's phrase, 'carried off a portrayal of the king as a kind of demonic halfwit in whom loathsome amorality and devious plotting were concentrated to an unusually abominable degree'.[2] The church called for the play to be withdrawn, and the last dregs of royal power were used to

---

[1] *Mémoires de J.-F. Talma*, t.2, p.38.
[2] Simon Schama, *Citizens: a Chronicle of the French Revolution* (London: Penguin Books, 1989), p.487.

issue the order; but this only increased the play's influence. Louis Camille Desmoulins believed that the play had profoundly aided the radical agenda as well as hardening the attitudes of the public towards the monarchy. Danton was said to have declared, 'If Figaro killed the nobility, Charles IX will kill the monarchy'. The following year, the leaders of the Revolution led a campaign for the return of the play. Inspired by Talma, the Comédie-Française's theatre had become a nightly battleground, with radicals in the audience disrupting performances and royalist members of the troupe placed under intolerable levels of stress. Fleury recalled: 'My hand trembled as I rubbed the rouge on my cheeks, at the thought of the vulgar attacks to which I was in the next moment to be subjected.' He summed up those surreal and frightening days with an evocative phrase: 'Nothing appeared burlesque, not even the grimaces of the street-buffoons.'[1]

On the evening of 22 July 1790, as the curtain fell on a performance of Voltaire's *Alzire*, a man with the imposing build and stony demeanour of a 'buste colossal'[2] stood on a bench at the centre of the pit and called for silence. This was Danton. At that time, Danton was president of the Cordeliers Club, in whose district the Théâtre de la Nation stood. 'Messieurs, in the name of our brothers, the deputies from Provence, I am charged to ask the members of the Comédie-Française to perform *Charles IX*, and as the deputies are departing after tomorrow, the play must be given tomorrow night. Do you agree? Would you like to see *Charles IX* again?' Behind the curtain and in the wings, the actors heard the frenzied response of the crowd, the stomping of feet and the unison cry of 'Oui, oui, *Charles IX*.' With unfortunate timing, a member of the stage crew hoisted the curtain, exposing the only actors on the stage, Naudet and Mlle Lange. Danton stepped onto his bench and shouted in Naudet's direction: '*Charles IX*.' Beside Danton stood Desmoulins. The chant was taken up once again by the whole house, for under Danton's skilful direction the mood of the volatile crowd had turned to fury. Fearing that Mlle Lange was about to

---

[1] Fleury, *The French Stage and the French People as Illustrated in the Memoirs of M. Fleury*, vol.2, p.285, 287.

[2] Talma's description of Danton.

faint, the courageous Naudet advanced to the footlights. Talma, who would later write an account of this event in his memoirs,[1] was watching from the wings. 'Messieurs,' Naudet said, 'it is impossible for us to fulfil your wishes.' 'Why's that?' Danton demanded. 'Because Mme Vestris is ill and Saint-Prix is not in Paris.'

With impeccable timing, Talma chose this moment to walk on stage and join Naudet at the footlights. 'I realised that it was the right moment to strike a blow,' he wrote in his memoirs. He told the audience: 'Naudet is following the orders of the gentlemen of the chamber, but I am a patriot, and must tell you that Mme Vestris is not so ill that she can't perform and Saint-Prix's role can be read by another actor.' Once the curtain had fallen, Naudet struck Talma in the face.

Later in the evening, Danton and Desmoulins asked the actors to meet them in the foyer of the theatre to confirm that *Charles IX* would be performed. Naudet accused Talma of orchestrating the night's events by plotting with Danton. Danton told Naudet that that wasn't true. In fact, the two men were meeting for the first time. Early the next morning, probably in the Bois de Boulogne, Talma and Naudet fought a duel with pistols. Because of the mist, Talma couldn't see Naudet. To the dismay of his seconds, Naudet bravely walked closer than the agreed twenty steps. Talma fired and missed. Naudet then shot in the air. In his memoirs, Talma would acknowledge Naudet's courage.

That evening, *Charles IX* was performed as agreed. Fleury was outraged by the behaviour of his former student, and the consensus view within the troupe was that Talma had betrayed the Comédie.

2   Olympe des Gouges

In 1784, the Comédie received a play – sent anonymously – called *Zamore et Mirza, ou l'heureux neufrage*.

Its author was Olympe de Gouges. Born in Montauban, near

---

[1] See *Mémoires de J.-F. Talma*, t.2, p.203-13.

Toulouse, she had made her way to Paris following the death of her husband – a man she had reluctantly married at the age of sixteen. In Paris, she became the lover of a rich man but refused to marry him. She was taken up by Mme de Montesson, the mistress (secretly the wife) of Louis Philippe d'Orléans, the First Prince of the Blood, and was seen regularly at her salon. Olympe de Gouges had radical views on social issues. During the first years of the Revolution, she published a stream of pamphlets on topics such as the rights of women and the immorality of slavery. Her assertion that illegitimate children should have equal inheritance rights with legitimate children, made her many enemies; and her support of Marie-Antoinette made her a target of the mob. Although there was a new tolerance for women who wanted to express a political opinion, for most men there was a line which they should not cross. Gouges proclaimed women to be superior to men and called Robespierre 'an amphibious animal'.[1]

While Gouges was waiting to hear if the Comédie's reading committee had accepted her play, she went to see the Comédie's production of Beaumarchais's *Le Mariage de Figaro*, an experience that led her to write, in quick time, her own sequel, which she called *Les Amours de Chérubin*. Beaumarchais heard about the play and immediately accused Gouges of plagiarism, as well as dismissing her work as mediocre. Instead of cowering, Gouges printed her play and published an open letter to Beaumarchais in which she wrote 'My Chérubin, protected by you, could have [...] found a place at the Comédie-Française to give a little rest to your Figaro, who tires himself more than he tires the public' before declaring: 'Ah! Caron de Beaumarchais, you are the true friend of women! Let me tell you that you deceive us, no-one is falser than you in favour of my sex.'[2]

As a result of this episode, the Comédie became aware that the author of *Zamore et Mirza* was a woman. Gouges later meticulously recorded her exchanges with the actors in *Mémoire pour Mme de*

[1] Quoted in Lucy Moore, *Liberty* (London: Harper Press, 2006), p.166.
[2] Quoted (in French) in Tomasz Wysłobocki, 'Olympe de Gouges à la Comédie-Française: un naufrage dramatique', in *Fabula / Les colloques, Théâtre et scandale*, at http://www.fabula.org/colloques/document5884.php (accessed 22/6/2019).

Gouges contre la Comédie-Française, published in 1790. She described how she was cruelly mocked by the actors, led by Molé, during a reading of her play. They didn't hide their prejudices. Curiously, though, they accepted the work. No guarantee was given as to when it might reach the stage. Gouges sent Molé gifts in an attempt to speed up the process. This led some of the women in the troupe to accuse her of offering to pay the Comédie to stage her play. When Gouges made the quarrel public, the actors were so outraged that – according to Gouges's memoir – they used their connections at court to arrange for a *lettre de cachet* to be issued against her. But because of her closeness to Mme de Montesson and the duc d'Orléans, the order was rescinded. The actors became conciliatory. Molé paid her a visit. 'This is the Comédie-Française, Madame. This is how even the great writers start.'

However, the years went by and the play remained unperformed. The actors' disdain for Olympe de Gouges wasn't necessarily the most important factor. The subject matter of her play, calling for the compassionate treatment of slaves, made it not only highly original but also a risky proposition. The powerful influence of the colonialists at court – the importance of the colonies to trade and commerce – meant that Gouges's play was unlikely to pass the censor. It is unclear why the actors accepted the play if they never intended to perform it, but it may have been because the duc d'Orléans wished his wife's protégé to be indulged.

It was only after the storming of the Bastille and the loss of the troupe's privileges, and in the climate of greater freedom that marked the first phase of the Revolution, that the Comédie-Française finally staged the play, now entitled *Esclavage des Noirs, ou l'heureux naufrage*. A cabal supporting the colonialists disrupted the premiere, on 28 December 1789, but the disruption wasn't needed – the play didn't impress the public. The Comédie withdrew *Esclavage des Noirs* after three performances. The mayor of Paris told Gouges that the play could incite an insurrection of slaves. Naudet told her that patrons of the Comédie with interests in the colonies had threatened to end their subscriptions and that the Comédie couldn't afford such a hit. She expressed her bitterness in the preface to the published edition of the play, and in an essay called

Lettre aux littérateurs français (1792). By then, she was using pamphlets and posters to advocate the causes she passionately believed in with seemingly little concern for her own safety. In 1791, she published her most important work, the pamphlet *Déclaration des droits de la femme et de la citoyenne*.

In February 1793, nine months before Gouges was sent to the guillotine, Talma staged her final play, *L'Entrée de Dumouriez à Bruxelles, ou Les vivandiers*, at the Théâtre de la République. The audience hissed and laughed throughout the performance. At its end, Gouges, who had been watching the play from one of the boxes, stood up and told the pit: 'There is nothing wrong with my play, these actors are to blame.' Talma's leading actress, Julie Candeille, replied from the stage: 'The citizen is mistaken. We have done everything possible to support her play.' In Talma's unsympathetic account, Gouges – 'an elderly woman, her bonnet askew, her hair dishevelled, her eyes popping out of her head' – fled the auditorium for the corridors, accompanied by waves of sarcastic laughter.[1]

In contrast, Fleury was compassionate. He depicted Mme de Gouges as a rather eccentric and volatile creature, but went on to write of her that she was 'humane and generous; and in one passage of her life at least, sublime.' This referred to her request to the National Assembly to be allowed to defend the king at his trial, an act of compassion that effectively signed her own death warrant. When dozens of people descended upon her house, she had the courage to go out to face them, and calmly parried the cruel jibes and menacing threats that they spat at her. Enraged by her composure, a man grabbed hold of her and pulled off her bonnet. 'Here goes the head of Mme de Gouges... for four-and-twenty sous! Once! Twice! Does nobody bid? Twenty-four sous for this wonderful head!'[2]

---

[1] *Mémoires de J.-F. Talma*, t.3, p.308-10
[2] Fleury, *The French Stage and the French People as Illustrated in the Memoirs of M. Fleury*, vol.2, p.221.

3   Terror

The rift within the troupe couldn't be repaired. In September 1790, the Comédie-Française suspended Talma, but only until his fellow radical, Dugazon, protesting, provoked a riot in the auditorium. The mayor, Bailly, asked the troupe to reinstate the actor. The troupe refused, but then gave in when Bailly threatened to close their theatre. Talma returned to the stage playing the minor role of Proculus in Voltaire's *Brutus*. He made his entrance wearing an 'authentic' Roman costume of toga and sandals, wigless, his hair cut short, his arms and legs bare. This look, obviously based on Jacques-Louis David's depiction of Brutus in his painting *The Lictors Bring to Brutus the Bodies of His Sons*, was an innovation that made dramatic sense, but Talma's main purpose was to show up his fellow actors – dressed normally for a tragedy – as relics of the *ancien régime*. Louise Contat, a member of the conservative group, was heard to say 'How ugly he looks'. Louise Contat and Fleury were among those members of the Comédie who, even as their situation became precarious, refused to abandon their principles or their loyalty to the king and queen. If Fleury's portrait of Talma in his memoirs was an attempt to set the record straight, it wasn't devoid of understanding. Fleury believed that Talma was a young man in a hurry, and that his actions were motivated by ambition and a longing for fame. 'His enthusiasm for the Revolution was merely that of a great artist,' wrote Fleury, continuing:

> In truth, in the eyes of the sublime Talma and of the comic Dugazon nothing appeared as it really was; the one being characterised by an almost childish freshness and simplicity of feeling, the other by a turn for drollery, which prevented his putting together two serious ideas. They had imagined that a Revolution was to present itself all at once, like the shifting of a scene on a stage.[1]

The managing committee of the Comédie-Française refused to

---

[1] Fleury, *The French Stage and the French People as Illustrated in the Memoirs of M. Fleury*, vol.2, p.213-15.

cast Talma in leading roles. In April 1791, he led his group – which included Dugazon, Grandmesnil, Monvel, Louise Desgarcins, and Mme Vestris – out of the Comédie and into the new theatre designed by Victor Louis at the Palais-Royal (today's Salle Richelieu). Molé didn't join Talma, but decided not to stay at the Comédie-Française either. The new troupe began by staging Chénier's *Henri VIII*. Talma played the title role, with Mme Vestris as Anne de Boulen and Louise Desgarcins as Jane Seymour. Talma continued to take advice from his friend Jacques-Louis David, whose studio was across the rue Saint-Honoré in the Louvre, on the visual aspects of production. As the Revolution started its descent into darkness, Chénier, believing in an ideal revolution, unforgiving but underpinned by legal process (which made him, relatively speaking, a moderate), wrote the Roman tragedy *Caïus Gracchus*, staged by Talma – who, despite his confrontational passion for the cause, shared Chénier's fear of anarchy – at the Palais-Royal in February 1792. One extraordinary line in the play – 'Des lois et non du sang' (laws and not blood) – would resonate across Paris. Talma followed *Caïus Gracchus* with revivals of Voltaire's tragedies *Brutus*, *La Mort de César*, *Mahomet* and *Sémiramis*.

Following the National Convention's proclamation of the abolition of the monarchy, on 21 September 1792, Talma's theatre at the Palais-Royal was renamed the Théâtre de la République. In November, Talma produced Jean-François Ducis's version of Shakespeare's *Othello*. In an age when English productions of Shakespeare's plays cut scenes and changed endings so as not to offend or shock, Ducis's sanitised *Othello* was not untypical. He wasn't of Voltaire's mind; on the contrary, he admired Shakespeare's art, writing of *Othello* that it was 'one of the most touching and terrific plays brought forth by the creative genius of this great man: the menacing Iago is painted with extraordinarily powerful brushstrokes';[1] but he did not believe that the French public would tolerate Iago's malignant nihilism and cut the character as written by Shakespeare from his version. Talma reluctantly acquiesced. The

---

[1] Jean-François Ducis, *Othello, ou Le more de Venise, tragédie* (Paris: chez André, imprimeur-libraire, rue de la Harpe, 1799), p.iii.

play was still controversial. Talma's decision to place a bed on the stage was viewed by some as a scandalous lapse in taste and the depiction of Desdemona's murder (acts of violence were normally reported rather than enacted in French tragedies) an affront to dignity. The commonplace of violence and killings in Paris increased people's sensitivity to depictions of violence in plays. A few women fainted and a man cried out: 'This play must have been written by a Moor and not a Frenchman.'[1] Ducis wrote an alternative ending but Talma, determined to be as true to Shakespeare as possible, preferred not to use it. Talma's performance, inspired by the English style of Shakespearean acting, was unrestrained and visceral. An English visitor to Paris wrote that '[Talma] burst out [...] with a force against which all critical scorn was helpless – he broke down all rules and carried away his audience with a torrent of emotions new and strange to the French stage.'[2]

Louise Desgarcins played Desdemona (named Hédelmone in Ducis's version). Her increasing frailty in real life was almost certainly reflected in her playing of the role. André Grétry set the willow song to music for her, and the scene was particularly admired. Mlle Desgarcins's life ended tragically. During an argument with her lover, she picked up a knife and stabbed herself in the chest several times. Forced to retire from the stage, she withdrew to an isolated house in Sceaux. Further grave misfortune followed in the form of thieves who imprisoned her in the cellar of her home. She died soon afterwards at the age of twenty-eight.

A letter published in the *Journal de Paris*, quoted by Julie Hankey in her introduction to the Cambridge edition of Shakespeare's play, linked *Othello* to the Revolution, for republicans seized upon Talma's production as an assault on the hypocrisy of the *ancien régime*. In Julie Hankey's phrase, the letter 'reassures [Talma] that times have changed: that classical tragedy has gone out with formal gardens and the monarchy, that whereas five years ago "les hommes de la cour" would have laughed at the idea of a beautiful young white girl marrying a Moor, now philanthropy has triumphed,

---

[1] *Mémoires de J.-F. Talma*, t.3, p.232.

[2] Quoted in Julie Hankey (ed.), *Othello* (Cambridge: Cambridge University Press, 2005), p.51.

mulâtres have the rights of citizens, and the aristocracy of colour is dead'.[1] However, the French critics, still living in Voltaire's shadow, were mostly appalled by the play. Talma was exasperated by what he considered to be their false judgements on Shakespeare.

During the king's trial, the actress, composer and writer Julie Candeille joined Talma's company and appeared in her own hit comedy, *Catherine ou la belle fermière*. Mlle Candeille had been a member of the Comédie-Française before the fracture: she'd joined the troupe at the age of eighteen in 1785, having previously performed at the Opéra. Talma's repertory at the Théâtre de la République oscillated between sentimental comedies, such as *Catherine*, that provided the public with a means of escape, and works of patriotism, such as *Le Jugement dernier des rois* by Sylvain Maréchal, that pleased the Committee of Public Safety. For Talma's theatre and even more so for the Comédie, choosing the wrong play could have perilous consequences. The Comédiens-français continued to perform at their home in Saint-Germain, but did so under constant threat from the revolutionary committees. Actors were expected to be functionaries of the Revolution even when on stage, obliged to attach the tricolour cockade to their costumes. A savage band of men and women, notorious for mocking victims and orchestrating hysteria in the place de la Révolution, would, at the end of a day of executions, cross the river to enter the auditorium of the Théâtre de la Nation. The men wore distinctive waistcoats and wide pantaloons, and looked like sinister clowns; the women's dresses were blood-splattered. They harassed the actors and drowned out the play by singing patriotic songs.

The troupe tried to take refuge in the classical repertoire, but it was a repertoire that, understandably, didn't attract a public caught up in the extreme events of the time: the theatre was often half-empty. In January 1793, seeking a success, the Comédie-Française made a grave error by staging a provocative comedy, *L'Ami des lois* by Jean-Louis Laya. It was clear to everyone that Laya had based the two principal characters on Robespierre and Marat. The first night audience responded positively, but the Jacobins and the

---

[1] Julie Hankey (ed.), *Othello*, p.51.

Commune de Paris, led by Pierre Gaspard Chaumette, denounced the play and forbade further performances. The public, though, were determined to see Laya's scandalous play. During one particularly fraught evening, when a full house refused to watch a scheduled performance of Vigée's *Matinée d'une jolie femme* and called for Laya's play, Dazincourt pleaded with the spectators from the footlights: 'Messieurs, do not demand the performance of this work, for the consequences could be fatal for us.'[1] Dazincourt's fear was well-founded.

Louis XVI was executed on 21 January 1793. Across the Channel, people who cared about France and the enlightened ideas of the century, looked on in horror at the unfolding tragedy. Horace Walpole, who had, in happier times, corresponded with Voltaire and attended performances at the Comédie-Française, expressed his rage in an impassioned letter to Anne FitzPatrick:

> It remained for the enlightened eighteenth century to baffle language and invent horrors that can be found in no vocabulary. What tongue could be prepared to paint a Nation that should avow Atheism, profess Assassination, and practice Massacres on Massacres for four years together: and who, as if they had destroyed God as well as their King, and established Incredulity by law, give no symptoms of repentance! These Monsters talk of settling a Constitution – it may be a brief one, and couched in one Law, 'Thou shalt reverse every Precept of Morality and Justice, and do all the Wrong thou canst to all Mankind'.[2]

At the beginning of August 1793, the Committee of Public Safety decided that it was necessary to pass a law to ensure that plays and performances were true to the ideals of the Republic and to enable the removal of directors who were not politically correct. Georges Couthon of the Committee took the lead, writing that 'theatres have too often served tyranny, now they must serve liberty'. The National Convention duly passed, on 2 August, a decree written by Couthon. The decree required designated theatres to

---

[1] Quoted (in French) in *Mémoires de J.-F. Talma*, t.4, p.10.
[2] Horace Walpole to Anne FitzPatrick: 29 January 1793.

perform three times a week, from 4 August to 1 September, a republican tragedy (directors could choose between Voltaire's *Brutus*, Lemierre's *Guillaume Tell* and Chénier's *Caïus Gracchus*) and other plays that 'extol the glorious events of the Revolution and the virtues of the defenders of liberty'. The second article of the decree was alarming in the extreme:

> Any theatre that performs a play that has the effect of corrupting the public spirit or of awakening shameful superstitions, will be closed and its directors arrested and punished according to the full extent of the law.[1]

Later that month, the Comédie went ahead with the premiere of François de Neufchâteau's adaptation of Samuel Richardson's *Pamela*, with Mlle Lange as Pamela and Fleury as Mr B. The production attracted a large audience dominated by the Comédie's most loyal patrons. At the end of the work, the heroine was revealed to be a member of the aristocracy. The play failed to meet the requirements of the new law. The Jacobins accused the actors of showing sympathy for the aristocracy and the Committee of Public Safety banned the play. Neufchâteau made some changes and the Committee surprisingly allowed performances to resume but made a chilling statement in its official journal: 'The dagger that killed Marat was sharpened at the Théâtre de la Nation.' During the first performance after the lifting of the ban, an argument broke out in the pit when Fleury spoke the line 'Les persécuteurs sont les seuls condamnables, et les plus tolérants sont les plus raisonnables'. A patriot who shouted out that the line was treasonous was roughed up and evicted from the theatre by some of his fellow spectators. The man told all at the Club des Jacobins.[2] Robespierre and his colleagues on the Committee of Public Safety decided that the time was right to move against the members of the Comédie. The Committee issued the order for their arrest on 2 September:

---

[1] *Archives parlementaires de 1787 à 1860*, t.70 (Paris: Paul Dupont, 1906), p.134-35.
[2] See F.W.J. Hemmings, *Culture and Society in France 1789-1848* (Bloomsbury Reader, 2011).

The Committee of Public Safety has considered the disturbances that arose at the last performance at the Théâtre-Français, during which patriots were insulted; [and has found] that the actors and actresses of this theatre have been constantly guilty of incivism since the start of the Revolution and have performed anti-patriotic plays. 1. The Théâtre-Français will be closed; 2. The actors of the Théâtre-Français and the author of *Pamela*, François de Neufchâteau, will be arrested and imprisoned and their papers seized; 3. The Paris police is ordered to enforce more severely the law of 2 August last, as it relates to theatre productions.[1]

The Théâtre de la Nation was closed on 3 September. Naudet had already left France for Switzerland, but the other men were taken to the prison des Madelonnettes; and the women were confined in the prison des Anglaises. Some of the younger members of the troupe would subsequently be released. The actor and playwright Jean-Marie Collot d'Herbois, president of the Convention and general secretary of the Committee of Public Safety, declared unequivocally that the Comédiens-français were counter-revolutionaries. In December 1789, soon after Collot's return to Paris from Geneva, the Comédie had accepted for performance his five-act prose comedy *Le Paysan magistrat*, an adaptation of Calderón de la Barca's *El Alcalde de Zalamea* that had been premiered in Bordeaux in 1781. The cast included Naudet, Talma, Dugazon and Mlle Lange. The Comédie withdrew the play after only five performances. It is impossible to know whether Collot was motivated in part by a personal grudge against the Comédie. This fanatical terrorist went on to oversee the judicial murder of nearly 2,000 people in Lyon.

Collot let it be known that the famous actors of the Comédie were to be executed. It was a way of increasing the size of the crowds in the place de la Révolution and along the roads between the prisons and the scaffold. Every morning, during the eleven months of

---

[1] Comité de salut public (ed. F.-A. Aulard), *Recueil des actes du Comité de salut public*, t.6, entry for [2 sept. 1793] (Paris: Impr. Nationale, 1893), p.236-37.

their captivity, Dazincourt (Beaumarchais's Figaro), Fleury, Florence, Larive, Louise Contat (Beaumarchais's Suzanne), Emilie Contat, Mlle Raucourt and Mlle Lange expected to go to the guillotine. Fleury's sister Felicité (Mme Sainville) knew Collot, having acted alongside him in Bordeaux. Collot granted her request for an audience, but coldly dismissed her petition on behalf of her brother and his colleagues. Collot wrote to the public prosecutor, Fouquier-Tinville, asking him he speed up the process against the most prominent actors – Dazincourt, Fleury, the Contat sisters, Mlle Raucourt, and Mlle Lange. In the last week of June 1794, the portfolios relating to the six actors were marked with the letter G (for guillotine) in red ink, to which Collot added a note that no appeal should be considered. The Committee having condemned the actors, the expectation was that they would be brought before the Tribunal within a few days and then dispatched to the guillotine.

However, when Fouquier-Tinville asked for the portfolios to be sent to the Tribunal they could not be found. The actors were being protected by an official of the Committee of Public Safety, a former actor called Charles de La Bussière who worked in the *Bureau des pièces accusatives* – the office of documents relating to prisoners. Fortunately, there was no system in place to track documents or register their arrival. For some months the courageous La Bussière had been saving lives by destroying documents. Now, with only a brief window in which to act to save the actors, he smuggled the accusatory documents out of his office in the palais des Tuileries by submerging the sheets of paper in water so that they could be squashed up and hidden in his clothing. He then released them into the Seine from the public baths.

The actors would not have survived for much longer had the Terror continued. Fouquier-Tinville, embarrassed by this high profile failure, was determined to identify the person responsible for the disappearance of the papers. The sudden fall of Robespierre on 28 July 1794, must have felt like a miracle. The prisoners, including François de Neufchâteau, were released.

As for Talma, he too lived under the threat of condemnation. Aligned to the Girondins, when this faction was ousted from government and dispatched to the guillotine, in October 1793, he became acutely vulnerable. The support of David, close to Robespierre, may have saved him. The execution of Robespierre and his supporters ended the reign of terror, but the new government would need time to bring stability; and the people would need time to recover from the profound trauma of the previous two years. Talma's Théâtre de la République closed in 1796.

4   Napoléon

Under the Directorate, in May 1799, the Comédie-Française reformed, with the two groups reunited. It was François de Neufchâteau, appointed Minister of the Interior by the new government, who oversaw the troupe's rebirth. Neufchâteau knew that Talma was the natural leader of the troupe. He decided that the Comédie-Française's home would be Talma's Théâtre de la République (Salle Richelieu) at the Palais-Royal[1] and asked the actors to move forward in a spirit of reconciliation. Molé and Naudet would return to the company.

The name of the Théâtre de la République reverted to the traditional Théâtre-Français, and the new era began on 30 May 1799 with performances of Corneille's *Le Cid* and Molière's *L'École des maris*. Talma, who had triumphed in *Le Cid* during the Revolution, deliberately gave this play precedence to underscore the reformed Comédie-Française's loyalty to the Republic.

It was Napoléon, however, who restored to the Comédie-Française the prestige it had enjoyed during the *ancien régime*. Napoléon loved the theatre above all of the other arts – when he was in Paris he went to the theatre at least once a week and he brought his favourite actor, Talma, into his social circle. He admired Corneille above all other writers, and perhaps saw aspects of his own life and personality in the master's plays. Like Louis XIV, he understood the political benefits of placing France's premiere theatre under

[1] The Odéon in Saint-Germain, already in a poor state of repair, was destroyed by fire in 1799.

state control.

The theatre flourished during the Consulate, with new venues opening across the capital. Napoléon moved to monitor and restrict theatrical output after his coronation as emperor in 1804. In restoring the rights of the Comédie-Française, which included a state subsidy, he took away the actors' independence. Once more, the troupe was managed by ministers; and the real estate of the Théâtre-Français was taken into state ownership. By 1807, Napoléon had, by official decree, created a theatrical scene that consisted of only eight licenced theatres: the Comédie-Française, the Opéra, the Opéra-Comique and the Opéra-Buffa; and the less important Vaudeville, the Variétés, the Ambigu-Comique, and the Gaîté. Each of these theatres performed a protected repertoire, and the censor was vigilant. New plays had to be approved by Napoléon's Surintendant des théâtres.

Napoléon's friendship with Talma was genuine and lasting. Talma was a regular guest at the château de Saint-Cloud and the other imperial palaces, and would be summoned frequently to join Napoléon for breakfast or lunch at the palais des Tuileries, during which the emperor would freely critique his interpretations of roles such as César in *La Mort de Pompée* by Corneille: 'Vous fatiguez trop vos bras,' he told the actor. 'Les chefs d'empire sont moins prodigues de mouvements; ils savent qu'un geste est un ordre, qu'un regard est la mort; dès lors ils ménagent le geste et le regard.'[1] ('You gesture too much with your arms. Emperors are reserved in their movements; they know that a gesture is an order, that an expression is death. So they use both sparingly.')

A new generation of players emerged at the Comédie-Française during the first decade of the 19th century, among them three iconic actresses. Mlle Mars[2] excelled playing Molière and Marivaux's young women, among other parts. Her parents were actors, and she made her debut at the age of fourteen. As Agnès in *L'École des femmes*, Silvia in *Le Jeu de l'amour et du hasard*, Chérubin in *Le*

---

[1] 'Napoléon amateur de théâtre et admirateur de Talma', in Alain Decaux (ed.), *L'Histoire pour tous*, n.96 (1968), p.570-71.

[2] Anne-Françoise-Hippolyte Boutet, dite Mlle Mars (1779-1847, b. Paris). CF j1795 s99 d1841.

Mariage de Figaro, and, later, as Elmire in *Tartuffe* and Célimène in *Le Misanthrope*, she turned heads and won hearts: she was the first actress since Louise Contat to make these parts her own. A contemporary portrait by Nicolas Jacques confirms the Comédie-Française's description of Mlle Mars as a 'maigre jeune fille aux beaux yeux noirs'. Napoléon admired Mlle Mars, but it is unclear whether she became one of his mistresses. In contrast, Napoléon's affair with Mlle George[1] was documented. Mlle George made her debut at the Comédie-Française in the role of Clytemnestre in Racine's *Iphigénie*. The 1802/03 season was a personal triumph for the sixteen-year-old actress, for she played Émilie in Corneille's *Cinna*, the title role in Racine's *Phèdre*, and Hermione in Racine's *Andromaque*. This was the repertoire that Napoléon most admired. He invited Mlle George to Saint-Cloud, where, according to her own account, written decades later, she held out for three nights before surrendering her virginity.

Mlle George's main rival was Mlle Duchesnois,[2] who played many of the same roles (she made her debut as Phèdre). Their rivalry – played out in public by their partisan fans – was exciting for patrons of the theatre but very difficult to manage within the company. Talma admired Mlle Duchesnois, and often chose her as his partner, but she had to overcome the repeated insult that she was ugly, which she achieved through the expressiveness and informality of her acting.

Few contemporary plays succeeded at the Comédie-Française during the Napoléonic era. Molé scored a big success in Fabre d'Églantine's *Le Philinte de Molière*, inspired by *Le Misanthrope*, in December 1799; but, new work couldn't compete with the rivalry of Mlles George and Duchesnois in the tragedies of Corneille and Racine, or the performances of Talma in the same repertoire. In 1803, Talma played Hamlet in the version by Ducis. He asked Ducis for changes, but these did not bring the text closer to Shakespeare's original. Talma's Hamlet was hugely admired, and not

---

[1] Marguerite-Joséphine Weimer, dite Mlle George (1787-1867, b. Bayeux). CF j1802 s04 d17.

[2] Catherine-Joséphine Rafuin, dite Mlle Duchesnois (1777-1835, b. Saint-Saulve). CF j1802 s04 d29.

only by French spectators. The Scottish historian Archibald Alison, who saw *Hamlet* at the Comédie in 1807, was so overcome by the performances of Talma and Mlle Duchesnois (playing Hamlet's mother) that he considered Ducis's closet scene to be 'better managed for dramatic effect' than Shakespeare's original.

> At the conclusion of this great tragedy, which has become so popular in France, and in which the genius of Talma is so powerfully exhibited, the applause was universal; and after some little time, to our surprise, instead of diminishing, became much louder; and presently a cry of Talma burst out from the whole house. In a few minutes the curtain drew up, and discovered Talma waiting to receive the applause with which they honoured him, and to express his sense of the distinction paid to him.[1]

Molière's plays had presented a problem since the beginning of the Revolution. His one-act satires were frequently performed before Napoléon's decree of 1807, but the great comedies only reached the stage in heavily adapted versions that disguised their *ancien régime* origins. This attempt to appropriate the plays for the Republic was eventually abandoned. After Napoléon came to power, Molière's relevance declined even further – for the emperor didn't appreciate dramatic comedy, and compared it to 'salon gossip': 'C'est comme si l'on voulait me forcer à m'intéresser aux commérages de vos salons.'[2]

Napoléon's use of the Comédie-Française both to enhance his personal prestige and to proclaim the grandeur of France reached its height October 1808, when he ordered the actors to give performances during his summit meeting with Alexander I of Russia in the central German town of Erfurt. During the three weeks of the Congress, before an audience drawn from the great and the good of Central European politics, high society and intellectual life (Goethe and Wieland attended the gathering), the troupe, led by

---

[1] Archibald Alison, *Travels in France, During the Years 1814-15*, 2nd ed., vol.1 (Edinburgh: Macredie, Skelly and Muckersy, 1816), p.204-15.

[2] Quoted in Hélène Tierchant and Gérard Watelet, *La Grande histoire de la Comédie-Française* (Paris: Éditions SW Télémaque, 2011), p.83.

Talma, performed more than a dozen tragedies, including Corneille's *Cinna*, Racine's *Phèdre* and *Britannicus*, and Voltaire's
Œdipe. Culture, though, had no real impact on politics. Alexander
gave the impression that he was impressed by this barrage of French
dramatic poetry, and prepared to show acquiescence to Napoléon
and to accept his domination of Europe, but his courtesy hid a
steely agenda: 'Bonaparte thinks that I'm a dunce,' he wrote to his
sister, 'but he who laughs last, laughs longest.'[1] Alexander agreed to
support the French in their conflict against Great Britain and Aus-
tria, but, in the months that followed, failed to honour the articles
of the Erfurt Convention. Russia regularly ignored the Continental
System, Napoléon's attempt to block the import of British goods
into the Continent.

Napoléon took the fateful decision to go to war, and in June
1812 the *grande armée* invaded Russia. Four months later, during
the bleak days of the Russian campaign, Napoléon signed an imperial decree that set in stone the regulations under which the
Comédie-Française operated. It was as if he was seeking solace in
addressing a domestic cultural matter that gave him pleasure. The
eighty-seven articles of the 'décret de Moscou' contained rules that
still underpin the governance and structure of the troupe today.
The decree stated that the government would continue to oversee
the company and its work; but also, crucially, that the Comédie-
Française would continue to be a society of actors, divided into two
categories, sociétaires and pensionnaires. The managing committee
would be chaired by a government official but would contain six
members of the troupe; and all members would have a voice via the
troupe's general assembly. The superintendent would retain ulti-
mate authority over the selection and promotion of actors. Actors
would not be given the freedom to turn down roles. The decree
protected the founding principles of the Comédie-Française and
secured its long-term future.

---

[1] Quoted (in French) in *La Grande histoire de la Comédie-Française*, p.84.

4

Le Drame Romantique

1825-1843

7. *Roméo et Juliette* by Shakespeare, Richelieu, 2015. Éric Ruf (mise en scène),
Éric Ruf (décor), Christian Lacroix (costumes), Bertrand Couderc (lighting).
Jérémy Lopez (Romeo), Suliane Brahim (Juliette).
Photograph by Alain Richard.

1   The Shakespeare Effect

The 1820s saw a major shift from classicism to the avant-garde movement of the age already flourishing in other parts of Europe – Romanticism. In this new artistic climate, Shakespeare's work profoundly influenced the music of Berlioz and the paintings of Delacroix; and adaptations of Byron, Scott and Schiller internationalised the Parisian stage.

The death, in 1826, of Talma, the actor who had dominated the French theatre throughout all the years of the Revolution and the Napoléonic wars, opened up new possibilities, if the troupe was willing to take them. The author, art critic and traveller Isidore Taylor, appointed Royal Commissioner of the Comédie-Française in 1825, was the right man for this moment. Taylor is best known today for his series of illustrated books recording the monuments of France (*Voyages pittoresques et romantiques dans l'ancienne France*); but, as philanthropist and facilitator, he was at the forefront of the artistic movements of his time. In Manet's 1862 painting depicting fashionable Parisians attending an afternoon concert beneath the trees of the jardin de Tuileries, *La Musique aux Tuileries*, we find Taylor alongside Baudelaire, Gautier and Manet himself.

Taylor supported a new generation of writers eager to revolutionise the theatre. Alexandre Dumas, Victor Hugo and Alfred de Vigny, all in their twenties, were the leading exponents of a new genre that became known as *drame romantique*. They would become members of a literary circle (le Cénacle) that met in the rooms of Charles Nodier at the Bibliothèque de l'Arsenal, where Nodier was librarian. Nodier, a progressive who admired Shakespeare as well as less well-known masters of English such as Laurence Stern, was a mentor to younger writers who embraced romanticism: Alfred de Musset, Alphonse de Lamartine and Gérard de Nerval were also members.

Dumas's first major play, *Henri III et sa cour*, was a great success at the Comédie in 1829. Victor Hugo's *Hernani* provoked arguments and fistfights when it was premiered in 1830, for the new drama was the subject of a heated intellectual debate that resulted in pro-Romanticism and anti-Romanticism cliques clashing violently in the Salle Richelieu. Alfred de Vigny's *Chatterton*, about the English poet, followed in 1835.

Dumas revered Shakespeare, Byron and Walter Scott, but had contempt for the second-rate adaptations of English plays that were fashionable in Paris in the 1820s. 'It was the age of limitations,' he wrote, 'no-one was strong enough to be original.' Nicholas Rowe's *Jane Shore*, performed in a bastardised version at the Comédie in 1824, was one such play, although Dumas admired Talma's performance as Richard, and provided a description of the great actor for which we can be grateful:

> Talma was wonderful in this play, poor though it was. In it he attempted what was in those days looked upon as a very extraordinary thing. He, a man of fine presence, graceful in bearing, full of poetry, lofty in mind and eloquent, played the part of the hunchbacked cripple Richard. The way he managed to make his right shoulder look higher than his left and his arm appear paralysed, was a miracle of skill, and the denunciatory scene was a miracle of talent.[1]

Talma died without having achieved his ambition of performing a Shakespearean role in England. Not long after Talma's death, in 1827, the director of the Odéon Theatre invited the actor-manager William Abbott to bring a company of actors over from London to perform a season of English plays on the Odéon's stage. Although

---

[1] Alexandre Dumas (trans. E.M. Waller), *My Memoirs*, vol.3 (New York: Macmillan Company, 1908), p.42.

Abbott assembled the company in haste, he was able to persuade Charles Kemble, Edmund Kean and William Macready to play the leading roles. Attitudes towards Shakespeare were changing: Voltaire's view of the playwright, so deeply-held, and passed down from generation to generation, was confidently dismissed by the young of the 1820s, and the ground-breaking season at the Odéon further increased Shakespeare's influence. For young writers like Hugo and Dumas, the dominance of the French classical tradition had made it a kind of tyranny and something of a bore. Hugo was brilliant at cutting down to size previous great writers who didn't fit into his ideology. Voltaire was an 'ape of genius sent by the Devil to do his work'.[1] On Racine, he wrote: 'Listening to Racine's tragedies and fishing with a rod – same sort of pleasure.'[2] Shakespeare represented creative freedom, unruliness, emotion and all the mutable mess of human life. Put simplistically, Shakespeare represented the triumph of genius over the dogma of the classical unities. Hugo and Dumas built on the ideas of Stendhal, expressed in the essay *Racine et Shakespeare* (1825).

Dumas was working as a humble office clerk in the administration of Louis-Philippe, duc d'Orléans, at the Palais-Royal. He borrowed money so that he could attend the season. The first play was *Hamlet*. Dumas knew some of the lines by heart, but was not prepared for the depth of his response to watching the play in performance. 'This was the first time that I had seen real passions on the stage, inspiring men and women of real flesh and blood,' he wrote in his *Memoirs*.

> Now I understood Talma's moans over each fresh part he created; I understood that everlasting aspiration for a literature that could give him the chance of depicting a hero who should be a living being; I understood his despair at dying before he had given expression to that side of his genius which perished unknown within him.[3]

[1] From *Les Rayons et les ombres* (1840): 'Voltaire alors régnait, ce singe de génie, chez l'homme en mission par le diable envoyé.'
[2] Quoted in Graham Robb, *Victor Hugo* (London: Picador, 1998), p.232.
[3] Dumas, *My Memoirs*, vol.3, p.201.

Romeo and Juliet followed. Kemble's performances as Hamlet and Romeo were much admired, but it was the relatively unknown actress playing Ophelia and Juliet who became the talk of the town. Twenty-seven-year-old Harriet Smithson had only been cast because Abbott had not been unable to engage one of the star actresses of the time. She approached the roles somewhat modestly; she wore little or no makeup and acted with a naturalism that seemed new in France. She would never achieve recognition in England, but in France it was as if she *was* Ophelia and Juliet.

Hector Berlioz was still finding his way as a composer, and searching for romantic inspiration from dramatic literature and poetry, when he took his seat at the first performance of *Hamlet*:

> [...] there, in the part of Ophelia, I saw Miss Smithson. I can only compare the effect produced by her wonderful talent, or rather her dramatic genius, on my imagination and heart, with the convulsion produced on my mind by the work of the great poet whom she interpreted. It is impossible to say more. This sudden and unexpected revelation of Shakespeare overwhelmed me. The lightning-flash of his genius revealed the whole heaven of art to me, illuminating its remotest depths in a single flash. I recognised the meaning of real grandeur, real beauty, and real dramatic truth, and I also realised the utter absurdity of the ideas circulated by Voltaire, in France, about Shakespeare.[1]

Berlioz's creative imagination was transformed by the Shakespearean universe he encountered at the Odéon, and the *Symphonie fantastique*, written three years later in 1830, would chart this universe in music. When *Romeo and Juliet* was announced, Berlioz hurried to the box-office to secure a seat at any cost.

> After the harrowing sufferings, the tearful love, the bitter irony, the black meditations, the heartrending sorrows, the madness, the tears, mourning, catastrophes, and malign fortune of Hamlet

[1] Hector Berlioz (trans. Rachel Holmes and Eleanor Holmes), *The Autobiography of Hector Berlioz, from 1803 to 1865*, vol.1 (London: Macmillan and Co., 1884), p.90.

– the dark clouds and icy winds of Denmark – the change was too great to the hot sunshine and balmy nights of Italy – to the love, quick as thought, burning as lava, imperious, irresistible, inimitably pure and beautiful as the smile of an angel; the raging revenge, heartbreaking embraces, and desperate struggles between love and death. And so, at the end of the third act, scarcely able to breathe, stifled with a feeling as though an iron hand held my heart in its grip, I cried out, 'Ah, I am lost!' I must add that I did not then know a syllable of English, that I only dimly discerned Shakespeare through the misty medium of Letourneur's translation, and had no conception of the exquisite poetry in which his wonderful creations were clothed. Nor indeed am I much better off even now. It is far more difficult for a Frenchman to sound the deeps of Shakespeare's style, than it is for an Englishman to appreciate the subtlety and originality of Molière or La Fontaine. Our two poets are rich continents, Shakespeare is an entire world. But the play of the actors, and especially of the actress, the succession of scenes, the action, and the tones of voice, penetrated me with the Shakespearian ideas and passions, as our poor, pale translations never could have done.[1]

Now infatuated with Harriet Smithson, Berlioz became something of a stage door stalker, leaving dozens of letters for the actress and persevering despite her initial indifference. They married in 1833.

The season was remarkable in scope. Following *Romeo*, the company performed *Othello*, *The Merchant of Venice*, *Richard III*, *King Lear* and *Macbeth*. Dumas appreciated all aspects of Shakespeare's art; he enjoyed Abbott's Mercutio as much as Kemble's Romeo. 'I recognised,' he wrote, 'that, after the Creator Himself, Shakespeare had created more than any other being.'[2] Dumas wrote about the season as if he had witnessed unadulterated Shakespeare when, in fact, Abbott's company performed the heavily cut and modified versions of the time. *Romeo and Juliet* and *Hamlet*, although cut, were not drastically changed; but in *King Lear*, Cordelia fell in love

---

[1] Hector Berlioz, *The Autobiography of Hector Berlioz, from 1803 to 1865*, vol.1, p.90-94.
[2] Dumas, *My Memoirs*, vol.3, p.255.

with Edgar and the Fool was cut; and in *Othello*, the willow scene was missing. Some of the French critics who covered the season in the press knew the plays in English and were disappointed by the omissions. Nevertheless, there was enough original content in these performances to transport young spectators like Dumas and Berlioz, and the productions clearly created an extraordinary atmosphere in the theatre. Most of the words were Shakespeare's own, spoken in his own language – this was the essential factor.

Some of the most influential writing on the significance of Shakespeare could be found in Victor Hugo's long preface to his verse drama *Cromwell*, published in 1827. In viewing the whole of literature, and identifying three distinct periods – the ode, the epic and the drama – within the progress of civilisation, Hugo declared Shakespeare to be the great modern writer: 'Shakespeare is the drama; and the drama [...] moulds the grotesque and the sublime, the terrible and the absurd, tragedy and comedy.'

Hugo turned Voltaire's view of Shakespeare on its head. Voltaire found the grotesque in Shakespeare unforgivable; in contrast, Hugo proclaimed this aspect of Shakespeare's art to be not only 'one of the supreme beauties of the drama' but also a 'necessity'. The grotesque, he wrote,

> finds its way in everywhere; for just as the most commonplace have their occasional moments of sublimity, so the most exalted frequently pay tribute to the trivial and ridiculous. Thus, often impalpable, often imperceptible, it is always present on the stage, even when it says nothing, even when it keeps out of sight. Thanks to it, there is no thought of monotony. Sometimes it injects laughter, sometimes horror, into tragedy. It will bring Romeo face to face with the apothecary, Macbeth with the witches, Hamlet with the gravediggers. Sometimes it may, without discord, as in the scene between King Lear and his jester, mingle its shrill voice with the most sublime, the most dismal, the dreamiest music of the soul. [...] That is what Shakespeare alone among all has succeeded in doing, in a fashion of his own, which it would be no less fruitless than impossible to imitate – Shakespeare, the god of the stage, in whom, as in a trinity, the three characteristic geniuses of our stage, Corneille, Molière,

Beaumarchais, seem united. […] It is lyric poetry above all that befits the drama; it never embarrasses it, adapts itself to all its caprices, disports itself in all forms, sometimes sublime as in Ariel, sometimes grotesque as in Caliban. Our era being above all else dramatic, is for that very reason eminently lyric.[1]

If, today, we might recoil from the polemical nature and the sweeping generalisations of Hugo's analysis, his desire to elevate Shakespeare into a divinity to justify the whole rationale of the romantic school, in the 1820s it was revolutionary: at this moment of change, it was necessary to try and burn down the house of classicism. Above all, we find in the *Préface de Cromwell*, one great writer's affinity with another, a shaking of hands across national borders and, indeed, the chasm of time.

2   Dumas

Charles Nodier arranged for Dumas to present his play *Christine* to Isidore Taylor at Taylor's home in the rue de Bondy. Dumas provided a vivid, semi-comedic account in his *Memoirs*. When he entered the room, Taylor was in his bath, held captive by another would-be writer who was half-way through reading a five-act tragedy of tortuous tedium. The writer had 'surprised Taylor as Charlotte Corday had surprised Marat when she stabbed him in his bath'. Protocol dictated that Taylor allow the interloper to finish before asking him to leave and turning his attention to his invited guest.

Christine was a verse tragedy written in the classical style, but with innovations. Taylor admired the play, and arranged for Dumas to appear before the committee of the Comédie-Française. In

---

[1] Victor Hugo, 'Preface to Cromwell', in Charles W. Eliot (ed.), *Prefaces and Prologues*. Vol.39. *The Harvard Classics*. (New York: P.F. Collier and Son, 1909-14); Bartleby.com, 2001: www.bartleby.com/39/ (accessed 8 October 2018).

an elegant room at the Salle Richelieu, Dumas recited his play before a formidable gathering of famous actors, among them Mlle Mars, who was now, at the age of almost fifty, the de facto leader of the troupe, Firmin and Anne Demerson.[1] Dumas particularly admired Mlle Demerson, 'an engagingly clever *soubrette*, who played Molière with great freshness and Marivaux with such finished style'. The actors responded enthusiastically but wanted the opinion of an established author. The manuscript was sent to Louis-Benoît Picard, an author of the old school whom Dumas didn't rate. Dumas's fears were confirmed when Picard, smiling, told him that he preferred short comedies to 'grandes machines romantiques'. He annotated Dumas's manuscript with multiple exclamation marks and told the boy to return to his clerk's desk. Dumas would take his revenge in his *Memoirs* by bringing Picard to vivid life as a small, deformed, bright-eyed weasel.

Taylor would not accept Picard's judgement and sought support from Nodier. With Nodier's endorsement, the work was once more presented to the actors. They asked for revisions, but accepted *Christine* for performance. However, this was not the end of the matter. Mlle Mars and Firmin,[2] who were to play the leading roles, thought rather more highly of Picard than of Nodier, and withdrew. Then, with unfortunate timing, a second play about Queen Christina of Sweden was offered to the Comédie-Française. The actress Mlle Valmonzey,[3] noted more for her beauty than her talent, wanted to play the title role. Mlle Valmonzey was the mistress of the journalist Évariste Dumoulin. Placed under pressure by the machinations of Dumoulin, Dumas reluctantly agreed to give way and allow the other *Christine* to be performed ahead of his own play.

Dumas wrote a new play, inspired by Shakespeare. *Christine* was relatively conservative; in *Henri III et sa cour*, the great storyteller in waiting came up with a strong plot and wrote innovatively in the

---

[1] Anne Demerson (1786-1872, b. Marbéville, Haute-Marne). CF j1810 s13 d30.

[2] J.-B. François Becquerelle, dit Firmin (1784-1859). CF j1811 s17 d31.

[3] Catherine-Caroline Comte, dite Mlle Valmonzey (1799-1835). CF j1821 s28 d34.

romantic style. The actors were once again enthusiastic, but this time Dumas demanded assurances that the play would proceed to production. Company politics ended Dumas's idealistic view of theatrical life. He had to fight to secure the actors he wanted, since the code of seniority, and perhaps also jealousy of the young, led Mlle Mars to oppose his choices. In place of Dumas's nominations, Michelot[1] (as Henri) and nineteen-year-old Louise Despréaux[2] (as the page), Mlle Mars put forward two senior actors – Armand and Mme Menjaud.[3]

Mlle Mars played the Duchess of Guise. Despite their differences of opinion, Dumas admired her honesty and absolute commitment to the troupe. On one occasion, during an interval in a play at the Salle Richelieu, he entered her dressing room to find her covered in her own blood. She had been struck down by a kind of fit, and instead of abandoning the show had called for leeches which she applied to her chest between acts.

Henri III et sa cour was a revolutionary play, the first *drame romantique* performed at the Comédie-Française. As the first night approached, Dumas waited nervously for the censor to pronounce on the play. When an influential critic, known to be corrupt, published an attack on the play, declaring it to be too shocking to be produced, Dumas went to his office and threatened to beat him with his cane if he refused to agree to fight a duel. The critic retracted his comments on the play in the next day's edition. Meanwhile, the rehearsals were tense affairs. The actors had to adapt to meet the style of the play. Mlle Mars objected to Dumas's interest in Virginie Bourbier, a pensionnaire who was playing a very minor part. However, the work was sound and some luck went Dumas's way – the censor demanded only minor changes and the premiere went ahead as planned. The duc d'Orléans attended, as did Hugo and de Vigny: Dumas met them for the first time that night. Dumas began the night as an unknown playwright; he ended

---

[1] Pierre-Marie-Nicolas Michelot, dit Théodore Michelot (1786-1856, b. Paris). CF j1805 s11 d31.

[2] Louise Rosalie Allan-Despréaux (1810-1856, b. Mons). CF j1820.

[3] Armantine Émile Devan, dite Mme Menjaud (1794-1844, b. Paris). CF j1815 s28 d36.

it as one of the most famous men in all of literary Paris. With fame came criticism, and, within a few days of the opening night, Dumas had challenged yet another man to a duel because of a libellous article in the press. The matter was settled before a shot was fired, but only because Dumas's opponent was injured in a duel with someone else.

The success of Dumas's play, provoked a number of authors, including Lemercier, to protest openly by sending a petition to the king demanding the reconfirmation of the special status that had always been afforded to Molière, Corneille and Racine. They saw themselves as the legitimate heirs of these French masters; whereas Dumas and the other new playwrights were the 'bastard sons' of Shakespeare, Goethe and Schiller. The actress Mlle Duchesnois, passed over for the role of the Duchess of Guise in *Henri III*, was particularly vocal on the matter.

The petition was wrapped in patriotic rhetoric. Its authors declared that the Comédie-Française had been created to honour and preserve the glory of French culture; and this glory should not be diluted by the staging of lesser plays that imitated the work of foreigners. Those who had turned their backs on the core repertoire, and particularly on the presentation of tragedies, were guilty of 'depravity of taste'.

It was as if the Revolution had never happened. Charles X, though, politely declined to get involved: 'I only occupy one seat in the theatre, like every other Frenchman,' he replied.

3   Hugo and the Battle of Hernani

Following the premiere of Dumas's *Henri III*, Victor Hugo wrote the play *Marion Delorme*. The play was accepted by the Comédie-Française and went into rehearsal; but because the piece contained a portrait of Louis XIII, the censor declared that it could only be performed with the permission of the king. Hugo was granted an audience with Charles X, but to no avail. With the piece banned, and Taylor's winter season at the Comédie in jeopardy, Hugo wrote a new play, *Hernani*, at speed.

Although Hugo was only twenty-seven, he was already well-known as a poet and novelist. Baron Taylor had first approached Hugo about writing a play for the Comédie-Française in 1825, when Hugo joined Taylor and Talma for supper at a restaurant in the rue Montorgueil. By the end of the night it was agreed that Hugo would write a Shakespeare-inspired play about Oliver Cromwell and that Talma would create the title role. By the time Hugo had completed the play, Talma had died and, anyway, the piece was deemed to be unperformable.

Hugo's arrival at the Comédie-Française was an event. If Dumas had knocked down the doors, Hugo – who liked a military metaphor – strode through with the arrogant demeanour of a literary Napoléon. Hugo's confidence was necessary because most of the senior actors were at best ambivalent about *drame romantique*. On behalf of his fellow romantics, Dumas complained that the comédiens, led by Mlle Mars, looked upon the new drama as an 'invasion by barbarians to which they were laughingly obliged to submit'. We cannot know whether Dumas was being unfair when he told his readers that 'underneath the flattery paid us by Mlle Mars, there was always the mental reservation of an outraged woman'.[1] It was true that the actors, along with the majority of theatre-going Parisians, viewed the Comédie-Française as the hub of France's cultural life: it was a place of reverence. The writer Léon Halévy, a purist, directed his contempt at Baron Taylor, writing, 'Le Théâtre-Français est un temple et non une boutique'.[2]

The rehearsals were long and stressful. Mlle Mars, playing the teenage heroine at the age of fifty-one, tested Hugo constantly, but in Hugo she found someone who more than met her match. Dumas recorded Mlle Mars's habit of constantly halting proceedings to pedantically challenge Hugo on particular words and phrases. These interjections would always start in the same way: Mlle Mars would advance to the footlights and enquire, 'M. Hugo are you

[1] Dumas, *Memoirs*, p.508.
[2] Quoted in *La Grande histoire de la Comédie-Française*, p.96.

there?' A duel of words, extremely polite, but poison-tipped, would then ensue. Rebuffed, albeit politely, by the author, Mlle Mars would try the same objection the next day. In one of the play's pivotal scenes, Doña Sol is required to sit motionless in silence for many minutes listening to Don Carlos and Gomez debate whether Hernani, her lover, should die. This long silence, finally broken by the despairing line 'Roi don Carlos, vous êtes un mauvais roi', is crucial to the power of the scene, but Mlle Mars found it intolerable that she had no lines for so many minutes. Silence was unusual in the plays of Molière and Corneille, but Hugo, true to the code of romanticism, wanted his characters to behave like real people, and was interested in the 'poetry of silence'. Finally exasperated by the demands of the actress, Hugo told her that he would take the part away from her if she didn't start to treat him with respect. He would, he said, cast young Mlle Despréaux in her place. Mlle Mars did as she was asked from that moment on. Professional pride ensured that Mlle Mars, M. Michelot – 'a man of the world, with finished manners, showed us his most gracious side; but at heart he loathed us'[1] – and Firmin performed the piece with conviction: such are the paradoxes, now as then, of the actor.

Before *Hernani* opened, the Comédie-Française staged Shakespeare's *Othello* in a new verse translation by de Vigny. Joanny[2] scored a personal success as Othello; Mlle Mars played Desdemona. While there were still significant omissions, de Vigny's text, published as a translation of Shakespeare's play rather than as a new work based on Shakespeare, was revelatory. De Vigny conceived his *Othello* as an antidote to French classicism. He retained sexual references that were normally cut (on English stages as well as French) and did not flinch from presenting the flaws in Othello's character. Whereas previous translators had substituted a bracelet for the handkerchief, deeming a woman's handkerchief to be too intimate an item in the context of the play, likely to provoke embarrassed laughter, de Vigny realised that its intimacy was the point. This is just one example of how de Vigny was true to the meanings behind

---

[1] Dumas, *Memoirs*, p.508.
[2] Jean-Bernard Brisebarre, dit Joanny (1775-1849). CF j1807 s28 d41.

Shakespeare's choices.[1] De Vigny's achievement was recognised by Victor de Broglie, who wrote of the production:

> From the moment Iago says 'Ha, I like not that', to the moment the curtain falls, the spectator cannot draw breath. You could hear a fly buzz. The spectator looks at the stage with something of that anxiety which takes hold of us when in a court of justice we witness the vain efforts of the miserable ones dragged off to execution.[2]

The premiere of *Hernani* on 25 February 1830 represented the shock of the new. Hugo's supporters rounded up the radical young men of the city to ensure that the *claqueurs*, paid to hiss, would be outnumbered. Mostly young and republican in their views, and dressed in a new style inspired by Spain and by romantic notions of earlier times, they outraged the theatre's regular attendees. Loud, disruptive and disrespectful of the traditions of the Comédie-Française, they ate, drank and urinated on the plush scarlet carpets:[3] to gauge the culture shock, think of the first appearance of punks on the King's Road in London a hundred and fifty years later.

The play's plot – Hernani, a noble outlaw, and Doña Sol are in love; but Doña Sol is coveted by both her elderly guardian and the king Don Carlos – was hackneyed and unoriginal; but, in his style and choice of words, Hugo hit his targets mercilessly. While Hugo was notoriously shifty when it came to political allegiances, the most radical among his supporters thought they saw a clear meaning in the play. Hernani and Doña Sol represented individual rights and the force for change; Gomez and Don Carlos represented political repression and tyranny.

The aggressive enthusiasm of Hugo's supporters carried the first night, but this was just the first exchange in what became known

---

[1] See Alfred de Vigny, 'Lettre à Lord *** Earl of *** sur la soirée de 24 octobre 1829' in William Shakespeare (trans. Alfred de Vigny), *Le More de Venise, Othello* (Paris: Levavasseur, 1830).

[2] Victor de Broglie, *Sur Othello traduit en vers français par M. Alfred de Vigny et sur l'état de l'art dramatique en France en 1830* (Paris: Didier, 1852). Quoted in Julie Hankey (ed.), *Othello*, p.53.

[3] See Robb, *Victor Hugo*, p.149.

as the battle of *Hernani*. All thirty-nine performances were punctuated by arguments and fistfights in the stalls, but overall the Hugoists were out-numbered and the boos and hisses grew in impact as the run neared its end. Hugo received death threats. *Hernani* was adored by the radical young and hated by the conservative old for the same reason: it was, in Graham Robb's phrase, 'the banner which united a generation',[1] a generation that was about to show that it was revolutionary: the July Rebellion (the violent three-day insurrection that ended the reign of Charles X) was only a month away.

4   Le Roi s'amuse and Lucrèce Borgia

Hernani was the high watermark of romantic drama at the Comédie-Française. Hugo's *Marion Delorme* was finally staged at the Comédie in August 1731, but despite the emergence of a new star actress, Marie Dorval,[2] the reception was somewhat lukewarm. Hugo's next play, *Le Roi s'amuse*, was banned after only one performance, in November 1832, because the government deemed it to be subversive and immoral. The authorities feared that the play would out-perform *Hernani* as a rallying-point for republicanism.

Le Roi s'amuse (the source material of Verdi's opera *Rigoletto*, composed twenty years later) was a strange concoction, part melodrama, part forerunner of absurdist drama. It reaches its grotesque denouement when the king's fool Triboulet (Hugo's second hunchback[3] in little more than a year) discovers that his plot to have François I murdered has misfired – the body in his sack is not that of the king but that of his own daughter. Hugo, who during these years had suffered the pain of his wife's affair with his close friend,

[1] Robb, *Victor Hugo*, p.147.
[2] Marie Dorval (1798-1849). CF j1834.
[3] The first being Quasimodo in *Notre-Dame de Paris*, published in March 1831.

Sainte-Beuve, and who may have been struggling with his complicated feelings for his beloved daughter Léopoldine, was in no mood
to be fair to women or to tolerate any kind of authority, reacted
defiantly when the play was banned by the government. Because
censorship had been ended after the fall of Charles X, Hugo declared that the troupe had no right to suspend performances and
took the Comédie-Française to court.

Hugo spoke at the proceedings, a *tour de force* of oration that
showed that the writer's political views were starting to harden and
to settle. Here, Hugo translated his feelings of victimisation into a
grand personal statement: 'Today, my freedom as a poet is taken
by the censor; tomorrow, my freedom as a citizen will be taken by
a policeman. Today, I am banished from the theatre; tomorrow, I
shall be banished from the land.' The speech came to a conclusion
with the defiant prophecy, 'Today, a state of siege exists in literature; tomorrow, it will exist in the city'.[1]

Hugo lost the case, but had at least made his points in the full
glare of public opinion. With his fractious relationship with the
actors of the Comédie-Française under great strain, Hugo gave his
new play, *Lucrèce Borgia*, to Charles Jean Harel at the Théâtre de la
Porte-Saint-Martin. The Porte-Saint-Martin Theatre lacked the
prestige of the Comédie-Française, but it also lacked all of the baggage that the troupe carried. The play – Hugo's first in prose – was
a huge success. Mlle George, who had left the Comédie-Française
in 1817, played the title role. Frédérick Lemaître, a big name and
a big personality (perhaps too big for the Comédie-Française),
played Gennaro. A beautiful young courtesan called Juliette
Drouet, who was trying her hand at acting, was given a minor role
on Hugo's insistence: he had fallen in love with her and was in the
process of making her his mistress. Hugo's gothic imagination produced a black tale of incest and murder that was shocking for the
time. By now, Hugo had acquired a reputation for writing scenes
that pushed the boundaries of decorum and taste by depicting sexual desire, malignant thoughts and acts of gruesome violence: the
full houses contained people – including working-class people from

---

[1] Quoted in Robb, *Victor Hugo*, p.178.

the *faubourgs* – who didn't normally go to the theatre.

Alfred de Vigny's most significant contribution to romantic drama, *Chatterton*, was premiered at the Comédie in February 1835. De Vigny's mistress Marie Dorval played Kitty Bell to great acclaim.

Dumas and Hugo had not given up on the Comédie-Française. Hugo's play *Angelo, tyran de Padoue*, concerning the conflict between a tyrant's wife (Catarina) and his mistress (Tisbe), opened at the Salle Richelieu in April 1835. Understandably, Hugo wanted the youthful Marie Dorval to play the courtesan ('You are beyond pretty,' he told the actress) and Mlle Mars to play the faithful wife, but Mlle Mars insisted that it should be the other way around: she knew that her younger rival (and junior colleague – Marie Dorval was still only a pensionnaire) would overshadow her if she played the more dynamic role. Marie declared that she didn't care; she was happy to play either part. Marie was too free-spirited to be offered lasting membership of the troupe.[1] Hugo's mistress Juliette was unaccustomed to being in competition with another woman. In a letter to Hugo she wrote: 'I'm jealous of a woman, Marie Dorval, who has the sluttiest character imaginable, who is with you every day, giving you the eye and touching you.'

Hugo's hopes for the play weren't realised. Dumas was equally disappointed by the reception given to his verse drama *Caligula*, premiered in December 1837. Neither play came close to generating the excitement of *Henri III* or *Hernani*. Dumas and Hugo were disappointed if they hoped to wipe classical tragedy from the corpus of living works. A new actress, Mlle Rachel,[2] excelled in this repertoire, and was the impetus needed to make it popular once again. She made her debut at the age of seventeen in 1838, playing Camille in Corneille's *Horace*. The audience members were not immediately on Mlle Rachel's side when she walked on stage. People commented on her black eyes and hair and on how strange she

[1] Marie Dorval's life as a girl hadn't been easy (an orphan, she was married at fifteen to a much older man), and she would not cope well when she reached middle-age and her career went into decline.

[2] Elisabeth Félix, dite Mlle Rachel (1821-1858, b. Mumpf, Switzerland). CF j1838 s42 d55.

looked; it didn't escape the prejudiced that she was Jewish. But, Mlle Rachel had remarkable poise for one so young, and her striking appearance set her apart from other ingénues. There was something deathly about her. For Musset, she was a 'vraie princesse bohémienne, une pincée de cendre où il y a une étincelle sacrée'; for Théophile Gautier, she was 'pale comme son proper fantôme'.[1] It was noted immediately that she spoke the verse beautifully. After Camille, in 1838 alone she played Émilie in Corneille's *Cinna*, Hermione in Racine's *Andromaque*, Aménaïde in Voltaire's *Trancrède*, Ériphile in Racine's *Iphigénie en Aulide*, Monime in Racine's *Mithridate*, and Roxane in Racine's *Bajazet*.

The 1840s belonged to this actress. In 1841, she appeared on the London stage;[2] and in 1843 she scored her biggest success playing the title role in *Phèdre* at the Comédie. In this climate, the relative failure of Hugo's final play for the Comédie, *Les Burgraves*, in March 1843, signalled the end of his career as a playwright. Hugo decided that politics was a higher calling than writing for a theatre-going public he had always partly despised. More significantly, personal tragedy of the most terrible kind was about to befall him. In September 1843, Hugo's daughter Léopoldine and her new husband went boating with his uncle and cousin on the Seine at Villequier: the yacht capsized and they were all drowned.

5   Aftermath

Hernani wouldn't be produced again at the Comédie-Française until much later in the century. When it was finally revived, in 1867, it was once more a *cause célèbre* that unified and emboldened opponents of the government. Hugo, living in political exile in Guernsey, was delighted to learn that, for the French, his fame and

[1] Quoted in *La Grande histoire de la Comédie-Française*, p.117.
[2] Matthew Arnold, writing in the journal *Nineteenth Century* in August 1879: 'I remember how in my youth, after a first sight of the divine Rachel at the Edinburgh Theatre, in the part of Hermione, I followed her to Paris, and for two months never missed one of her representations.'

influence were greater than ever. In 1877, after Hugo's return to France, Mounet-Sully and Sarah Bernhardt starred in a new production at the Comédie that the author supervised. This staging became a constant fixture at the Comédie.[1]

[1] New productions were mounted in 1927 (Émile Fabre); 1937 (Georges Le Roy: Marie Bell played Doña Sol); 1952 (Henri Rollan); and 1972 (Robert Hossein). The Comédie-Française's current production of *Hernani* was premiered in 2013. Nicolas Lormeau directed Félicien Juttner, Jennifer Decker, Bruno Raffaelli and Jérôme Pouly.

5

From the Second Empire to the Commune

1848-1871

8. Sarah Bernhardt by Nadar, ca.1864.

1   Alfred de Musset

Alfred de Musset, born into an aristocratic family in Paris in 1810, was even more precocious than Victor Hugo. He started to attend Charles Nodier's salon while still at school, and published his first collection of poems, *Contes d'Espagne et d'Italie*, at the age of nineteen in 1829. His doomed love affair with George Sand brought him public notoriety during the early 1830s, for, at this time, Sand was also believed to be sharing her bed with Marie Dorval: Musset would explore his feelings for Sand in the anonymously published *Gamiani ou deux nuits d'excès*, an illustrated erotic novel based, it was assumed, on Sand's scandalous reputation (1833), and in *La Confession d'un enfant du siècle*, published in 1836.

Musset was a child of Romanticism, but too young and too singular to be fully embraced by Hugo and its other leaders. He attempted to join Hugo as an author of romantic dramas, but his play *La Nuit vénitienne*, premiered at the Odéon in 1830, was a failure: the performance was disrupted by the anti-Romantics and plagued by laughter-inducing mishaps – wet paint from the set ended up all over the leading actress's white dress. Musset continued to write plays, and published them in the *Revue des Deux Mondes*. They were conceived to be read and not performed – Musset's feverish imagination, soon to burn itself out, was the product of a nervous disposition and physical frailty; it was influenced by both Shakespeare and Marivaux but was very much his own. This linking of English lyricism with French elegance, set Musset apart from an anti-classicist like Hugo, and, in terms of his artistic temperament, Musset was, perhaps, more in tune with the great

English romantics – he translated De Quincey's *Confessions of an English Opium-Eater* into French when he was eighteen (1828) – than with Hugo, for among the characteristics he shared with them were narcissism and detachment. Musset's work realised one of the key concepts of Hugo's *Préface de Cromwell* – the Shakespearean shift from comedy to tragedy.

Musset's originality and modernity are best revealed by his three short *proverbes dramatiques* (as long as they are read in French – sadly, Musset's style has not been captured in the available English translations): *On ne badine pas avec l'amour* (1834), *Il ne faut jurer de rien* (1836), and *Il faut qu'une porte soit ouverte ou fermée* (1845). He unexpectedly found success in the theatre in 1847 when his 1837 work *Une Caprice*, a comedy, was produced at the Comédie-Française. The actress Louise Despreaux[1] had selected this work for performance at the French Theatre in Saint Petersburg, and brought it with her when she returned to Paris and re-joined the Comédie-Française.

After the Revolution of February 1848 and the establishment of the Second Republic, Musset was dismissed from his post as librarian at the Ministry of the Interior. The loss of his salary, along with fading health and the realisation that his creativity was spent (he tried to write a new work for Mlle Rachel), meant that he faced an uncertain future. Fortunately, his theatre was suddenly in demand. On 7 April, *Il faut qu'une porte soit ouverte ou fermée* was premiered at the Salle Richelieu (renamed Théâtre de la République), alongside Molière's *L'École des maris* and Racine's *Les Plaideurs*. Musset's elegant duologue, lasting only forty minutes, fitted well as an interlude between these two established masterpieces. The critics were divided, but the piece had the stealth to sneak into the hearts and minds of a public facing, once again, political upheaval and violence. 'Putting into plain words the truthfulness, refinement, heart and wit of Musset's writing,' wrote his friend Théophile Gautier, 'would be like brushing the dust off the wings of a butterfly to reveal its true colours'.[2]

---

[1] For ten years from 1837 Louise Despreaux worked in Saint Petersburg.

[2] Quoted (in French) in Comédie-Française, *Dossier de presse - Il faut qu'une porte soit ouverte ou fermée* (2017). 'Ce ton si vrai et si fin, cette allure à la fois

The Comédiens-français went on to perform Musset's *Le Chandelier* in 1850 and *Les Caprices de Marianne* in 1851. *Lorenzaccio*, arguably Musset's most dazzling and compelling play, was deemed to be too long and convoluted for performance. It would be staged during the 20th century by Jean Vilar at the Théâtre national populaire (1958) and, at the Comédie, by Franco Zeffirelli in 1976 and Georges Lavaudant in 1989. In England, the play was produced at the RSC by Ron Daniels (in a version by Paul Thompson, 1977), and at the National Theatre by Michael Bogdanov (in a version by John Fowles, 1983).

The Comédie-Française staged *Il faut qu'une porte soit ouverte ou fermée* every year from 1910 to 1970, and mounted a new production in the Studio-Théâtre in 2017. *Fantasio* was last performed in 2010 and *On ne badine pas avec l'amour* in 2012. *Les Caprices de Marianne*, staged in 1980 with Ludmila Mikaël as Marianne, is due for revival, as is *Lorenzaccio*.

Musset's theatre proved to have greater relevance for future generations than Hugo's, in that the melodramatic and conventional aspects of Hugo's plays were very much of their own time. By writing plays to be read and not staged, Musset, with his imagination unshackled from the constraints imposed by practical matters of stagecraft (as they existed in the mid-19th century, before modern lighting and swift set changes), created theatre pieces that would come into their own once the art of theatre production had advanced both technically and aesthetically. The subject of Musset's modernity was first expressed by Jacques Copeau in the 1920s:

> [Musset] possesses the secret of light composition. […] An agility, a joyousness. True power in art is delicate and explosive. It abolishes real duration at one stroke. […] [Musset] is in command of everything. An image, an allusion, a passage, a break, a balancing of scenes or speeches, and perhaps even less, is enough for him to stir up the powers of illusion, to awaken a desire in the

délicate et dégagée, ce mélange de cœur et d'esprit, cet inattendu qui ne tombe jamais dans le baroque, cette originalité si aisée et si franche, tout cela ne peut se transporter dans un sec compte rendu. Autant vaudrait-il racler la poussière des ailes d'un papillon, pour en montrer les couleurs.'

imagination and to satisfy it at the same moment.[1]

Musset's work predicts the modern meaning of the theatre as an art form concerned with the poetry of light and space and with irony and illusion. Jean Renoir's 1939 film *La Règle du jeu* was inspired in part by Musset's *Les Caprices de Marianne*. It felt right when the Comédie-Française decided to adapt Renoir's screenplay for the stage: Christiane Jatahy's production opened at the Salle Richelieu in 2017, with Suliane Brahim as Christine, Jérémy Lopez as Robert, and Laurent Lafitte as André.

'It wasn't my intention,' Renoir revealed, 'to make an adaptation, but let's just say that my reading of *Les Caprices de Marianne*, which I consider to be Musset's most beautiful play, helped me a lot. But, they are only distantly related.'[2] Renoir's Christine is, in fact, closely related to Musset's Marianne. As Doménica Brassel and Joël Magny identified in their introduction to Gallimard's 1998 edition of *La Règle du jeu*, Renoir's screenplay shares a number of elements with Musset's 'sombre comédie romantique': a nocturnal setting; a change of identity which goes wrong; the theme of love betrayed; and, at the end, a fateful 'accident' which is the price of the game. Renoir saw Musset's link to Marivaux and Beaumarchais, but also the closeness to film of a text like *Les Caprices de Marianne*. In Yifen Beus's phrase, 'the shifting perspectives of *Les Caprices de Marianne* provided a dramatic base for Jean Renoir's film technique'.[3]

In *Les Caprices de Marianne*, Marianne, a young woman believed to be pure and cold, is married to an elderly judge, Claudio. A shy young man, Célio, is in love with her. Marianne only vaguely knows who he is. She ignores his letters and refuses to see him.

---

[1] Quoted in Yifen Beus, 'Alfred de Musset's Romantic Irony', in *Nineteenth-Century French Studies*, vol.31, no.3/4 (University of Nebraska Press, 2003), p.197-209.

[2] Quoted (in French) in Jean Renoir, *La Règle du jeu* (Paris: Gallimard, 1998). 'Je n'ai pas eu l'intention de faire une adaptation; disons que lire et relire *Les Caprices de Marianne*, que je considère comme la plus belle pièce de Musset, m'a beaucoup aidé; mais il est évident que cela n'a que des rapports bien lointains.'

[3] Yifen Beus, 'Alfred de Musset's Romantic Irony'.

Célio's charismatic friend Octave intercedes on his behalf by going up to Marianne in the street and talking to her; but this good deed goes wrong, for Marianne falls for him and asks him to meet her later that night. Octave resists the temptation, and arranges for Célio to go to the rendezvous in his place. Marianne tries to warn the man she takes to be Octave that her jealous husband has posted an assassin to kill any man who enters his garden. Célio isn't told in time. Marianne tells Octave that she loves him. Octave rejects her by revealing the ironic truth: 'Je ne vous aime pas, Marianne; c'était Célio qui vous aimait.' This unexpectedly tragic and bitter ending forces the audience to reconsider everything that has gone before.

In the premiere production at the Comédie, Marianne was created by eighteen-year-old Madeleine Brohan,[1] who had only joined the troupe the year before but who had already been singled out as a major talent. Octave was played by Édouard Brindeau,[2] Célio by Louis-Arsène Delaunay,[3] and Claudio by Jean-Baptiste Provost.

Musset died in 1857, at the age of fifty-six.

2   Theatre Under the Second Empire

In the 1860s, during the Second Empire, the area around the Salle Richelieu became a huge building site, for much of the quarter was demolished to create the avenue de l'Opéra, part of Napoléon III's grand project, managed by baron Haussmann, to modernise the capital by clearing the medieval slums and replacing them with modern housing and a modern sanitation system. As part of the development, the Salle Richelieu was enlarged by the architect Prosper Chabrol. Chabrol created a new public foyer in which he placed full-size statues in white marble of Molière and Voltaire. Under the Second Empire, the economy boomed; and Paris was cleaner and brighter. At night, it offered new levels of debauchery

---

[1] Madeleine Brohan (1833-1900, b. Paris). CF j1850 s52 d85.
[2] Édouard Brindeau (1814-1882, b. Paris). CF j1842 s43 d54.
[3] Louis-Arsène Delaunay (1826-1903, b. Paris). CF j1848 s50 d86.

and vice. Writers such as Baudelaire mourned the destruction of the old Paris. In the *faubourgs*, activists believed that the rebuilding of Paris was entirely about neutralising the rebellious nature of its citizens: the warrens of stone, in which working-class revolutionaries had built their barricades, were replaced by wide boulevards down which the militia could ride their horses, should the people rise once more.

The Comédie-Française was once more placed under direct political control. In 1849, Napoléon III created the new position of Administrator under the authority of the Interior Minister. Édouard Thierry,[1] appointed to the position in 1859, stayed in post for twelve years. Thierry had been librarian of the Bibliothèque de l'Arsenal before taking up his post at the Comédie. He had made his name as a theatre critic, writing for the *Revue du théâtre* and other journals during the 1830s. The government lessened the Comédie-Française's dominant status by issuing a decree (in January 1864) that opened up the Paris stage commercially. Anyone could open and run a theatre; the market would decide whether these independent theatres flourished or failed. The Comédie-Française was no longer afforded a monopoly over the performance of the repertoire it had always considered its own. At the same time, the government hardened up censorship. The aim was to turn the French theatre into a money-making industry while, through censorship, ensuring it had no political bite.

Within this new climate, a new genre emerged – *comédie bourgeoise* – and a new actress who would flit between the classical and commercial theatre and who would become one of the first world stars: Sarah Bernhardt.[2] The daughter of a courtesan of Dutch-Jewish lineage, Bernhardt was placed in a boarding school and then a convent while her mother and her mother's powerful lover the duc de Morny (the half-brother of Napoléon III) decided what to do with her. By her mid-teens, she had grown into a beautiful young woman with dark eyes and a mass of unruly black hair (her appeal

---

[1] Édouard Thierry (1813-1894, b. Paris).
[2] Sarah Bernhardt (1844-1923, b. Paris). CF j1862 s75 d80.

would be captured for posterity a few years later by the photographer Nadar). Dumas, a friend of Morny, was impressed by the girl's intensity. It was decided that she should become an actress. She was given a place at the Paris Conservatoire, where she was taught by Provost. In 1862, Édouard Thierry brought her into the Comédie-Française as a pensionnaire. Perhaps because of Morny's influence, she made her debut playing no less a role than Iphigénie in Racine's tragedy. At the age of eighteen, she was too nervous and too inexperienced to succeed in such a part. The critics said so; while other members of the company resented the promotion of a girl who had yet to prove herself. Bernhardt slapped the senior actress Mlle Nathalie during a heated argument. She refused to apologise so Thierry let her go. Following an unsuccessful season at the Théâtre du Gymnase, she quit the stage and considered entering her mother's profession. She had a child, but refused to name the father. To support her son, she took on minor roles in one of the boulevard theatres. In 1866, she was given a chance by the director of the Odéon, Felix Duquesnel, and it was at the Odéon that she made her name. She played Ophelia in her first season, followed by the boy Zacharie in Racine's *Athalie* (1867), Anna Danby in Dumas's *Kean* (1868 – Dumas had kept faith with her all along) and the troubadour in François Coppée's *Le Passant* (1869).

The Odéon, on the edge of the Latin Quarter, was frequented by students and artists: it was quite different from the Comédie. 'It is the theatre I loved most,' Bernhardt would reveal in her memoirs.

> I was very sorry to leave it, for everyone liked each other there, and everyone was gay. The theatre is a little like a continuation of school. The young artistes came there, and Duquesnel was an intelligent manager, and very polite and young himself. During rehearsal we often went off, several of us together, to play ball in the Luxembourg, during the acts in which we were not on. I used to think of my few months at the Comédie-Française. That little world I had known there had been stiff, scandal-mongering, and jealous. At the Odéon I was happy. We thought of nothing but putting plays on, and we rehearsed morning, afternoon, and at

all hours, and I like that very much.[1]

At the premiere of the revival of *Kean*, the political tensions of the late 1860s were played out in the auditorium. The curtain was delayed for an hour while young republicans in the audience chanted the name of the exiled Hugo and turned on the pleasure-loving Dumas, who was sitting in a box with an unknown woman, presumed to be a courtesan, because he wasn't Hugo. Dumas, in a rage, tried to talk them down. Eventually, Duquesnel decided to start the play. Bernhardt's entry on the stage calmed the house and the play succeeded.

3 The Siege

During the terrible days of the Prussian army's siege of Paris, from September 1870 to January 1871, the foyer of the Comédie-Française was turned into an ambulance (field hospital). The actresses worked as nurses in the ambulance.

The French army had been crushed at Sedan at the beginning of September. The Second Empire fell and a government of national defence proclaimed the Third Republic. The new government refused to surrender. By 19 September, the Prussians had surrounded Paris and the officers of the high command were enjoying life at their new HQ – the palais de Versailles. It was now up to the Garde Nationale (civilian militia) and the Garde Mobile (reserve troops) within the city walls to take the fight to the Prussians. Paris was protected by a system of defences, constructed in the 1840s. A high wall[2] enclosed the city; within the wall there was a wide trench and strategically placed forts. Initially, the Germans decided not to bombard Paris, believing that an effective blockade would lead to the city's surrender.

Men in the uniform of the Garde Nationale – blue trousers with

[1] Sarah Bernhardt, *My Double Life* (London: Heinemann, 1907), p.127.
[2] Today's Boulevards des Maréchaux mark the location of the wall.

a red stripe, kepi cap – were suddenly everywhere, but they lacked the military bearing, the discipline, of professional soldiers. The Garde Nationale at ease was something of a fractious rabble. The parks were turned into military parade grounds and shooting ranges in a last-ditch attempt to transform these men into battle-ready soldiers. In the faubourgs, socialists were organising against the provisional government. General Trochu, president of the government of national defence and commander of the city's defences, was understandably concerned about a politicised Garde Nationale dominated by those battalions formed in, and administered by, the working-class districts of Paris.

The privileged classes carried on with life as usual for as long as they could: the boulevards and cafés were busy during the evenings. A state of shock, of unreality, was common. A blockade was an affront to progress and modernity. Sieges belonged in the Middle Ages. Patriotic fervour, inspired by the rebirth of the republic and heightened by the rhetoric of Victor Hugo ('Those who attack Paris attack the whole human race'), survived for some weeks. Hugo had returned home after nearly twenty years of exile on 5 September. Thierry wrote in his journal: 'Victor Hugo has returned to Paris. Triumphant entry. He gave a speech from the balcony of the hôtel Saint-Quentin and then led a procession down the boulevards. Stone eagles, torn from the barracks of the Cité, were hurled into the Seine from the pont Notre Dame.'[1] Hugo had arrived at the Gare du Nord late in the evening. 'He was planning to slip away through the darkened streets and find somewhere to spend the night,' writes Graham Robb. 'A masterpiece of false modesty – the exiled son snuggling into the old city like an animal returning to his lair. […] An open carriage was brought and

> Hugo was paraded through the streets like a saviour or a circus act. The boulevards were thick with promenaders and café-goers, dazzling in gaslight – nothing like a change of regime and an approaching enemy to create a carnival atmosphere.[2]

---

[1] Édouard Thierry, *La Comédie française pendant les deux siéges (1870-1871): journal de l'Administrateur Générale* (Paris: Tresse et Stock, 1887), p.60-61.
[2] Robb, *Victor Hugo*, p.447-48.

On the train with Hugo that night was a significant figure in this narrative, the critic, novelist and dramatist Jules Claretie, who, fifteen years later, would become the administrator of the Comédie-Française. Claretie, like Hugo, was filled with hope for the new republic. The carnival atmosphere fizzled out in the coming weeks. Claretie described a Paris that looked as beautiful as ever under the luminous blue skies of early autumn, a Paris that was proudly itself despite the surreal intrusion of soldiers and canons:

> In the distance, beyond the flowerbeds, the fountains and the *al-*
> *lée des Tuileries*, there is a golden haze into which the crowds of
> people move. The Arc de l'Étoile glows in this light. But the
> crowd is made up of battalions, artillery batteries and squadrons
> of horsemen. War waits at the end of these peaceful images. In
> the gardens, white marble statues stand out against a black back-
> ground formed by canons. Sentries pass. The ponds are deserted.
> No longer do happy children launch tiny boats onto the water.[1]

The theatres were closed by order of the authorities at the beginning of the siege. At the end of October the restrictions were relaxed to allow benefit performances. The government did not believe that it would be appropriate to sanction 'normal' shows.

The authorities wanted the Comédie-Française to organise a series of benefit concerts on top of its own programme and to release actors to give readings at other venues, but Thierry did not have the resources – his actresses, working in the ambulance, had little left to give as it was.[2] The Comédie was in a delicate situation given its ties with the Second Empire and its hope of receiving the funding it needed from the new republic. Some ministers believed that the Comédie was a 'nest of reactionaries'. They wanted to abolish the principles of the decree of 1812, particularly the rule that allowed the Comédie-Française to remain a society of actors, semi-autonomous from the state. Thierry wanted to feature a reading –

[1] Jules Claretie, *Paris assiégé: journal, 1870-1871* (Paris: Armand Colin, 1992), p.22.

[2] See Thiery, *La Comédie française pendant les deux siéges*, p.119.

by Marie Favart[1] – of the poem *Stella* from Hugo's *Les Châtiments* during the matinee that would re-open the Salle Richelieu. He went to see Hugo at Paul Meurice's house in the avenue Frochot.[2] Hugo knew, and exerted influence over, many of the people of standing in politics and the arts, but he did not know Thierry. Hugo indicated that he would grant permission but rebuked Thierry for still using the title Comédiens ordinaires de l'Emperor on the troupe's posters.[3] Thierry had a strong character. When, later, Hugo wanted the Comédie to recite his poem *L'Expiation* as part of a benefit matinee devoted to his work, Thierry refused. 'If such a thing were to take place,' he wrote in his journal, 'I would immediately resign. Hugo does not insist, and Coquelin agrees with me that we must not politicise our benefit concerts'.[4]

Thierry recorded in his journal that the re-opening of the Salle Richelieu, on 25 October, drew a huge crowd. In a gesture that could have been interpreted as a political statement, almost certainly incorrectly, Thierry placed recovering combatants from the ambulance in the former imperial box. Final permission hadn't been given to perform the Hugo, but overall Thierry was content. He wrote: '*Horace* and *Le Misanthrope* spoke to every soul and lost nothing for being performed in ordinary clothes.'[5] A few weeks later, Thierry refused to allow the fifth act of Hugo's *Hernani* to be performed at the Porte-Saint-Martin Theatre as part of a benefit concert for the victims of Châteaudun (the Comédie co-owned the rights with the author). Hugo wrote in his notebook: 'A peculiar obstacle this M. Thierry!' Hugo didn't prevent the Comédie from

---

[1] Maria Pingaud, dite Marie Favart (1833-1908, b. Beaune, Cote d'or). CF j1848 s54 d79.

[2] Hugo had sexual encounters with many women here, including actresses who sought guidance on how to recite his verse. In the words of Edmond Goncourt: 'Every night […] he would leave the Hôtel Rohan where he had quartered Juliette … He would then return to the Meurice home where one, two or three women would be waiting for him – all sorts of women, from the most distinguished to the dirtiest of drabs.' Quoted in Robb, *Victor Hugo*, p.453-54.

[3] Thierry, *La Comédie française pendant les deux siéges*, p.119-20.

[4] Thierry, *La Comédie française pendant les deux siéges*, p.162.

[5] Thierry, *La Comédie française pendant les deux siéges*, p.121.

performing the fifth act of *Hernani* (for the victims of the war) at the Salle Richelieu a week later (25 November). Thierry invited the actors of the Porte-Saint-Martin to perform the last act of *Lucrèce Borgia* during the second half of the evening. Between these performances, extracts from Hugo's *Les Châtiments* were recited. Before the concert, Marie Favart visited Hugo in the avenue Frochot to receive instruction from the master.

Theatrical performances during the siege were sombre affairs. The Comédie's auditorium was unheated and lighting was minimal. Patriotic poems and extracts from the plays of Corneille and Racine were the mainstays. Nevertheless, people flocked to the theatre and found solace there. The blockade had started to work and the winter months stretched ahead like a dark tunnel. Food was running out, starvation a reality for the poor. Dogs, horses, rats and eventually even the unfortunate animals in the zoo in the Jardin des plantes, including two elephants, were killed to be eaten. Gautier wrote that the Salle Richelieu, during the siege, 'felt like a military camp': '[The] duskiness flattered the stage and the actors. There were relatively few ladies and their austere outfits, in black or grey, had no need of glittering illumination. The men, for the most part, hadn't bothered to take off their National Guard uniform.' The wounded men in the imperial box made the deepest impression:

> All eyes turned on them with tender interest. There were arms in slings, hands and heads wrapped in bandages; but what commanded most attention was a young fellow, his face covered by a large strip of cloth – he looked like one of Tuareg in the Sahara, veiled up to their eyes … in one of his nostrils was a bullet which, so they said, could not be removed – it didn't stop him from being very attentive to the tears of Andromache and the passions of Hermione.[1]

Ambulances were established not only in public buildings but

---

[1] Théophile Gautier, *Tableaux du siege* (Paris, 1886). Quoted in Rupert Christiansen, *Paris Babylon: Grandeur, Decadence and Revolution, 1869-1875* (London: Pimlico, 2003), p.221.

also in the private homes of the rich. The eagerness of famous actresses and society ladies to transform themselves into nurses provoked, initially, some mocking voices, and there was, perhaps, a theatrical element at play – 'At the Comédie-Française,' writes Rupert Christiansen in his vivid account of the siege, 'beautiful young actresses such as Madeleine Brohan moved seraphically from one fallen hero to another, wiping the sweat from the fallen heroes' brows with cambric handkerchiefs and reciting the more ethereal passages of Byron'[1] – but then the beds became full, the agony all too real, the actresses' white aprons blood-splattered, and the mortality rate from post-amputation infections (these makeshift wards in rooms with germ-infested carpets and curtains were death-traps) took away all hope.

In January, the Prussians changed their strategy and started to fire shells into central Paris, day and night, killing hundreds of civilians. Male members of the Comédie-Française aged under thirty joined their battalions in the Garde Mobile. These included Ernest Coquelin, Jules Boucher, Jules Laroche, Charles Prud'hon and Jules-Didier Seveste. Thierry pledged to help their families. Sociétaires took on the roles normally played by these pensionnaires. Jules-Didier Seveste (b. 1846) had joined the Comédie-Française in 1863, and, at the age of twenty-four, was one of the troupe's most promising actors. A lieutenant in the *Carabiniers parisiens* (a unit formed of middle-class volunteers that operated as an advanced guard beyond the posts), he was fatally wounded on 19 January during the battle of Buzenval, at Saint-Cloud, just west of Paris. This was the final attempt to break out of Paris: the Prussians forced the French back into the city. Seveste was taken to the ambulance in the Salle Richelieu. Édouard Thierry wrote in his journal: 'The poor boy was screaming horribly. He told me that his leg had been shattered into four pieces and every grating movement of the fragments caused him dreadful pain. Never mind: he was in his theatre, surrounded by his own. He thought that he was saved.'[2] The actresses who nursed Seveste hid from him their distress. His

---

[1] Christiansen, *Paris Babylon*, p.191.
[2] Thierry, *La Comédie française pendant les deux siéges*. Quoted in Christiansen, *Paris Babylon*, p.257.

leg was amputated but he died on the 31st.

The authorities surrendered on 28 January. The Prussians imposed humiliating terms. They took Alsace and part of Lorraine. The French agreed to pay a staggering amount of money in reparations. The armistice was signed by Adolphe Thiers, leader of the conservatives in the National Assembly (sitting in Bordeaux). The great fear of the provisional government was that the people of Paris, led by radical socialists and supported by their own armed militia, for republicans controlled the rank and file of the Garde Nationale, would form a revolutionary government. In Paris, even moderates felt betrayed. Anxiety and hunger was replaced by mistrust of the provisional government. The articles of capitulation were published in the *Journal official*. Thierry commented: 'On les trouve insidieux et pleins de menaces. Ce qui blesse surtout, c'est l'article des correspondances qui doivent passer, non cachetées, par Versailles.'[1] His journal is a powerful record of how the unrelenting tension of those days infected all sections of his staff. His work to ensure that the theatre functioned as it should – on the day of the armistice the actors performed *Le Misanthrope* and *Le Jeu de l'amour et du hasard*, with Henri Lafontaine and Mlle Croizette in the leading roles – was straight-forward compared to the time he spent dealing with politicians, overseeing the ambulance and managing his on-edge staff. One evening, the *feutier* (the staff member in charge of heating) burst, drunk, into the committee room looking for Marie Favart: 'He wanted to kill Mlle Favart,' wrote Thierry, 'because he said she had made his wife cry.'[2] The man was subdued and then sacked.

The general election of 8 February returned a conservative government. The Prussian army's victory parade down the boulevards and the election of a conservative government that working-class and radical Paris believed would betray the new republic, meant that the mood in the city was bitter and volatile.

---

[1] Thierry, *La Comédie française pendant les deux siéges*, p.277.
[2] Thierry, *La Comédie française pendant les deux siéges*, p.285-86.

4   The First Voyage to England

When the Garde Nationale and socialist revolutionaries seized power in Paris, on 18 March 1871, and formed a government, the Comédie-Française's position became precarious. A public institution like the Comédie-Française, with its historical links to France's kings and emperors, would face an uncertain future if the Commune maintained its hold on power. With no subsidy, and with the Salle Richelieu requiring major repairs, the troupe faced financial ruin. Some of the actors on the administration committee didn't think that the theatre should stay open if the subsidy wasn't restored. They were unhappy to go on stage in these circumstances. Thierry, though, was determined to keep going, and said he would bring in outsiders if necessary. It was agreed not to close. To raise money, the committee decided to investigate the possibility of performing in London. The troupe would split into two groups, one in London and one at the Salle Richelieu. Edmond Got,[1] who was widely admired as the finest comic actor of his generation, was nominated to take the plan forward. Got had the stature to lead the troupe abroad. 'He is really a *philosophic* actor,' wrote Henry James. 'His comicality is sometimes colossal; but his most striking quality [is his] profundity [...], the impression he gives you of having a general conception of human life and of seeing the relativity, as one may say, of the character he represents.'[2] Got named the actors he wanted to take to London and Thierry agreed. The London group included the troupe's biggest names – Got himself, Constant Coquelin[3] and Louis-Arsène Delaunay. Coquelin was twenty years younger than Got but considered his equal in classical comedy. The leading French theatre critic Francisque Sarcey said so, and Sarcey's opinion was the one that mattered in Paris: 'No one is better cut

---

[1] Edmond Got (1822-1901, b. Paris). CF j1844 s50 d94.

[2] Henry James, *French Poets and Novelists* (London: Macmillan, 1878), p.426.

[3] Constant Coquelin, dit Coquelin Aîné (1841-1909, b. Boulogne). CF j1860 s64 d92.

out to represent those bold and magnificent rascals of the old repertory, with their boisterous gaiety, their brilliant fancy and their
superb extravagance.' At the age of forty-five, Delaunay was still the
troupe's most popular leading man, the actor with the largest number of female admirers.

Got travelled to England to make the arrangements. Less than a
year before, the impresario Sefton Parry had opened a new theatre
in London with the intention of presenting French works: he gave
the theatre, built just off the eastern end of the Strand in Wych
Street, the French name Opera Comique. In building a theatre on
this site, Parry may have been speculating, for he knew that the old
streets and houses of the district had been earmarked for demoli-
tion, and that the owners would be entitled to huge compensation
payments.

The Opera Comique was inaugurated in October 1870 by a
French company led by the actress Virginie Déjazet. The theatre
struggled from the start. Although attractively decorated, it was
small, cramped and partly underground; and French drama was a
hard sell beyond connoisseurs and Francophiles. Got would have
preferred a larger, grander and more prestigious venue, but the
Opera Comique was available for long term rent and sympathetic
Londoners already knew the venue as the French theatre in London.[1]

Got and twenty-three other members of the troupe – including,
as well as those already mentioned, the actors Bressant, Febvre and
Talbot,[2] and the actresses Émilie Dubois, Marie Favart, Clémentine
Jouassain and Zélia Ponsin (all of whom had been active in the
running of the ambulance in the Salle Richelieu during the siege)
– arrived in London on 27 April, perhaps a little surprised that they
had been able to raise the advance needed to secure the theatre and

---

[1] The Opera Comique was subsequently leased by Gilbert and Sullivan.
HMS Pinafore, premiered in 1878, ran for over 500 performances. The Opera
Comique went into decline after D'Oyly Carte departed for the Savoy. It
closed in 1899 and was demolished in 1902 as part of the redevelopment
scheme that created the Aldwych crescent. Today, Bush House occupies the
site.
[2] Denis-Stanislas Montalant, dit Talbot (1824-1904). CF j1856 s59 d79.

obtain the permission of the officials of the Commune to allow them to leave Paris.

The troupe had travelled to Dijon, Lyon, Toulon and Marseilles in the summer of 1868, but the London adventure was its first overseas tour (if one discounts the command performances during Napoléon's summit at Erfurt). Forty-four years after the English season in Paris introduced the French to the masterpieces of English drama, the Comédie-Française repaid the favour with a programme that was full and ambitious, although stronger on comedy than tragedy and missing any play by Hugo. The troupe performed *Tartuffe*, *Le Misanthrope*, *L'Avare*, *Les Fourberies de Scapin*, *Le Malade imaginaire*, and *L'École des maris* by Molière; *Le Menteur* by Corneille; *Les Plaideurs* by Racine; *Le Barbier de Séville* by Beaumarchais; *Le Jeu de l'amour et du hasard* by Marivaux; but also contemporary pieces by Émile Augier and Alfred de Musset. Musset's *Il ne faut jurer de rien*, *On ne badine pas avec l'amour*, *Les Caprices de Marianne*, *La Nuit d'octobre*, and *Il faut qu'une porte soit ouverte ou fermée* were all performed.

The importance of the Comédie-Française, its history, and the rules that governed it, were well understood in England, and looked upon with a certain envy, for there was nothing like it in England, a country, that despite its remarkable corpus of dramatic literature and the great theatre troupes of its past, would not establish a national theatre company until 1961 when Peter Hall transformed the Stratford theatre into the Royal Shakespeare Company. More members of the educated classes understood French in 1871 than today, so the full houses at the Opera Comique were knowledgeable and appreciative of the plays performed by the Comédie-Française. There was even some sympathy for the old enemy because of the suffering of its citizens during the siege. Disraeli attended performances, as did the leading figures of literary London. The great and the good of London society wanted to be seen in such company. *The Times* summed up the significance of the Comédie-Française for its readers:

A greater novelty could not have been presented to the London public than a theatrical performance by the entire troupe, which dates its existence from the days of Molière. [...] It brings with it its traditions intact. The respective times at which Molière, with his 'Theatre de Monsieur', established himself at the Palais Royal, and our Charles II granted letters patent to Thomas Killigrew closely correspond, and thus in round numbers the age of the Comédie-Française is identical with that of Drury Lane, but there is this marked difference between the histories of the two institutions, that the Theatre Royal has been perverted to all sorts of uses, including the exhibition of equestrian feats, while the Comédie remained true to its purpose. [...] The acceptance of a dramatic work by its rulers was always esteemed by literary Frenchmen as a peculiar honour, such as no other theatrical establishment could bestow, and though some of the most popular dramatists of Paris have never seen their pieces acted on its boards, and it has frequently been preached against by innovators in art for its extremely conservative tendency, it has always held its own, and those who have assailed it most have been only too glad if special exceptions have been made in their own favour. One of its old glories, that classical school of tragedy, which is never heartily relished in England, has, indeed, faded even in France, and only some singular genius, like the late Mlle Rachel, can galvanise it into vitality, but the hold of classical comedy to its boards is as firm as it was in the days of Louis XIV. Theoretically, perhaps, Shakespeare is more worshipped in England than Molière in France, but whereas, till within the last twelvemonth, there was not a week in which some *chef-d'oeuvre* of the great comic writer could not be seen at Paris, perfectly acted by a company chiefly formed to immortalise his genius, the times in which Shakespeare has been confined to the studies in London have been neither few nor far between.[1]

To open their season, the actors performed Molière's *Tartuffe* and extracts from *Le Dépit amoureux*. 'All the performers make the most of the parts assigned to them,' wrote the theatre critic of *The Times*, 'but in none is there the slightest appearance of a conscious exercise of art':

The hypocrite is represented by M. Bressant, whose figure is in

[1] *The Times* (3 May 1871), p.12.

itself a picture, and who preserves with eminent consistency his show of sanctity till his inner nature is revealed by the intensity of passion. […] Elmire, a character demanding all the finish of which high comedy is susceptible, is played by Mlle Favart with a quiet force that cannot be described, and the keenness of her irony while receiving the addresses of Tartuffe is marvellous. Talbot is Orgon – the part which Molière assigned to himself – stout in figure, boisterous in rage, and with all his attempts at sanctimony, evidently intended for anything rather than a devotee.

Le Dépit amoureux […] serves to introduce M. Delaunay, who, as Eraste, gave within the smallest limits a superb representation of the young French gallant of the 17th century, and M. Got, who played the valet Mascarille, now almost reduced to a nullity, and for whom occasions for greater distinction are reserved. Perhaps the most striking portion of the little piece is the diatribe against womankind put into the mouth of the valet Gros-René. […] The manner in which M. Coquelin, amazed at the rapid development of his own wisdom, bounded not only mentally but physically from proposition to proposition was a marvel of gesticulating declamation.[1]

Édouard Thierry, back in Paris, was delighted by the reviews in the British papers and by the takings at the box office. He was also pleased by the way the troupe's younger players were holding the fort in Paris. 'Our pensionnaires,' he wrote to Got, 'are learning three substantial roles a week […] and our young girls are blossoming.' Thierry had to deal with the constant demands of officials of the Commune, and was anxious because he feared they wanted to evict the troupe from the Salle Richelieu and use it for the government. He was under pressure to stage a tragedy written by a communard, but had the skill to fend off this person with polite excuses. However, reaching a compromise with the leaders of the council of the Commune, such as the socialist Édouard Vaillant, in charge of education, was impossible. Vaillant was behind a new statute which abolished subsidy and monopoly and required actors to self-manage their theatres by forming associations.

The council ran out of time to implement the statute. At the end

[1] *The Times* (3 May 1871), p.12.

of May, the Commune was violently crushed by the regular army – many atrocities were committed by both sides during a week of fighting – and the government of the Third Republic asserted its authority. When the news reached London, some of the actors understandably wanted to return to Paris at once, but Got wanted to extend the season to capitalise on its success and Thierry agreed: he insisted on unity and asked all the actors to continue in London until August. 'You must finish as you started,' he told Got. Parisians, though, were not pleased that most of the star actors were in London. In the end, a compromise was reached and the actors returned home on 9 July.

The day before the actors departed, a banquet was held in their honour at Crystal Palace. Senior members of the political class (including Disraeli), writers and men of the theatre (such as Tennyson and Macready), and the usual gaggle of aristocratic hangers-on, sat down to lunch with the actors, while the band of the Grenadier Guards played music from French operas. 'The banquet honours all of us,' Thierry wrote to Got. 'We owe a debt of gratitude to the hosts, who do things with such good grace and who offer such respect to our old Comédie-Française.'[1] Although a minor footnote in the history of Anglo-French relations, it was somewhat extraordinary – a sincere demonstration of mutual admiration and respect. Lord Dufferin,[2] president of the organising committee, and Lord Granville,[3] vice-president, both spoke at length in French with wit and erudition, as well as a sprinkle of self-deprecation: 'I would venture to remind you,' Lord Dufferin told the guests, 'that when anyone wishes to make a speech in a foreign language he will find it much easier to do so after dinner than at an early hour in the

[1] Quoted (in French) in George d'Heylli, *La Comédie-française à Londres (1871-1879): journal inédit* / de E. Got. Journal de F. Sarcey (Paris: Paul Ollendorff, 1880), p.xlix.

[2] Frederick Hamilton-Temple-Blackwood. In 1871, Lord Dufferin was a minister in the Liberal government. He later served as Viceroy of India.

[3] Granville Leveson-Gower, 2nd Earl Granville. In 1871, Lord Granville was Foreign Secretary in the Liberal government.

morning.'[1] Got replied on behalf of the Comédie. The actor-manager Alfred Wigan expressed the hope that the example of the Comédie-Française would persuade the English to establish an equivalent company that would serve Shakespeare and the other masters of English drama as the Comédie-Française served Molière and his peers.

[1] *The Times* (10 July 1871), p.12.

Previous double page:

9. *Les Trois sœurs* by Chekhov, Richelieu, 2010. Alain Françon (mise en scène), Jacques Gabel (décor), Patrice Cauchetier (costumes), Joël Hourbeigt (lighting). L-R: Michel Vuillermoz (Alexandre Ignatievitch Verchinine), Florence Viala (Olga), Elsa Lepoivre (Macha), Éric Ruf (Vassili Vassilievitch Saliony), Gilles David (Fiodor Ilitch Koulyguine), Coraly Zahonero (Natalia Ivanovna), Georgia Scalliet (Irina), Laurent Stocker (Nikolaï Lvovitch Touzenbach), Guillaume Gallienne (Andreï Sergueïevitch Prozorov), Bruno Raffaelli (Ivan Romanovitch Tcheboutykine), Stéphane Varupenne (Vladimir Karlovitch Rode), Hélène Surgère (Anfissa). Photograph by Raphael Gaillarde.

6

The Belle Époque

1871-1914

10. Edmond Got by Nadar.

1   Mounet-Sully and the Return of Sarah

The actors returned home to discover that Édouard Thierry was no longer in post. The Comédie's new Administrator was Émile Perrin, appointed by the government to bring glamour back to the Salle Richelieu. A painter by training, Perrin had, until recently, been the director of the Opéra. Known to be volatile and autocratic, he was feared and respected in equal measure.

Perrin offered a contract to Mounet-Sully,[1] an actor who had been an officer in the army during the recent war. Perrin recognised Mounet-Sully's commanding presence, the gravitas that came from living a dangerous life beyond the theatre; and then there was the deep tone of his voice. He made his debut at the Comédie in 1872, playing Oreste in Racine's *Andromaque*. He would excel in the great tragedies, ancient and modern, the first iconic actor in this repertoire since Talma. As Oedipus, and as Creon in *Antigone*, he silenced not only the Salle Richelieu but also the Roman arena at Orange. He would later triumph in Shakespeare's *Hamlet* and *Othello*. Mounet-Sully's style was not subtle. Henry James wrote, in 1876, that the actor's 'rantings and splutterings and contortions are altogether beside the mark'.[2]

To match Mounet-Sully, Perrin was determined to bring Sarah Bernhardt back to the Comédie. He went to see her at the Odéon, where she was starring in a hit production of Hugo's *Ruy Blas*. He

---

[1] Jean-Sully Mounet, dit Mounet-Sully (1841-1916, b. Bergerac). CF j1872 s74 d1916.

[2] Quoted in Julian Barnes, *The Man in the Red Coat* (London: Jonathan Cape, 2019), p.165.

offered her a financial deal that was far superior to her contract at the Odéon. The director of the Odéon refused to match Perrin's offer, so, in October 1872, Bernhardt broke her contract and crossed the river to the Salle Richelieu. The increase in her income was important to Bernhardt because her lifestyle was extravagant, but it was surely not the only motive. To fully realise the extent of her talent, she needed to play the great classical roles at France's preeminent theatre. Perrin wanted the kudos and profits that Bernhardt would bring; and presumably believed that he would be able to manage an artist who was famously independent-minded, mercurial and, despite herself, the cause of resentment and conflict within a company of players. He was soon struggling. When Bernhardt couldn't get her way with Perrin, she went above his head to the minister. Perrin pointedly called Bernhardt 'Mlle Revolt' to her face. He was exasperated by her refusal to play certain parts, and by her constant sick notes. Bernhardt was determined to stand up to a man she would later characterise as an 'icy mannequin'. When she went on a balloon trip without seeking permission, Perrin unwisely tried to fine her. Bernhardt went to the minister and threatened to resign.

Her performances, though, were acclaimed. Within a year, she had played Junie in Racine's *Britannicus*, Cherubin in Beaumarchais's *Le Mariage de Figaro* and the title role in Voltaire's *Zaïre*. In 1873, she starred opposite Mounet-Sully in Racine's *Phèdre*. The critics waxed lyrical over Bernhardt's musical verse-speaking and regal attitude. The slight pale young woman, most associated with the playing of vulnerable girls and young boys, had grown up. There were critical voices, people who compared her unfavourably to Mlle Rachel. Here's Matthew Arnold, writing in 1879:

> Temperament and quick intelligence, passion, nervous mobility, grace, smile, voice, charm, poetry – Mlle Sarah Bernhardt has them all; one watches her with pleasure, with admiration, and yet not without a secret disquietude. Something is wanting, or, at least, not present in sufficient force [...]: that something is high intellectual power. It was here that Rachel was so great; she began

almost where Mlle Sarah Bernhardt ends.[1]

Curiosity over Bernhardt and Mounet-Sully's off-stage relation-ship added to their box-office appeal. Bernhardt was condemned in respectable drawing rooms by people who pretended to be shocked by the stories of her promiscuity. It is impossible to know who suf-fered most within their relationship, Mounet-Sully or Bernhardt. When it ended, Bernhardt wrote a tender letter to Mounet-Sully it which she seemed to take the blame to appease his fragile ego: 'My heart demands more excitement than anyone can give it. My frail body is exhausted by the act of love. Never is it the love I dream of… What can I do? You must not be angry with me. I'm an in-complete person.'[2] They continued to share the stage. In 1877, they appeared together in Hugo's *Hernani*. Bernhardt was not unaware of her own vices. She would later write: 'The public treated me like a spoiled child. My comrades were a little jealous of me.' Hugo sent her a gold bracelet from which a single pearl dropped like a tear. 'You moved me – me, the old combatant,' he wrote in the accom-panying note. 'And at one moment, while the public whom you had enchanted cheered you, I wept.'[3]

Bernhardt's main rival was Sophie Croizette.[4] The two had known each other since their schooldays in Versailles, and now found themselves together at the Comédie. They had been close back then, playing together in the great park, and according to Bernhardt they remained fond of each other despite the forced competition of theatrical life. Bernhardt's memoirs make entertain-ing reading as an account (very much from her own point of view, of course) of company politics, and one can only wonder if things are as fraught and volatile between the young actors of today's troupe. Bernhardt believed that Perrin favoured Croizette over her because she was obedient, docile and eager to charm him; and

[1] Matthew Arnold, 'The French Play in London', in *The Nineteenth Century: a Monthly Review*, vol.6, no.30 (August 1879), p.230.
[2] Quoted in Julian Barnes, *The Man in the Red Coat*, p.164.
[3] Quoted in Sarah Bernhardt, *My Double Life*, p.282.
[4] Sophie Croizette (1847-1901, b. Saint Petersburg). CF j1869 s73 d82.

knew, because Croizette admitted it, that this was a calculated policy of manipulation to get the best roles. Bernhardt desperately wanted to play Célimène in *Le Misanthrope* and Camille in Musset's *On ne badine pas avec l'amour*, but lost out to Croizette.

When, in 1876, the dramatist of the moment, Dumas *fils*, wrote his new play for the Comédie-Française, the rivalry between the two actresses reached its zenith. *L'Étrangère* featured two leading female roles, Mrs Clarkson (the *étrangère* of the title) and the duchesse de Septmonts. In Bernhardt's account of the episode, Dumas, Perrin and Croizette conspired to deprive her of the role she had been promised – the Duchess – and when she acquiesced (for Mrs Clarkson was actually the more compelling role), Perrin plotted to change the title of the play to *La Duchess de Septmonts*. Bernhardt berated Dumas, and Dumas agreed that the title would not be changed. To complicate matters, Perrin scolded the unfortunate Croizette during rehearsals because she was failing to realise the Duchess as he wanted. Bernhardt comforted her and in so doing their friendship was restored. Here, as elsewhere, Bernhardt painted an unsavoury picture of male bullying of young women over whom they had power, on the one hand, and female rivalry on the other.[1]

2   The Second Voyage to England

At the beginning of June 1879, the Comédie-Française returned to London to perform a five-week season of work at the Gaiety Theatre. The visit had been planned for some years. Both Perrin and the manager of the Gaiety, John Hollingshead, believed that their organisations would make money from the enterprise. Perrin was motivated by the need to finance the closure of the Salle Richelieu for essential maintenance work. Whereas in 1871 only some of the actors had been involved, in 1879 the whole troupe decamped to London. *The Times* acknowledged this fact by telling its readers –

[1] See Sarah Bernhardt, *My Double Life*, p.272-275.

'There is no company of actors in the world the charm of whose performances consists so much in the perfection of its ensemble'.[1]

The Comédie's appeal, for the foreigner, was expressed by Henry James, who lauded the troupe in a long essay published in London less than six months before the season at the Gaiety. The essay is so revealing of the Comédie-Française during the Belle Époque, and so little known, it deserves to be quoted at length. James began by writing about the traditions of the Comédie and 'the charm of the place':

One feels this charm with peculiar intensity as a newly arrived foreigner. The Théâtre-Français has had the good fortune to be able to allow its traditions to accumulate. They have been pre-served, transmitted, respected, cherished, until at last they form the very atmosphere, the vital air, of the establishment. A stranger feels their superior influence the first time he sees the great cur-tain go up; he feels that he is in a theatre that is not as other theatres are. It is not only better, it is different. It has a peculiar perfection – something consecrated, historical, academic. This impression is delicious, and he watches the performance in a sort of tranquil ecstasy.

Never has he seen anything so smooth and harmonious, so ar-tistic and complete. He has heard all his life of attention to detail, and now, for the first time, he sees something that deserves the name. He sees dramatic effort refined to a point with which the English stage is unacquainted. He sees that there are no limits to possible 'finish', and that so trivial an act as taking a letter from a servant or placing one's hat on a chair may be made a suggestive and interesting incident. He sees these things and a great many more besides, but at first he does not analyse them; he gives him-self up to sympathetic contemplation. He is in an ideal and exemplary world – a world that has managed to attain all the fe-licities that the world we live in misses. The people do the things that we should like to do; they are gifted as we should like to be; they have mastered the accomplishments that we have had to give up. The women are not all beautiful – decidedly not, indeed – but they are graceful, agreeable, sympathetic, ladylike; [...] As for the men, they are not handsome either; [...] I can think of no

[1] 'La Comédie Française at the Gaiety', in *The Times* (3 June 1879), p.5.

one but M. Mounet-Sully who may be positively commended for his fine person. But M. Mounet-Sully is, from the scenic point of view, an Adonis of the first magnitude. To be handsome, however, is for an actor one of the last necessities; and these gentlemen are mostly handsome enough. They look perfectly what they are intended to look, and in cases where it is proposed that they shall seem handsome, they usually succeed. They are as well-mannered and as well dressed as their fairer comrades and their voices are no less agreeable and effective. [...] The comedians of the Théâtre-Français are never awkward, and when it is necessary they solve triumphantly the problem of being at once realistic to the eye and romantic to the imagination.

I am speaking always of one's first impression of them. There are spots on the sun, and you discover after a while that there are little irregularities at the Théâtre-Français. But the acting is so incomparably better than any that you have seen that criticism for a long time is content to lie dormant. [...] It used to please me, when I had squeezed into my stall – the stalls at the Français are extremely uncomfortable – to remember of how great a history the large, dim salle around me could boast; how many great things had happened there; how the air was thick with associations. Even if I had never seen Rachel, it was something of a consolation to think that those very footlights had illumined her finest moments and that the echoes of her mighty voice were sleeping in that dingy dome.[1]

For Henry James (and other Francophiles and theatre connoisseurs) the superiority of the Comédie's actors lay in their collective style; in their embodiment of good taste and their appreciation for aesthetics as revealed by how they dressed, spoke and moved. It was an age in which impeccable tailoring was considered a virtue both on and off the stage, and if this seems vaguely comical today, it survived in actors such as John Gielgud for at least half of the 20th century.

The Gaiety Theatre was situated on the Strand in the Aldwych quarter, very near to the Opera Comique. A large theatre able to accommodate two thousand spectators, it was built, in 1864, as a

---

[1] Henry James, *French Poets and Novelists*, p.408-15.

music hall. Under Hollingshead, it mostly presented musical comedies and operettas: Offenbach's *Les deux aveugles* played at the
Gaiety in 1872.

In advance of the tour, Hollingshead addressed the problem of
censorship. Since the Theatre Act of 1843, censorship in England
had been restrictive and rigorously enforced. Some of the plays that
the Comédie wished to perform, including *Le Demi-monde* by Dumas *fils*, were banned in England on moral grounds because they
addressed social taboos. *Le Demi-monde* was a highly regarded
work, on a serious theme, and London theatre-goers were eager to
see it. By granting the Comédie a special dispensation to perform
the play (without any cuts) at the Gaiety, the political class was, in
a sense, acknowledging the cultural superiority of the troupe over
any homegrown theatrical enterprise of the time.

To maximise the public's interest in the tour, Hollingshead insisted that Sarah Bernhardt appear on the opening night. This was
awkward for Perrin because, within the natural hierarchy of the
troupe, Bernhardt was not one of the most senior actors and company rules were more important than star-power. He reluctantly
agreed that the second act of *Phèdre*, starring Bernhardt, would be
performed on the opening night, alongside *Le Misanthrope* and *Les
Précieuses ridicules*. Tensions were already running high because
Bernhardt had made her own arrangement with a London impresario, Edward Jarrett, to give solo recitals in private homes, for
which she would make a small fortune. Perrin only found out when
he read an English newspaper.

On the eve of the visit, reports in the press that the Comédie
would be curtailing their advertised programme, and that Mlle
Bernhardt would not necessarily be performing, forced Hollingshead, worried that his subscribers would be scared off, to publish a
hurried response in *The Times*: 'The public,' he wrote, 'will get all
they have been promised, and probably more. A sudden illness may
prevent any particular performer appearing on a particular night
[Hollingshead knew of Bernhardt's reputation in this regard, so the
caveat was necessary]; but should no such illness occur, the entire
programme will be faithfully presented. *L'Étrangère* [by Dumas *fils*]
will be played, with Madame Sarah Bernhardt and the full cast, as

advertised.'[1]

The programme of work devised for the season repeated many of the plays of Molière, Racine, Marivaux and Musset performed in 1871, but added more contemporary works: as well as Dumas's *Le Demi-monde* and *L'Étrangère*, the troupe would perform plays by Hugo (*Hernani* and *Ruy-Blas*) and Jean Aicard.

On the evening of 4 June 1879, the whole company took to the stage (where busts of Molière and Shakespeare awaited them), and Edmond Got, so fondly remembered from 1871, began the night by reciting Aicard's poem *Molière à Shakespeare*. *Le Misanthrope* followed, with Delaunay as Alceste and Mlle Croizette as Célimène. The reviewer in *The Times* (a man with detailed knowledge of French theatre and a passion for the Comédie) praised Delaunay, but was ambivalent about Sophie Croizette, although his comments on her performance actually suggested a certain originality:

> We do not find in Mlle Croizette the Célimène either of our recollections or our idea. She is too modern in her looks, *allures*, and bearing, and her habit of dropping her voice almost to a whisper by way of accentuating certain *nuances* of her part interferes with the effect of many of its most telling passages.[2]

As expected, the performance of Sarah Bernhardt in *Phèdre* took most of the plaudits, with Mounet-Sully treated as little more than a bystander:

> The second act of *Phèdre* gives some opportunity to Mounet-Sully in the *farouche* Hippolyte's avowal of his hidden flame for Aricie; and a great opportunity to Phèdre when, tearing off the thin veil of propriety in which she at first tries to conceal her guilty love, she stands revealed before her horror-stricken stepson, a creature all aglow with the white heat of passion and after pouring out the lava-flood of her unreturned flame, in a transport of shame and despair, snatches the sword from the belt of Hippolyte with a hoarse cry of 'Donnez' and tries to thrust it into her heart. This tremendous scene Mlle Bernhardt rendered with a self-

[1] 'John Hollingshead to the editor', in *The Times* (9 May 1879), p.11.
[2] 'La Comédie Française at the Gaiety', in *The Times* (3 June 1879), p.5.

abandonment that took no measure of her strength. She seemed like a leaf whirled away on the torrent of her passion. And when at last the storm seemed to shatter her being, and she sank inert and insensible into the arms of Oenone, the house seemed rather to be relieving its pent-up feelings in its tumult of applause than offering a tribute to the fair, frail creature, who had so held their breaths suspended on hers. We remember Rachel's sombre grandeur, the concentrated passion that seemed to be glowing as a red heat in the core of her heart. Her Phèdre might be more terrible and intense, but it was, perhaps, less womanlike, less sympathetic, less *entrainante* than the Phèdre of Sarah Bernhardt.[1]

On the second night, the Comédie performed the highly-anticipated *L'Étrangère*, a work, according to *The Times*, of 'morbid social anatomy' relieved by 'the striking portrait of Mrs Clarkson', a woman born into slavery, sold and dishonoured, who seeks vengeance on all of mankind. The debate was centred on whether Dumas *fils* was right to believe that the theatre was a legitimate forum in which to expose the darkest corners of society. Because the play was performed by a foreign company, there was a sense in which the spectators at the Gaiety felt free to put Victorian propriety to one side and to enjoy the slight frisson of shock that the performance provoked. As *The Times* declared: 'The morality of the play was less the subject of consideration with last night's audience than the power, point, and pith of the dramatist's work and the skill of his interpreters.'

The editor of *The Times* gave his theatre critic many column inches to dissect the production.[2] Coquelin's performance as the duc de Septmonts was 'a masterpiece of stage art, all the more remarkable when it is borne in mind that this embodiment of varnished vice and well-bred wickedness is the best actor of the broadest low comedy of Molière, and the same man who was convulsing the house last night in the Mascarille of *Les Précieuses ridicules*'. Mounet-Sully, as Gerard, was 'somewhat over-measured and solemn, [but] he gave the part both the weight and dignity it

---

[1] 'The Comédie Française at the Gaiety', in *The Times* (3 June 1879), p.5.
[2] 'The Comédie Française at the Gaiety', in *The Times* (4 June 1879), p.10.

wants to keep his very questionable virtue from utter collapse'. As for the performances of Sarah Bernhardt, playing Mrs Clarkson, and Sophie Croizette, playing the Duchess, the reviewer returned to his theme of the previous day. Whereas Bernhardt 'reigned supreme', Croizette was miscast. On Bernhardt:

> It is impossible to overpraise Sarah Bernhardt's impersonation of this dangerous *charmeuse*, half Siren, half Serpent, with the lithe and sinuous beauty of the one, and the witching voice and seductive wiles of the other, nor the subtle art with which, in telling the Duchess the secret story of her life, she betrayed the bitterness of her recollections under the mask of cynicism and the show of superiority to all human feeling.

On Croizette:

> Mlle Croizette, as the Duchess, had her own ovation, too, in the scene of the fourth act where the outraged wife empties the vials of her wrath on her vile husband's head. In her case, too, there was a contrast between the handsome and splendidly dressed actress and her part, but it was not a contrast that worked in her favour like that in Sarah Bernhardt's case. The Duchess of Dumas's play suggests something younger, frailer, gentler at least, and more delicate than Mlle Croizette. She seemed to be suffering, too, from a hoarseness which impaired the effect of her more quiet passages, though in the great scene where she turns on her husband she triumphed over this and all other natural disqualifications for the part and showed herself the Croizette of the Sphinx, who in certain of her moments can carry her public away and make herself the sensation of Paris.

Dumas's *Le Fils naturel* and Alfred de Musset's *Les Caprices de Marianne* were both performed the following night. Perrin was making a statement about the contemporary relevance of the troupe. The troupe was able to switch from Dumas's social realism to Musset's 'graceful but sickly fantasies' in a heartbeat. London particularly admired Musset's *Les Caprices de Marianne*, recognising that there was nothing quite like it in the English language. *The*

Times's critic commended this 'lightest of tragedies and saddest of comedies', and recalled how Madeleine Brohan, playing the elderly Hermia in the current production, had, in the 'first flush of her youth and beauty', created the role of Marianne back in 1851.[1] For this critic, Mlle Croizette could not compete with his memory of Mlle Brohan.

Hugo's *Hernani*, presented on 10 June, was one of the most eagerly anticipated shows of the season. This was because it featured Mlle Bernhardt, and not because Hugo's play was held in high regard. By seeking inspiration from Shakespeare, Hugo was inevitably compared to Shakespeare and found wanting.

> There is one great and fundamental distinction between [Hugo] and the great English master of the historical drama – that the object of the first seems to be to utter himself in all his characters; that of the latter, to make his personages reveal, not Shakespeare, but themselves. Victor Hugo, as a magnificent rhetorician when he is not a consummate lyrist, with a strong instinct of melodrama, which is still melodrama though mounted on the tallest stilts that melodrama ever walked in, gives us stirring and stately rhetorical talk about passion by way of passion, and highly sensational melodramatic incident by way of tragic action; but it is impossible for an English public, trained on even as much Shakespeare as is known through the theatre, to accept M. Hugo's work in a more serious light. To name the men in the same breath as dramatists is to us a practical joke. The interest of *Hernani* here must mainly depend on its interpreters.[2]

Perrin and Francisque Sarcey could not understand the marked preference of the public and the English press for Bernhardt over their own favourite Croizette. In its review of *Hernani*, *The Times* gave an explanation for Bernhardt's appeal as an actress:

> The specially feminine elements of grace, fragility, physical delicacy, a slender figure, a sweet voice, whatever most suggests purity, tenderness, even weakness and the need of protection –

---

[1] 'The Comédie Française at the Gaiety', in *The Times* (6 June 1879), p.8.
[2] 'The Comédie Française at the Gaiety', in *The Times* (11 June 1879), p.8.

all the points, in short, that most distinguish woman from man are of paramount effect. Mlle Croizette's fullness of figure; a certain air of assured self-dependence and power to stand alone, have much to do, we are convinced, with the coldness which so puzzles M. Sarcey. But the specially feminine characteristics we have indicated meet in Sarah Bernhardt in a rare degree, united with a strangeness and originality which add to her womanly graces a piquancy of their own.

Such was Bernhardt's magic trick on the stage. People who knew the two women off stage, such as Perrin, must have read the above with a wry grin. Bernhardt's extraordinary success in London upset many of her colleagues for it went against the ethos of the ensemble and overshadowed everyone else. For her part, Bernhardt felt unappreciated and unfairly treated. When Bernhardt withdrew from a matinee performance of *L'Étrangère* because she also had to perform in the evening, few senior members of the company were inclined to be understanding. The London public was disappointed and the level of adulation dipped momentarily. Those sections of the British press that were in the business of being satirical and critical, went to work on Bernhardt and the declamatory style of French verse-speaking (some members of the troupe were offended, not understanding what journals like *Punch* were about). In Paris, some of the papers were writing negative articles about Bernhardt, suggesting that she was dishonouring the Comédie. Upset, Bernhardt wrote a letter to the editor of *Figaro* in which she said she was going to resign from the Comédie.

The news of Bernhardt's 'resignation' became public in early July, before the end of the tour. Hollingshead reassured ticketholders that the actress would not be leaving the Comédie until the tour ended, and indeed she held off from sending a resignation letter to Perrin and returned to Paris with her colleagues. Bernhardt had received an offer from America, but leaving the Comédie was not an easy matter for her.

By the end of the tour, some members of the troupe had become contemptuous of their London audiences. In 1871, the troupe had performed in a small theatre and had attracted audiences in which

Francophiles and French-speakers dominated. In 1879, the size of the Gaiety and the draw of Sarah Bernhardt, meant that non-French speakers dominated: it must have been disconcerting to perform night after night in a theatre where the majority of the spectators couldn't understand the language and didn't react in the expected way. The archivist of the Comédie, Georges Monval, told Perrin: 'Tomorrow, we will no longer need to have anything to do with the English. With a few exceptions, these people have remained our enemies. We will therefore return to Paris with joy.'[1] It seems that the troupe was divided between men like Monval and those members who cared about their work being seen and admired in the land of Shakespeare and who wanted to engage in a creative exchange of ideas with their English equivalents. The admirable Got was firmly in this camp. He did not dismiss out of hand the English opinion that French acting was too artificial and he thought deeply about the benefits of the English style. 'English actors,' he wrote, 'are more natural; they follow their instinct and their temperament, and are not slaves of dogma. They arrive at effects that we produce only by dint of art.'[2]

While the general public in London were only really interested in Sarah Bernhardt, as Hollingshead had predicted, there was an enthusiastic core of people, passionate about the theatre, who were interested in the Comédie-Française as a whole, in its style and its repertoire (the plays in which Bernhardt didn't appear were well attended).

Perrin achieved his objective – a renovated Salle Richelieu and the money to pay for it. Overall, the tour, so ambitious in scale, had been a success. The Comédie's share of the ticket sales amounted to 243,685 francs, while the expenses were 127,788 francs. The troupe had been feted in London by the cultural elite and the leading newspapers. Perrin reported to his political masters that the tour had enhanced the reputation of the Comédie.

[1] Quoted (in French) in Nicole Bernard-Duquenet, *La Comédie-Française en tourne ou Le Théâtre des cinq continents 1868-2011* (Paris: L'Harmattan, 2013), p.57.
[2] Quoted (in French) in Nicole Bernard-Duquenet, *La Comédie-Française en tourne ou Le Théâtre des cinq continents 1868-2011*, p.57.

Back in Paris, Perrin insisted that Bernhardt appear in a new play, *L'Aventurière* by Émile Augier, that she didn't rate. After the opening, she resigned.

3   'Organise the theatre!'

As in 1871, but more so, the Comédie-Française's London residency in 1879 fed into the ongoing national debate on the state of the British theatre (dramatic literature was in the doldrums, waiting for the emergence of Harley Granville-Barker and Bernard Shaw) and increased the longing for the establishment of a national theatre organised along the same lines as the Comédie, the view expressed by the poet and critic Matthew Arnold in a long essay published in the journal *Nineteenth Century*.

Arnold began by reflecting on the public's sudden passion for French plays and actors that saw 'lords, lawyers, statesmen, squires of low degree, men known and men unknown, of those acquainted with the French language perfectly, of those acquainted with it a little, and of those not acquainted with it at all'[1] rush to the Gaiety Theatre.

> I am not going to join the cynics, and to find fault with the *engouement*, the infatuation, shown by the English public in its passion for the French plays and players. A passion of this kind may be salutary if we will learn the lessons for us with which it is charged. Unfortunately, few people who feel a passion think of learning anything from it.[2]

Arnold's admiration for the actors of the Comédie was greater than his admiration for the authors of the plays they performed. The French lack a genius for high poetry, he told his readers. They

[1] Matthew Arnold, 'The French Play in London', in *The Nineteenth Century: a Monthly Review*, vol.6, no.30 (August 1879), p.228. Arnold here quotes Wordsworth.

[2] Matthew Arnold, 'The French Play in London', p.228-29.

have no Shakespeare. He admired Molière as a 'comic poet' – 'he has insight, a masterly criticism of life, a profound seriousness' – but concluded that the 'highest sort of poetic power was wanting in him'. In a manner that was highly contentious, he dismissed the alexandrine form as stilted and inflexible; and explained France's adulation of Corneille and Racine (the view expressed by Voltaire – 'These men taught our nation to think, to feel, and to express itself') by writing:

> The French had no Shakespeare to open their eyes to the insuffi-ciencies of Corneille and Racine. Great artists like Talma[1] and Rachel, whose power as actors was far superior to the power as poets of the dramatists whose work they were rendering, filled out with their own life and warmth the parts into which they threw themselves, gave body to what was meagre, fire to what was cold, and themselves supported the poetry of the French classic drama rather than were supported by it.'[2]

Arnold dismissed Hugo's *Hernani* – 'we are not in the world of poetry at all, hardly even in the world of literature' – but recognised that, in such works as Dumas's *Le Demi-monde*, plays concerned with the 'average sensual man', as he put it, France was ahead of England, a country that had 'no modern drama at all'.

The final part of the essay was the most important, for it amounted to a manifesto for a reformed theatre in England:

> What are we to learn then from the marvellous success and at-tractiveness of the performances at the Gaiety Theatre? [...] Surely it is this: 'The theatre is irresistible; organise the theatre.' [...] The performances of the French company show us plainly, I think, what is gained [...] by organising the theatre. Some of the drama played by this company is, as we have seen, question-able. [...] An older and better drama, containing many things of high merit, some things of surpassing merit, is kept before the public by means of this company, is given frequently, is given to

---

[1] Arnold's argument was weakened by the fact that he had never seen the actor perform. He was six when Talma died.

[2] Matthew Arnold, 'The French Play in London', p.236.

perfection. Pieces of truth and beauty, which emerge here and there among the questionable pieces of the modern drama, get the benefit of this company's skill, and are given to perfection. The questionable pieces themselves lose something of their unprofitableness and vice in their hands; the acting carries us into the world of sound and pleasing art if the piece does not. Secondly, the French company shows us not only what is gained by organising the theatre, but what is meant by organising it. The organisation in the example before us is simple and rational. We have a society of good actors, with a grant from the State on condition of their giving with frequency the classic stage-plays of their nation, and with a commissioner of the State attached to the society and taking part in the council with it. But the society is to all intents and purpose self-governing. In connexion with it is the school of dramatic elocution of the Conservatoire. [The Comédie-Française has] traditions, effect, consistency, and a place in the public esteem.

In contrast:

We have in England everything to make us dissatisfied with the chaotic and ineffective condition into which our theatre has fallen. We have the remembrance of better things in the past, and the elements for better things in the future. We have a splendid national drama of the Elizabethan age, and a later drama which has no lack of pieces conspicuous by their stage-qualities, their vivacity and their talent. We have had great actors. We have good actors not a few at the present moment. But we have been unlucky, as we so often are, in the work of organisation. In the essay at organisation which we had, in the patent theatres with their exclusive privilege of acting Shakespeare, we find by no means an example, such as we have in the constitution of the French Theatre, of what a judicious man, seeking that good of the drama and of the public, would naturally devise. [...] So far as we have had a school of great actors, so far as our stage has had tradition, effect, consistency, it had them under the system of the privileged theatres. The system had its faults, and was abandoned; and, then, instead of devising a better plan of public organisation for the English theatre, we gladly took refuge in our favourite doctrines of the mischief of State interference, of the blessedness of leaving every man free to do as he likes, of the impertinence of presuming to check any man's natural taste for bathos and to press him to relish the sublime. We left the English theatre to take its chance. Its present impotence is the result. It seems to me that every one of us is concerned to find a remedy […], and that the pleasure we have had in the visit of the French company is barren, unless it leaves us with the impulse to do so, and with the lesson how alone it can be rationally done.[1]

Arnold turned his aspirations into a practical plan of organisation. To summarise his key points: accept the principle that the state ('the nation in its collective') should involve itself in the arts; form a company from England's best and most promising actors; give that company the Drury Lane Theatre and a state grant; agree a core repertoire; establish a training academy.

The Comédie's 1879 London season greatly increased the number of people interested in the creation of an English national theatre building and company and, by example, strengthened the argument for their creation. Exposure to the players and repertoire of the Comédie crystallised thinking and prompted the press and the public to compare the state of the English stage unfavourably with that of the French. It provoked, in Arnold's essay, not only the most articulate contribution to the national theatre debate, but also, given his status, the most influential. The tireless work of the Flower family to open a theatre dedicated to Shakespeare in Stratford-upon-Avon, already underway, was a separate but equally important factor.

The theatre owners and actor-managers who were the masters of the English theatre took an active interest in the national theatre movement, but not always sincerely. Despite their public utterances of support, the real motive of some of them was to slow down its work and to water down its ideals. Progress was painfully slow despite the clarion call at the end of Arnold's manifesto and the support of the preeminent actor of the time, Henry Irving. When the Comédie-Française returned to London in June 1893 to take up a residency at the Drury Lane Theatre, Irving, speaking at the

[1] Matthew Arnold, 'The French Play in London', p.241-43.

official reception, called for the creation of a national theatre 'so that the [dramatic] art may grow with the progress of the times, till in the end it becomes like that great institution which is honoured here today, and which honours us by their presence, a source not only of civic but of national pride'.[1] It was only when a younger generation of theatre writers and directors, led by William Archer and Harley Granville-Barker, took up the cause during the first decade of the 20th century – Archer and Granville-Barker's book *A National Theatre: Scheme and Estimates*, a blueprint of practical solutions, published in 1907, was particularly important – that an organised movement emerged under the banner of the Shakespeare Memorial National Theatre Committee, supported by Bernard Shaw and others. Securing political support and funding took many more decades to achieve.

4   Thermidor

In the early 1880s, productions at the Comédie-Française were characterised by a visual opulence. An artist by training, Perrin had long wanted to bring to the Comédie the design-orientated aesthetic that he had developed during his time running the Opéra. He employed the best design studios and costume houses in Paris to fulfil his vision. His production of *Œdipe roi*, in which Mounet-Sully starred, was played before an exquisitely painted backcloth depicting temples and cypresses (1881).

To finance this new approach, Perrin introduced a practice that had been in operation at the Opéra for some time. Wealthy male patrons of both companies had always enjoyed backstage access to the performers as invited guests, but the Opéra had established a stream of revenue by opening up access to the public. Perrin followed suit by reserving performances on Tuesdays for subscribers,

---

[1] Quoted in Ignacio Ramos Gay, 'The Comédie-Française in London (1879) and the Call for an English National Theatre', in the *Revue de littérature comparée*, vol.345 (January-March 2013), p.13.

who were invited to mingle with the actors in the backstage areas of the theatre. The 'mardistes', as they became known, tended to be middle-aged and conservative, as well as affluent. They were more interested in the actresses than the plays. Perrin would have had no illusions about that. Sarcey was dismissive of this 'public of penguins'.

The 1870s saw the rise of a new literary movement, naturalism. An adaptation of Émile Zola's controversial novel *L'Assommoir*, staged at the Théâtre de l'Ambigu-Comique in 1879, was a terrific success, and in his essay *La Naturalisme au théâtre*, published in 1880, Zola called for plays that reflected modern life. Perrin's attempt to bring Zola's conception of a modern theatre to the Comédie by producing Henry Becque's *Les Corbeaux* provoked rage at its premiere in September 1882 because, once again, the conservative core of its public (made stronger by the influence of the 'penguins') wanted the Salle Richelieu to be a temple of traditional values and not a studio of daring and risk. Octave Mirbeau told Becque not to worry, for it was an 'honour to fail at the Comédie-Française'. The previous year, the premiere of Victorien Sardou's *Thermidor* showed that the Comédie could still become, albeit unwittingly, the focal-point of profound political divisions. While regular patrons of the Comédie appreciated the reactionary tone of Sardou's historical drama about the last days of the Terror during the Revolution, radical socialist republicans, led by the journalist Prosper-Olivier Lissagaray, were outraged by the critical portrait of Robespierre which they interpreted as an attack on the Revolution itself. The second night performance was halted by a near riot. In an attempt to shame the actors, coins were thrown onto the stage. With great style, one of the actors slowly picked up the money and dropped it into his pocket. As the mood became more violent, the police arrived.

The affair opened up old wounds that the government feared would provoke working-class radicals and students to take to the streets once again. Further performances of *Thermidor* were banned. There was a strong feeling that the republic still wasn't secure, and that its guardians needed to be ever vigilant. The affair was debated in the National Assembly. Georges Clemenceau, who had been in the audience with his children when Lissagaray's faction started to disrupt the performance, and who was on that side of the argument, told his fellow deputies: 'The French Revolution is a bloc, a bloc from which nothing can be separated, because historical truth does not permit it.' He went on:

> If you want to know why, as a result of this insignificant staging of a bad play at the Comédie-Française, there has been so much emotion in Paris, and why there is at present so much emotion in the chamber, I will tell you. It is because the great Revolution is not finished, it continues, and we are its actors, for the same men are still fighting the same enemies.[1]

Perrin could not have predicted the affair. He wasn't taking a political side by staging *Thermidor*. It was simply a well-made play that meant something to the troupe because it dramatised the heroism of the clerk who had saved the lives of previous members during the Terror.

5   Hamlet

Perrin's death in 1885 ended an era of innovation and high drama. His successor, the critic and author Jules Claretie,[2] would stay in post until his death in 1913, and oversee a period of work that was rarely of historical interest. One of the few productions of historical note occurred at the very beginning of Claretie's reign in 1886, when he brought to fruition a new staging of Shakespeare's *Hamlet* conceived by Perrin. Perrin had been working on the production

[1] Quoted (in French) in 'Georges Clemenceau (29 janvier 1891)', Assemblée Nationale website, at http://www2.assemblee-nationale.fr/decouvrir-l-assemblee/histoire/grands-moments-d-eloquence/georges-clemenceau-29-janvier-1891 (accessed 20/3/2019).

[2] Jules Claretie was a prolific writer of novels, works of history and theatre criticism. Before taking up his post at the CF he wrote reviews for *Le Figaro* among other journals.

at the time of his death, and was responsible for the spectacular design – the costumes, by Charles Bianchini, emulated the dress of Shakespeare's own time, and the naturalistic setting, by Lavastre, showed a view of Elsinore inspired by Carcassonne. The Comédie used Dumas's version of the play, co-written with Paul Meurice during a stay in Florence in 1841, and later revised (1864). For all his appreciation of Shakespeare's greatness, Dumas believed that French taste would still not tolerate a wholly faithful version of *Hamlet* in the French language. Dumas allowed Hamlet to live at the end of the work, and his approach overall was surprisingly insipid. He was right, though, in his understanding of the kind of *Hamlet* his fellow Parisians wanted to see: the play, premiered at the Théâtre Historique in December 1847, was a huge success for both Dumas and the actor playing the title role – Rouvière. 135 performances were given during the initial run. Théophile Gautier was bowled over by the play, writing, without irony: 'This is the first time that I have really seen Hamlet.'[1] The 1864 revision, used by the Comédie, was much more faithful – Hamlet dies – and stronger.

Something of Voltaire's critical view of Shakespeare's art still lingered at the Comédie-Française despite the progress made by *drame romantique* and the modern attitudes expressed and explored by novelists and poets. Dumas had written his *Hamlet* for the Comédie, and only produced it at the Théâtre Historique because the reading committee demanded changes to the text. Claretie faced opposition in 1886, despite the presence in the troupe of Mounet-Sully, an actor born to play the title role. When Meurice read the revised text to the actors – a text, remember, cleansed of puns and metaphors that might offend polite taste – some of the actors tittered and sneered. Shakespeare, though, had acquired a special status, even in France. Responding to one of the interruptions made by the senior actress Augustine Brohan, Meurice said simply 'Madame, ce n'est pas de moi, c'est de Shakespeare.'

---

[1] Quoted in Paul Benchettrit, 'Hamlet at the Comédie Française: 1769-1896', in *Shakespeare Survey*, vol.9 (January 1956), p.62.

By the time the production opened at the Comédie, in September, *Hamlet* was very much in vogue. This was because a version was staged that February at the Théâtre de la Porte-Saint-Martin, with Sarah Bernhardt as Ophelia. Bernhardt's presence distracted the audience – and the critics – away from the actor playing Hamlet, Garnier. The Comédie-Française's production was much anticipated, and Claretie delivered. He released the 150,000 francs needed to achieve Perrin's grand concept, and rehearsed the company for over a month. In his diary, Claretie recorded small disputes with the actors, some of them genuinely comic. The actor playing the ghost didn't want to appear during the opening scene, and Suzanne Reichenberg, playing Ophelia, demanded the kind of entrance enjoyed by Sarah Bernhardt despite lacking Bernhardt's status. Got, playing Polonius, suggested that Ophelia's line 'On dit que la chouette était fille d'un boulanger' ('They say the owl was a baker's daughter') would provoke laughter because of the recently failed *coup d'état* by General Boulanger. Mounet-Sully also tried Claretie's patience, mostly because he kept changing his mind about Hamlet as he strove to interpret the character, but occasionally because of vanity. Rehearsing the final scene, Meurice and Claretie wanted Hamlet to be scratched on the hand by Laertes's rapier, as Shakespeare had written; but Mounet-Sully wanted to be cut on the chest so that he could open his shirt in a big dramatic moment.

The opening night, on 28 September, was a triumph for Mounet-Sully. Accounts of the performance suggest that, despite the compromises of Dumas and Meurice's text, he was one of the first 'modern' interpreters of the role. Reviewers wrote of how Mounet-Sully incorporated brooding silences into his performance as well as sudden outbursts of emotion; of how he carried a notebook in which he would suddenly write something (on one occasion he tore a leaf from the book and handed it to Ophelia); and of how he spoke the soliloquies quietly with real contemplation. Remarkably, during the closet scene, Gertrude was seated on a chair with castors and Hamlet pushed the chair violently back and forth across the stage to force her to confront the two portraits. It is an idea that the young Peter Brook might have come up with seventy years later. Mounet-Sully was ahead of his time in allowing the character to be mercurial and enigmatic as well as melancholic and tender. Sarcey acknowledged this ambiguity when he wrote of the first night performance: 'We neither know what Hamlet is nor what he wants.' At the same time, Mounet-Sully satisfied the public's idea of the character as a noble prince.

The production generated interest across the Channel. *The Times* began its review by commenting on the deficiencies of the text – 'the translators [...] introduced, for the necessity of French versification, a quantity of things which Shakespeare never said and never would have said' – but went on to praise the *mise en scène* and, with reservations, Mounet-Sully's performance, highlighting its 'passion, irony, and melancholy':

> Mounet-Sully contrived to speak with a restrained violence, and yet with a clearness which made everything he said intelligible, and brought into play his wonderful voice. He was powerful and affecting in the final scene of the play within the play, and his uncontrolled passion amid the general confusion and terror produced a wonderful effect.[1]

The Comédie performed the play in London in July 1893. It was the centrepiece of the troupe's four-week residency at the Drury Lane Theatre. This third visit to London in little over twenty years had less impact than its predecessors, partly, perhaps, because the novelty had worn off, but also because the troupe decided to devote most of the season to new and recent plays, lightweight comedies by such writers as Émile Augier, Jules Sandeau, Jean Richepin, Édouard Pailleron and Alexandre Parodi. The critic who reviewed the London performance of *Hamlet* for *The Times* found it too wild and intense for his taste: 'Generally speaking, the court of Elsinore is depicted as a ruder and more barbarous place than is compatible with the conception of the philosophic and cultured Hamlets of the English and the German stage.'[2]

---

[1] 'Hamlet in Paris', in *The Times* (30 September 1886), p.3.
[2] 'Drury Lane Theatre', in *The Times* (4 July 1893), p.5.

Dumas and Meurice's *Hamlet* would remain the version performed by the Comédie-Française until 1924.

6   Tragedy

Claretie was, by and large, a cautious Administrator who avoided controversy. The Comédie, charged with supporting French writers, did not stage plays by living foreign authors. The plays of Ibsen became available after 1906 but, because they explored taboo topics that some people deemed to be obscene, they were not produced by the Comédie until after the Great War. It was left to the Théâtre-Libre and the Théâtre de l'Œuvre, theatre clubs exempt from censorship, to champion the work of Ibsen. Claretie, though, also missed out on the uncontroversial but dazzlingly brilliant *Cyrano de Bergerac* by Edmond Rostand.

Rostand's first play *Les Romanesques* was premiered by the Comédie in 1894. *Cyrano* was written for Constant Coquelin, but the great comic actor, angered by Claretie's refusal to let him organise his own tours, had left the Comédie in 1892. Coquelin was running the Théâtre de la Porte-Saint-Martin, so *Cyrano* was presented there in December 1897. Coquelin's performance became iconic. The first night audience was said to have applauded for over an hour, and Coquelin went on to perform Cyrano at the Lyceum Theatre in London (1898) and in New York with Sarah Bernhardt as Roxanne (1900). Rostand wrote his other major plays for Bernhardt – *La Princesse lointaine* (1895), *La Samaritaine* (1897) and *L'Aiglon* (1900). Actors who emerged during the period included Julia Bartet,[1] who in the 1880s replaced Bernhardt as the troupe's most admired young actress and who remained with the troupe until 1919. Mlle Bartet was especially admired for her performances in plays by Racine (Bérénice, Andromaque), Musset (Camille in *On ne badine pas avec l'amour*), Hugo (Blanche in *Roi s'amuse*,

---

[1] Julia Regnault, dite Mlle Bartet (1854-1941, b. Paris). CF j1879 s81 d1919.

Doña Sol in *Hernani*), Molière (Armande in *Les Femmes savants*), and Marivaux (Silvia in *Le Jeu de l'amour et du hasard*).

The vulnerability of theatres to fire had long been a cause of anxiety. In London, conflagrations destroyed Drury Lane in 1809, Covent Garden in 1808 and 1856, the Lyceum in 1830, and the Garrick in 1846. In Paris, the Odéon was set ablaze in 1799 and 1818, the Opéra-Comique in 1887, and the Opéra in 1763, 1781 and 1873. The devastating fire of 1781 raised the Opéra's theatre at the Palais-Royal to the ground and killed eleven members of the company. Tragedy befell the Comédie-Française on 8 March 1900. As the staff were preparing the Salle Richelieu for a schools' matinee performance of *Bazajet*, a fire broke out at the back of the stage and climbed rapidly up the highly inflammable scenery. The iron safety curtain was raised at the time, and the firemen who attended every performance had yet to arrive. By the end of the afternoon the allegorical ceiling painting by Alexis-Joseph Mazerolle that had adorned the cupola since 1879 had been consumed and the building was open to the sky. Theatre staff managed to save most of the pieces of sculpture, including Houdon's statue of Voltaire, and many of the priceless manuscripts. In the confusion, thieves impersonated staff and walked away with some of the paintings.

Thankfully, the fire struck before the public had entered the auditorium. Two actresses, though, were trapped in the upstairs dressing rooms. Mlle Dudlay[1] was able to open a window and cry out for help. 'I was nearly dressed,' she told reporters, 'when I smelled smoke, which entered under the door. I flung the door wide open and found utter darkness. The corridor was filled with smoke, which choked me. I rushed along the corridor and reached a window, where I shouted for help. My cries were heard below and a fireman mounted a ladder, tied a rope around me and led me to the ground, just in time as I could feel that I was about to faint.'[2]

The young actress Jane Henriot, a pensionnaire, left her dressing room on the fourth floor but panicked in the thick smoke: instead of descending, she ran up the stairs and sought refuge in a small

[1] Adeline-Elie-Françoise Dulait, dite Mlle Dudlay (1858-1934, b. Brussels). CF j1876 s83 d1908.

[2] Reported in the *San Francisco Call*, vol.87, no.99 (9 March 1900).

room. Jane Henriot's mother, also an actress, had modelled for Renoir; and it is believed that Renoir's *Fillette au chapeau bleu* is a portrait of Jane. A fireman found her body lying on the floor.

> The body was carried out and placed in an ambulance car. As her face was so much burned that she was unrecognisable, the body was taken to the morgue, where it was identified by [Ernest] Coquelin[1] and other members of the Comédie-Française by the clothing. Meanwhile the mother of Mlle Henriot had hurried to the scene, bareheaded and crying wildly for her daughter. The truth was concealed from her as long as possible, and when it was finally told to her she was distracted with grief.[2]

Other reports stated that Mlle Henriot was trying to find her little dog. The tragedy, covered extensively by the popular press (*Le Parisien* placed on its cover an artist's depiction of the moment Jane Henriot's body was found), preoccupied the public for many weeks.

The government released funds immediately so that the theatre could be rebuilt (to Victor Louis's original design, under the supervision of the architect Julien Guadet). Remarkably, the work was finished by the end of the year. It was decided not to replicate Mazerolle's ceiling design; instead, Albert Besnard was commissioned to create a new painting called *Apollon accueille sur l'Olympe les grands dramaturges*.

The theatrical scene was in the process of changing. Romain Rolland's manifesto for a people's theatre, published in the *Revue d'Art Dramatique* in 1902, formed part of a movement to democratise the theatre. Rolland, and other members of the intellectual left, dismissed the mainstream theatre as bourgeois, decadent and exclusive. Rolland compared the Comédie-Française to the Louvre and the Panthéon to indicate that it was a pillar of the establishment, and expressed the view that the troupe's work was moribund, outdated and irrelevant to the lives of ordinary people. The accusation would resurface at intervals throughout the 20th century.

---

[1] Constant Coquelin's younger brother.
[2] *San Francisco Call*, vol.87, no.99 (9 March 1900).

The fact that Claretie was still in post, and seemed irremovable, had become an issue of concern for the actors. Claretie had asserted his authority over the actors by suspending the reading committee in 1901. This was later overturned, but Claretie remained in post until 1913, by which time he had served for twenty-seven years.

11. *Ruy Blas* by Hugo, 1879. Sarah Bernhardt, Mounet-Sully
and Frédéric Febvre.

7

The Great War

12. Béatrix Dussane, 1910.

1   In Paris

At the beginning of 1914, the government appointed Albert Carré to succeed Claretie as the Administrator of the Comédie. Carré had been in charge of the Opéra-Comique since 1898, and had overseen an era of modernisation which saw the premiere of Debussy's *Pelléas et Mélisande* (1902) and the French premieres of Puccini's *Tosca* (1903) and *Madame Butterfly* (1906).

The outbreak of the Great War meant that Carré's career at the Comédie ended before it had really started. On mobilisation, Carré, a lieutenant-colonel in the territorial army, joined his regiment in Besançon; and he only returned to the Comédie briefly before joining military intelligence in November 1915. During his short time in charge, Carré started to engage a new generation of actors and to commission young authors such as Sacha Guitry.

Carré was replaced by the playwright and director Émile Fabre for the duration of the war. A writer of naturalistic plays on social themes, Fabre's membership of the radical generation of writers who wrote for André Antoine's Théâtre-Libre, and not the state theatre, did not mean that he was unsympathetic to the principles of the Comédie-Française; on the contrary, he was passionate about the Comédie and, at a time of war, believed that it should act as a focal point for patriotism and a source of comfort.

Other than for a period of a few months at the beginning of the war, when Paris was in peril until the Allies halted the German advance at the Marne river in September 1914, the theatres stayed open. Many of the Comédie's actors joined up at the beginning of the war, but most received permission to return to the Comédie before its end. Two members of the troupe were killed in action – Raymond Reynal and Fontaine. Reynal was a highly-regarded comedian who, although only in his twenties, had played Harpagon in Molière's *The Miser* (1912) and Bartholo in Beaumarchais's *Le Barbier de Séville* (1914). Reynal was killed during the battle of the Ourcq, at Barcy, in September 1914. Fontaine was killed at Verdun in 1916.

Inspired by Édouard Thierry's courageous leadership during the Franco-Prussian war, Fabre worked tirelessly to make the most of what he had. With so many actors at the front, he had to engage young players who perhaps otherwise would not have been selected for the Comédie. The Comédie's normal regulations were suspended. A percentage of the box office receipts were allocated to good causes, and seats were reserved for soldiers. In this climate of austerity, evening dress was banned. The Comédie did what it could to support the war effort: for instance, the company's seamstresses made clothes for the soldiers. The *Marseillaise* was played at every performance. During the final months of the war, on nights when the Germans bombarded the city, the public took shelter with the actors in the basement of the Salle Richelieu.

Fabre wanted to serve all sections of society, including soldiers on leave in Paris, and selected plays that were diverting but that had some relevance to the war. One of his first choices backfired: Pierre Frondaie's *Colette Baudoche*, a play in which a young Frenchwoman (played by the pretty and vivacious Marie Leconte) living in German-controlled Lorraine in 1913 is tempted by the advances of a Prussian teacher (Maurice de Féraudy), premiered in 1915, was considered to be unpatriotic by some even though Colette finally rejects her pursuer.

The military censor was vigilant. Playwrights wrote about patriotic duty and the sacrifice of war but did not attempt to depict life in the battle zone. No-one wanted to be confronted by the terrible reality during a night at the theatre, when husbands, sons and brothers were facing that reality in real-time. Soldiers in these plays were either waiting to be mobilised or had returned home. The war was something that happened offstage.

Of the new works presented at the Salle Richelieu, the most

prominent was *L'Élévation* by Henry Bernstein. The Comédie's only previous production of a play by Bernstein, *Apres Moi*, a melodrama targeting anti-Semitism, had provoked a riot following its premiere in 1911. The far-right Action française organised a protest against the play that resulted in demonstrators trying to force their way into the theatre. The police only held them back by charging on horseback. Claretie's son Georges fought a duel against the editor of *Action française* Leon Daudet because Daudet had insulted his father in print. Having missed each other with pistols, the two men fought with swords: Georges Claretie was seriously wounded. To prevent further demonstrations, Bernstein withdrew his play. He later fought a duel of his own, against the editor of the newspaper *Journal*. For Henry Bernstein, any insult was a matter that required satisfaction: he had fought five duels during the previous twelve years. The duel took place in the Parc des Princes. Both men missed, probably deliberately. Duels were rarely fatal because they were stopped as soon as an injury took place.

Bernstein was serving in the flying corps when he wrote *L'Élévation*. In the play, a young woman married to an ageing professor has an affair with a young man. The young man joins his regiment and is fatally wounded at the front. All three characters are reconciled through the realisation that the fate of France has far greater meaning than their personal drama. *L'Élévation* was a typical boulevard play, with a typical love-triangle plot, given a redemptive ending because of the war.

The Comédie premiered the work in June 1917. It chimed with the public, and stayed in the repertory. The critic Émile Mas was not convinced, writing: 'During these harsh years of war, the French family is symbolised by a weak husband, a cynically adulterous woman and a dandy who believes himself absolved from his bad behaviour because he does his duty at the front.'[1] Many of the soldiers attending the show with their relatives surely must have felt ambivalent about a play that turned the injured soldier into a symbol of sacrifice and drenched the stage in pathos. This was the

---

[1] Émile Mas, *Comoediana: journal d'Émile Mas*, no.1, 7 octobre 1917 (Paris, 1917), p.13.

attitude of the fascist writer Pierre Drieu La Rochelle, who, in misogynistic language, compared the 'bourgeois theatre' to a prostitute. In his semi-autobiographical novel *Gilles*, published by Gallimard in 1939, Drieu La Rochelle inserted a scene in which the hero and his cynical friend, Bénédict, on leave from the front, go to see *L'Élévation* at the Comédie and are disgusted by its depiction of a 'suffering soldier [...] presented like a soiled host to the devouring pity of the public'. Bénédict calls the play, 'cette saloperie de pièce héroique'.[1] 'Although half the theatre was filled with soldiers and their relatives,' the narrator writes, 'the audience was ecstatic.' Sitting in the theatre, Gilles's mind is at the front; he is marked by death and can no longer see any purpose in a life that does not risk death.

Fabre kept the plays of Corneille, Racine and Molière at the heart of the repertory, alongside those of Marivaux and Beaumarchais, Hugo and Dumas, Musset and Dumas fils. Performances of Shakespeare were expressions of Anglo-French unity, not only on the Paris stage – the Comédie staged extracts from *Macbeth*, with Paul Mounet[2] in the title role, *The Merchant of Venice* (*Shylock*), *The Taming of the Shrew* (*La Mégère apprivoisée*), and *Hamlet* – but also in towns along the Western Front, in amateur performances for the troops and local people. *Henry V*, with its final scenes of Anglo-French reconciliation, was particularly resonant in this regard. *Hamlet* was evoked by Paul Valéry in an attempt to make sense of the European tragedy of the war: 'From an immense terrace of Elsinore which extends from Basle to Cologne, and touches the sands of Nieuport, the marshes of the Somme, the chalk of Champagne, and the granite of Alsace, the Hamlet of Europe now looks upon millions of ghosts.'[3]

[1] Quoted in Mary Ann Frese Witt, *The Search for Modern Tragedy: Aesthetic Fascism in Italy and France* (Ithaca: Cornell University Press, 2001), p.170.

[2] Paul Mounet (1847-1922, b. Bergerac). CF j1889 s91 d22. The younger brother of Mounet-Sully.

[3] See Ton Hoenselaars, 'Great War Shakespeare: Somewhere in France, 1914-1919', *Actes des congrès de la Société française Shakespeare* [online], 33, 2015, mis en ligne le 10 mars 2015, consulté le 06 avril 2019. URL: http://journals.openedition.org/shakespeare/2960 ; DOI : 10.4000/shakespeare.2960

For soldiers who cared for art and literature, the classical repertoire offered solace and meaning. François Mauriac, during brief furloughs in Paris, found himself drawn to the Comédie, where a performance of Racine's *Britannicus* restored his faith in his country. In 1916, he wrote to a friend:

> I found myself feeling a sudden and infinite tenderness for Junie, pale and bathed in tears, to whom the young Roman murmurs: 'Your eyes, your sad eyes...' It was really, for me, the ineffable face of France. France is not the virago of Rude screaming with an open mouth – it is the Racinian virgin clothed in linen, the proud princess. Compared to her, other nations are drunken slaves.[1]

2   At the Front

Fabre's great achievement was to establish the Théâtre aux Armées, a touring troupe that entertained soldiers at the front. Members of the Comédie-Française were joined by actors from the Odéon and other theatres, as well as singers and dancers from the Opéra and the Opéra-Comique. Fabre was inspired by the example of the maréchel de Saxe, who during the War of the Austrian Succession of the 1740s engaged Charles-Simon Favart to provide a theatre troupe to accompany the army during the campaign. The government and military endorsed Fabre's idea, but there was no funding so everything had to be achieved on a shoestring. The Théâtre aux Armées did not need to be an extravagant enterprise, with sets and lighting of the standard of the Salle Richelieu; on the contrary, the rough and ready intimacy of the concerts, bringing performers into close proximity with the soldiers, so that they shared the same space, was exactly what was needed.

The performers, directors and musicians worked on a voluntary basis and accepted the dangers of being so close to the front line

---

[1] Quoted (in French) in *La Grande histoire de la Comédie-Française*, p.154.

(artillery bombardments were a constant threat), as well as the extreme cold of the winter, and the profound shock of seeing wounded and dying men in the field hospitals. The eclectic programme included short pieces (by writers such as Georges Courteline, Max Maurey and Sacha Guitry); arias from the operas of Bizet, Gounod, Massenet and Delibes; popular songs from the Paris cafés and music halls; and dramatic monologues and poems recited by members of the Comédie. The theatre's archive contains evocative photographs of the Théâtre aux Armées in action. The photographer of one of these images, captured row upon row of young men standing shoulder to shoulder before a simple wooden platform, backed by trees and shrubs, protected from the elements by a canopy of tarpaulin. On the stage, an upright piano and one or two performers. Many of the soldiers wear their helmets. All are watching the stage, except for a single man who has turned his head to stare directly into the camera, a cigarette hanging from his lips. Another image, tinted, shows the distinctive grey-blue colour of the uniforms. Soldiers are standing in a wood, stretching their necks to see the stage.

The first performance was given by the Comédie-Française near the village of Crèvecœur-le-Grand, north of Beauvais, on 9 February 1916. Among the players, was the young actress and writer Béatrix Dussane.[1] Mlle Dussane had won the prize for comedy at the Conservatoire and had joined the Comédie at the age of fifteen in 1903. She was a natural player of Molière and Marivaux, especially admired for her playing of Dorine in *Tartuffe* and Marton in *Les Fausses confidences*. She wrote an account of her experiences in the Théâtre aux Armées, beginning with the performance at Crèvecœur-le-Grand. The company arrived at a farm, driving through an archway into a large courtyard, like Molière's troupe of the 1650s. A barn was converted into a makeshift theatre. Performing for the soldiers was a profound thing for the actors. Here is part of Béatrix Dussane's tender recollection:

Night had come. In the courtyard, the silhouettes of the soldiers

[1] Béatrix Dussane (1888-1969, b. Paris). CF j1903 s22 d41.

were pressed against each other, and shadows were cast by the dazzling glare of the headlights of automobiles. Above us, in a piece of nocturnal sky cut by the quadrilateral roofs, there could be seen two blue stars under a crescent moon. Our stage was framed by garlands and flags, a beautiful image. None of the players who were there will ever forget what they saw, as a corner of the Indian curtain was lifted: this stone building with its exposed carpentry was scarcely illuminated by a few small electric lamps suspended from the beams; in this half-light, the soldiers were shifting in their seats, and their uniforms were like a great sheet of blue shadow. We heard murmurs and laughter. We looked at all these unknown faces, and saw the ardent gaze that sought ours. We felt that these men, who had done so many courageous things, were waiting for us to bring joy and comfort. At that moment, Mme Bartet started to sob, and all of us, I tell you, had tears in our eyes.[1]

That evening, the programme consisted of Eugène Brieux's *Lettre pour le petit soldat*, recited by Julia Bartet; extracts from Jean-François Regnard's *Démocrite* (1700), performed by Mlle Dussane and Henry Mayer; Georges Courteline's *Gros chagrins* (1897), performed by Dussane and Thérèse Kolb; and Abraham Dreyfus's *Le Klephte* (1883), performed by Dussane, Kolb, Mayer, and Charles Siblot. Marguerite Carré of the Opéra-Comique sang arias by Massenet (*Manon*) and Offenbach. The show was directed by Jean Dax.

Another member of the Comédie, the young pensionnaire Elisabeth Nizan,[2] recorded her impressions in her journal, poignantly describing her encounter at Pont-sur-Meuse, during the bloodiest

---

[1] Quoted (in French) in Jacqueline Razgonnikoff, 'La Comédie-Française au Théâtre aux armées', in *Mission Centenaire 14-18*, at http://centenaire.org/fr/espace-scientifique/arts/la-comedie-francaise-au-theatre-aux-armees-souvenirs-du-front (accessed 8/4/2019). Jacqueline Razgonnikoff's fascinating essay includes long quotes from the testimonies of Béatrix Dussane and Elisabeth Nizan (in French) and a selection of photographs from the archives of the CF. I encourage readers of French to access this page. More pictures can be viewed on the CF's website at https://www.comedie-francaise.fr/fr/expositions_virtuelles/la-comedie-francaise-au-theatre-aux-armees (accessed 8/4/2019).

[2] Elisabeth Nizan (1896-1969, b. Bucarest). CF j1915 s32 d36.

phase of the year-long battle of Verdun in July 1916, with these 'poor boys' soon to go into battle:

> We stayed, Dussane and I, for part of the afternoon in the midst of them, chatting with them, not only without the slightest fear, but touched by the effort they were making to avoid in their language any word that might shock or offend us. We had the impression of symbolizing for them the girl they loved but were too shy to approach.[1]

Earlier, during the concert, Mlle Nizan recited Miguel Zamacoïs's 'Le Salut des comédiens aux soldats du front' and the music hall singer Lise Fleuron performed several popular songs. And all the while they could hear the sound of artillery fire.

Béatrix Dussane's exceptional character and appeal were captured in a number of photographs.[2] More of her testimony:

> Joining the Théâtre aux Armées is neither a heroic act nor a source of pleasure. It is not a question of being brave under shell-fire. It is a very humble way of showing solidarity with the boys of France.
>
> It is getting up very early, and travelling in trains with uncertain schedules or in clapped-out motors near the end of their service; it is to sleep little, to freeze in winter and to be too hot in summer, to eat at unusual times or to go without; it is to perform in the open air, in the bright sunlight or in the night mist, to be choked with heat in a room that is too small or chilled to the bone in a hangar open to all winds; it is to give up to three performances a day […], dancing on a four-square-metre stage without getting burned by the candles that form the ramp, and stretching your voice to be heard by four thousand men assembled in a meadow. [...]
>
> To be a member of the Théâtre aux Armées is to bring joy, wherever the soldier takes rest, whether it is the rest of just a few days taken 1500 metres from the lines, or the rest of a few weeks

---

[1] Quoted (in French) in Jacqueline Razgonnikoff, 'La Comédie-Française au Théâtre aux armées'.

[2] See http://centenaire.org/fr/tresors-darchives/archives/en-images-les-comediens-theatre-aux-armees (accessed 8/4/2019).

away from the front. [...] At the end of our concerts, we all felt, in our souls, the living bond that connected us to these men.[1]

In May 1916, during the battle of Verdun, Sarah Bernhardt joined the troupe at Boucq, in Meurthe-et-Moselle. The aim of the Théâtre aux Armées wasn't normally to rouse the troops into a state of patriotic fervour (see the above quote from Mlle Dussane), but Sarah Bernhardt wasn't a normal actress and came to Boucq with a patriotic text that she had commissioned – *Les Cathédrals* by Eugène Morand. She had recently been seriously ill, the consequence of an injury to her knee that had become gangrenous; to save her, the surgeon amputated her right leg at the hip. She refused to use a wheelchair, so two soldiers carried her from the car on a palanquin she had designed herself. Mlle Dussane watched as the *grande dame* of French acting, wrapped from head to foot in a voluminous leopard skin fur coat, silenced a restless audience of exhausted soldiers, who cared little for her fame, by the intensity of her delivery. As she pronounced the final words – 'Aux armes!' – and the pianist began the *Marseillaise*, three thousand men rose as one.

[1] Quoted (in French) in Jacqueline Razgonnikoff, 'La Comédie-Française au Théâtre aux armées'.

8

The Interwar Years

1919-1939

14. *Asmodée* by Mauriac, 1937. Jacques Copeau (mise en scène).
L-R: Gisèle Casadesus (Emmanuelle), Germaine Rouer (Marcelle).
Photograph by Lipnitzki.

1   Changes to the Repertoire

At the end of the war, Albert Carré did not return to the Comédie-Française. It was agreed that Fabre would remain at the Comédie and that Carré would once again run the Opéra-Comique.

Fabre stayed in post until 1936, a term of twenty-two years. It harmed his reputation that he stayed beyond the point at which it would have been sensible to hand over to a younger director. In the final phase of his tenure he came under heavy criticism that didn't recognise the scale of his achievement, both during the war and after. His international standing remained high. In 1934, he was invited by William Bridges-Adams to direct a production at Stratford-upon-Avon, but his commitments wouldn't allow it.

Fabre oversaw a broadening of the repertoire to include works by foreign writers, and was a forceful advocate of new writing. In 1921, he took the pragmatic decision to clear the Comédie's backlog of unperformed plays by returning them to their authors. This caused anger, since the plays had been accepted. Fabre, though, had inherited most of them, and his priority was to stage new plays of the 1920s and not plays that had been written before the war and which belonged to a different age.

Among the more than thirty young writers supported by Fabre were Jean-Jacques Bernard and Paul Raynal. Bernard's *Le Feu qui reprend mal* was presented at the Comédie in 1929. *Martine*, premiered at the Théâtre de la Chimère in 1922, followed in 1934. Bernard used silences and sparse dialogue to convey the inner life of his characters, and to explore the difficulty of human understanding. In his own words, 'The theatre is above all the art of the unexpressed'. On a hot summer day, an impressionable young country girl meets a young man who has recently returned from the war. Martine falls in love, but for Julien, despite his feelings, the affair can only be a summer dalliance; he has a fiancé and, anyway, he comes from a different world. *Martine* is like a Marivaux play re-written by Chekhov. Desire, longing, hurt and regret are poignantly implied. Because of this understatement, *Martine* stands out from the other French plays of its time. Madeleine Renaud,[1] whose significance in the history of French theatre in the 20th century was equivalent to Peggy Ashcroft's significance in England, played Martine. She had joined the Comédie in 1921 and by the age of twenty-two had played Cécile in Musset's *Il ne faut jurer de rien* and Agnès in Molière's *L'École des femmes*.

Bernard's play was admired abroad. It was staged in London at the Gate Theatre in 1929, and revived in the West End in 1933. Peter Hall directed the play, in a version by John Fowles, at the National Theatre in 1985, and Fowles's version was also seen at the Finborough Theatre in 2014. The play deserves a modern revival at the Comédie.

Paul Raynal is forgotten today, but his play *Le Tombeau sous l'Arc de Triomphe* caused a scandal when it was premiered at the Comédie in February 1924. The subject of *Le Tombeau sous l'Arc de Triomphe* was the war and feelings were still raw. Raynal dared to expose the tragic disconnect between the men who fought and their families at home. A soldier is given four days leave so that he can return home and marry his fiancé. He arrives to find a telegram waiting, ordering him back to the front. During his one night at home, he is acutely aware that the members of his family are living a life of comfort and ease. His fiancé tells him that she no longer loves him, but sleeps with him anyway. The soldier returns to the front, believing that he will be killed in the next attack. René Alexandre[2] played the soldier.

Ibsen entered the repertoire of the Comédie-Française in 1921,

---

[1] Madeleine Renaud (1900-1994, b. Paris). CF j1921 s28 d45.
[2] René Alexandre (1885-1946, b. Reims, Marne). CF j1908 s20 d44.

when Fabre fought off opposition from some members of the reading committee – who agreed with the widely-held view in France that Ibsen was 'cadaverous, misogynistic and deadly dull'[1] – and produced *Un Ennemi du peuple*. *Hedda Gabler* followed in 1925. Marie Thérèse Piérat played Hedda, with Madeleine Renaud as Mme Elvsted, Denis d'Inès[2] as Lœvborg, Charles Granval as Tesman, Jacques Guilhène as Bracke and Catherine Fonteney as Julie Tesman. D'Annunzio's *La Torche sous le boisseau* was staged in 1927; and Pirandello's *Chacun sa vérité* in 1935. The other important playwrights of the first decades of the 20th century would not be first produced by the Comédie until decades later: Chekhov in 1944, August Strindberg in 1970, Anouilh in 1971, George Bernard Shaw (*Heartbreak House*) in 1999, Sean O'Casey (*The End of the Beginning*) in 2008, and Frank Wedekind in 2018.

2   Internal Disputes

In January 1922, Fabre organised a festival to celebrate the tercentenary of Molière's birth. Nearly thirty of Molière's plays were performed across the Paris theatres, with the Comédie and the Odéon leading the way. Some rarities were staged – including *Les Fâcheux*, *L'Impromptu de Versailles* and *La Princesse d'Elide*. In May, the troupe continued the festivities by travelling to London to perform *L'Avare* and *Le Misanthrope* at His Majesty's Theatre on the Haymarket. The leading players were Maurice de Féraudy (Harpagon) and Huguette Duflos (Elise); and Raphael Duflos (Alceste) and Cécile Sorel (Célimène). The performances raised money for the Reims cathedral restoration fund.

The troupe returned to the English capital in October to perform a month-long season at the Coliseum. The programme included

---

[1] Quoted (in French) in *La Grande histoire de la Comédie-Française*, p.161. The quote is by Léon Daudet.
[2] Denis d'Inès (1885-1968, b. Paris). CF j1914 s20 d54.

Édouard de Max[1] in two scenes from *Hamlet*, *Gringoire* by Theodore de Banville, and two acts from *Tartuffe*. The flamboyant and charismatic Édouard de Max, protégé of Gide, friend of Sarah Bernhardt and Cocteau, had made his name at Bernhardt's theatre and at the Odéon in French tragedies and such Shakespearean roles as King Lear and Antony in *Antony and Cleopatra* (directed by André Antoine). He was forty-five when he joined the Comédie in 1915, admired for his gravitas on stage but notorious, within Paris's artistic community, for his hedonism off-stage. 'His Hamlet,' wrote a critic, 'is consciously the centre of a tragedy of the stage: the more formal speeches are deliberately and beautifully formalised, and are delivered again and again straight at the audience; the emphatic phrase, the immense, decisive gesture, and the movements across stage have been timed and brought into accord with an accuracy upon which no English Hamlet would expend the same labour.'[2]

In-between, in July, the troupe travelled to Provence to perform Sophocles's *Œdipe roi* in the Roman arena at Nîmes, and the occasion was vividly described in *The Times* by Harold Hannyngton Child:

> Last Saturday was a summer night of windless, cloudless beauty. Daylight was still lingering as the audience gathered in the amphitheatre. On one side the higher walls and arches to that tremendous mass were a 'saint-like grey'; on the other a deep violet. The swallows that haunt these Midi towns in myriads flitted restlessly over the palace of Œdipus, and about the sweep of sparse electric lamps that were beginning to assert themselves against the twilight. And all over the arena were the people […]; the blaring hues of crimson and orange and scarlet affected by these women of the South slowly fading with the waning light. The eyes insisted on leaving the stage now and then to note how the sky above the Theban palace was turning from blue to impenetrable purple, and thence to a star-set black, while the ear persisted in exchanging sometimes the pleasure of French verse, spoken by French players, for the awful thrill of the vast silence,

[1] Édouard de Max (1869-1924, b. Iasi, Romania). CF j1915 s18 d24.
[2] 'Comédie Française: M. de Max in Hamlet', *The Times* (31 October 1922), p.10.

the concentrated silence of thousands intent on the tragedy, the silence of a large town in which only the chimes are awake. And it must be admitted that our friends of the Comédie Française gave us a chance now and then of a little forgetfulness. Their art is built upon the technique which in England too soon becomes the tricks of the 'old pro'; and it is just possible that before the good folk of the provinces they like to display the technique more frankly than they would before critical Paris. Not M. de Max as Tirasias, nor M. Dorival as the old shepherd who had received the infant Œdipus; theirs were acting and speaking which thrilled and filled the vast amphitheatre. […] But M. Silvain, as the priest of Jupiter, perhaps, too, Louise Silvain as Jocaste and certainly Albert Lambert fils as Œdipus, these showed themselves conscious of the size of the stage and of the house. But better than anything was the chorus. Led by M. Albert Raynal, with Mlles Guintini and Marie Bell to share the speaking with him, the chorus moved seldom, moved broadly, moved always with dramatic effect. It was they, in the end, who filled that mighty stage under the towering pillars, and set the lovely summer night a-tremble with the dreadful tale of ancient sin and agony and doom.[1]

In 1927, Fabre marked the hundred-year anniversary of romanticism by reviving some important plays, including Musset's *À quoi rêvent les jeunes filles*, in which Madeleine Renaud and Marie Bell[2] shone.

Fabre's post-war management of the Comédie came under stress from a number of sides. Madeleine Renaud and Marie Bell wanted more of a voice and felt that they deserved to be promoted, but this couldn't happen until two of the senior sociétaires retired. At the Comédie, it was still not uncommon for an actress of over fifty to play a woman of twenty. In May 1919, the minister in charge, Louis Lafferre, agreed to change the rules. Napoléon's decree of

[1] 'Comédie-Française in Provence', in *The Times* (28 July 1922), p.12. The name of the critic was not published with the article. I'm grateful to Nicholas Mays, archivist of *The Times*, for providing the information on Harold Hannyngton Child. Child wrote for *The Times* as assistant theatre critic from 1902 to 1920 and then as a special writer and leader writer from 1920 to 1941.
[2] Marie Bell (1900-1985, b. Bègles, Gironde). CF j1921 s28 d45.

1812, establishing a governing committee of six members, all nominated by the minister, was revised: the committee would now consist of twelve members, and three of these would be actors elected by the sociétaires. Lafferre also lowered the retirement age so that places in the society would become available more often. Retired actors would remain connected to the troupe as honorary members. In 1926, though, the minister backtracked on actor representatives, prompting one of the troupe's most stylish and intelligent actors, Pierre Fresnay, to resign. Fresnay was possibly already committed to a career in films that would see him work for Hitchcock (*The Man Who Knew Too Much*) and Renoir (*La Grande illusion*). Fabre feared that if Madeleine Renaud and Marie Bell continued to feel unappreciated they would also choose the cinema over the Comédie. *The Times* of London explained to its readers the complex arrangements of the Comédie's organisational structure:

> The Comédie-Française is passing through one of the small crises which recur periodically. Two of the younger artists, Mlle Madeleine Renaud and Mlle Marie Bell, have threatened to resign unless they are admitted sociétaires – that is, as full members of the society enjoying a share of the profits – or are given a promise of that promotion for next year. Unfortunately, the whole of the profits for 1928 are already apportioned out among the present sociétaires and nothing remains to furnish emoluments for newcomers. There is no dispute as to the artistic qualifications of the two actresses, and the managing committee appears to have given them assurances – but only verbally – that their cases would be favourably considered at the end of next year. Money for their promotion may then be rendered available by the creation of vacancies in the ranks of the society. It is suggested alternatively that the Minister of Education and Fine Arts may conceivably solve the immediate difficulty by surrendering the full share to which he has a right. In reality, however, the present crisis is part of a larger and more serious crisis caused by the relatively inadequate reward obtained by artists of the first rank who are asked to remain throughout their careers at the state theatre. Two sociétaires, Mme Huguette Duflos and M. Fresnay, have recently left to make striking successes in other theatres, and there is no

question of the pecuniary advantages of such a course. Artists who remain faithful sociétaires are claiming advances in their payment. A full member proceeds gradually to the maximum payment receiving a proportion only during the earlier part of his career. The system is to divide the maximum into 12 parts, so that a sociétaire receives so many 'twelfths'. At the end of next year an indeterminate number of 'twelfths' may be at the disposal of the committee. They are the nine-twelfths allotted to M. Desjardins, who is retiring, and the shares of Mlle Duflos and M. Fresnay, if these artists do not return to the fold. To facilitate a settlement Mme Cécile Sorel has offered to surrender her whole share, which is the maximum, but the committee is said to be indisposed to accept an arrangement which would involve her retirement.[1]

Madeleine Renaud and Marie Bell were both promoted as promised in 1928.

3   Jacques Copeau and the Vieux-Colombier

In February 1930, the Comédie premiered Jean Cocteau's monologue *La Voix humaine*. This enfant terrible of the avant-garde had, as a child, attended matinees at the Comédie, and the place had left its mark. 'The Comédie-Française,' he told the *Écho de Paris*, '[represents for me] a beautiful auditorium with a mysterious public, unsure of the name of the author but willing to queue in the snow to see an actor.' The premiere attracted the great and the good of Paris society, and polarised opinion into two camps. Conservatives found it shocking that a work by the decadent and openly homosexual Cocteau should be seen at the Comédie-Française, but the clever conceit of the play – a woman talks to her lover over the phone, and the audience only hears her side of the conversation – won many people over. Berthe Bovy's performance was universally

---

[1] 'A Comédie-Française Dispute', in *The Times* (14 December 1927), p.17.

admired.[1] It so happened that earlier in the day Prime Minister André Tardieu had dissolved his cabinet. Most members of the political elite attended the premiere. It was well known that the actress Mary Marquet[2] was Tardieu's mistress, and that Marquet was not the only sociétaire involved with a senior politician. The premiere was one of those theatrical occasions when different factors collided in a way that amused the public.

The decision to produce *La Voix humaine* indicated that some members of the Comédie-Française were ready to embrace new ideas. Since early in the century the Comédie's productions had suffered in comparison with the work of a new generation of artists. From 1913 to 1914 and from 1920 to 1924, Jacques Copeau's company at the Théâtre du Vieux-Colombier was widely viewed as an alternative Comédie-Française, more exciting and more innovative.

Copeau had started out as a journalist, the co-founder, with André Gide and others, of the influential literary journal *La Nouvelle Revue Française* (NRF). When Copeau decided to put his ideas on the theatre into action, he looked for a venue on the Left Bank, far away from the commercial theatre district, and chose the vacant and crumbling Athénée-Saint-Germain in the rue du Vieux-Colombier. Copeau formed a company, and wrote a manifesto which he published in the NRF as *Un Essai de rénovation dramatique: le théâtre du Vieux-Colombier*. Influenced, in particular, by Elizabethan and Jacobean drama, Copeau wanted to replace artifice and melodrama with a simpler, truer and more analytical style of theatre. The Théâtre du Vieux-Colombier would be the antithesis of the commercial boulevard theatre, but also different from the Comédie-Française, for Copeau believed that the House of Molière was too grandiose and too resistant to new ideas. It would appeal to the young, and to people who wanted to see foreign works. It would train its actors in its own academy. Copeau, decades before Peter Brook, believed in a theatre of first principles, without spectacular effects: 'Pour l'œuvre nouvelle,' he wrote, 'qu'on nous laisse

---

[1] Berthe Bovy (1887-1977, b. Visé, Belgium). CF j1907 s20 d41.
[2] Mary Marquet (1895-1979, b. Saint Petersburg). CF j1923 s28 d45.

un tréteau nu.' ('For the work of the future let us have a bare platform.')[1]

The Théâtre du Vieux-Colombier opened to the public in October 1913. The first season began with the Elizabethan rarity *A Woman Killed With Kindness* by Thomas Heywood (a play that the RSC would revive in 1991 in a production by Katie Mitchell), and ended with Shakespeare's *Twelfth Night* (*La Nuit des rois*), not then widely known in France. The English painter Duncan Grant designed the production. In-between, Copeau staged Alfred de Musset's *Barberine*, Molière's *L'Avare* and *La Jalousie du Barbouillé*, Paul Claudel's *L'Échange*, and his own adaptation of *The Brothers Karamazov*. It was an adventurous programme. The principal roles were played by Copeau's close collaborators Suzanne Bing (Viola in *Twelfth Night*), Charles Dullin and Louis Jouvet. Copeau cast himself as Malvolio. The war intervened. Most of the men in the company were mobilised. Instead of trying to keep the Théâtre du Vieux-Colombier open, when Copeau returned from active service he accepted an invitation to take the available members of the company to New York. They mounted two full seasons at the Garrick Theater. On returning to Paris, he re-opened the Théâtre du Vieux-Colombier in January 1920 with a remarkable production of *The Winter's Tale* (the translation was by Copeau and Suzanne Bing), for which the setting was a bare stage surrounded by the walls of the theatre, with a linen curtain drawn across the forestage for some scenes, and lighting used to change the mood as the play progressed.

However, by 1924, the troupe, for all its success, had started to disintegrate. Dullin and Jouvet had both gone their own way. Copeau closed his theatre and disappeared from sight. Considering Copeau's significance, and the reason for his withdrawal, John Palmer wrote:

> There was always a faint suggestion at the Vieux-Colombier of the evangelist. The theatre was for Copeau a vocation – excellent fun, of course, but there must be a limit in any reference one

[1] Jacques Copeau, 'Un Essai de rénovation dramatique: le théâtre du Vieux-Colombier', in *La Nouvelle Revue Française*, no.57 (1 September 1913), p.353.

might make to a sacred subject. To a man so devout, theatrical Paris in 1920 was a far from congenial environment. To succeed in such a world was almost as disconcerting as to fail. The Vieux-Colombier, to the mind of the ordinary playgoer, carried with it no suggestion of luxury or sophistication. But the whole idea was wrong – this performing of highly elaborate entertainments for the pleasure of a highly cultivated audience. The ascetic temperament of Jacques Copeau resented its own enjoyment. To realise something of this you had only to look at his face – the face of one who might have been a great cardinal in a period of counter-reformation. The disappearance of Jacques Copeau was, nevertheless, a shock to most of us, and it has never ceased to be a subject of expostulation. [...] He is sorely needed in Paris, and must return.[1]

Copeau had in fact retreated to Burgundy with his most dedicated followers, settling first in Morteuil near Beaune and then amid the vines in a grand house at Pernand-Vergelesses. His troupe became a local phenomenon, performing in village squares and halls. The locals called Copeau's actors Les Copiaus. In 1929, Michel Saint-Denis formed an off-shoot of Les Copiaus called La Compagnie des Quinze. This group performed in Paris and later travelled to England, where they were embraced by the London theatre community. Saint-Denis established Copeau's ideas in England and eventually joined Peter Hall and Peter Brook as a co-director of the newly-established Royal Shakespeare Company (1961).

Albert Camus would later write of Copeau: 'Dans l'histoire du théâtre français, il y a deux périodes: avant et après Copeau.'[2] Increasingly, during the 1920s, Fabre was undermined by Copeau's supporters. In 1929, two of the Comédie's senior members, Pierre Fresnay and Berthe Bovy, pressed Copeau to accept the position of Administrator, should it be offered, as did Gabriel Boissy (drama critic of Comœdia) and a number of the most important writers of the time, including Édouard Bourdet, André Gide, Paul Claudel,

---

[1] John Palmer, 'Jacques Copeau', in The Times (28 November 1928), p.14.

[2] Albert Camus, 'Copeau, seul maître', in Théâtre, Récits, Nouvelles (Paris: Éditions de la Pléiade, 1962), p.1698.

Jean Giraudoux and Jean Cocteau. The campaign intensified that summer with articles of support in *Comœdia* and other newspapers. Copeau tried to remain calm, writing to his wife: 'I have everything that matters to me, and the difficulty is to moderate the newspapers, for they are too aggressive in their advocacy and risk upsetting the government. Everyone has a lot of zeal and is confident of success. Me, I do not know.'[1] In October, *Les Nouvelle littéraires* and *Comœdia* published an *adresse* to Pierre Marrault, Minister of Education and Fine Arts, and André François-Poncet, Secretary of State for Fine Arts, in which over a hundred of Copeau's supporters called for his nomination to lead the Comédie.[2] Copeau wrote a piece for *Les Nouvelle littéraires* in which, without asking for the job, he set out his ideas on how to reform the 'old theatre'. There can be little doubt that he wanted the position.

In November, André Tardieu replaced Aristide Briand as prime minister. He called Copeau to a meeting and indicated that he was in favour of Copeau replacing Fabre at the Comédie, but that he wouldn't be ready to make a decision until March. March came and went. In May, Tardieu told Copeau that 'the moment has still not come',[3] at which point Copeau lost patience and accepted that the matter was dead.

4   The 1930s

During the final decade of the Third Republic, with French politics dangerously polarised between Left and Right, and with an institution like the Comédie-Française so easily politicised, Fabre came under political, as well as intellectual, pressure. In December 1933, he directed a production of Shakespeare's *Coriolanus* (*Le Coriolan*), spectacularly conceived and executed, that was initially admired.

---

[1] Quoted in Jacques Copeau (ed. Claude Sicard), *Journal, 1901-1948*, t.2 (Paris: Seghers, 1991), p.279.

[2] *Comœdia* (18 October 1929).

[3] Jacques Copeau, *Journal*, p.291.

During the run, the Stavisky financial scandal broke, exposing corruption within the radical socialist government. The Prime Minister, Camille Chautemps, resigned. His replacement, Daladier, immediately dismissed the head of the Paris police, Jean Chiappe, a right-wing sympathiser. Because René-Louis Piachaud's loose translation was appropriated as an anti-democratic work supporting the oligarch Coriolanus over the representatives of the people, Fabre and the Comédie-Française were accidentally caught up in the affair. The right embraced the production as a critique of corruption within the political elite of the Third Republic – the right-wing newspaper *Le Figaro* went so far as to compare Coriolanus with Hitler[1] – and the left accused Fabre of creating a 'fascist' production. Daladier agreed, and sacked Fabre, appointing in his place the head of the Sûreté-Générale, Georges Thomé. The appointment of a policeman to manage a theatre company was greeted with as much laughter as dismay. The political right, galvanised by the Stavisky scandal, took to the streets on 6 February: the police fired into the crowd, killing fifteen people. Daladier's one-week-old premiership fell as a result and a coalition government led by the conservative politician Gaston Doumergue took over. Doumergue reinstated Fabre, but Fabre was left in no doubt that, in these politically volatile times, the Comédie-Française's work would be misinterpreted and misappropriated. The actors, although glad to be rescued from Thomé, were not universally behind Fabre. After the election of the socialist Popular Front government, in May 1936, the Comédie-Française came under the jurisdiction of the new Education and Fine Arts Minister, Jean Zay, a young man of talent and conviction who wanted to make the theatre an agent of social change. Fabre stepped down that August.

Zay believed that France's national theatre had become self-regarding and complacent. To rejuvenate the Comédie, he instigated a policy of reform. He gave the Administrator the power to impose his will on the actors, over repertoire, casting and promotions. The man Zay appointed to reform the Comédie-Française was the playwright Édouard Bourdet, who had made his name during the

[1] See *Le Figaro* (1 January 1934).

1920s. Bourdet's first major play, *La Prisonnière*, written for the Théâtre Fémina in 1926, dealt, sensitively, with a lesbian relationship between a girl and an older woman. The girl feels damned, but cannot break free of the relationship. A *cause célèbre*, it was staged in Berlin (by Max Reinhardt) and in New York. Bourdet went on to write dark comedies for the Théâtre de la Michodière – *Vient de paraître* (1927); *Le Sexe faible*, a comedy in which a woman in search of a fortune pushes her sons into finding rich wives (1929); *Les Temps difficiles* (1934), about a family business facing bankruptcy, and the moral corruption that follows; and the farce *Fric-Frac*, starring Arletty, which was later turned into a film (1936). The Comédie's production of *Les Temps difficiles* at the Vieux-Colombier in 2006 revealed that Bourdet was a major writer. Philippe Tesson wrote of the play: 'Quel savoir-faire en effet! Quelle vivacité dans le dialogue! Quelle lucidité, quelle cruauté dans le regard! Quelle intelligence dans la construction! Le premier acte, qui expose une situation plutôt complexe, est un petit chef-d'oeuvre.'[1]

Bourdet would be supported (at his own request) by a committee of management, consisting of the artists who still represented all that was innovative about the contemporary French stage – Copeau and his former students from the pre-war Vieux-Colombier, Charles Dullin and Louis Jouvet, plus Gaston Baty. The four would not work full-time at the Comédie (Dullin, Jouvet and Baty had their own theatres[2] to run), but the expectation was that their contributions would be significant. Bourdet used his power sensitively. He gave greater opportunities to young actors, but respected the principles of the troupe. In terms of the repertoire, he reduced the number of revivals of plays by Corneille and Racine.

Understandably, some senior members of the troupe were unhappy with the changes, and initially viewed Bourdet as a dictator. Émile Mas was one of the conservative journalists who objected on the basis that the Comédie's unique status as a society of actors would be undermined; he also believed that avant-garde directors

---

[1] Philippe Tesson, 'Bourdet, l'anti-Brecht', in *Le Figaro Magazine* (1 December 2006).

[2] Théâtre de l'Atelier (Dullin), Théâtre de l'Athénée (Jouvet), Théâtre Montparnasse (Baty).

had no place at the Comédie, since they would not respect the classical tradition. Those actors who were more progressive in their thinking, such as René Alexandre, Dussane and Berthe Bovy, were delighted that the leading directors of the time would be working at the Comédie.

Copeau, then, was finally at the Comédie. But before discussing the impact of the new management structure, it is worth recording a unique performance that took place at the Salle Richelieu in May 1936. The great English actor Charles Laughton was invited to appear with the Comédiens-français during a gala performance, playing the leading role, Sganarelle, in the second act of Molière's *Le Médecin malgré lui*, alongside Madeleine Renaud, Béatrix Dussane, Saffon, Ledoux and Weber. The invitation was regarded as a singular honour, as well as a serious challenge – for Laughton had to perform in French and adapt his English style to the style of the troupe ('Are not English acting and French acting two different processes, the one a strict art, the other a gallant adventure?' wrote an English commentator). His fellow actors told him that he spoke French with a Breton accent, which very much suited the character. As for Laughton, he approached the performance with a self-deprecating modesty. 'I hope to be good,' he remarked, 'but I have often been bad. If I am bad this time, I shall come back another time to do better.'[1]

The gala, presented before president Lebrun, was organised to raise money for the children of the late Jacques Guilhène. The Molière was the main event, starting at two in the morning and not ending until 4.30. *The Guardian* reported that Laughton was a success: 'Time and time again the curtain rose and fell, but the applause went on, while the first Englishman ever to act on this classic stage smiled nervously, shaking his head as if he felt he did not deserve their praise.'[2] *Le Figaro* wrote that Laughton's performance was of an 'enormous buffoonery rendered the more pleasing

[1] Quoted in 'Mr Charles Laughton at the Comédie Française', in *The Guardian* (8 May 1936), p.13.
[2] 'Mr Laughton in Molière: Ovation at the Comédie', in *The Guardian* (10 May 1936), p.26.

by his accent' and that he 'preserved an easy style […], at once hesitant and definite, which gives his interpretation a very telling relief'.[1] The good feelings generated by Laughton's appearance continued for the rest of the decade. The actors were moved by the warmth of the welcome when they travelled to London at the end of February 1939[2] – they performed Molière's *L'École des maris*, Musset's *Le Chandelier* and *À quoi rêvent les jeunes filles* and Jean-François Regnard's *Le Légataire universel* during a week-long residency at the Savoy Theatre. This was the Comédie's eighth visit to the English capital since 1871.

After his first meeting with Bourdet to discuss the new arrangements at the Comédie, in September 1936, Copeau wrote in his journal: 'He is young, modern, direct and sufficiently communicative. It seems to me that he accepted the position in the same spirit as myself, so as to experience things in the moment and to address issues as they are raised by the working conditions. I hope I wasn't too fiery, that I didn't say too much.'[3] Bourdet held the first team meeting at Maxim's, over lunch. Copeau recorded his impressions of a meeting that left him feeling uneasy about the future:

> Bourdet very good, calm, attentive and objective. Dullin in good form, smiling, modest, cautious. Baty rather shy, although pretentious, dumb. Jouvet quite unbearable, full of bluff, whimsical, not fully in control, inarticulate. He made some hateful comments about his old comrade Le Goff. I walked a few steps with him on leaving the restaurant. Hardly spoke. A Corneille cycle: *Le Cid* directed by Baty, *Cinna* by Dullin, *L'Illusion* [comique] by Jouvet. I would direct *Le Menteur* and perhaps *Polyeucte*. A feeling of unease that I will have to master.[4]

[1] Quoted in 'Paris Acclaims Laughton' in *The Guardian* (11 May 1936), p.9.

[2] See P.S. Marsh, *The Theatre in Paris During the German Occupation, 1939-1944*. PhD Thesis, University of Warwick (1973), p.157.

[3] Jacques Copeau, *Journal*, p.406.

[4] Jacques Copeau, *Journal*, p.407. A full Corneille cycle didn't materialise, but Jouvet staged *L'Illusion comique* in 1937 and Copeau staged *Le Cid* in November 1940.

A short while later he wrote about 'impermeable vanities' and expressed his belief that Jouvet and Baty were 'hostile and especially anxious to win or not to be eclipsed'.[1] Perhaps Copeau's distrust was motivated by past betrayals. At any rate, the bond that connected him to his former students was extremely fragile. It is unclear whether Bourdet was aware of the fractious nature of Copeau's relationship with Jouvet in particular.

Despite these issues, Bourdet kept the team together while maintaining his authority as Administrator. He successfully rejuvenated the Comédie. Ageing sociétaires who had monopolised the same parts for years were persuaded to give way. Decades-old costumes and pictorial settings were discarded in favour of uncluttered settings, utilising the depth of the stage. The repertoire was extended to include plays by Giraudoux, Lenormand, Mauriac, Romain Rolland and Pirandello, and masterpieces by Shakespeare not previously seen at the Comédie.

In 1936, Copeau directed Marie Bell and Aimé Clariond[2] in *Le Misanthrope*. In 1937, Racine's *Bajazet* and the premiere of Mauriac's *Asmodée*. Creating productions at the Comédie and working with the actors didn't lift Copeau's mood. He complained to his wife of dreary rehearsals. 'I am so bored in this theatre,' he wrote, 'and feel so little at home that I wonder if I can stay here for long.'[3]

In Mauriac's play, his first work for the theatre, a rich widow, the owner of an estate in the Landes, lives under the controlling influence of her son's tutor, Blaise Coûture, but is unaware of Coûture's malignancy. Coûture moves against the English student who threatens to charm both the widow and her daughter Emmanuelle. Germaine Rouer played the widow, with Aimé Clariond as Coûture and Jean Weber as the student. Copeau initially cast Renée Faure in the pivotal role of the innocent Emmanuelle, but during rehearsals replaced her with Gisèle Casadesus,[4] who was

---

[1] Jacques Copeau, *Journal*, p.409.

[2] Aimé Clariond (1894-1959, b. Périgueux, Dordogne). CF j1936 s37.

[3] Quoted in Jacques Copeau, *Journal*, p.416.

[4] Gisèle Casadesus (1914-2017, b. Paris). CF j1934 s39 d62 sh67. She made her debut playing Rosine in Beaumarchais's *Le Barbier de Séville*. Blessed with a very long life, she made her last appearance with the Comédie in 2011.

only in her third year with the troupe. Copeau felt that the play was slight, but the critical response was very positive. The production would run for over a hundred performances during the next two years. In 1938, Copeau revived Roger Martin du Gard's *Le Testament du Père Leleu* and Marivaux's *La Surprise de l'amour*. Duncan Grant's daughter, Angelica Garnett, who knew Copeau at this time, wrote that 'he was cardinal-like, with white hair, black eyebrows, and magnificent dark eyes.'[1]

Most of Copeau's productions received mixed reviews. Some of Copeau's critics were openly hostile (right-wing papers viewed the Comédie-Française as a Jewish-led hotbed of socialism); others objected to Copeau's style and found the intellectual rigour of the work cold and static. It seems that Copeau was struggling to update his own ideas and was not working at his very best. By the end of 1938 he had changed his opinion of Bourdet's abilities, writing to his wife that 'Bourdet's reign is faltering, he is making a lot of mistakes and displeases everyone' and recording in his journal that 'Bourdet has become discouraged and I fear very much that his reign will lead to a rapid decline'.[2] Copeau comes across at this stage of his life as someone who held standards that were impossible to meet.

Copeau's fellow directors had better luck with the critics, and the productions did well at the box-office. Overall, Copeau, Dullin, Jouvet and Baty directed fewer productions than had been expected; but their work amounted to a small revolution. For Bourdet, the four 'not only bring to the productions they direct their perspicacity and their talent, they also offer to the sociétaires and pensionnaires who work with them the opportunity to choose, and to use one day, what is best in their method and their conceptions'.[3]

In May 1938, Bourdet, like a number of men of letters before him, became embroiled in an argument with the veteran dramatist,

---

[1] Angelica Garnett, *The Unspoken Truth* (London: Chatto & Windus, 2010), p.79.

[2] Jacques Copeau, *Journal*, p.425.

[3] Quoted in P.S. Marsh, *The Theatre in Paris During the German Occupation, 1939-1944*, p.190.

and serial duellist, Henry Bernstein, who had fought three duels in as many days back in 1911. Bourdet had never fought a duel and surely must have found the whole affair farcical until the moment he found himself standing opposite Bernstein in a Neuilly garden with a sword in his hand. He had been taken to the location – the private garden of a house in the rue Peronnet – by car, with the scrambled press pack following at speed. The quarrel concerned Bernstein's play *Judith*, selected by the Comédie in 1937. Bernstein accused Bourdet of deliberately delaying the premiere of the work until the very end of the season, thereby denying it a good run of performances. He withdrew his play and wrote to Bourdet: 'A dramatic author who lays down his pen to direct a state theatre, and whose first administrative preoccupation is to maltreat a colleague whom he has pretended to admire, plays a part which none of your predecessors would wish to fill.'[1]

Bourdet's elegantly scornful reply was worthy of Voltaire: '[Your letter is] decked out with the eulogies which you bestow on yourself in accordance with your favourite and rather comic method. I am obliged to declare, weighing well my words, that with the best will in the world I am unable to attribute to you any of the qualities requisite for passing a valid judgement on the conduct of other people in general, or of myself in particular.'

Several journalists climbed a wall and had a good view of the duel.

At the words 'Allez, messieurs', Bourdet attacked vigorously; M. Bernstein remained strictly on the defensive at first without giving ground, as if studying his adversary. After three minutes it looked as if either man might have been touched, and M. Renaud called a halt to satisfy himself whether there had been a wound, but there had not been. M. Bernstein, who is 62, sat down for a moment streaming with perspiration, while M. Bourdet walked up and down with one of his seconds, M. Pierre Benoit. When the fight was resumed M. Bourdet again attacked and twice seemed near to wounding M. Bernstein – first in the head and

[1] Quoted in 'French Dramatists to Fight Duel', in *The Times* (19 May 1938), p.14.

then in the chest. M. Bernstein continued to hold his ground and began to reply more vigorously. M. Bourdet withdrew slightly and then attacked vigorously, this time in the low lines. M. Bernstein parried his opponent's epée, disengaged his own weapon, and wounded him with a stop hit. The doctor at once called 'Halt', and after having examined the wound insisted that the duel should be broken off in spite of M. Bourdet's protest. The point of the weapon had penetrated to the bone of the arm. M. Bourdet walked to his car without even putting on his coat.[1]

Bernstein was magnanimous in victory. 'Please don't congratulate me,' he told the waiting journalists. 'I hope Bourdet isn't seriously hurt.' Bourdet was soon back at his desk, and this strangest and most anachronistic of episodes would soon be as forgotten as the play that was its cause.

[1] 'Nine minute duel in Neuilly Garden', in *The Times* (21 May 1938), p.13.

Previous double page:
15. *Les Damnés*, Palais des Papes, Avignon, 2016. Ivo van Hove (mise en scène),
Jan Versweyveld (décor and lighting), An D'Huys (costumes), Tal Yarden (video).
Christophe Montenez (Martin von Essenbeck), Elsa Lepoivre (Sophie von Essenbeck).
Photograph by Anne-Christine Poujoulat.

9

The Occupation

1940-1945

16. The Liberation of Paris, August 1944.

1   Copeau as Administrator

Following the fall of France in the summer of 1940, the German occupation of Paris and the establishment of the Vichy government under Marshal Pétain, Jean Zay slipped out of Bordeaux on board the Massilia, bound for Casablanca. He planned to establish a resistance government in north Africa, but was arrested for desertion by the Vichy authorities in Casablanca and sent back to France. Even before the war, Zay was hated by right-wing opponents such as Vichy's Minister of the Interior, Philippe Henriot, because he was both Jewish and a radical socialist. The military tribunal, though, resisted calls for his execution and he was placed in the prison at Riom in the Auvergne. During the final months of the Occupation, in 1944, he was taken from the prison by members of the Milice and shot dead in the woods of Cusset, near the village of Molles.

Jacques Copeau, who had never really felt at home at the Comédie-Française, became the troupe's interim Administrator just before the Occupation. In February 1940, Bourdet was knocked down by a car on the Champs-Elysées and seriously injured. From his hospital bed, he offered Copeau the position of Administrator on a temporary basis (Jouvet, Dullin and Baty had all declined). Copeau was on a lecture tour of Turkey at the time. He agreed to a term of six months, and returned to Paris on 12 May. The Comédie-Française closed its doors on 10 June, just two days before the Germans occupied the city. Copeau went home to Burgundy, but returned to Paris in the middle of July. It is unclear whether Copeau wanted the position permanently, but he was soon facing accusations from Jouvet, Dullin and Baty that he was conspiring against Bourdet. Letters were exchanged in the *Les Nouveaux temps*. The question of Bourdet's future was not in Copeau's hands. The Vichy government viewed Bourdet as a Jewish sympathiser and a writer of decadent plays, and did not intend for him to resume leadership of the Comédie.

Copeau was in an unenviable position. The Germans ordered the dismissal of all Jewish members of the troupe. An anti-Semitic poem published in *Le Pilori* named the actors; then, the German officer with responsibility for the theatre, Badenmacker, demanded to be given an official list of names. After his first meeting with Badenmacker, in July, Copeau wrote in his journal:

> Lieutenant Badenmacher, 'führer' of the Paris theatres, a small fair-haired man, wanted to talk about the Jewish question. He told me that as long as the Germans are in Paris, no work by a Jewish author or composer will be performed, and not a single Jewish actor will appear on the stage or screen. The wave of anti-Semitism surging through Paris, not least in the newspapers, is sickening.[1]

Copeau believed that Badenmacher was being influenced by French *arrivistes*. 'He has taken,' he wrote, '[Henry] Bernstein's apartment and is living with *la petite* Michèle Alfa.'[2]

Copeau delayed declaring the names, but began the unsavoury business of asking those actors suspected of being of Jewish descent to provide documents proving otherwise. Marie Ventura[3] was able to produce the marriage certificate of her parents to show that they weren't Jewish. Copeau continued to procrastinate; but the Germans were unequivocal – the theatre would not reopen unless the matter was settled.

Copeau gave in, and moved to exclude the actors (Vichy's anti-Jewish legislation of 3 October, the *Statut des Juifs*, would have forced their exclusion). To the profound regret of Copeau and the

---

[1] Jacques Copeau, *Journal, 1901-1948*, t.2, p.507.
[2] Jacques Copeau, *Journal*, p.507. Michèle Alfa (1911-1987), actress.
[3] Marie Ventura (1888-1954), b. Bucharest, Romania). CF j1919 s22 d45.

managing committee, René Alexandre and Jean Yonnel[1] were told to leave the troupe. The committee recorded in its minutes (5 September) the great contribution made by these actors to the Comédie, and their heroism during the Great War. Robert Manuel[2] and Véra Korène,[3] away at the time, were told not to return. Béatrice Bretty[4] resigned so she could be with the politician Georges Mandel (she accompanied him on the ill-fated voyage to North Africa). The Germans were later persuaded that Yonnel wasn't Jewish, so he was permitted to return.

Copeau was in no sense pro-German but did have friends and acquaintances who were fascists, such as Alphonse de Châteaubriant, the editor of the weekly paper *La Gerbe*. He didn't judge Châteaubriant. Unlike Dullin, he declined to write for *La Gerb*, but did so politely. 'I admire some of Châteaubriant's books,' he recorded in his journal, 'and believe him to be profoundly honest. He treats me with kindness and respect, but there is something about him that I don't understand and which leaves me cold.' Copeau shouldn't have been surprised nor hurt when Châteaubriant used *La Gerbe* to attack him, but it seems that he was both.[5]

From the stage of the Salle Richelieu, on the night of the reopening, 8 September, Copeau made a remarkable speech, idealistic in its patriotism but honest in its intellectual defiance; a speech that, in its recognition that France had suffered a catastrophe and in its prediction of hope and renewal, angered the Germans, for the French were expected to believe in the new world order:

> Actors will appear before you. They are ready to resume the work that is their *raison d'etre*, that of perpetuating the genius of France by the performance of its ageless masterpieces. [...] They are aware of the particular solemnity of the hour. This great house, whose foundation dates back three centuries, whose patron is one of the greatest, most universal and most human of poets, this House of Molière, as it is called, has always overcome national

[1] Jean Yonnel (1891-1968, b. Bucharest, Romania). CF j1926 s29 d55.
[2] Robert Manuel (1916-1995, b. Paris). CF j1936 s48 d62.
[3] Véra Korène (1901-1996, b. Bakhmout, Ukraine). CF j1931 s36 d55.
[4] Béatrice Bretty (1893-1982, b. La Fère, Aisne). CF j1915 s29 d55.
[5] See Jacques Copeau, *Journal,* p.512.

catastrophes. The latest of these is one of the most severe, the most serious and the most radical in our history. It will have repercussions, currently incalculable, to our consciences, our ideas and our work. It will leave us for a long time in a state of suffering and mourning. And we have everything to fear – political, social and moral uncertainties plunging us into the abyss. [...] Something shudders, something ignites and rises, which we hesitate to name, but which we must call, tomorrow, hope. In spite of catastrophes, we preserve a secret but irrevocable faith in the virtues of our country and in the power and durability of the French spirit. Of this spirit, the society of the Comédiens-français is one of the most faithful witnesses. I would like to compare it to those ancient domains of our soil to which time, venerable wear, revolutions and invasions have periodically modified the physiognomy. Here is a building that we have constructed. The trees of the park have been replanted; the flower beds reshaped. The furniture in the apartments has been changed according to taste and according to the needs of the guests who have passed from generation to generation. But, whatever the change, one recognises it as French. [...] It seems to me, that the misfortunes of the homeland do not forbid me, on the contrary, they command me, this evening, in the presence of the public, and on behalf of the sociétaires and pensionnaires and all those who work here, to pledge an oath to make this house more beautiful and more alive than ever before.[1]

There was a long standing ovation after which Copeau recited *L'Espérance* by Charles Péguy. Copeau made a more personal speech to young people attending a matinee: 'You will be happier than us, because you will have experienced, at the dawn of your life, a great and painful lesson [...]. You will have before you the greatest and most beautiful of tasks: that of rebuilding your fallen country.'[2]

Copeau's journal reveals the stress he was under: 'Every day, vestiges of bile and a tremendous inclination to resign.'[3] In letters to his wife, that October, he wrote: 'The Germans are watching me.

[1] Quoted (in French) in *Opéra* (16 October 1945).

[2] Quoted (in French) in Jean-Pierre Thibaudat, 'La jour où Copeau a exclu les acteurs Juifs du Français'.

[3] Jacques Copeau, *Journal*, p.510.

They care only for slaves. […] I will be happy to leave this Comédie-Française to its mistakes, its nonsense, its intrigues. I will return to the road of solitude, the road of my youth.' But a sense of duty kept him going. He brought Jean-Louis Barrault[1] into the company and reprised his production of Shakespeare's *La Nuit des rois*. Renée Faure and Jeanne Sully alternated the role of Viola, alongside Lise Delamare[2] as Olivia and Aimé Clariond as Orsino. Copeau's strong ensemble also included Pierre Bertin as Malvolio, André Brunot as Belch and Denis d'Inès as Feste.

In December 1940, the Vichy government decided to make Copeau's position permanent (Baty, Jouvet and Dullin immediately resigned). However, the Germans were unhappy with Copeau over his slowness to exclude the Jewish members of the Comédie and his general reluctance to engage with the occupying authorities. They vetoed the appointment. A representative of the Vichy government, Lavelle, told Copeau that the Germans would close the Comédie if Vichy disobeyed. He also told Copeau that 'it is an honour for you to be considered undesirable'.[3] Copeau sent his letter of resignation on 8 January. On the 23rd, he noted in his journal: 'This adventure is over. It is a great relief.' Then, back home in Pernand-Vergelesses, he wrote a highly revealing sentence: 'Return to reality after eight months spent with the ghosts in that monument to vanity and cabotinage, the Comédie-Française. How much richer is the world when one rediscovers the freedom to offer it one's heart.'[4] The entry is consistent with his previous private comments, but contrasts with the speech of 7 September and reveals that Copeau's private feelings about the Comédie were complicated indeed. The chance to direct the Comédie-Française came too late and under impossible circumstances. His reputation – at least among directors, writers and actors – would remain high. Giorgio Strehler echoed Albert Camus when, on his appointment to direct the Théâtre de l'Europe at the Odéon in 1983, he said of

---

[1] Jean-Louis Barrault (1910-1994, b. Le Vésinet, Yvelines). CF j1940 s43 d46.

[2] Lise Delamare (1913-2006, b. Colombes, Seine). CF j1934 s52 d66.

[3] Quoted in Jacques Copeau, *Journal,* p.511.

[4] Jacques Copeau, *Journal,* p.513.

Copeau and the Théâtre du Vieux-Colombier (at that time unused and derelict): 'Copeau is the father of us all. The first time I went on stage I was an angel in a pageant he directed for the May celebrations in Florence. We can't allow his theatre to die; it exists, a little less alive each year, and we must make it live again.'[1]

2   Jean-Louis Vaudoyer

Jean-Louis Vaudoyer became Administrator of the Comédie-Française in March 1941. Vaudoyer was a distinguished art historian and minor novelist, and the director of the Musée Carnavalet. At the Comédie, he had been responsible for the Saturday 'Matinées poétiques' since 1936. His friends Jean Giraudoux and François Mauriac encouraged him to take up the appointment.

Any Administrator of the Comédie during the Occupation would have had to deal with the Vichy authorities and the Germans on an almost weekly basis. What was simply a matter of practical necessity could look like collaboration. Vaudoyer worked under constant pressure, and was worn down by the responsibility. Most of the actors felt supported by Vaudoyer. Because he was neither a dramatist nor a leading director, he was not an Administrator like Baudet or Copeau, exerting artistic power over the troupe. Photographic portraits show a rather melancholy face with a drooping moustache, and indeed, Béatrix Dussane wrote of him: 'I can and I must reveal here that I have seen him repeatedly concerned, in his discreet and melancholy way, to limit, as far as possible, the influence of the Germans over the life of the Comédie-Française.'[2]

We know that Vaudoyer tried to resist the call to stage a play by the German dramatist Gerhart Hauptmann by putting up obstacles and delaying the production as long as possible. However, many

[1] Quoted in Colette Godard, 'Strehler at the Odéon: a French institution for Europe', in *The Guardian* (20 March 1983), p.13.
[2] Quoted (in French) in P.S. Marsh, *The Theatre in Paris During the German Occupation, 1939-1944*, p.221.

people believed he should have fought harder, or resigned, when the German authorities wanted the Schillertheater of Berlin to appear at the Salle Richelieu, as happened in 1941 and 1943. When Vaudoyer asked his actors to attend the reception for the German troupe at the German embassy, some objected strongly. More troubling, though, was his invitation to Robert Brasillach, the rabidly fascistic and pro-German editor of *Je suis partout*, to give a reading from Corneille at a matinée poétique in June 1941. Mauriac fell out with Vaudoyer over Brasillach's invitation. An exchange of letters between Mauriac and Georges Duhamel revealed that Vaudoyer, in an angry outburst, bitterly attacked writers who were unsympathetic to Pétain and Vichy.[1] Here, then, we possibly have the measure of the man: conservative but not extremist; pro-Vichy but not pro-German, although Mauriac, in the heat of argument, wouldn't accept the distinction, calling Vaudoyer 'the director of the Germans' Comédie-Française'. In criticising Vaudoyer, Mauriac was on shaky ground, for although he ended the war as a brave and committed member of the Resistance he had started it by expressing sympathy for the aims of the Vichy government.

Members of the Resistance understandably had a low opinion of writers and theatre directors who maintained cordial relations with the Germans, accepting invitations to attend the parties of the cultivated and socially charming German Ambassador, Otto Abetz, in the rue de Lille, as Cocteau did, and of actors who performed before German officers and their French mistresses enjoying a night out at the theatre. Jean-Louis Barrault would claim that ignoring the Germans and simply carrying on was the best response.[2] The claim was sincere, but there was a contradiction: the actors were entertaining the occupiers on a nightly basis.

Like Fabre during the First World War, Vaudoyer believed that the Comédie-Française's primary task was to sustain the public by performing the great works of French dramatic literature, from

---

[1] See John E. Flower, 'An Armchair Dispute: François Mauriac, Jean-Louis Vaudoyer, the Académie Française and the Occupation', in *Journal of War and Culture Studies*, vol.2, no.1 (2009), p.70.

[2] See Antony Beevor and Artemis Cooper, *Paris After the Liberation* (London: Hamish Hamilton, 1994), p.152.

Molière to Rostand. This allowed people to put the hardships of the Occupation to one side for a few hours. 'La permanente mission du théâtre,' he remarked in an interview, 'est une mission poétique. Cette mission est double: elle consiste, d'une part, à faire de la vie rêvée une vie réelle, et, d'autre part, à conférer à la réalité le prestige du songe.'[1] All plays had to be approved by the German censor, and multiple small cuts were made even to plays written centuries ago. The authorities were particularly concerned to identify anything that might promote French patriotism. This was a mostly pointless exercise, since the censor didn't spot many of the phrases that had meaning to French audiences, and those audiences took pleasure in collectively identifying double meanings. As Marcel Thiébaut, wrote: 'We went back to the theatre, above all to look for the slightest allusion that, at a stroke, would make the whole room hostile or complicit.'[2] The performance of a play by Molière, even with cuts, was a patriotic act that made people feel good about being French.

The censor looked out for any line that could be appropriated to mock Germany or Vichy; any passages that reminded people that they were hungry or cold; and any phrases that referenced the British in anything other than a negative way. For instance, the censor cut from Musset's *André del Sarto*, performed in May 1941, the line: 'Est-ce que les Anglais ont une patrie? J'aime autant les voir ici que chez eux.'[3] In this context, it is perhaps surprising that the authorities allowed plays by Shakespeare to be performed. In 1940, the Comédie revived Copeau's *La Nuit des rois*, and in March 1942 Jean-Louis Barrault played the title role in *Hamlet*, directed by the former sociétaire Charles Granval who had also directed the troupe's previous production of the play. The translation was by Guy de Pourtalès.

Vaudoyer relied upon Barrault's talent as both actor and director. Barrault, who studied acting under Dullin and mime under

---

[1] Quoted in P.S. Marsh, *The Theatre in Paris During the German Occupation, 1939-1944*, p.164.

[2] See Patrick Marsh, 'Censorship in France During the German Occupation', in *Theatre Research International*, vol.4, no.1 (1978), p.27.

[3] See Patrick Marsh, 'Censorship in France During the German Occupation', p.28.

Étienne Decroux, had already made his mark on both stage (running an experimental troupe at the Grenier des Augustins studio) and screen when he accepted Copeau's invitation to join the troupe. He accepted in part so that he could join Madeleine Renaud at the Salle Richelieu. The two had met on the set of the film *Hélène* in 1936, and married in September 1940. In 1942, Barrault directed a new production of Racine's *Phèdre*. Marie Bell played the title role.

3   Montherlant's La Reine morte

In 1942, Vaudoyer asked Henry de Montherlant to write a play for the Comédie, and suggested that he find inspiration in Spanish drama of the 16th century. Spanish history played well with the Germans because of their alliance with Franco's Spain. The commission had significance beyond the ordinary, for Montherlant's play would be the first new work staged at the Comédie since the beginning of the war.

Montherlant's disdain for the Third Republic and admiration for Hitler's Germany had been a feature of his journalism since 1933. He wrote regularly for *La Gerbe* and his public reputation was that of a fascist writer and, in the broadest sense of the word, a collaborator. Despite his open stance in his writing, Montherland was constantly troubled in his life, forever fearful that his sexual activity with young boys would be revealed to the Germans. He mostly kept his distance from the Germans in Paris; he refused invitations to go to Germany, and he didn't write articles for the German press. When it became clear that Germany was losing the war, he wisely stopped writing for French papers and journals associated with collaboration.

Montherlant was an acclaimed novelist. He published *Les Célibataires* in 1934 and the anti-feminist tetralogy *Les Jeunes filles*, written in prose that is as cruel as it is elegant, between 1936 and 1939. A British reviewer of *Les Jeunes filles* wrote of Montherlant that 'he is both pitiful and detached; he mixes a warm sympathy with a cold lucidity, and pity with power'. He had written very little for the stage. Vaudoyer's bringing of Montherlant into the Comédie was another reason why, for some, he was a fascist sympathiser. In fact, the invitation was motivated by friendship – the two had been close for many years – and we simply can't know whether Vaudoyer had any sympathy with Montherlant's extreme political ideas or simply over-looked them.

Vaudoyer was right to believe that Montherlant would write a major work that would find a big audience. Montherlant took Guevara's *Régner après sa mort* as his starting point but created a new three-act drama, *La Reine morte*.

To cement a political alliance, the king of Portugal, Ferrante, arranges the marriage of his son Pedro to the young Infanta of Navarre. The Infanta tells Ferrante that Pedro has rejected her. He cares for another. Pedro confesses to the king that he loves Inès de Castro, and has married her in secret. In doing so, he has placed his personal feelings above his duty to the state. Ferrante, who already has contempt for his son, has the boy arrested. Ferrante's courtiers advise him to order the murder of Inès. Ferrante at first refuses. He talks to Inès about his troubles, almost tenderly, and, although Inès has been warned by the Infanta that her life is in danger, she trusts the king and reveals to him that she is pregnant. The king tells his captain to arrange her murder. She is ambushed and killed on the road. Ferrante suddenly collapses and dies. Pedro mourns Inès and becomes king.

There is no action as such in the play: it is a psychological drama weighed down by Montherlant's nihilism. The ageing king is world-weary, cynical and difficult to read. His complex nature is expressed in lines such as: 'Pourquoi je la tue? Il y a sans doute une raison, mais je ne la distingue pas.' Pedro is weak; Inès is naïve. Montherlant has contempt for all of them. He wrote the play away from the stresses of Paris during a short sojourn in Grasse in Provence; but this southern idyll didn't prevent the war from influencing his play. On the contrary, Montherlant would later reveal that there was a direct connection between the atmosphere of his play and contemporary events in France.

The play, premiered on 8 December 1942, was a great success:
it attracted full houses and was performed over one hundred times.
The production, by Pierre Dux,[1] with designs by Roland Oudot,
was admired. Dux's interpretation, and the actors' performances,
may have subtly altered the tone of Montherlant's text, making the
work more appealing. Jean-Louis Barrault and Madeleine Renaud
played Ferrante and Inès. These were all important factors. However, the very great popularity of the work can only be explained by
the curious malleability of the text when considered from different
points of view. The audiences were quick to see meanings in the
play that chimed with their own ideas. For Pro-Vichy spectators,
Pedro represented weak young men who refused to do their duty
for the new France. For spectators in despair over the Occupation
and the Vichy regime, Pedro was a *résistant* imprisoned by a tyran-
nical state. When Pedro is arrested, he remarks: 'C'est curieux, les
hommes de valeur finissent toujours par se faire arrêter.' ('It's curious how men of worth always end up being arrested.') The line
provoked instantaneous applause. This was certainly not Montherlant's intention, and the line, and lines like it, were missed by the
German censor. Montherlant was dismayed that his text was being
used to encourage 'acts of terrorism' (his phrase for acts of resistance).

Actual members of the Resistance knew that Montherlant was
no closet supporter of their fight. They despised Montherlant and
they despised his play, or rather used it to make the point that
needed to be made, over and over again, as the war entered its final
year. The underground paper *Les Lettres françaises clandestines* told
its readers:

> And Montherlant, who has always been fond of celebrating viril-
> ity and greatness – in his writings if not in his life – takes sides,
> making us feel at every moment the will of the state against feel-
> ing and human happiness. This is the secret of the official support
> for *La Reine morte*. The racist critic of *Je suis partout*, this dirty
> police informer named Alain Laubreaux, is also responsible for

[1] Pierre Dux (1908-1990, b. Paris). CF j1929 s35 d45 AG 70-79.

warning us about 'the reasons of state'. For, through M. de Montherlant, the idea is to desensitize us and to make us dismiss as negligible the persecutions and the tortures inflicted on our people by the masters of the hour.[1]

The play's popularity and literary merit didn't shield the Comédie from criticism, but certainly mitigated the consequences. The play would survive the circumstances of its creation, and stay in the repertoire. It was revived, triumphantly, in 1948, and in 1954 Montherlant joined the cast to celebrate its 250th performance at the Comédie.

4   Claudel's Le Soulier de satin

Vaudoyer continued to support new work. In 1943, he accepted a new play by Jean Cocteau. Thirteen years after *La Voix humaine*, Cocteau, who was living in an apartment at the Palais-Royal, remained fascinated by the mythical history of the Comédie-Française. Looking out from his office window at the garden's arcades and statues, white paths and symmetrical rows of lime trees, Cocteau was inspired to write a drama in the manner of Racine. Following the controversial *Les Parents terribles*, revived at the Théâtre du Gymnase in 1941, Cocteau was perhaps looking for a project that would be less newsworthy and that would bring him the respect of the literary establishment. In writing the new play he set himself the challenge of writing in verse and observing the unities of time, place and action. The result, *Renaud et Armide*, was a moderate success. Cocteau created the part of Renaud for Jean Marais but Marais had left the Comédie. The role was played by Maurice Escande.[2] Marie Bell played Armide. Jacques Dacquemine and Mary Marquet were also in the production.

---

[1] Quoted (in French) in P.S. Marsh, *The Theatre in Paris During the German Occupation, 1939-1944*, p.229.
[2] Maurice Escande (1892-1973, b. Paris). CF j1918 s36 d70 AG 60-70.

The big event at the Comédie in 1943 was the staging, by Barrault, of Paul Claudel's *Le Soulier de satin*. The poet and playwright Paul Claudel was a very different figure from Cocteau. While pursuing a literary career, he worked as a senior diplomat, representing France in China, America and Brazil. In this sense, he was a 'man of action' with an intimate knowledge of public service and politics. A devout Catholic, Claudel's religious faith informed nearly all of his writing. He wrote in a highly original free style, densely metaphorical, and he ignored theatrical conventions, writing plays that were as long and as intricate as the subject matter and themes required.

On a ship bound for China, Claudel started an affair with a married woman. The experience inspired the greatest of his early plays, *Partage de Midi* (1906), which explored the conflict between temptation and salvation. Claudel published his plays, but they rarely reached the stage, partly because he was mostly abroad until his retirement from the diplomatic service, but also because his form of theatre (integrating text, *mise en scène*, visual motifs and original music) was vastly challenging for producers to realise on the stage. *L'Annonce faite à Marie* and *L'Otage* were both premiered at the Théâtre de l'Œuvre, in 1912 and 1914 respectively. Copeau directed *L'Échange* at the Vieux-Colombier in 1913. *Partage de Midi*, written before the First World War wouldn't be staged until after the Second. The Comédie-Française mounted a revival of *L'Otage* in 1934. Émile Fabre directed Marie Ventura, Jean Hervé, André Bacqué and Fernand Ledoux.

Claudel expressed admiration for Pétain in 1940 by writing an ode to the Marshal, but his mind was changed by Vichy's defeatist mentality and subservience to Germany. Claudel despised the Nazis and was pro-British. In June 1940, at Churchill's request, he secretly flew to Algeria to investigate establishing a resistance government. The mission failed. Claudel felt too old to join de Gaulle in London.

Claudel's diary makes his support for England and the Free French clear. Publicly, he kept his head down and mostly stayed in his chateau at Brangues. In December 1941, he wrote to the grandrabbin to express his 'disgust and horror' at the treatment of the

Jews. He was understandably fearful when the letter was made public. The Vichy government had no doubts about Claudel's real feelings, writing in his file: 'Sur le plan extérieur: semble dévoué au Maréchal. Désigné comme anglophile et gaulliste.'[1]

At the end of the war, though, Claudel faced criticism that he had collaborated. For some, it was an act of collaboration to give a play to the Comédie, a theatre under the control of the Germans. Claudel gave interviews to the collaborationist press to publicise his work; more damaging, he was a director of a company – Gnôme et Rhone – that made engines for the Germans.

Claudel remains a controversial figure, especially for people on the left. Outside of politics, his reputation was most damaged by his treatment of his sister, Camille Claudel. Having been exploited and betrayed as a young woman by her teacher and lover Rodin (the exact truth is debated), Camille was deserted by her mother and brother, who judged her severely because of her 'immoral' lifestyle. After Camille suffered a mental breakdown, her brother committed her in the asylum at Neuilly-sur-Marne (1913). It was Claudel who kept her in mental hospitals for the rest of her life, ignoring the advice of her doctors that she should be released. And it was certainly not because of Claudel that at least some of her great sculptures were preserved for posterity. As the Comédiens-français were rehearsing Claudel's *Le Soulier de satin*, the play that would be widely acclaimed as his masterpiece, in October 1943, his sister died forgotten and alone in the Montdevergues asylum near Avignon and was buried in a communal grave.

The idea to stage the play was the brainchild of Barrault. Claudel had published the play in 1929, with little hope of ever seeing it produced on the stage. A symbolist epic set in the Spanish golden age, it was of a great length and required magical stage effects and ever-present music. Barrault visited Claudel at Brangues and asked the writer to authorise a shortened version that would allow the work to be performed in two parts. In the end Claudel agreed to an even shorter text that could be played in a single evening. A close

---

[1] Quoted in Edward Boothroyd, *The Parisian Stage During the Occupation, 1940-1944: a Theatre of Resistance?* PhD Thesis, University of Birmingham (2009), p.233.

working relationship developed between the two that would last for the rest of Claudel's life. Barrault was passionate about Claudel's work because it aligned with his own ideas about 'total theatre'. Vaudoyer was enthusiastic about the project and persuaded the reading committee to accept the play.

The production was very expensive to mount, and all-consuming. The opening was delayed more than once. This angered Claudel but aided the publicity campaign that was whetting the public's appetite to see the play. Barrault cast himself in the leading role of Rodrigue, Marie Bell as Doña Preuhèze, Madeleine Renaud as Doña Musique, and André Brunot as Balthazar. Arthur Honegger was commissioned to write the music. The sets were by Lucien Coutaud.

Le Soulier de satin opened on 27 November. The play began with the line: 'La scène de ce drame est le monde.' Barrault's production played with the nature of theatre to dramatise the theme of divine providence. The spectators were reminded at all times that they were watching a conceit: the actors moved the scenery and the usually hidden mechanisms of stagecraft were revealed. The Announcer, played by Pierre Dux, acted as a master of ceremonies. The play provided grand spectacle, a tragic love story, episodes of comedy, and a redemptive ending. It contained some of Claudel's most beautiful poetry, but its ideas were rarefied. Claudel gave an explanation in an interview published in the fascist paper *La Gerbe*:

> Man is two-sided: on one side, he is an animal of pleasure, whose instinct for life is tainted by flaws; and on the other, he desires to achieve great things, has noble aspirations, and yearns for God. It is this double instinct which is the subject of human drama and which culminates in this claudication of man, symbolized by the slipper which the heroine, on the point of sinning, hands to the Virgin.[1]

The play was an extravagant success. In part, this was because the production was an early example of 'event theatre' and a piece of

---

[1] Quoted (in French) in P.S. Marsh, *The Theatre in Paris During the German Occupation, 1939-1944*, p.263.

art that represented all that was good and magnificent about French theatre and poetry at a time of shame and austerity. In those dark days, people craved the kind of patriotic cultural experience that *Le Soulier de satin* provided. The play's final line – 'Délivrance aux âmes captives!' – was especially resonant. Overall, the censor didn't have a problem with the play, but, as usual, individual lines were cut that were deemed to have a topical resonance – for instance most references to England were cut. It is therefore surprising that the play's final line was allowed to stand. The censor didn't foresee that the play would embolden people yearning for the end of the Occupation.

This was an extraordinary time for Barrault. Before, during and after working on *Le Soulier de satin*, he was closely involved in the preparation and shooting of *Les Enfants du paradis*, in which he co-starred as the mime Deburau. It was Barrault who, over drinks one evening in Nice, presented Marcel Carné with the idea of making a film about Jean-Gaspard Deburau and some of the other notorious figures of the Boulevard du Temple theatre quarter during the 1830s.

5   The Liberation

Members of the Comédie-Française were active in the Resistance. In 1942, four members – Marie Bell, Pierre Dux, Julien Bertheau and Pierre de Rigoult – joined Jean-Paul Sartre and others in the establishment of a Comité de Résistance. One of the publications of the Front national (communist resistance), *Lettres françaises clandestines*, was printed in the home of Aimé Clariond of the Comédie.

By the time of the Liberation, Jean-Louis Vaudoyer was no longer in post. He had come under constant pressure after Abel Bonnard became the Vichy minister in charge of the Comédie in 1942. Bonnard expected the Comédie to act unequivocally in the interests of the New France, and, has already been said, Vaudoyer always tried to keep the authorities at arm's length. By March 1944,

Vaudoyer could no longer abide Bonnard's interference and angry rebukes and suddenly resigned. Vaudoyer's colleagues on the management committee interceded on his behalf, but Bonnard was glad to see Vaudoyer go. The veteran sociétaire André Brunot was appointed in Vaudoyer's place as interim Administrator. Bonnard wanted Alain Laubreaux, the fascist critic of *Je suis partout* who had constantly attacked Vaudoyer, to take charge of the Comédie, but a majority of the sociétaires voted this down.

One of Vaudoyer's last acts was to offer a contract to the popular star Raimu. This raised eyebrows since Raimu wasn't a classically trained actor but a protégé of the music hall entertainer Félix Mayol. Raimi made his name as a comic actor at the Folies Bergère and became an international figure because of his work on screen in the 1930s. He played César Olivier in Marcel Pagnol's play *Marius* in 1928 and again in the film version, directed by Alexander Korder and released to acclaim in 1931. Raimi went on to play César in the final two films of Pagnol's Marseille trilogy, *Fanny* (1932) and *César* (1936), as well as the baker in *La Femme du boulanger* (1938). In 1942 he co-starred with Marie Bell in *Le Colonel Chabert*, and it was Mlle Bell who suggested to Vaudoyer that he engage Raimu. A character actor somewhat similar to Charles Laughton, Raimu was in his sixties and very much his own man: his entry into the Comédie was an event that divided opinion. Raimu made his debut playing Jourdain in Molière's *Le Bourgeois gentilhomme* in March 1944. His performance was widely admired. For Cocteau, writing in *Comœdia*, Raimu had 'humanised' Jourdain. 'The dancing lesson is a masterpiece,' he wrote.[1]

The Allies landed on the Normandy beaches on 6 June. The Comédie closed on 21 July. During the battle for Paris in August, the Comédie-Française was among those buildings that the Resistance moved quickly to occupy and protect. The sociétaire Julien Berthau[2] was one of the young members of the troupe ready to join the street fighting. Between them they only had four shotguns.[3] Members of staff used sandbags and chairs from the nearby café de

---

[1] Quoted (in French) in *La Grande histoire de la Comédie-Française*, p.187.

[2] Julien Berthau (1910-1995, b. Algiers). CF j1936 s42 d58.

[3] See Antony Beevor and Artemis Cooper, *Paris After the Liberation*, p.42-

l'Univers to construct a makeshift barricade between the columns in front of the theatre.

Charles Danglade, chairman of the committee of the Croix-Rouge Française in the 1st arrondissement, and Dr André Meunier, responsible for first-aid workers, established medical stations throughout the quarter. The Comédie-Française offered the Salle Richelieu on 19 August, and its actors and staff joined nurses and Red Cross volunteers. René Alexandre, Jean Chevrier and Lise Delamare took charge of logistics. Jacques Charon,[1] who had joined the Comédie in 1941 and was still a pensionnaire, drove one of the ambulances (hastily converted vans or cars). Another pensionnaire, Jacques Dacqmine, just out of the Conservatoire, fought with the FFI in the 1st arrondissement (a protégé of Barrault's, Dacqmine would be among those actors who went with him to the Marigny in 1946).

Fighting in the arrondissement was intense. People were killed or injured by gunfire or explosions. People with severe burns needed to be cut free from vehicles by the emergency teams while the fighting continued. Medical volunteers were killed as they attempted to save others. The team at the Comédie treated ninety-four wounded and eighteen dead.[2]

The relief of liberation was quickly followed by the brutal settling of scores that became known as the *épuration sauvage* (savage purge). In the confusion and lawlessness of those first days of freedom, before De Gaulle's provisional government had established control, mob violence and summary executions despatched thousands of people in towns and villages throughout France. While members of the hated Milice were understandably targeted, some of the victims were falsely accused of collaboration.

De Gaulle's great achievement was to unite the country. The arts were used as a means of promoting national pride. In September

43.

[1] Jacques Charon (1920-1975, b. Paris). CF j1941 s47 d75.

[2] See the website of the *Croix-Rouge Française*, at https://www.croix-rouge.fr/La-Croix-Rouge/La-Croix-Rouge-francaise/Historique/Seconde-Guerre-mondiale/Aout-1944-liberation-de-Paris-le-poste-de-secours-de-la-Comedie-francaise-1791 (accessed 2/1/2020).

1944, one of the first tasks of René Capitant, the Minister of Education in the provisional government, was to appoint a new Administrator of the Comédie: his choice, Pierre Dux, had impeccable credentials – not only a brilliant actor but also a member of the Resistance. He had made his debut with the troupe in 1929, playing the iconic role of Figaro in *Le Barbier de Séville*, and his achievements as a director included the Comédie's production of *La Reine morte*. The Comédie re-opened on 27 October with a gala performance in honour of the 'poets of the Resistance', presided over by De Gaulle. The programme was compiled by Mauriac. The first play staged after the re-opening was *Le Malade imaginaire*. Raimu played Argan. His short time at the Comédie soon came to end because he wasn't given the freedom to pick his own roles.

De Gaulle instigated an *épuration légale* to investigate politicians and officials but also prominent figures in journalism and the arts. The process was extremely complex and required a high level of pragmatism since the legal profession, the civil service and the police had worked for Vichy and were badly compromised. It simply wasn't realistic to remove from office everyone in these professions below the top few tiers. Similarly, in the cultural sphere, the commissions concentrated on the most prominent offenders. Alain Laubreaux escaped to Franco's Spain, but Robert Brassilach was tried and sentenced to death. Mauriac, Camus, Claudel and Cocteau signed a petition calling on De Gaulle to commute the sentence on the grounds that a writer should not be executed for expressing an idea, however vile that idea might be. De Gaulle, though, was not prepared to show leniency to a man who had published the names and last known addresses of Jews and who had called for the execution of Georges Mandel and all members of the Resistance. Brassilach didn't ask for leniency. He refused to retract anything he had said or written. He was executed by firing squad in the fort de Montrouge. Some writers on the Left who had been active in the Resistance took a different line from the great names who had signed the petition. They called for the severe punishment of writers who had collaborated, with Montherlant at the top of their list. Montherlant was investigated by the *Commission d'épuration* examining the conduct of writers, but no clear evidence of collaboration was identified. Montherlant's prudence during the Occupation had saved him from public humiliation and censure. The actress Arletty, the most prominent of the women accused of *collaboration horizontale*, was tried for treason and imprisoned for eighteen months.

The Comédie-Française was investigated by a *Commission d'épuration*. Four members of the Comédie – René Alexandre, Maurice Donneaud, Jean Meyer[1] and Pierre de Rigoult – sat on the Commission; Dux decided not to participate. 'Collabos' within the troupe were easily identified because they had been members of the theatre section of Groupe Collaboration, the body set up to foster close cultural links with the Germans. Groupe Collaboration published *La Gerbe*. The following members of the troupe were found guilty of collaboration: André Brunot (sacked as interim Administrator, he retired from the troupe); Geneviève Auger; Antoine Balpétré (who had appeared in films produced by the German firm Continental as well as participating in a ceremony of homage to Philippe Henriot); Pierre Bertin; Jean Debucourt; Maurice Escande; Yves Furet (who had worked for Radio-Paris); and Louis Seigner. Debucourt, Escande and Seigner were suspended for a period of between three and six months. Furet and Auger were ejected from the troupe.[2]

The commission did not investigate Vaudoyer, for the consensus view was that, while he had committed errors of judgement, such as his invitation to Brassilach, he had not actively collaborated. Vaudoyer's critics, though, would not let the matter drop. His former friend François Mauriac publicly objected when Vaudoyer sought election to the Académie Française. A committee of honour investigated Vaudoyer and found in his favour.

The actors excluded in 1940 – René Alexander, Béatrice Bretty, Véra Korène and Robert Manuel – re-joined the Comédie. Manuel was one of the nearly 70,000 Jews rounded up by the French police and placed in the Drancy internment camp. Only an accident of

---

[1] Jean Meyer (1914-2003, b. Paris). CF j1937 s42 d59.

[2] See Jean Knauf, *La Comédie-Française: 1944*, available online at https://www.lesarchivesduspectacle.net/Documents/P/P85857_8.pdf (accessed 3/5/2019).

fate saved him from transportation to Auschwitz. Manuel resumed his distinguished career at the Comédie playing Fleurant in Molière's *Le Malade imaginaire.*

Paul Bonifas returned from London. A pensionnaire at the Comédie since 1938, Bonifas joined the army at the beginning of the war. Seriously injured during the battle for France, he was evacuated along with his unit from Dunkirk. He joined the Free French and was a member of Michel Saint-Denis's team at the BBC, broadcasting daily into France. During his time in England, Bonifas formed the Molière Players and appeared in films, including the Ministry of Information propaganda shorts *Venture Malgache* (directed by Hitchcock) and *Two Fathers* (directed by Anthony Asquith), and the commercial movies *The Foreman Went to France* (1942) and *Champagne Charlie* (1944). *Two Fathers* consisted of a dialogue between two strangers, an Englishman, played by Bernard Miles, and a Frenchman, played by Bonifas. The Englishman's son is an airman, missing in France. The Frenchman's daughter is a member of the Maquis, risking her life to help men like the Englishman's son. The film's purpose was to tell the public that, despite Vichy, the English and the French were still allies.

Barrault continued his work as a director at the Comédie by staging Mauriac's *Les Mal-aimés* in March 1945, a failure, and then André Gide's translation of Shakespeare's *Antony and Cleopatra* in April. The production's stylish semi-abstract design and imaginative stagecraft confirmed Barrault's reputation as one of the most innovative young directors of the time. Clariond and Marie Bell played the title roles. However, all was not well at the Comédie. The denunciations of the épuration, and the verdicts of the commission, had understandably caused conflict and unhappiness. Pierre Dux had not taken his place on the commission because he didn't want to judge his colleagues. He did not want to preside over the implementation of the judgements, so he stepped down as Administrator in July 1945.

6   The Old Vic and the Comédie

Just before his departure, Pierre Dux led the troupe to London. To celebrate the victory in Europe, the British Council had facilitated a unique event. For two weeks in early July, the Comédie-Française and the Old Vic Company exchanged theatres. This was the first time that a foreign company had been invited by the Comédie to appear at their home (the visit of the German actors having been imposed on the troupe).

The Old Vic was hit by a bomb in the Blitz. While the theatre was being re-built, the Old Vic company was based at the New Theatre in St Martin's Lane (today's Noël Coward Theatre), so it was here that the Comédie performed. In 1945 the Old Vic company was co-directed by Laurence Olivier, Ralph Richardson and John Burrell, and Michel Saint-Denis was appointed to realise the ambitious plans for the restored Old Vic – a new centre that would include a school and a studio for experimentation.

Olivier and Richardson, not yet formally discharged from their regiments, arrived at the Salle Richelieu in uniform. Olivier starred in *Richard III*, and Richardson, directed by Tyrone Guthrie, in *Peer Gynt*. Shaw's *Arms and the Man* completed the repertory. Sybil Thorndike and Joyce Redman were prominent in a very strong ensemble. On 14 July, the Old Vic company's performance of *Arms and the Man* formed part of the first Bastille Day festivities since before the war. It seemed that *tout-Paris* wanted a piece of Olivier. Paris was showing the world its extraordinary capacity for renewal (previously seen in 1795 after the Terror and in 1871 after the Franco-Prussian war and the Commune). In 1945, despite the double trauma of the Occupation and the Épuration, the feeling of freedom released a *joie de vivre* in the young that was lacking in England, a country that would have to wait until 1963 for its own renaissance.

In London, the Comédiens-français performed a double-bill of Beaumarchais's *Le Barbier de Séville* and Molière's *L'Impromptu de Versailles*, Hugo's *Ruy Blas*, a double-bill of Molière's *Tartuffe* and Georges Courteline's *Le Boulingrin*, and Racine's *Phèdre*. Dux played Figaro (with 'a fine comic verve', underpinned by melancholy). Tartuffe was played by Jean Yonnel and Phèdre by Marie Bell. Ashley Dukes, reviewing the production of *Tartuffe* in *The Observer*, commended 'the calm grace of Mlle Germaine Rouer's Elmire and the sincerity of M. Louis Seigner's Orgon'. The production revealed that 'Molière is a modern playwright uttering our thoughts in the liveliest words'.[1]

At the end of the tour, Pierre Dux issued a statement on behalf of the troupe:

> I am happy to say how much the reception we have received from the London public has touched all members of the Comédie-Française. Many people have been unable to be present at our performances, so great has been the demand for tickets; and after sixteen performances proof has been given that there is a large public in London for French repertory. I wish especially to thank the British Council, whose practical goodwill has enabled us, after the end of a tragic war, to come and experience the understanding, in the artistic and literary world, of our friends and allies.[2]

---

[1] Ashley Dukes, 'Theatre and Life', in *The Observer* (8 July 1945), p.2.
[2] Quoted in *The Guardian* (16 July 1945), p.3.

17. *La Machine à écrire* by Cocteau, Odéon, 1956. Jean Meyer (mise en scène), Suzanne Lalique (décor). L-R: Lise Delamare, Jean Serviere, Cocteau, Robert Hirsch, Annie Girardot, Jean Meyer.

10

The Fourth Republic

1946-1959

18. *Les Espagnols au Danemark* by Prosper Mérimée. Jean Meyer (mise en scène).
Jeanne Moreau, backstage, 1948.

1 The Post-War Years

The task of implementing the reforms fell to Dux's successor, André Obey. The actors were used to managing their own careers; to remaining in the troupe while taking up opportunities to work in films. Now, each actor was restricted to appearing in one film a year, shot during the summer months, and that film needed to be approved by the management. The actors saw the new regulations as an attack on their freedom and their dignity. On 9 June 1946, Barrault, Clariond, Escande, Bertin, Debucourt, Chevrier, Madeleine Renaud, Marie Bell and Renée Faure resigned. An exodus on this scale hadn't been seen at the Comédie since the Revolution.

Barrault's departure was a blow, but, given his ambition and creative drive, surely only the directorship – and a free hand over policy – would have persuaded him to stay in the longer term. By the end of the year he had formed a new company with Renaud at the Théâtre Marigny and had starred in his own production of Gide's translation of *Hamlet*, a landmark moment in the history of the Paris stage. Barrault and Renaud were joined at the Marigny by some of their former colleagues – Brunot, Bertin, Catherine Fonteney, Le Roy, Desailly and Dacqmine. The young Pierre Boulez was engaged as music director.

The character and culture of the theatre scene in Paris hadn't significantly changed in over a century and was quite different from the scene in London. Individuals ran theatres in line with their own prejudices and maintained particular traditions. Few theatres had the very latest lighting rigs or stage machinery. Most actors made their own decisions without the help of managers or agents. There was no Binkie Beaumont. No unions. When Peter Brook started to work in Paris in 1957, he felt liberated from the regulations and restrictions of theatre-making in the West End. In London, for instance, sets were constructed by a firm of builders and detailed architectural plans were essential. In Paris, a designer such as Christian Bérard would draw his design on a café napkin and the skilled *machinistes* of the theatre would work out how to realise the drawing technically. 'When, the night before an opening, [Bérard] suddenly decided to change it all, this did not lead to anger, to strikes, or to hard-bargained overtime deals but only to a few bottles of red wine that made the same machinistes work happily to dawn, with a genuine satisfaction in bringing their skills to a creation that they loved and shared.'[1] Theatre practices would change in Paris during the next few decades, but the picture painted by Brook has not entirely faded away.

Obey had made his name in the 1920s as a novelist. It was through Copeau and Michel Saint-Denis that he started to write for the theatre. His play *Noé*, written for Saint-Denis's Compagnie des Quinze, was feted in Paris and London. As Obey was taking charge of the Comédie, Benjamin Britten's opera *The Rape of Lucretia*, based on Obey's play of the same name, opened at Glyndebourne.

With so many departures, Obey was running a depleted company just as the government re-assigned to the Comédie, after a gap of one hundred and sixty-two years, the theatre de l'Odéon, inaugurated by the Comédie in 1784. The Odéon was re-named the Salle Luxembourg to compliment the Salle Richelieu. The actors' workload doubled. Often, an actor would perform in a matinee at the Salle Richelieu and then rush by car across the river to the Salle Luxembourg for an evening show. 'We didn't even have time,' Gisèle Casadesus remembered, 'to notice people's bewilderment at seeing someone in 17th or 18th century clothes at the wheel of a car speeding across the pont du Carrousel.'[2] Among the important actors who joined the troupe at this time was Micheline Boudet,[3]

---

[1] Peter Brook, *Threads of Time: a Memoir* (London: Methuen, 1998), p.94.
[2] Quoted (in French) in *La Grande histoire de la Comédie-Française*, p.193.
[3] Micheline Boudet (b. Metz, Moselle, 1926). CF j1945 s50 d71 sh72.

who had abandoned a career as a dancer at the Paris Opéra to train at the Conservatoire. She quickly made her name at the Comédie in the plays of Molière, Marivaux and Beaumarchais.

After little more than a year in post, Obey quit. Without the actors on side, the demands of running the Comédie were too dispiriting. The minister struggled to find someone from within the theatre community who had been active in the Resistance (still, three years after the end of the Occupation, an important requirement) and who wanted to take on the Comédie at this difficult time. The minister turned to the eminent scholar of the theatre, Pierre-Aimé Touchard. The new regulations stipulated that the Comédie's Administrator would serve for no more than six years, and Touchard would see out his contract.

Touchard's first act was to suspend the hated anti-cinema rule. Most of the actors who had departed with Barrault and Renaud returned to the fold. Not Barrault and Renaud, who had everything they could wish for at the Marigny, and not Marie Bell, although she accepted the position of sociétaire honoraire. Five years later, though, in 1953, she asked to be readmitted to full membership: the committee turned her down. The Comédie had been central to Mlle Bell's life since she was twenty-years-old so this ending must have been hurtful; but she was a formidable woman, perhaps the last of those great female stars – Lecouvreur, Dumesnil, Clairon, Contat, Mars, George, Rachel, Bernhardt (et al) – who defined whole epochs of work at the Comédie. Peter Brook got to know her in 1960 when she was running the Théâtre du Gymnase and he was looking for a theatre manager brave enough to put on Jean Genet's *Le Balcon*. Brook would later write in his memoirs:

> Marie Bell had stepped straight out of the 19th century. She had played all the great leads at the Comédie-Française, there were leopard-skin rugs over the divan in her dressing room, she had an apartment on the Champs Élysées that was draped in crimson velvet, she wore large hats, strong make-up, had the panache and style that belonged to her role, and in her extravagant diva way was a free woman. […] As she had a great respect for Genet, she was delighted to wage a battle on his behalf, being fearless for

herself and contemptuous of the police. She wanted to play the overliterary part of the *maîtresse du bordel*, and later she proved to be one of the few actresses I have ever known with the practical sense to urge me to cut more and more of her lines: 'The less I say,' she would insist, 'the better I will appear.'[1]

Touchard was a patrician figure who was able to bring some stability to an expanded troupe that contained different factions. Disputes, though, were frequent. In 1952, Touchard brought Jean Marais back into the Comédie. Since Marais's earlier brief spell with the troupe in 1943, he had fought under Leclerc in the armoured division of the French army in Alsace and had starred in some major films. Among the films that resulted from Cocteau's infatuation with Marais were *L'Éternel retour* (1943) – Alain Laubreaux, in *Je suis partout*, mocked Marais as 'L'homme au Cocteau entre les dents' – and *La Belle et la bête* (1946). Public knowledge of Cocteau and Marais's relationship didn't define the actor for the public. He was both a war hero and the first *bona fide* French movie star of the new age. The theatrical part of Marais's personality – serving with his tank regiment in eastern France, he was accompanied by his dog Moulouk – added to the myth of Marais. His stature in France was similar to Olivier's in England, and the two men made sure to meet during the Old Vic's residency in Paris in 1945.

In signing his new contract with the Comédie, Marais declared his desire to work as a director as well as an actor, and the right to make two movies a year. The committee granted his wish to direct and design Racine's *Britannicus*, and to play the role of Néron, but Marais's ideas were quickly deemed to be alien to the traditions of the Comédie. Many members were unhappy that a star had been parachuted into the troupe, so their willingness to accept Marais's approach to the classical repertory was limited. The committee told Marais that they would cancel the production unless he agreed to be supervised by Bertheau. Two opposing camps quickly formed and the opening night, in a throwback to the theatrical battles of

---

[1] Brook, *Threads of Time*, p.104-05.

the 19th century, was disrupted by people either cheering or hissing. It was clear to Marais that to continue in the troupe would be folly.

2 The Era of Jean Weber

Touchard's successor, Pierre Descaves, would build on his work. Running the two theatres was challenging, but it offered new possibilities. Classics were mounted at the Salle Richelieu; modern pieces at the Salle Luxembourg. Touchard and Descaves were greatly aided by the presence of Jean Meyer. Initially an acclaimed actor, Meyer emerged as an important director during the war. He enjoyed an early success directing Raimu in Molière's *Le Bourgeois gentilhomme* in March 1944. Meyer was prolific as both an actor and a director. He was a Molière specialist, but his work was broad, ranging from Shakespeare to contemporary playwrights such as Édouard Bourdet, Montherlant, Gide and Cocteau. He rediscovered the work of Prosper Mérimée. He directed Shakespeare's *Othello* in 1950 and *Coriolanus* in 1956. Clariond played Othello, alongside Jean Debucourt (Iago) and Renée Faure (Desdemona). Paul Meurisse played Coriolanus. Meyer was a classicist, and perhaps something of a puritan, but his work was not old-fashioned. His productions were informed by his understanding of actors, his intelligence and his good taste.

In 1950, Touchard and Meyer courted Gide by visiting him in Provence. Weber wanted to mount a stage version of Gide's novel *Les Caves du Vatican* and the old master agreed. He even followed Meyer's advice and wrote some new scenes. Meyer's production opened at the end of 1950. It had literary prestige, but wasn't the grand success that Touchard and Meyer had hoped for. Gide wrote in his journal: 'Décidément je n'aime pas le théâtre.'[1] He died a little over a year later in February 1951.

[1] Quoted in *La Grande histoire de la Comédie-Française*, p.202.

The Comédie-Française remained faithful to the two great writers who had brought literary prestige to the troupe during the difficult years of the Occupation. The golden premieres of Montherlant's *La Reine morte* and Claudel's *Le Soulier de satin* had stayed in the collective memory while criticism of the two authors' political views had diminished. Four plays by Montherlant were produced. Meyer premiered *Port-Royal*, a tremendous success, in 1954 and *Brocéliande* in 1956. Revivals of *Pasiphaé* (starring Véra Korène) and *Le Maître de Santiago* were staged by Bertheau in 1953 and Henri Rollan in 1958. Montherlant's *Port-Royal*, based on Sainte-Beuve, and set in the Jansenist abbaye de Port-Royal, formed the final part of his Catholic trilogy. The tone of the writing was unrelentingly austere and sombre. A play of ideas, its great popularity was perhaps explained by the fact that in secular France in the 1950s Catholicism remained deeply rooted. Annie Ducaux and Renée Faure were outstanding in the principal roles. A student at the Conservatoire called Jean-Paul Belmondo played one of the chaplains.

Bertheau's staging of Claudel's *L'Annonce faite à Marie* opened in 1955. The play, written in 1892, was produced by Jouvet at the Théâtre de l'Athénée in 1942 and again in 1945. Bertheau's production, created in the presence of Claudel, was compared unfavourably with Barrault's *Le Soulier de satin*, for it lacked the passion of the latter as well as the profound circumstances that turned it into a landmark event.

During the Touchard and Descaves eras, 1947-59, a remarkable generation of actors emerged, actors who would remain at the core of the troupe for many years. These included Robert Hirsch, Michel Aumont, Jacques Toja, Jean Piat, Jean-Paul Roussillon, and Jacques Sereys. A few young pensionnaires made a great impression, but didn't stay to become sociétaires. These included two actresses who would become iconic stars of the Nouvelle Vague – Jeanne Moreau and Annie Girardot.

Jeanne Moreau's talent was recognised by Denis d'Inès, doyen of the Comédie, who coached her for entry into the Conservatoire in the spring of 1947, when she was nineteen. By the end of the year she had appeared at the first Avignon festival, cast by Jean Vilar as

Ophélie in *La Terrasse de midi*, and had made her debut at the Comédie as Joas in Racine's *Athalie*. Auditioned by Meyer, she was made a pensionnaire at the start of 1948. During the next four years she played more than twenty roles, including Chérubin in *Le Mariage de Figaro* (Meyer, 1948), Angélique in Marivaux's *L'Épreuve* (1948), Doña Maria in Prosper Mérimée's *L'Occasion* (Meyer, 1948), Anne-Marie in Bourdet's *Les Temps difficiles* (Dux, 1949), Camille in Musset's *On ne badine pas avec l'amour* (1949), Bianca in Georges Neveux's translation of Shakespeare's *Othello* (Meyer, 1950), Perdita in Claude-André Puget's translation of Shakespeare's *The Winter's Tale* (Bertheau, 1950), Carola in Gide's *Les Caves du Vatican* (Meyer, 1950) – 'She made us understand,' Meyer declared in his memoir *Place au théâtre*, 'that a girl of barely twenty can be aged prematurely by prostitution'–, Silvia in Marivaux's *La Double inconstance* (1951), and Clara in Feydeau's *Le Dindon* (Meyer, 1951). Photographed for the cover of *Paris Match*, her face stared out from news kiosks all across Paris and beyond. Filmmakers took note of the young actress, and Vilar, too, was keen to direct her again. He offered her a contract to join the TNP and to return to Avignon. Moreau faced a difficult decision – whether to commit her future to the Comédie or to spread her wings and explore the myriad of possibilities that were coming her way. She chose the latter. 'My departure was painful,' she would later reveal. 'Friendships were broken for a time. But I will never forget those four years at the beginning of my career. From this first experience was born the rest of my life as an actress and as a free woman.'[1] On leaving the Comédie, as well as appearing with the TNP, Moreau played Eliza to Jean Marais's Higgins in Shaw's *Pygmalion* at the Théâtre des Bouffes Parisiens (1955), and Maggie in Peter Brook's production of Tennessee Williams's *Cat on a Hot Tin Roof* at the Théâtre Antoine (1956). The young directors of the Nouvelle Vague were not interested in glamourous movie queens, but sought to cast actresses who had the appeal of normal young women, and Jeanne Moreau and Annie Girardot were the first representatives of

---

[1] Quoted (in French) in *La Grande histoire de la Comédie-Française*, p.334.

this new breed of performer. Moreau's success in Louis Malle's *Ascenseur pour l'échafaud* and *Les Amants* initiated a life in film that would dominate much of the rest of her career.

Annie Girardot joined the Comédie on graduating from the Conservatoire in 1954 and stayed until 1957. She played Lisette in Marivaux's *Le Jeu de l'amour et du hasard* (1955), and, directed by Jean Meyer, Martine in *Les Femmes savants* (Salle Richelieu, 1956), Armandine in Feydeau's *Le Dindon* (Richelieu, 1956), La Jeune Dame in Jules Romains's *Amédée et les messieurs en rang* (Luxembourg, 1956), Margot opposite Hirsch[1] in a revival of Cocteau's *La Machine à écrire* (Luxembourg, 1956) and the tragic Éponine in *Les Misérables* (Luxembourg, 1957). She achieved iconic status because of her youth, style and modern 'look' as Margot in the Cocteau and as Christiane in Jacques Deval's *Mademoiselle* (1957) – her hair cut boyishly short four years before the Jean Seberg of Godard's *À bout de souffle*. For Cocteau, twenty-four-year-old Annie Girardot was 'le plus beau tempérament dramatique de l'après-guerre'. The Comédie is possessive of its actors. Like Moreau a few years before, Girardot soon felt imprisoned. Things came to a head when she accepted a role in the movie *L'Homme aux clefs d'or* and needed to spend part of the week in the south of France, where the production was being shot. After performing at the Salle Luxembourg, she hurried to the airport to catch a night flight to Marseille. The next afternoon she flew back to Paris and rushed to the Comédie to perform in the evening. This routine was repeated for a number of weeks. When Descaves found out that his young star was a 'francs-tireur' he insisted that she accept becoming a sociétaire. This declaration of faith in her talent was also a means of asserting control. So Girardot declined the contract and soon left the Comédie to star opposite Jean Marais in Luchino Visconti's production of *Deux sur la balançoire* (*Two for the Seesaw*) at the Théâtre des Ambassadeurs, a success that led to her movie breakthrough as the tragic prostitute in Visconti's *Rocco et ses frères* (1960). Visconti's camera captured all of Girardot's sadness and mystery.

---

[1] Robert Hirsch (1925-2017, b. L'Isle-Adam, Val-d'Oise). CF j1948 s52 d73.

Two actresses of Annie Girardot's generation would remain with the Comédie for the rest of their long careers – Claude Winter[1] and Catherine Samie.[2] Catherine Samie played many of Molière's *soubrettes* in her twenties, often directed by Jean Weber; her wit and mischievousness delighted audiences in this repertoire but her grasp extended from Shakespeare to Strindberg.

In 1954, at the height of the Cold War, the Comédie-Française travelled to Russia, the first theatre company to do so since the 1917 revolution. The troupe performed Molière's *Le Bourgeois gentilhomme* and *Tartuffe*, Corneille's *Le Cid*, Musset's *Une Caprice* and Jules Renard's *Poil de carotte* in Moscow and Leningrad. The actors were greeted by enthusiastic audiences in both cities.

The volatility that had marked the internal politics of the troupe since the war, was a factor in the strange case of Bernard Shaw's play *Mrs Warren's Profession*. In 1952, the reading committee accepted the work for performance. The Comédie had not previously produced a play by Shaw, but a revival of interest in the great playwright, perhaps provoked by the Old Vic's presentation of *Arms and the Man* at the Comédie in 1945, was underway in the French capital. It took some years for a selected play to reach the stage. *Mrs Warren's Profession* was finally scheduled for performance, at the Salle Luxembourg, in March 1955. During rehearsals, the reading committee looked at the text again and decided that the work, even with cuts, was 'amoral' and unsuitable for presentation at France's national theatre. To the consternation of the company members working on the production (including Béatrice Bretty as Mrs Warren and Hélène Perdrière as her daughter), their colleagues on the committee banned the play. Descaves didn't have the power to overturn a decision that would lose the Comédie a considerable sum of money. He admitted to the press that the decision was 'unprecedented in the company's history'. Costumes and sets designed by Jean Oberle would have to be destroyed. A French critic responded to the announcement by wryly commenting: 'It can only be regretted that we shall never know what Shaw's own comment

---

[1] Claude Winter (1931-2011, b. Tianjin, China). CF j1953 s60 d88.
[2] Catherine Samie (b. 1933, Paris). CF j1956 s62 d2006.

would have been on hearing, that the Comédie-Française had come round sixty years later to the view of the Lord Chamberlain who banned the play in London in 1894.'[1] It is unclear what motivated this inexplicable outbreak of prudery at the Comédie. Admirers of Shaw flocked instead to the Théâtre des Bouffes Parisiens to watch Jean Marais and Jeanne Moreau.

In 1957, the tension over retirements and promotions that often divided senior and junior members of the troupe broke into a major dispute, as it did every ten years or so. On this occasion the conflict spread to audiences in the Salle Richelieu. Jean Meyer was a powerful advocate of younger members of the company, and was blamed when Descaves decided to retire Jean Yonnel, Béatrice Bretty and Véra Korène so that three talented pensionnaires could be promoted. This caused outrage in sections of the press, and admirers of the three retirees scattered leaflets of protest in the auditorium. Meyer was hissed when he took his curtain call on the first night of a revival of *Le Barbier de Séville*.

[1] Quoted in 'Shaw Play Banned in Paris', in *The Times* (23 February 1955), p.7.

11

The Return of Pierre Dux

1960-1982

19. Michel Aumont, Isabelle Adjani and Pierre Dux, 1973. Photograph by Patrice Picot.

1   Maurice Escande

The Comédie-Française had always been impacted, in large and small ways, by the political revolutions and crises that marked France's national life, and it was no different in 1958/59, when the uprising in Algeria precipitated the collapse of the Fourth Republic and the return of Charles de Gaulle. The new Minister of Culture, the imposing André Malraux (intellectual, novelist and politician), was a man on a mission to establish a network of national theatres and to revitalise all aspects of France's cultural life. Malraux's analysis of the current state of the theatre left him believing that, since the war, the actors of the Comédie had assumed too much power which had resulted in the programming of too many light comedies and too few performances of the tragedies of Racine and Corneille. The requirement to programme plays in a second house had similarly resulted in the production of too many inferior plays. One of Malraux's officials had gathered statistics to back up his analysis: out of the last 556 performances, only six were of plays by Racine.

For Malraux (and others), the troupe had fallen short of fulfilling its obligation 'to develop the national culture and to improve taste with productions of quality'. A theatre that received such a large subsidy (amounting to two-thirds of its operating costs) could not expect to be left alone by a government that needed both to account for the money and, in theory, to distribute it evenly. Malraux, like many politicians before and since, came face to face with the troupe's peculiar and antique governing structure, laid out by Napoléon in 1812. The Comédie-Française was both a state theatre and a society whose members had a say in policy and a share of the profits. There was a conflict here. And the rules that governed how the actors shared the profits, based on length of service and seniority, were fundamentally divisive. The issue for men like Malraux, tasked with reforming the Comédie-Française, was this: was it possible to dismantle the Comédie's structure of governance (so as to turn the Comédie into a state-owned national theatre in which actors were merely employees) without wrecking what was special and unique about the troupe? In the end, the answer to that question had always been 'no'.

Malraux moved to reassert the government's authority over the Comédie-Française, and the Administrator's authority over the sociétaires, by removing actor representatives from the executive committee. Descaves's contract came to an end in 1959. Malraux formulated new rules to increase the Administrator's powers and caused dismay by appointing a distinguished diplomat – Claude Bréart de Boisanger – to the post. Malraux invited Michel Saint-Denis to advise the Administrator. Next, he took back the Odéon from the Comédie and handed it (along with part of the Comédie's subsidy) to Jean-Louis Barrault's company. The Comédie would now have a competitor able to compete at the same level, but, arguably with a more modern outlook. Given that the Comédie was often overshadowed by Vilar's TNP, this should have been a matter of concern, but, from the outside, it sometimes looked as if members of the troupe were complacent.

Jean Meyer resigned, and other sociétaires were poised to follow. Malraux backtracked. He annulled the new rules, dismissed Boisanger and appointed the veteran sociétaire Maurice Escande in his place. Michel Saint-Denis joined Peter Hall at Stratford. Boisanger appealed to the Conseil d'Etat, was reinstated, but then resigned anyway. These farcical events dragged on for over two years, during which Escande just kept on working. While a part of Malraux's scheme had unravelled, the separation of the Odéon from the Comédie-Française was carried through.

Escande was given wide powers by Malraux but, as a member of the company, he sought consensus in exerting them. It seems that he shared Peter Hall's conviction that a national theatre needed to balance the old with the new, the classical with the modern, if it was to be a living organism. Malraux would be satisfied as long as the Comédie did more Racine and less Feydeau. In February 1960, Escande gave his first press conference as Administrator. He announced that he would address discontent within the company by changing the 'Statut des Comédiens' so that members could retire after fifteen years rather than the current twenty. To bring in new ideas, he would invite leading directors to work with the company, including Peter Brook, who he hoped would stage a play by Shakespeare and Sheridan's *The School for Scandal* during the 1960/61 season. Following the tour of his Stratford production of *Titus Andronicus* to Paris and his work with French actors at the Théâtre Antoine, Brook was the most coveted young director of the time. Sadly for the Comédie, he decided to join Hall at the RSC. Escande also planned to add the works of Albert Camus and Jean-Paul Sartre to the repertoire.

Escande was widely supported. For the Paris correspondent of *The Times*,

> The recent appointment to the post of Administrator of M. Maurice Escande, the most senior of the Comédie-Française actors, marks to some degree a return to traditional practice and will, it is to be hoped, restore peace to this renowned theatre company, whose chronic state of crisis or supposed crisis has never seriously prevented it from carrying out its appointed role as guardian of the heritage of the French classical theatre. When the Comédie-Française was already 175 years old, Sainte-Beuve wrote of it that it lived 'in spite of all vicissitudes and of political and literary controversy, because it remains a school of good taste and good language'. There can today be few, if any, whatever their urge to reform it, who would wish to end the days of an institution whose habitual complacency is more than balanced by its lustre. [...] The great building at the bottom of the Avenue de l'Opéra is heavy with the spirit of the past: elegant green-rooms, dressing rooms, and offices, red-carpeted passages lined with marble busts, walls covered with paintings of former actors, dressmakers' and tailors' workshops capable of dressing any play of any date, a lift with the floors marked not numerically but by the names of famous actors (if you want to fit a wig, you press the button marked

'Rachel' and are carried up to the wigmaker's workshop on the seventh floor) – all these create an atmosphere and ambience which even the casual visitor is able to sense immediately.[1]

Despite his popularity and charm, Escande found it a challenge to realise the more radical aspects of his plans. If the desire was there, consensus within the troupe often wasn't. The traditional French repertoire of the Comédie was overwhelmingly in evidence throughout the 1960s, and the pioneering spirit of that decade rarely penetrated the palatial walls of the Salle Richelieu. Camus, Sartre, Genet, Beckett were conspicuous by their absence. Of active or recently active playwrights, only Montherlant and Claudel were truly favoured and their plays were hardly at the cutting edge. However, there were notable exceptions when it came to extending the repertoire. Escande mounted Pirandello's *La Volupté de l'honneur* in 1969; Sheridan's *The School for Scandal* (*L'École de la médisance*), with costumes by Cecil Beaton, in 1962; Bernard Shaw's *La Grande Catherine* in 1962; an adaptation of Dostoevsky's *Crime et Châtiment*, directed by Michel Vitold, in 1963, with Hirsch as Raskolnikov; the troupe's first-ever production of Shakespeare's *A Midsummer Night's Dream* (*Le Songe d'une nuit d'été*), in a production by Jacques Fabbri, in 1966; and Ionesco's *Le Soif et la faim* in 1966. This last caused a minor scandal, for conservative patrons were outraged by, as they saw it, the play's immorality. Perhaps the finest production of a foreign masterpiece at the Comédie during the Escande era was Jacques Mauclair's *Oncle Vania*, premiered in April 1961. This was only the second play by Chekhov staged by the Comédie – his early one-act comedy *L'Ours* (*The Bear*) had been performed by Jean Meyer, Madeleine Renaud and Robert Manuel in November 1944. The troupe's famously rigid and declamatory style when performing the French classical repertory had started to be questioned by some of the younger critics, who believed it to be outmoded, so there was curiosity as to how the actors would approach Chekhov. They confounded their critics by performing with 'the touching realism that Chekhov demands':

[1] 'House of Molière Rides a Storm', in *The Times* (18 June 1960), p.9.

Daniel Ivernel's performance is beautifully modulated and delicately observed. Renée Faure is too experienced an actress to allow the weight of her years to stand between her and her intriguing portrayal of Sonia as an awkward but sensitive young girl. Jean Marchat and Yvonne Gaudeau play their respective roles of the cantankerous Professor and his almost indecently feckless wife as though they had never performed on the stage in any style but the one most suited to convey the smouldering underground fires which so impressed Leonìdov after the first performance in Moscow. René Arrieu illuminates the doctor's role with a proper blend of childish enthusiasm and cynical indifference and even the smallest roles belong to the general human pattern like pieces in a tightly fitting jigsaw puzzle.[1]

Ivernel came to the Comédie after a long run playing Henry II in Anouilh's *Becket* at the Théâtre Montparnasse. Despite his success in *Oncle Vania*, he decided not to stay with the troupe. The same thing had happened in 1943, when his debut at the Comédie was also a one-off performance. He made his name at the TNP.

There were significant new productions of Racine's *Bérénice* (1961) and *Andromaque* with Denise Noel in the title role (1968), Corneille's *Le Cid* (1963) and *Le Mort de Pompée* (1964), and Rostand's *Cyrano de Bergerac* (1964), directed by the great comic actor Jacques Charon. Charon's production starred, as Cyrano, another master, Jean Piat,[2] supported by Jacques Toja as Christian and Geneviève Casile[3] as Roxanne. Piat would play Cyrano over four hundred times in the period up until 1972.

The depth of talent in the company was exceptional. Alongside the players already mentioned, we find Charon, Aumont, Arrieu, Catherine Samie – this is just to name a handful. Young actors who came through included Françoise Seigner, Alain Pralon, Catherine Salviat, Catherine Hiegel and Ludmila Mikaël. Jean Marchant and Paul-Émile Deiber emerged as important directors of the classics.

During the De Gaulle presidency, foreign leaders on state visits

---

[1] 'Comédie Adapts its Style to Chekhov', in *The Times* (3 April 1961), p.12.

[2] Jean Piat (1924-2018, b. Lannoy, Nord). CF j1947 s53 d72.

[3] Geneviève Casile (b. 1937, Boulogne-Billancourt, Hauts-de-Seine). CF j1961 s65 d93.

were usually taken to see a performance of a French play at the Comédie-Française, and the troupe was asked to fly the flag abroad by touring. De Gaulle's attitude towards the state theatre, then, wasn't that different from Napoléon's. The troupe toured to the USA and Canada in 1961, Japan in 1962, Mexico in 1963, the Soviet Union in 1964 and Israel in 1965. They took part in the RSC's World Theatre seasons at the Aldwych in 1964 and 1967, performing *Tartuffe* (Louis Seigner, Annie Ducaux and Lise Delamare), Feydeau's *Un Fil à la patte* (Charon, Hirsch, Roussillon), Corneille's *Le Cid* (Deiber, Casile, Claude Winter), and Marivaux's *Le Jeu de l'amour et du hasard* (Escande, Roussillon, Toja, Winter, Madeleine Boudet).

2   May 1968

The Comédie-Française's position as the state theatre separated it from the largely left-wing radicalism of the wider theatre community. This was vividly revealed by the student and workers' revolt of May 1968.

The avant-garde of post-war French theatre had been driven by a belief in decentralisation and democratisation. At local level, this meant engaging with working people who felt excluded by the theatre. Ideologically, it meant using theatre as an agent of social change. These ideas united many theatre managers and directors. Jean Vilar had established the Avignon Festival to bring young people together from all countries and all walks of life, and Roger Planchon's Théâtre de la Cité de Villeurbanne was the most prominent of the many left-wing theatre organisations that worked in local communities. The desire for change didn't belong solely to the left. A key goal for Malraux, minister in the Gaullist government, was to decentralise the theatre. Planchon and Malraux were political opposites but they both wanted to make culture accessible to all. The difference was that, whereas Planchon and Vilar saw the theatre as a public service enabling self-expression and social change, Malraux saw it as a means of enriching people's lives through exposure to high art. The Comédie-Française, as the state theatre, was condemned by the left (as it always had been since the beginning of the century) for its supposedly right-wing and bourgeois tendencies. The truth was subtler. Members of the troupe had their own politics, left or right, but publicly the Comédie needed to be politically neutral, or above politics: its role required it and its survival depended upon it.

During the student revolt, theatre people tended to be sympathetic to the ideals being expressed and therefore opened the doors of their theatres to the protestors so they could be used for public debates and meetings. Barrault welcomed the students who occupied the Odéon. He was caught up in events that were happening at lightning speed. The RSC's Peter Brook, who, at Barrault's invitation, was directing a workshop production of *The Tempest* for the Théâtre des Nations festival, described those surreal days of May in his memoir *Threads of Time*:

> I sat with a friend in a little Greek restaurant. She had her back to the window. As we chatted, the little street outside was suddenly full of panic-stricken figures running, ducking, trying to avoid the police with their black helmets and shields who were charging and plying their truncheons. Inside the restaurant there was no reaction, no acknowledgement of what was on the other side of the door, so I too curiously accepted this strange unreality, seeing the face of my friend in close-up as in a film, with the dangerous incidents of the street out of focus behind.[1]

A crisis in which the Catholic, conservative, paternalistic France of De Gaulle came face to face, for a few weeks, with the sexually, culturally and politically liberated young of the 1960s, quickly evolved into a general strike. For a few days the government was so fearful that they were facing a revolution that De Gaulle was flown to an army base in Germany.

Police violence persuaded many people to come down on the

---

[1] Brook, *Threads of Time*, p.145-46.

side of the students. These included intellectuals, filmmakers, actors and theatre workers. The student leader Jean-Jacques Lebel, holding meetings at the Sorbonne, called for symbolic action, and decided that that action would be the occupation of the Odéon, also known at that time as the Théâtre de France. The students took the theatre on the evening of 15 May. Barrault followed the advice of the ministry, which was not to resist. However, he subsequently disobeyed the government when he was instructed to switch off the electricity and the phones. When he was criticised by the right-wing press, Barrault replied: 'Serviteur oui, valet, non.' Soon the anarchists' red and black flags were flying over his theatre and the slogan 'Quand l'assemblée nationale devient un théâtre bourgeois, tous les théâtres bourgeois doivent devenir des assemblées nationales' ('When the National Assembly becomes a bourgeois theatre, all the bourgeois theatres should be turned into national assemblies') had been scrawled across the ancient stones. The students renamed the Odéon the 'ex-Théâtre de France'. Along with the occupied Sorbonne, the Odéon became the headquarters of the student revolt.

The Comédie-Française's theatre was undamaged by the events of May. Actors and staff manned the Salle Richelieu day and night and prevented protestors from entering the building. Technical and administrative staff, though, were inevitably caught up in the general strike and demanded joint-management of the backstage and technical operations at the Comédie. They went on strike for twenty days, during which at least some of their concerns were addressed.

Staff of the TNP went on strike to demonstrate solidary with the protestors. In Villeurbanne, directors of the Maisons de Culture and the popular theatres signed a joint declaration in favour of a politized theatre. They refused to enter into a dialogue with the Ministry of Culture unless the declaration was acknowledged.

Late one night, Brook was approached by a young man in the Café de Flore and invited to a meeting at the Odéon. He found a theatre in which events had slipped into anarchy:

Onstage, a nonstop marathon of speech making, which had begun on the first evening, had now become repetitive and self-indulgent. The hedonistic sex in the corridors was sinking into an apathy of drugs and squalor; dealers, thugs and operators were taking over the theatre, and boredom was overcoming the last handful of listeners still scribbling notes in the stalls.[1]

Brook was introduced to a student leader who was in fact a police informer. He returned to London and continued to work on *The Tempest* at the Roundhouse.

With the protests fizzling out, the police took back control of the Odéon on 14 June. Barrault had participated in student meetings and was badly compromised. A survey of the building revealed that it required major repairs. Among the manuscripts destroyed were Boulez's scores for Barrault's productions at the Marigny. Malraux, who had supported Barrault at the time of his company's production of Genet's controversial play *Les Paravents* in 1966, waited until September but then announced that the Odéon would not be returned to Barrault's company.

3 Pierre Dux

Ill-health forced Escande to retire in 1970. Twenty-five years after his first, abortive, spell in charge, Pierre Dux returned as Administrator.

During the intervening years Dux had worked as an actor and director in the boulevard theatre. Together with Marcel Karsenty, Dux directed the Théâtre de Paris from 1948 to 1952. He taught at the Conservatoire from 1953 to 1956. He had remained connected to the Comédie as an honorary sociétaire: he directed new productions of Bourdet's *Les Temps difficiles* in 1948, Giraudoux's *Électre*, in which he played the role of the beggar, in 1959, and Racine's *Andromaque* in 1964.

---

[1] Brook, *Threads of Time*, p.146.

A large man, Maigret-like, Dux had an old-world charm, but he was formidable as well as wise and much admired within a profession that was notably competitive. Dux read De Gaulle's speeches on the radio and the great man referred to him as 'the master'. Dux was willing to take risks to achieve his goal of making the Comédie not only envied abroad for its long history and ensemble model, but also admired as one of the most dynamic of all the major theatres of Europe. The Comédie's actors, trained at the Conservatoire (by former sociétaires of the troupe) to within an inch of their lives in the French style, could perform Molière and Racine in their sleep. Dux believed passionately in the French style and the formal training that kept it alive, and opposed new methods of teaching at the Conservatoire; but he wanted to see what would happen when the actors were confronted by foreign styles, particularly when performing foreign plays. The idea, for instance, of inviting an English director to direct the actors in Shakespeare had been discussed before but never realised.

The Odéon had been dark since the events of 1968. Dux, realising that the RSC had benefitted greatly from additional theatres, pressed for the Odéon to be returned to the Comédie-Française. Malraux's successor at the Ministry of Culture, Jacques Duhamel, agreed. The Odéon re-opened in September 1971 as a 'National Theatre' under the direction of the Comédie. Dux invited Jean-Pierre Miquel to take charge. The troupe performed new and contemporary plays in the Odéon for half of the season; the other half was given over to transfers from the major regional theatres and from foreign theatres – from 1983, the Odéon was the part-time home of the Théâtre de l'Europe project under Giorgio Strehler. The Odéon would remain under the direction of the Comédie until 1990.

Dux's decade in charge would be marked by a major renovation of the Salle Richelieu (in 1975/76 – during the renovation the troupe rented the Marigny Theatre); by the broadening of the repertoire into the Odéon and the Petit Odéon; and by the troupe's most significant, up until this point, exposure to outside influences and styles. It was also marked by changes to the governance of the Comédie. Dux understood the need of actors to work outside of the troupe, and made changes to the regulations, including a reduction in the number of years the sociétaires were contracted to serve, designed to give his colleagues more freedom to make their own choices (decree of November 1975). He reduced the number of plays from the existing repertoire performed each season so that he could programme more new works. Dux was assisted by Georges Guette, appointed to the position of General Secretary. Guette previously worked for Vilar at the TNP. Dux and Guette had to deal with the discontent of technical staff and the threat of strikes (Peter Hall at the National Theatre in London faced the same predicament). They closed the Salle Richelieu during the 1972-73 season until an agreement was reached with the unions. During the closure the troupe performed in a marquee erected in the jardin des Tuileries.

At the beginning of his tenure in August 1970, Dux announced that he would invite to the Comédie-Française directors who had not worked there before. By the end of September he had travelled to London with Robert Hirsch to meet with the RSC's Terry Hands. The meeting was arranged by Peter Daubeny, director of the RSC's World Theatre seasons at the Aldwych, and took place at his apartment over lunch. It was agreed that Hands would direct Shakespeare's *Richard III* during the 1971/72 season. Hands could not speak French at the meeting, but was fluent by the time he arrived in Paris a little over a year later to start work on the production. At twenty-nine, he was the youngest of the RSC's associate directors. Since 1968, he had directed Shakespeare's *Pericles*, *Richard III* and *The Merchant of Venice*, the Jacobean thriller *Women Beware Women* and Jean Genet's *The Balcony*. Trevor Nunn's closest colleague, he combined Nunn's textual scholarship with a vivid theatrical imagination that created images from space and light and limited abstract décor. His work, often designed by Farrah, was atmospheric, audacious and provocative, three things that no-one associated with the Comédie-Française at this time. Dux instantly liked the young director, and believed that he would fit in at the Comédie as well as bringing a new approach and a deep understanding of Shakespeare – the authentic Shakespeare – that would benefit French actors. Dux told *The Times*: 'We found his person-ality entirely engaging. Both Hirsch and I were delighted with our choice of this Shakespearean director to stage a Shakespeare at the Comédie-Française. I am sure our players, too, will warm to him as we did. Incidentally, we're using a new translation by Jean-Louis Curtis for the occasion.' Hands took a close interest in the transla-tion – several drafts were needed before he was happy.

Rehearsals for *Richard III* began in January 1972. Hands worked with his regular collaborators from the RSC, Farrah and the com-poser Guy Woolfenden. As well as Hirsch, the cast included Jacques Charon (Buckingham), Michel Duchaussoy (Clarence), Ludmila Mikaël[1] (Lady Anne), Catherine Samie (Elizabeth), and Denise Gence (Marguerite). Part of Hands's process was to gently steer the actors into the foreign territory of English Renaissance drama, where, in the same work, black humour and irony often co-existed with the classical concept of tragedy. 'In France,' Hands noted in his diary, 'You don't normally laugh during tragedies nor weep at comedies. Shakespeare on the other hand puts a fool into *King Lear*, Malvolio into a dungeon and Richard laughs his way to eleven murders. Equally, at the Comédie-Française "tragic" and "comic" actors tend to be divided. You are one or the other.'[2] Hands quite deliberately cast great comic actors in his *Richard III*. Although the actors arrived at the first rehearsal expecting to act in a tragedy, they were courteous and open to Hands's ideas, especially to the notion that there are no rules in Shakespeare – one scene is 'virtually Vaudeville', the next classical.

Hirsch came to Richard with no preconceived ideas: he was happy to work from the text and let the character emerge during the rehearsals. At the Comédie, unlike in England, Hands didn't need to spend time negotiating with star actors who had strong preconceived views and who wanted to discuss 'motivation'. How-ever, Hands found that the actors were too reverential, both towards the senior members in the cast and towards himself as the

---

[1] Ludmila Mikaël (b. 1947, Bois-Colombes, Hauts-de-Seine). CF j1967 s75 d86 sh87.

[2] Terry Hands, 'Hands Across the Sea', in *The Guardian* (23 April 1973), p.6.

director. They didn't ask any questions, or express any ideas: they simply reacted, dutifully and with great precision. In ensemble scenes, actors simply stopped acting when a senior player was giving a long speech, so as not to 'show up' the star. Hands needed many days to animate those scenes.

Hands discovered an irony. 'Where the English actor finds no difficulty in accepting the idea of variation in style [demanded by Shakespeare] he has trouble accomplishing it. [...] The Comédie Française actors on the other hand find difficulty in accepting the idea of variability but have all the training to accomplish it.' Within days Hirsch had mastered this style, switching from 'laughing clown to pathetic clown by an inflexion', and where Hirsch led the others followed.

At the Comédie-Française at this time, there were no dedicated rehearsal rooms. The first weeks of rehearsal took place in the red plush grandeur of the *foyer du public*, the last weeks on the stage. Hands found it difficult to rehearse in the foyer, where it was not possible to mark out the stage nor to create the world of the play and where his eyes were constantly drawn to the marble busts of Molière and Voltaire, to the chandeliers and to the ancient arm-chair used by Molière's troupe. 'Le Théâtre-Français n'est pas un théâtre comme less autres,' wrote Dumas fils during the Belle Époque. 'Quand on y apporte un manuscript, il y a les bustes qui vous regardent.' When rehearsals transferred to the stage, the union threatened to call the stage-hands out on strike. Dux called a general assembly of all staff. Hands, excluded, observed this gathering of hundreds of people in the auditorium of the Salle Richelieu:

It is an extraordinary sight. The *Richard* cast in costume scattered amongst the blue-overalled stage-hands and electricians, wardrobe staff, administrators, wig-makers, scene builders, prop men, prompters, stage managers and dressers. The full staff of a great and famous theatre. And to the sentimental observer it suddenly is a great theatre. Muddled, illogical but rooted in traditions of dedication to a common cause. A strange world of charade, perhaps, and illusion maintained with a kind of dogged self-sacrifice and madness. Many speak. The strike is called off. We are called back. Not as director, designer, composer so much as employees of the troupe, hired to help them with what they have decided, their play.[1]

Dux's faith in Hands was rewarded. The production, which opened on 29 March, was a great success – the ovation at its end lasted for many minutes and the critical response was enthusiastic. *Le Monde*, prone to unfairly dismissing the Comédie as a heritage house, saw the production as a landmark, a work that revealed that the Comédie could confound expectations by being alive and modern. The production was an 'eloquent rehabilitation of the great repertoire and one of the most imposing Shakespearian stagings of the decade'.[2] Hands's *Richard III* won the Syndicat de la critique's grand prix for best production of the year, the most prestigious theatre award of the time. That summer, Dux took the show to Avignon, the troupe's debut at the festival, and in 1973 to the RSC's Aldwych Theatre in London. Reviewing the London performances, Michael Billington commented that 'the company that brings us this hurtling, spring-heeled, voluptuously theatrical *Richard III* is barely recognisable as the same troupe that last week picked its way daintily through Molière'. Alongside the *mise en scène*, Billington particularly admired the playing of Robert Hirsch:

> What gives the production its blazing vitality is Robert Hirsch's bustling, sweat-stained, chalk-faced Richard. In essence Hirsch follows the traditional, Olivier-influenced reading of Richard the satanic joker and consummate role-player; but he adds his own inimitable brush-strokes. [...] [He has] an exuberant athleticism (at Baynards Castle he exultantly leaps from the parapet on to Buckingham's back) and a coiled-spring rage that constantly bursts through the jocular façade (the young Duke of York, clambering on to his back, finds himself whirled round like a teetotum and flung to the floor). Hirsch begins as the smiler with half a dozen knives under his cloak; and he ends as a frothing, cornered paranoid.[3]

---

[1] 'Hands Across the Sea', in *The Guardian* (23 April 1973), p.6.

[2] *Le Monde* (31 March 1972).

[3] Michael Billington, 'Richard III at the Aldwych', in *The Guardian* (24 April 1973), p.12.

Hands, appointed to the unique position of Consultant Director, would, for the rest of the decade, divide his time between the RSC and the Comédie-Française. In 1974, he directed Ludmila Mikaël as Marina in Shakespeare's *Périclès prince de Tyr*, the play's debut at the Comédie. Ludmila Mikaël had joined the Comédie at the age of twenty in 1967, making her debut as Elvire in Molière's *Dom Juan* and quickly demonstrating a darker side to her playing as the queen in Hugo's *Ruy Blas* (1968). She excelled in the work of Claudel – Lumîr in *Le Pain dur* (1970) – and Montherland – Mariana in *Le Maître de Santiago* (1972) and Sister Gabrielle in *Port-Royal* (Meyer, 1973).

Périclès called upon most members of the troupe. Shakespeare's sprawling romance, with its abrupt changes of mood and, in Hands's staging, episodes of music and dance, must have taken many of the actors out of their comfort-zones. The ensemble included François Beaulieu[1] in the title role and Michel Aumont[2] as Gower. Since joining the troupe from the Conservatoire in 1968, Beaulieu had played roles in plays by Corneille, Racine, Marivaux, Molière and Montherlant and was admired for his verse-speaking and versatility. He first worked for Hands as Richmond in *Richard III*. Aumont, who had played the title role in *Richard III* for Hands at Avignon, was breaking free from the character parts that had been his forte since he was a young man (he joined the troupe in 1956). An actor of remarkable range and subtlety, his performance as Harpagon in *L'Avare*, directed by his friend and fellow actor Jean-Paul Roussillon,[3] was considered by many to be definitive (1969). He would go on to play Amalric, to Mikaël's Ysé, in Claudel's *Partage de Midi* (1975), Puntila in Brecht's *Maître Puntila et son valet Matti* (1976), Berenger in Ionesco's *Le Roi se meurt* (Odéon, 1975), Vladimir to Roussillon's Estragon in Beckett's *En attendant Godot*, revived by its original director Roger Blin (Odéon, 1978), Malvolio in *Twelfth Night* (Hands, 1980) and Trigorin in Chekhov's *The Seagull* (1980).

[1] François Beaulieu (b. 1943). CF j1968 s74.
[2] Michel Aumont (1936-2019, b. Paris). CF j1956 s65 d93.
[3] Jean-Paul Roussillon (1931-2009, b. Paris). CF j1950 s60 d82.

Hands and Mikaël married in 1974 and named their daughter, born in 1975, Marina. In 1975, Mikaël was granted permission by the Comédie to join the RSC to play Katherine in Hands's production of *Henry V* at Stratford. In 1976, Hands returned to the Comédie to stage *Twelfth Night* (*La Nuits des rois*) at the Odéon. The designer was the RSC's John Napier. Rather like Copeau in 1914, Hands saw the play as a chamber work that required minimal design. He presented the actors on an empty stage decorated with a few bare trees to represent the melancholy of winter, and evoked mood with light. Dissatisfied with the Odéon's lighting rig, he brought extra projectors over from London. Mikaël starred as Viola alongside Geneviève Casile as Olivia and Beaulieu as Orsino.

Hands began rehearsals with a French translation, by Curtis, that used the alexandrine. This attempt to see if Shakespeare's lyricism would work in the verse norm of the French language failed. Only after Hands asked Curtis to change the text into iambics did the play come alive in rehearsals. Even then, Hands discovered that emotions in Shakespeare's text that were typically English, such as wryness and ruefulness, emotions that allowed, in Hands's phrase, an 'ambiguity of response',[1] were not translatable into French. 'If you were Viola,' he wrote, 'you couldn't do a rueful grin as you made yet another mistake.'[2] Hands worked to introduce these emotions into the playing. 'By building up the passionate, vibrant, secure, sure way that the French have of playing, it began to work.'[3] The scenes between Viola and Orsino and Viola and Olivia came alive in French, moving the centre of the work away from the social comedy of the Sir Toby and Malvolio scenes (exceptionally well played by Jacques Eyser and Pierre Dux) into a comedy of heartache and desire – a comedy in which the French concept of *passion* (the madness of love) was the central theme.

During rehearsals, as the actor playing Feste, Dominique Rozan, spoke, in French, the line 'For what says Quinapalus?' (act 1, scene

---

[1] Bill Alexander, John Barton, John Caird, Terry Hands (ed. Michael Billington), *RSC Directors' Shakespeare: Approaches to Twelfth Night* (London: Nick Hern Books, 1990), p.105.

[2] *RSC Directors' Shakespeare: Approaches to Twelfth Night*, p.105.

[3] *RSC Directors' Shakespeare: Approaches to Twelfth Night*, p.105.

5), Hands discovered a convincing possible meaning of this obscure name, for Rozan naturally spoke the word as the phrase 'Qui n'a plus lu' – 'Who has not read'.[1] This could suggest that Shakespeare's knowledge of French was deeper than is usually thought.

Hands cast the emerging star Francis Huster[2] as Sebastien. Huster, who had joined the troupe in 1971, was made a sociétaire in 1977. *La Nuits des rois* won Hands a second grand prix.

Huster next played the title role in a production of Musset's *Lorenzaccio* directed by Franco Zeffirelli, followed by Don Rodrigue in Hands's version of Corneille's *Le Cid*. Zeffirelli's operatic production opened the restored Salle Richelieu and was arguably the most newsworthy event of the Dux era. Ingmar Bergman declined an invitation from Dux because he didn't believe his French was good enough. In 1978 the Italian master Giorgio Strehler arrived from Milan to stage Goldoni's *La Trilogie de la villégiature* at the Odéon, and Hands directed Beaulieu as Thomas Becket in T.S. Eliot's *Meurtre dans la cathédrale* at the Chaillot. Strehler's cast included Beaulieu, Dux, Catherine Hiegel,[3] Ludmila Mikaël and Françoise Seigner.

Hands's success in Paris opened up the prospect of further links being made between the English and French theatre communities, with both benefiting. Dux, who had fond memories of the reception he had received when he had brought the Comédie to London in 1946, was eager to try. A kind of summit meeting between the leaders of both country's national theatres was even held in London, but without achieving a positive outcome:

> When the late Lady Hartwell brought together on the South
> Bank in 1976 the leaders of the British and French subsidised

---

[1] See *RSC Directors' Shakespeare: Approaches to Twelfth Night*, p.123. Hands wrote to the editor of the *New Arden Shakespeare*, T.W. Craik, but Craik rejected the idea. The editors of the RSC *Shakespeare Complete Works*, Jonathan Bate and Eric Rasmussen, published in 2007, do acknowledge the idea in their explanatory notes: 'Quinapalus: an invented authority perhaps playing on the French *qui n'a plus lu*.'

[2] Francis Huster (b. Neuilly, Hauts-de-Seine, 1947). CF j1971 s77 d82.

[3] Catherine Hiegel (b. 1946, Montreuil, Seine-Saint-Denis). CF j1969 s76 d2009 sh10.

theatres, the two sides – having donned their headphones for a simultaneous translation – stared at each other across a long table in mutual bemusement. What could possibly come of it? Pierre Dux as head of the Comédie-Française led the French party of actors, actresses, playwrights and producers; and the British had Albert Finney and a matching bunch of other players, writers and directors with the bilingual Terry Hands in the chair. The French were voluble, the British almost mute. Never was the gap between the London and Paris stages made to seem wider. And everyone except Dux was disappointed. He had seen it all before. He knew that the differences in theatrical thought, word and deed between London and Paris ran so deep that the only hope of better appreciating each other's work lay with the individual – a producer like the late Peter Daubeny; visiting critics with some of the language; directors like Hands and actors like Hands's then wife, Ludmila Mikaël of the Comédie-Française, who acted the Princess in *Henry V* at Stratford with charming authority.[1]

Antoine Vitez's arrival at the Comédie in 1975 challenged the troupe's more conservative patrons. Radical in his ideas and his politics (he was an active member of the Communist party), Vitez had made his name as a teacher and as the founding director of the Théâtre des Quartiers d'Ivry. Dux took a risk in bringing Vitez to the Comédie, but it paid off: Vitez was a theatre artist first and foremost; he had a deep understanding of acting and stagecraft and the ability to inspire others. For his debut he directed Claudel's *Partage de Midi*. He took from Claudel's text the idea that even flawed men and women can be touched by grace. The production, created during the closure of the Salle Richelieu, opened at the Marigny Theatre to widespread acclaim. Visually beautiful, with an uncluttered design by Yannis Kokkos that placed the action before a blue cyclorama, and elements inspired by Japanese theatre, Vitez's dreamlike production was a departure for the Comédie.

Dux also invited Jean-Louis Barrault, who returned briefly to his former home to direct *Le Bourgeois gentilhomme* (1972), Robert Hossein, Georges Wilson, Jean Vilar, and Jacques Rosner. A young

[1] Adam Benedick, 'Obituary: Pierre Dux', in *The Independent* (28 December 1990), p.19.

pensionnaire of only seventeen played Lucile in Barrault's *Bourgeois gentilhomme*. This was Isabelle Adjani, a student of Hossein's from the Théâtre Populaire de Reims. In 1973, Adjani's youth and precocious talent made her a newsworthy Agnès to Dux's Arnolphe in *L'École des femmes*. As Marie-Françoise in *Port-Royal*, Adela in Garcia Lorca's *La Maison de Bernarda* and the title role in Giraudoux's *Ondine*, Adjani was so candid it was as if she was simply being herself. Not since Annie Girardot and Jeanne Moreau during the 1950s had a new actress at the Comédie-Française made such an impression. Her career at the Comédie ended abruptly when François Truffaut offered her the lead in his film *L'Histoire d'Adèle H*. The outstanding young actor of this period was Richard Berry. Berry joined the Comédie on graduating from the Conservatoire in 1973. Dux was too slow in making Berry a sociétaire, so he left in 1980, having delivered fine performances as Dubois in Marivaux's *Les Fausses confidences* (1977), Figaro in *Le Barbier de Séville* (1979) and Jon in Antoine Vitez's production of René Kalisky's *Dave au bord de mer* (1979). Other contemporary plays programmed by Dux included Guy Foissy's *Cœur à deux* (1972), Louis Calaferte's *Chez les Titch* (1973) and *Trafic* and *Mo* (1976), and Jacques Sternberg's *C'est la guerre M. Gruber* (1973), all of them directed by Jean-Pierre Miquel at the Odéon. In 1975 the troupe performed a rare American play, Eugene O'Neill's *Une Lune pour les desherites* (*A Moon for the Misbegotten*) in a production by Jacques Rosner.

At the end of the 1970s, Dux surprised many by advocating the Comédie's participation in the grand scheme to rejuvenate the Les Halles quarter. Dux believed that if the Comédie was to continue to modernise it needed to move into a modern complex that would provide new theatres and state of the art facilities. However, Dux's time in charge was about to end. He had served for nine years, three longer than the government wanted. His sudden dismissal in 1979 ended an era of innovation and high achievement.

4   Jacques Toja

Dux was succeeded by another veteran sociétaire, Jacques Toja.[1] Toja, who had been with the troupe since the early 1950s, was admired for the formal elegance of his playing in work that ranged from Molière to Pirandello.

If Toja was a conservative choice, he was not a reactionary. He strove to continue Dux's work: 'The Comédie-Française must be prepared to take risks. We must collaborate with others. The guiding idea is for the troupe to be comfortable in all styles, to be skilled at playing Molière but also Ionesco, Racine and Beckett.'[2]

Toja's short time in charge, brought to an end by Mitterrand's new socialist government, is best viewed as a coda to the Dux years.

[1] Jacques Toja (1929-1996, b. Nice). CF j1953 s60 AG 79-83.
[2] Quoted (in French) in *La Grande histoire de la Comédie-Française*, p.245.

20. *Dom Juan* by Molière, Polish tour, 2004. Jacques Lassalle (mise en scène). Production created in 1993, revived 2002-04. L-R: Odile Grosset-Grange (Mathurine), Andrzej Seweryn (Dom Juan), Emmanuelle Wion (Charlotte). Photograph by Mariusz Grzelak.

12

The Turn of the Millennium

1983-2001

21. *Les Fourberies de Scapin* by Molière, RSC Barbican, 2000. Production created at the Richelieu in 1997. Jean-Louis Benoit (mise en scène), Alain Chambon (décor and costumes), Alain Banville (lighting). L-R: Nicolas Lormeau (Léandre), Christian Blanc (Argante), Gérard Giroudon (Scapin). Photograph by Geraint Lewis.

1 Vitez and Lassalle

President Mitterrand's Minister of Culture, Jack Lang, wanted to shake things up. As tended to happen when there was a significant change in power, the new ruling class viewed the Comédie-Française as a branch of the previous regime. This had last happened when De Gaulle returned to power in 1959. Malraux had taken the Odéon away from the Comédie. It was a way of indicating that the government thought the troupe had too great an advantage over other theatres. Lang didn't go that far, but he did decide that the Odéon would be shared between the Comédie and the Théâtre de l'Europe project under Giorgio Strehler. Mitterrand was a leader who believed in culture as a continuation of politics by other means, as his *grands projets* would demonstrate. Lang was a high-profile minister, close to Mitterrand, who oversaw a budget for the arts (1% of France's state budget) that was the envy of his harassed, low-profile no-money counterpart in Britain. Lang, though, didn't give extra money to the Comédie-Française and the other national theatres: instead, a significant sum was allocated to new cultural organisations throughout France.

Lang ended the recent practice of selecting the troupe's director from within its society of actors. Escande and Dux had both been outward-looking, but Lang wasn't convinced, believing that, without change, the Comédie would remain the 'old museum she has become'. His verdict, while being unfair to Dux, was not wrong in principle. Lang sought someone 'young and dynamic' who would give the Comédie a 'new face'.[1] The flaw was this: if the sociétaires

---

[1] Quoted (in French) in *La Grande histoire de la Comédie-Française*, p.249.

didn't support the choice, success was unlikely.

Dux had hoped that Terry Hands would succeed him, but the appointment of a foreigner was too great a step. Finding a young director of the right stature, who would be willing to take on the burden of running France's pre-eminent theatre, a theatre that came with so much perceived baggage, and who would be supported by the troupe, was a challenge. The obvious candidate was Patrice Chéreau. Chéreau was running his own troupe at Nanterre. If he was asked to take on the Comédie-Française, he turned the offer down. The director appointed was his friend and contemporary Jean-Pierre Vincent, director of the Théâtre national de Strasbourg.

Vincent would struggle to produce work that reached the heights achieved by Dux. Nearly all of his ideas backfired. He challenged the French style of classical acting without taking the actors with him. A production of Genet's *Le Balcon* failed badly, and a new version of Racine's *Bérénice*, staged in the German style by Klaus-Michaël Grüber, left some of the players in tears. Vincent attempted to transform the Comédie-Française into an avant-garde theatre at too great a speed. The Dux era had shown that the actors would embrace radicalism and accommodate the ideas of leading young directors if the process was managed with skill and sensitivity by the Administrator. Vincent didn't seek the renewal of his contract at the end of his three-year term in 1986.

Lang's new policy had failed at the first attempt. Few people expected Lang to abandon the policy, but he did. To succeed Vincent he appointed a sociétaire, Jean Le Poulain,[1] a fine comic actor and a perceptive, if traditionally-minded, director. Le Poulain programmed a season of classics. Only a production of Shakespeare's *A Midsummer Night's Dream*, by Jorge Lavelli, was admired. Le Poulain's problems were exacerbated when the technicians went out on strike. In March 1988, he died suddenly of a heart attack. The troupe's most senior member Claude Winter took temporary charge until the government secured the appointment of Antoine Vitez. Vitez was running the Chaillot at the time.

[1] Jean Le Poulain (1924-1988, b. Marseille). CF j1978 s80 AG 86-88.

Vitez had a history at the Comédie, having directed important productions during the Dux era, but he had never been a member of the acting troupe. It was an appointment that had the chance of working for all parties – the government, the troupe and Vitez himself. Vitez was a major artist, a radical, but had shown that he could adapt and work well with the members of the Comédie. Vitez's first season coincided with the bicentenary of the beginning of the French Revolution. To honour the occasion, Vitez mounted the three Figaro plays of Beaumarchais, directing *Le Mariage de Figaro* himself. It was a sign that Vitez would bring to the Comédie the same ethos that had characterised his work at the Ivry and the Chaillot: the placing of theatre texts within the context of their ideas; finding contemporary relevance; and aspiring to make the theatre accessible for all. With Richard Fontana,[1] Vitez's former student at the Conservatoire, leading a cast that also included Jean-Luc Bideau, Jean-François Rémi, Geneviève Casile, Catherine Samie, and the young Véronique Vella,[2] Vitez's production – designed by his regular collaborator, Kokkos – was nuanced, bittersweet and elegant. The 1988/89 season also included the Comédie's first production of Musset's *Lorenzaccio* since the 1970s. Georges Lavaudant, of the TNP, directed the pensionnaire Redjep Mitrovitsa[3] in the title role.

A new production of Shakespeare's *As You Like It* (*Comme il vous plaira*), by Lluis Pasqual, starred another of the troupe's most talented younger players, the pensionnaire Valérie Dréville, as Rosalind, with Michel Aumont as Jacques and Claude Mathieu[4] as Celia. Pasqual's visually beguiling staging was based on his creation for the Teatre Lliure in Barcelona in 1983. Jack Lang subsequently placed him in charge of the Odéon. Valérie Dréville had previously worked for Vitez at the Chaillot. In 1989/90, Vitez also programmed Sartre's *Huis-clos*, Strindberg's *Père*, and Aimé Cesaire's *La Tragédie du roi Christophe*. In March 1990, he staged Brecht's

[1] Richard Fontana (1952-1992, b. Paris). CF j1979 s83 d92.
[2] Véronique Vella (b. 1964, La Tronche, Isère). CF j1988 s89.
[3] Redjep Mitrovitsa (b. 1959). CF j1989 pensionnaire 89-96.
[4] Claude Mathieu (b. 1952, Mont-Saint-Aignan, Seine-Maritime). CF j1979 s1985.

La Vie de Galilée as a response to the fall of the Berlin wall. Roland Bertin played the title role. The production received great acclaim. One critic wrote: 'Tableau aprés tableau, les acteurs infusent tant d'intensité, d'incandescence à cette magnifique représentation.' Vitez died suddenly that April. Catherine Samie, who had succeeded Claude Winter as *doyenne*, was named the troupe's interim administrator.

Jacques Lassalle, Vincent's successor at the Théâtre national de Strasbourg, became Administrator of the Comédie at this difficult time. He remained true to his predecessor's programme. He recognised that the Comédie had gone through a process of modernisation in recent times, and that Vitez had started something important that needed to be continued. 'The Comédie-Française has changed enormously,' he told *Le Monde*, 'it is no longer an extraordinarily hierarchical house, whose great examples are Mounet-Sully or Sarah Bernhardt.'

> Gradually, its repertoire and practices have been infiltrated, irreversibly. This house has become a point of reference and the last theatre of art to have the means to fulfil its ambitions. A spirit of reform is needed, but not revolution. I've been appointed to lead a theatre that has seen, in ten years, six directors arrive in quick succession, sometimes in a state of mourning and always on an emergency basis. I was not chosen to contradict the decisions of Antoine Vitez. For the first time in a long time, the Comédie-Française will experience continuity, of both policies and aspirations. My primary mission is to serve the great classical French and foreign repertory. Then we must add, with caution, contemporary texts.[1]

In planning ahead, his goal was to internationalise the Comédie by inviting foreign directors to the Salle Richelieu. Lassalle went further than Dux in this respect. He issued many invitations and gave his guest directors a free hand to realise their visions, and he looked mostly east rather than west. Artists who came included Youssef Chahine from Egypt, Anatoli Vassiliev from Russia, Lucian

[1] 'Entretien avec Jacques Lassalle', in *Le Monde* (21 March 1991).

Pintilié from Romania, and Otomar Krejča and Jiri Menzel from the Czech Republic. Lassalle's compelling and eclectic programming included Camus's *Caligula*, Tennessee Williams's *La Nuit de l'iguane*, Italo Svevo's *Un mari*, Sophocles's *Antigone* (starring Muriel Mayette), and Racine's *Iphigénie* (starring Valérie Dréville).

In Lassalle's first season, 1990/91, the Italian master Dario Fo directed Molière's rarely performed *Le Médecin malgré lui* and *Le Médecin volant* in a single evening. Lassalle ran the show in repertory with his own staging of Marivaux's *La Fausse suivante*. Fo combined vivaciously performed slapstick with a compelling visual poetry. The players were Richard Fontana, Catherine Hiegel, Christian Blanc, Marcel Bozonnet, Isabelle Gardien, Philippe Torreton and a young actress who had just joined the Comédie – Céline Samie[1] (the daughter of Catherine Samie). Lassalle's sombre, enigmatic Marivaux starred Fontana, Muriel Mayette, Geneviève Casile and Gérard Giroudon.[2] Together, these productions showcased the troupe's versatility and sense of adventure. Michael Billington, writing in *The Guardian*, provided a snapshot of Lassalle's Comédie-Française following a four-day visit to the French capital:

> I was struck, as so often, by the variety available in Paris – not least at the Comédie-Française. The popular myth is that it's an ossified institution steeped in tradition – indeed Adrian Noble said as much on British television two weeks ago. But judging by the productions of Marivaux and Molière I saw, it revitalises the classic repertory just as assiduously as the RSC. I was very taken by Marivaux's *La Fausse suivante* (1724), marvellously directed by the Comédie's current administrator, Jacques Lassalle. [...] Lassalle offers a drastic re-evaluation of Marivaux. Instead of a dandified romp we get a sour, melancholic pastoral. A rustic wedding-party, straight out of Vigo's *L'Atalante*, degenerates into rampant promiscuity. A menacing Harlequin, rumbling the Chevalier's disguise, threatens her with rape. Darkly impressive in Marivaux, the company lets its hair down in a double-bill of Molière's *Le Médecin malgré lui* and *Le Médecin volant*. Both are

---

[1] Céline Samie. CF j1991 s2004 d16.
[2] Gérard Giroudon (b. 1949). CF j1974 s81 d2016 sh17.

directed by Dario Fo as vulgar, vaudevillian, over-the-top farce. Ladders are swung over the audience's heads, dummy-bodies are hurled from boxes, and wine passed off as urine is drunk from piss-pots. I have seen nothing like it since the Crazy Gang in their heyday, with Molière's satire on quack-medicine turned into a heady, gag-filled tonic.[1]

Lassalle continued his re-evaluation of Molière by producing new versions of *Le Malade imaginaire* (Gildas Bourdet directed Jean-Luc Bideau), *George Dandin* and *La Comtesse d'Escarbagnas* (Lassalle directed Alain Pralon, Muriel Mayette and François Beaulieu), and *Dom Juan*. This last, which Lassalle opened at the 1993 Avignon Festival, featured in the title role an actor new to the Comédie, the Polish star Andrzej Seweryn,[2] who had made his name in the films of Andrzej Wajda. Seweryn had settled in Paris after the suppression of Solidarity in 1981. During the 1980s he worked for Patrice Chéreau (*Peer Gynt*), Peter Brook (*Le Mahabharata*), Deborah Warner (*La Maison de poupée*) and Antoine Vitez (*L'Échange* by Claudel), and reached a large audience in France playing Robespierre in *La Révolution française* (1989). His entry into the Comédie in 1993 was an event. Also in the *Dom Juan* ensemble were Catherine Sauval[3] (Charlotte), Isabelle Gardien (Mathurine), Jeanne Balibar[4] (Elvire) and Éric Ruf[5] (Dom Carlos). Ruf and Balibar, fresh from the Conservatoire, were making their debuts with the troupe.

One of the highpoints of Lassalle's tenure was undoubtedly Vassiliev's languorous, meticulously designed and choreographed production of Mikhaïl Lermontov's verse drama *Le Bal masqué*, although some spectators found its modernist aesthetic alienating (1992). This landmark of Russian romanticism was written in 1835, six years before its author's death in a duel. Lermontov was

---

[1] Michael Billington, 'Michael Billington on the lessons we can learn from the richness of French theatre', in *The Guardian* (31 December 1991).

[2] Andrzej Seweryn (b. 1946, Heilbronn, Germany). CF j1993 s95 d2012 sh13.

[3] Catherine Sauval (b. 1962, Amiens, Somme). CF j1984 s90 d2015.

[4] Jeanne Balibar (b. Paris, 1968). CF j1993 pensionnaire 93-97.

[5] Éric Ruf (b. 1969, Belfort, Territoire de Belfort). CF j1993 s98 AG 14-.

inspired by the Shakespeare of *Othello*, by Hugo, Byron and Lamartine. Valérie Dréville played the innocent Nina, murdered by
her jealous husband, Arbénine, played by Jean-Luc Boutté, during
a masked ball. Richard Fontana, who played Kazarine, died not
long after the premiere in June 1992. The star of Vitez's *Mariage
de Figaro* and *Hamlet* (at the Chaillot) was only forty-one.

In 1993, the Comédie was assigned the renovated Théâtre du
Vieux-Colombier, Jacques Copeau's legendary pre-war theatre in
Saint-Germain. The Vieux-Colombier was about to be demolished
when Lang stepped in and issued the funds for its restoration. Las-
salle inaugurated the reborn theatre in April 1993 by staging
Nathalie Sarraute's *Elle est là* and *Le Silence*.

When the socialists lost control of the National Assembly in
1993, the conservative politician Jacques Toubon replaced Lang at
the Ministry of Culture. By the time Lassalle's dark and gripping
interpretation of *Dom Juan* opened in Avignon its director knew
that Toubon did not intend to grant him a second term as Administrator. It was a decision driven by party politics and not by artistic
sense. Not since Dux had an Administrator been in post long
enough to complete an artistic project. The directorships of Vitez
and Lassalle, despite their brevity, were among the most important
in the troupe's history.

2   Jean-Pierre Miquel

In 1993, Pierre Dux's colleague from the 1970s, Jean-Pierre Miquel, returned to the Comédie as Administrator. For the previous
ten years he had been the director of the Conservatoire. Miquel
shared with his predecessors the desire to make the Comédie as
open and as egalitarian as possible. Miquel, who began work in
September 1993, inherited the 1993/94 season from Lassalle. Re-
grettably, Valérie Dréville left the troupe.

Once again, the Salle Richelieu, that most temperamental of
buildings, required essential repairs. Miquel closed the théâtre and

the actors left Paris to tour the provinces. On their return to the capital, they performed Kleist's *Le Prince de Hombourg* at the Mogador and Hugo's *Lucrèce Borgia* at the Opéra-Comique. Jean-Luc Boutté directed Christine Fersen[1] in the title role. In January 1995, they returned home with a new production of Feydeau's *Occupe-toi d'Amélie*. The director was a surprise – Roger Planchon, making his debut with the company.

Miquel successfully pressed the government to change some of the regulations. For the first time, the Comédie-Française was allowed to receive private money in line with other public establishments. The conditions of the General Administrator's contract were changed. The length of contract was now five years, renewable for further terms of three years. This gave the Administrator time to formulate and see through an artistic project. Miquel would serve for eight years, during which the Comédie-Française acquired a third theatre, the new Studio-Théâtre at the Louvre.

The troupe of the Comédie-Française was in good health at the start of the 1990s and getting stronger. Some of the actors who came through under either Lassalle or Miquel, committing themselves to become sociétaires, are still with the troupe today: Éric Ruf, Sylvia Bergé, Cécile Brune, Éric Génovèse, Anne Kessler, Alain Lenglet, Denis Podalydès, Bruno Raffaelli, Julie Sicard, Florence Viala, Coraly Zahonero, Alexandre Pavloff, Guillaume Gallienne, Françoise Gillard, Clotilde de Bayser, Jérôme Pouly, and Laurent Stocker.

During his first months in office, Miquel formed a working group and conducted a thorough investigation of the Comédie's production history during the previous twenty-five years, discovering that only fifteen plays of the French classical repertoire had been performed with any regularity. This was especially the case with Racine – *Iphigénie*, *Britannicus* and *Bérénice* had only been staged occasionally, and *Phèdre*, *Bajazet*, *La Thébaïde*, *Mithridate*, *Athalie* and *Alexandre* hadn't been performed at all. Of the modern period, only the same one or two plays by Claudel, Montherlant, Ionesco

[1] Christine Fersen (1944-2008, b. Paris). CF j1965 s76.

and Beckett had made a mark at the Comédie. Miquel was determined to fill the gaps, and to do so by mounting cycles of connected work across two or more seasons, his chief innovation. He began with the Romantics, showing the links that connected French and German dramatic literature. Together with *Le Prince de Hombourg* and *Lucrèce Borgia*, Miquel produced *Hamlet* and Schiller's *Intrigue et amour*, followed by Lessing's *Nathan le sage* and Goethe's *Faust*, the last two directed by Alexander Lang. Alongside this exploration of romanticism, the troupe performed a Racine cycle, beginning in the 1994/95 season with the rarely performed plays *La Thébaïde*, directed by Yannis Kokkos, and *Bajazet*, directed by Miquel's former student Éric Vigner, and continuing in 1995/96 with Anne Delbée's *Phèdre* and Daniel Mesguich's *Mithridate* at the Vieux-Colombier. Kokkos's *La Thébaïde* was presented with striking simplicity, and featured remarkable performances from Anne Kessler[1] as Antigone and Catherine Samie as Jocaste, powerfully supported by Jean-Yves Dubois (Polynice), Michel Favory (Créon), and Alexandre Pavloff (Hémon). *Phèdre* was also powerfully acted, by Martine Chevallier[2] as Phèdre, François Beaulieu as Thésée, Éric Génovèse[3] as Hippolyte and Céline Samie as Aricie. *Mithridate* initiated Guillaume Gallienne's career at the Comédie. Having recently graduated from the Conservatoire, Gallienne[4] was working as an intern at the Vieux-Colombier when Mesguich cast him in the role of Arcas.

Miquel didn't add as many contemporary plays to the repertoire as he would have liked, but those that did make it to production were significant. Two works by Marguerite Duras, *Le Square* and *Le Shaga*, were directed by Christian Rist as a double-bill at the Vieux-Colombier in 1995. In January 1998, the Comédie staged Tom Stoppard's *Arcadia*, its first production of any work by this great playwright. Philippe Adrien directed the play at the Vieux-

---

[1] Anne Kessler (b. 1964). CF j1989 s94.

[2] Martine Chevallier (b. Gap, Hautes-Alpes). CF j1986 s88 d2018 sh19.

[3] Éric Génovèse (b. 1967, Nice). CF j1993 s98.

[4] Guillaume Gallienne (b. 1972, Neuilly-sur-Seine, Hauts-de-Seine). CF j1998 s2005.

Colombier. Françoise Gillard[1] and Jean-Pierre Michaël played Thomasina and Septimus, with Denis Podalydès as Valentin, Alain Pralon[2] as Noakes and Claire Vernet[3] as Lady Gray. The show did well enough for Miquel to transfer it to the Salle Richelieu during the following season, meaning that it entered the official repertoire. This was possible because, in 1995, Miquel had overturned, by statute, the decades-old regulation that prevented the Comédie from producing plays by living foreign authors (a rule designed to protect homegrown talent). Foreign plays still had to be considered important enough, and Stoppard was the first playwright to benefit. The critics, though, didn't understand or appreciate this masterpiece. In 2000, the Comédie staged Pinter's *The Homecoming* (*Le Retour*) in a production by Catherine Hiegel that was admired, and endorsed by Pinter himself. Muriel Mayette played Ruth, with Roland Bertin as Max and Bruno Putzulu as Lenny.

In 1998/99, Miquel launched a Russian cycle, consisting of Ivan Turgenev's *Un Mois à la campagne*, Chekhov's *La Cerisaie* (*The Cherry Orchard*) and Gogol's *Le Révizor* (*The Government Inspector*). Catherine Ferran, Florence Viala,[4] Nicolas Silberg and Thierry Hancisse[5] shone in Alain Françon's elegant staging of *The Cherry Orchard*, and Denis Podalydès[6] was remarkable as the government inspector, directed by Jean-Louis Benoit. Benoit was also responsible for acclaimed productions of Molière's *Les Fourberies de Scapin* in 1997 and *Le Bourgeois gentilhomme* in 2000. *Scapin* was notable for its darkness of tone, its recognition of the pain and anger that underpin much of Molière's art, and the virtuosic performances of Philippe Torreton[7] and subsequently Gérard Giroudon in the title role. The 'sack scene' was a masterpiece of spite and thuggery. When the show visited the RSC's Barbican Theatre, in 2000, with

---

[1] Françoise Gillard (b. 1973, Charleroi, Belgium). CF j1997 s2002.

[2] Alairen Pralon (b. 1939, Agen, Lot-et-Garonne). CF j1965 s72 d2005 sh06.

[3] Claire Vernet, née Chantal Pauline Françoise Andrée Versavaud (b. Paris, 1945). CF j1964 s74 d2001 sh02.

[4] Florence Viala. CF j1994 s2000.

[5] Thierry Hancisse (b. 1962, Namur, Belgium). CF j1986 s93.

[6] Denis Podalydès (b. 1963, Versailles). CF j1997 s2000.

[7] Philippe Torreton (b. Rouen, 1965). CF j1990 s94 d99.

Giroudon as Scapin, Michael Billington wrote: 'This scene becomes the comic centrepiece of Jean-Louis Benoit's wondrously cool, alert production. It has the cruelty of farce as the sack, containing the black-and-blue Géronte, goes swinging back and forth across the stage. But it also becomes about crime and punishment and a delight in role-playing.'[1]

Miquel ensured that the core repertoire was well served. His production of Marivaux's *Les Fausses confidences*, created in the same year as Benoit's *Scapin*, was chosen to spearhead the French season organised by the National Theatre and the Royal Shakespeare Company in London and Stratford in October 1997. It played in the National's Lyttelton Theatre. Benedict Nightingale, writing in *The Times*, admired an evening that

> combines Pinteresque subtlety and nuance with a wintry sophistication that chills the blood while tantalising the mind. [...] Marivaux wrote *Les Fausses confidences* in 1737, but the dark costumes and Satie-like piano chords of Jean-Pierre Miquel's production suggest an era nearer ours. Quite right, too, for you would have to look to Dickens, Balzac and their successors to find a piece in which money seems more contaminating to the spirit. The squashed, buckled, oddly humanoid tree at the back of the stage sums up much. After all, what is the first reason that Dorante gives to his lackey, Dubois, for becoming the widow Araminte's steward and trying to win her heart? Not the elegance, grace and low-voiced yearning Cecile Brune brings to the character. Indeed, he has never met her. It is her 50,000 livres a year that matters both to Laurent d'Olce's smooth young Dorante and to Gerard Giroudon's Dubois, a frighteningly cold, guarded creature who expects a share of the marital property in return for his Iago-like cunning. [...] Together, Dorante and Dubois work on Araminte's suppressed sensuality by suggesting to her that her new steward is a worthy man who is stifling a desperate love for her, and together they exploit chance and manipulate other people's follies to win her compassion. It is like watching a butterfly being so ruthlessly stalked that in the end she deliberately flies

---

[1] Michael Billington, 'Class Act', in *The Guardian* (10 June 2000).

into the net.[1]

The director of the National, Richard Eyre, did not care for the Comédie-Française or the production. On seeing the production in Paris he had written in his diary: 'I love going into that theatre, although I seldom like what I see there. I don't believe that in London the theatre has ever had the social cachet it has in Paris – an indelible part of the ritual of haut bourgeois life, like going to the opera in London. The show was wholly inert, as was the audience, but they didn't seem to mind.'[2]

Two plays by Shakespeare were performed during Miquel's time as Administrator – *Hamlet*, directed by Georges Lavaudant, in 1994, and *The Tempest*, directed by Daniel Mesguich, in 1998. The troupe hadn't staged *Hamlet* since 1942. Lavaudant used the translation by Yves Bonnefoy and cast Redjep Mitrovitsa in the title role. The superb ensemble included Jacques Sereys[3] as Polonius, Andrzej Seweryn as Claudius, Christine Fersen as Gertrude, Isabelle Gardien[4] as Ophelia, and Philippe Torreton as Laertes. The drama unfolded on a cavernous bare stage (the designer was Lavaudant's regular collaborator Jean-Pierre Vergier). Mitrovitsa's hair was cropped and dyed blonde, and he had a punk sensibility. The costumes were of period, heavy and restrictive, but the physicality of the acting, richly choreographed, and deliberately baroque, was unrestrained.

Administrators of the Comédie struggle to retain the loyalty of all members of the troupe, and Miquel was no different. The nature of the job requires decisions to be made that please some members and upset others. If an Administrator stays in post for long enough, the knives start to be sharpened. In January 1999, the sociétaire

---

[1] Benedict Nightingale, 'Chill comedy in this bleak French house', in *The Times* (2 October 1997).

[2] Richard Eyre, *National Service: Diary of a Decade* (London: Bloomsbury, 2003), p.366.

[3] Jacques Sereys (b. 1928, Saint-Maurice, Val-de-Marne). CF j1955 s59 d96 sh97.

[4] Isabelle Gardien. CF j1989 s95 d2010.

Philippe Torreton, who had won the best actor César for his performance in Bertrand Tavernier's *Capitaine Conan* in 1997,
resigned in the most public way possible, on air during a television
broadcast. 'The scheduling may look like artistic policy,' he said,

> but in fact it's all about doing favours for friends. The Comédie-
> Française? It's the Vatican. Just as in Rome, the company here
> has its pope who has total control and surrounds himself with
> cardinals, archbishops and Swiss guards.

It was felt by others, too, that Miquel worked with a clique. Torreton complained about the decision to stage Stoppard's *Arcadia*.
Miquel, under strain, gave a sharp response:

> As far as my choices are concerned, I would simply say that an
> artistic policy, by definition, can be challenged by anyone. The
> actors who criticise do not usually do so because of the nature of
> the plays but because they don't contain roles that they would
> like to play [or because the directors haven't cast them]. Philippe
> Torreton was very spoiled in this house. But he would have liked
> me to organise the seasons according to the roles he wanted to
> play.[1]

The episode went on to reveal the often cutthroat nature of theatrical life at this level. Miquel faced criticism in the newspapers,
the most damaging article being by Olivier Schmitt in *Le Monde*
(23 January 1999). In March, the Friends of the Comédie-Française were sent the annual newsletter, which included a defence of
Miquel and his policies by Philippe Adrien and a petition of support signed by over thirty directors who had worked at the
Comédie. Signatories included Jean Dautremay, Simon Eine,
Catherine Hiegel and Muriel Mayette (all members of the troupe),
plus Jean-Louis Benoit, Yannis Kokkos, Jorge Lavelli, Éric Vigner
and Jean-Pierre Vincent. A director who refused to sign the petition, Anne Delbée, went public. In an open letter published in *Le*

---

[1] Quoted (in French) in Brigitte Salino, 'Philippe Torreton et Jean-Luc
Bideau claquent la porte de la Comédie-Française', in *Le Monde* (23 January
1999).

Figaro, Anne Delbée wrote: 'Philippe Adrien's letter, far from enlightening us, is only a long, pious defence of the Administrator. Its content prevents me from associating myself with this approach. I had esteem for M. Jean-Pierre Miquel and I would have been with him if he had resigned or been sidelined for no reason. I do not dare to think that he was the accomplice of such a masquerade.'[1]

Then there was the political dimension. In 1998, when Miquel's contract came up for renewal, the Minister of Culture, Catherine Trautmann, came under pressure from President Chirac to appoint Francis Huster. She withstood the pressure and renewed Miquel's contract for three years, at the end of which he reached the age limit. A new minister, Catherine Tasca, considered applications from Andrzej Seweryn, Jean-Louis Benoit, Daniel Mesguich and Marcel Bozonnet.

Miquel could point to some notable achievements – the renovation of the Salle Richelieu, the opening of the Studio-Théâtre, and the modernisation of the statutes under which the troupe operated. He appointed talented new actors and added thirty plays to the official repertoire. On the debit sheet, it was felt by some that too many of the productions were below standard.

---

[1] Anne Delbée, 'La crise à la Comédie-Française: Les "suicidés" du Français', in *Le Figaro* (1 March 1999).

Previous double page:
22. *Tartuffe* by Molière, Richelieu, 2005. Marcel Bozonnet (mise en scène), Daniel Jeanneteau (décor), Renato Bianchi (costumes), Dominique Bruguière (lighting). Eric Génovèse (Tartuffe), Florence Viala (Elmire). Photograph by Raphael Gaillarde.

13

Towards the Present

2001-2014

23. *L'École des femmes* by Molière, Richelieu, 2011. Jacques Lassalle (mise en scène). Julie-Marie Parmentier (Agnès). Photograph by Raphael Gaillarde.

1   Marcel Bozonnet

Miquel's successor was the former sociétaire Marcel Bozonnet,[1] who had left the troupe in 1992 to take up the directorship of the Conservatoire. The directorship of the Conservatoire had become a stepping-stone to the top job at the Comédie.

It had become customary for a new Administrator of the Comédie to begin by expressing the importance of looking outwards, and Bozonnet was no different: 'We must develop a policy of exchange with the Piccolo of Milan, the Burgtheater of Vienna, the theatres of London, Norway, Ireland,' he told the press. 'Our children must have access to European culture.' Bozonnet revealed his commitment to new writing and the avant-garde, his desire to stage works by such writers as Bernard-Marie Koltès, Edward Bond, Olivier Py and Sarah Kane, but was careful to reassure the traditionalists: 'The Comédie-Française should be totally of its time, but I do not intend to destroy the repertoire or renounce the great classical legacy that I love.'

Bozonnet was inspired by the eras of Dux, Vitez, and Lassalle. He had strong ideas and the determination to take risks. His approach was cerebral and sometimes iconoclastic. One of Bozonnet's first decisions was to begin the 2001/02 season with a production of Shakespeare's *Merchant of Venice*. The director, Andrei Serban, appropriated Shakespeare's play and referenced the Holocaust. The production was controversial. Andrzej Seweryn played Shylock,

---

[1] Marcel Bozonnet (b. 1944, Semur-en-Auxois, Côte-d'Or). CF j1982 s86 d92 AG 2001-06.

with Clotilde de Bayser[1] as Portia and Michel Favory as Antonio.

The next show celebrated the bicentenary of Victor Hugo's birth – *Ruy Blas*, directed by Brigitte Jaques and starring Éric Ruf. As the queen, Bozonnet cast one of his recent students at the Conservatoire, Rachida Brakni, the young star of the recently released film *Chaos*. Media interest centred on Brakni's youth and Algerian heritage. Brakni received a Molière Award for her performance in *Ruy Blas*, but decided not to stay at the Comédie. In September 2002, Bozonnet mounted a production of Marguerite Duras's *Savannah Bay*, directed by Éric Vignet, at the Salle Richelieu. The production starred Catherine Samie and Catherine Hiegel. In October, he revived Jacques Lassalle's production of Molière's *Dom Juan*. Andrzej Seweryn returned to one of his finest roles, alongside Thierry Hancisse as Sganarelle, Éric Ruf as Dom Carlos, Nicolas Lormeau as Don Alonse, Jérôme Pouly as Pierrot, Françoise Gillard as Elvire, Florence Viala as Charlotte, and Emmanuelle Wion as Mathurine.

Bozonnet believed that familiar works should be reassessed. In 2002 he handed Molière's *Amphitryon* to Anatoli Vassiliev, who had a unique vision for the piece that Bozonnet knew his core audience would find provocative. Vassiliev essentially told the actors – 'I'm not interested in what you normally do'. The poetic setting of a tower in a desert and the white Japanese-inspired costumes, either amazed or alienated, depending on one's view. Placing this work by Molière, based as it is on a Greek myth, within a high concept was an experiment worth making, but Vassiliev's production raised more questions than answers. Bozonnet's interpretation of *Tartuffe* (2005) also challenged traditionalists, but it aimed to seduce them too. Daniel Jeanneteau's uncluttered setting of a sand-coloured courtyard overlooked by multiple windows was beautifully lit by Dominique Bruguière. The play was reinvigorated by Éric Génovèse's performance as a young and dangerous Tartuffe. His scenes with Florence Viala's Elmire were especially powerful.

Bozonnet's invitation, in 2004, to Robert Wilson to create a family show for the troupe based on the fables of La Fontaine proved to be inspired. This meeting of Wilson's visual aesthetic

[1] Clotilde de Bayser (b. 1963, Paris). CF j1997 s2004.

with La Fontaine's storytelling and the skill of the Comédie's actors produced a theatre work that would delight audiences at home and abroad. Wilson commissioned Michael Galasso to write the score and Kuno Schlegelmilch to design the animal masks that were such an important element of the show's charm. Nineteen of La Fontaine's fables were chosen. The actors created movements that matched the masks they were wearing. The *Fables de La Fontaine* was a genuine departure.

During the same season, there were new productions of Shakespeare's *Twelfth Night* (*La Nuit des rois*), directed by Andrzej Seweryn, and Corneille's *Le Menteur*, directed by Jean-Louis Benoit. Seweryn seemed to have Vassiliev in mind when he remarked: 'Why pretend to invent something. I want to be in the line of Copeau, Jouvet, Mnouchkine, Hands. We are their heirs. We have the right to reject the past, but, like it or not, we are created by the past.'[1] Benoit's visually beautiful, enigmatic *Le Menteur* (the setting and costumes were by his regular designer Alain Chambon) starred Denis Podalydès, Bruno Raffaelli, Isabelle Gardien, and the pensionnaire Elsa Lepoivre,[2] who, as Clarice, was performing one of her first major roles. In the Studio-Théâtre, Muriel Mayette directed a rare production of Shakespeare's *The Winter's Tale* (*Conte d'hiver*).

Bozonnet brought into the company Loïc Corbery and Clément Hervieu-Léger in 2005, and the young actress Marina Hands,[3] the daughter of Terry Hands and Ludmila Mikaël, in 2006. Marina Hands had already found success playing Aricie in *Phèdre* for Chéreau at the Odéon (2003): joining the Comédie-Française must have seemed like a matter of destiny. She made her debut playing the princess in Claudel's *Tête d'or*, directed by Anne Delbée, at the Vieux-Colombier. 2006 marked Catherine Samie's fiftieth anniversary as a member of the troupe: she retired as a sociétaire following a great final role – Winnie in Samuel Beckett's *Oh les beaux jours* at the Vieux-Colombier. She became a sociétaire honoraire.

[1] Quoted (in French) in *La Grande histoire de la Comédie-Française*, p.269.
[2] Elsa Lepoivre (b. 1972, Caen). CF j2003 s07.
[3] Marina Hands (b. 1975, Paris). CF j2006 pensionnaire 06-07 pensionnaire 2020.

In selecting contemporary work for performance at the Vieux-Colombier, Bozonnet looked for pieces that were little known and from the developing world. His interest in the avant-garde resulted in the premiere of Pascal Rambert's *Le Debut de l'A* in the Studio-Théâtre in 2005. Rambert directed the pensionnaires Alexandre Pavloff and Audrey Bonnet.[1] A superb revival by Podalydès of *Cyrano de Bergerac*, with Michel Vuillermoz[2] in the title role and Françoise Gillard as Roxanne, was the perfect piece to keep the faithful in the Salle Richelieu happy (2006). But Bozonnet's critics believed that there hadn't been enough of these evenings.

Bozonnet wasn't someone prepared to compromise his principles. When he learned that the Austrian author Peter Handke had attended and made a speech at the funeral of the former Serbian president Slobodan Milošević, who had died while on trial for crimes against humanity at the Hague, he withdrew a planned production of Handke's play *Voyage au pays sonore ou l'art de la question*. 'For my soul and conscience, it was impossible to welcome that person into my theatre,' Bozonnet said at a press conference to announce the 2006/07 season. 'For three weeks I have been plunged back into the horror of ethnic cleansing. I am not a muckraker, but I was scandalised by what Peter Handke said.'

Handke's compatriot Elfriede Jelinek expressed outrage on behalf of free speech. 'I am horrified that the Comédie-Française functions today like a censor,' she said in a statement. 'This is not censorship,' Bozonnet responded. 'It is one theatre director who has decided not to put on a play, but all the others can stage it. He is allowed a lot of freedom, so give me some too.'

Many intellectuals supported Bozonnet's stand, but it seems that the right-wing government of Dominique de Villepin was angered that he had used his position, and the Comédie, to make a political point that it didn't agree with. The Minister of Culture, Renaud Donnedieu de Vabres, invited Handke to a private meeting in his office, then denied Bozonnet the second term as Administrator that he had previously been promised. Donnedieu de Vabres stated,

---

[1] Audrey Bonnet (b. 1975). CF j2003 pensionnaire 03-06.
[2] Michel Vuillermoz (b. 1962, Orléans). CF j2003 s07.

without any conviction, that the Handke affair wasn't the reason, implying that he had discovered that the actors were unhappy with their Administrator. Leading members of the troupe refuted this claim, outraged that the minister was trying to make them the scapegoats. Anne Kessler, Éric Génovèse, Denis Podalydès and Éric Ruf expressed their dismay publicly, Podalydès and Ruf in a long joint letter to *Le Monde* which began with an emphatic statement of support for Bozonnet: 'After some days of reflection and consultation, the non-renewal of Marcel Bozonnet's contract as Administrator of the Comédie-Française seems to us – that is, to certain members of the troupe – inexplicable and unjustified.' The letter continued:

> We intend here not to make any judgment on the appointment of our colleague Muriel Mayette, whom we know to be capable of such a responsibility, other than to say that we do not know her vision for the troupe since she was caught off guard by her appointment and has not had the time to prepare a plan. [...] Would the departure of Marcel Bozonnet have been desired by the troupe? The question did not arise. As the renewal of his contract seemed to have been decided, no internal debate was held on this subject. In the spring, some of the actors met the Minister of Culture, at his invitation. [...] It was made clear that the current Administrator – he had received assurances – would continue in post until 2009, when he would reach the age limit set by the regulations. Because the three seasons to come have been partly planned, [...] nothing could induce a change of director at this point. Is this the Peter Handke affair? The controversy – interesting, dignified and philosophical when most controversies are scabrous and reflect a mediocre social debate – did not question the intrinsic qualities of the Administrator, and in no way compromised the cohesion of the troupe since the Administrator had the right to make his choice (a choice endorsed by a majority of the actors) and did not deserve to be sanctioned. Is it to camouflage the announcement of a budget cut? A circular said this year that 5% of the subsidy would be frozen. [...] Marcel Bozonnet has brought great masters of the national and international stage [to the Comédie]. Some shows were expensive. To

repeat the famous distinction of Antoine Vitez, we are in a 'théâ-tre-édifice', where the artistic mission, necessarily ambitious, cannot be achieved at a discount […]. Our budgets have re-mained balanced, and no bankruptcy is to be feared. Is it the result of a last-minute political intrigue, of which Marcel Bozon-net is the victim? We do not know. The worst thing would be to compare Muriel point by point with her predecessor. We refuse to consider her appointment as a negation, let alone a condem-nation, of Marcel's record. There were, of course, disagreements between them, but no more so than between others, and always over matters of artistic policy or the requirements of the theatre.

The wider theatre community was deeply concerned by a deci-sion that disregarded their views and which was both unjust and unwise given Bozonnet's achievements. The influential theatre critic, Georges Banu offered a summation: 'Marcel Bozonnet took the Comédie-Française to a place of first importance in the inter-national theatre. He invited great directors such as Robert Wilson, and added the work of writers such as Novarina to the repertoire.'[1]

According to *The Times*, when Muriel Mayette was asked about the controversy she said: 'Marcel Bozonnet had the right to his own opinion and the right not to want to shake Handke's hand. But his gesture was too impulsive.'[2] In August 2006, Donnedieu de Vabres formally placed her in charge of the Comédie – she was the first woman to lead a national theatre in France.

2   Muriel Mayette

Muriel Mayette joined the Comédie-Française at the age of twenty in 1985. Alongside her distinguished career as an actress, she taught at the Conservatoire. She hadn't planned to become the troupe's

[1] Quoted (in French) in Didier Mereuze, 'Nomination surprise de Muriel Mayette à la tête de la Comédie-Française', *La Croix* (21 July 2006), p.21.
[2] See *The Times* (29 July 2006), p.50.

Administrator, but when it came her way she embraced the opportunity. She had the resolve to deal with the difficult circumstances of her appointment.

She made the familiar statements about wanting the Comédie-Française to be 'more in the world', which for her partly meant international tours, but also announced that she wanted to increase the number of actors from the current sixty players. Over the years, the size of the troupe had been whittled down from the eighty players that Mayette, and others, believed to be the optimal number to fulfil the Comédie's role. She would have time to formulate her ideas because the programme for the upcoming season had been planned by her predecessor.

Interviewed by *Le Monde*, at the beginning of September, Muriel Mayette defended her position robustly. She denied that she had been appointed as a result of the Handke affair or because of her gender. While expressing admiration for her predecessor, she claimed that he hadn't addressed some underlying issues, particularly an 'internal heaviness' that prevented flexibility in the use of the three theatres and made touring difficult. Mayette was more convincing when talking about her aspirations:

> The Comédie-Française is the first theatre of France, and its influence must be much broader. This house must become once again a symbolic guardian of French culture, which is being steadily weakened. In short, I think it should have panache. I also think that the actors of this troupe, who are often remarkable, are not sufficiently celebrated: some of them have everything needed to become stars! There is too much anonymity. Just look at our posters. I do not find that we are festive enough. It's up to us to be less austere without being less intelligent or less creative.[1]

At her first press conference, Mayette talked about the primacy of the troupe: she wouldn't implement a personal project but rather a collective project. She spoke of her intention to end the practice

---

[1] Quoted (in French) in Fabienne Darge and Michel Guerrin, 'La Comédie-Française doit reprendre un peu de panache', in *Le Monde* (8 September 2006), p.26.

of using the Vieux-Colombier and the Studio-Théâtre as second class venues, dumping grounds for new and experimental work; of her desire to bring directors such as Deborah Warner and Declan Donnellan to the Comédie. She would seek an increase in the subsidy so that she could fulfil her promise to enlarge the troupe.

An early crisis came in February 2007 when the Comédie staged its first-ever production of a play by Bernard-Marie Koltès – *Le Retour au désert*. The performance of a play by Koltès at the Salle Richelieu was a significant moment. Mayette directed a committed cast, but Koltès's brother, who owned the performing rights, was unhappy when he learned that Mayette had disregarded Koltès's instruction that the character of Aziz should be played by an Arab. There were no Arab actors in the company at this time. Mayette had no choice but to follow François Koltès's instruction and cancel the remaining performances. Mayette instigated two court cases against François Koltès, the first claiming that he had 'abused his rights', and the second, a libel suit, claiming that he had falsely accused her of breaking her promises. The first case was won. François Koltès was ordered to pay the Comédie-Française damages of 30,000 Euros. He revealed that he would have to sell the manuscript of Koltes's *Roberto Zucco* to raise the money. The second case was lost. Mayette and the Comédie were ordered to pay François Koltès's costs of 50,000 Euros. Both sides appealed. However, Mayette and the Comédie-Française later had a change of heart, presumably because they realised that the decision to prosecute had been an error of judgement. They decided to cease contesting the abuse of rights case against Koltès. The decision coincided with the twentieth anniversary of his brother's death (April 1989). The theatre issued a statement: 'The Comédie-Française wishes François Koltès to continue in all serenity his mission to protect and promote his brother's work.'

Mayette invited the German director Lukas Hemleb to direct a new staging of *Le Misanthrope* and cast Thierry Hancisse as Alceste. Marie-Sophie Ferdane[1] and Marina Hands played Célimène. When the production was revived, in February 2008, the part was

---

[1] Marie-Sophie Ferdane (b. 1977). CF j2007 pensionnaire 07-13.

played by another young pensionnaire recently brought into the troupe by Mayette – Judith Chemla.[1] Hands next starred alongside Éric Ruf and Hervé Pierre[2] in a new production, by Yves Beaunesne, of Claudel's *Partage de Midi*, playing Ysé, a part played by her mother back in 1975. That September, though, Hands left the Comédie to take up the opportunities brought about by her success in the film *Lady Chatterley*. Denis Podalydès expressed the frustration that many members of the troupe had felt over the years: 'I think it's a pity that we are unable to keep an actress like Marina. It is obviously vital for the actors to be able to work outside the Comédie-Française when they have the opportunity and the chance.' Muriel Mayette told Marina Hands, 'When you are tired of your adventure, come home, we will be waiting for you'. The reality, of course, was more complicated. Administrators of the Comédie-Française had never been prepared to change the rules to accommodate the situations of individual players. Hands would reveal later that she couldn't cope with the heavy workload and pressures that came with being a pensionnaire at the Comédie: 'Physiquement, psychologiquement, je n'ai pas supporté.'[3]

In the summer of 2007, the troupe performed Robert Wilson's *Fables de La Fontaine* at the Lincoln Center in New York; in 2008 they took two productions on tour to eastern Europe, Spiro Scimone's *La Festa*, directed by Galin Stoev, and Molière's *Les Précieuses ridicules*, directed by Dan Jemmett; and in 2011 they visited China for the first time (Molière's *Le Malade imaginaire*, directed by Claude Stratz). Muriel Mayette's hope of increasing the size of the troupe remained on hold because the money wasn't there, but she was determined to secure another theatre for the company. The three existing theatres did not adequately serve the needs of the Comédie in the 21st century, when the troupe needed to expand and to continue to modernise. The Comédie had been weaker since the Odéon was taken away in 1983. The Salle Richelieu was cramped and needed constant repairs; the Vieux-Colombier was small and

---

[1] Judith Chemla (b. 1985, Paris). CF j2007 pensionnaire 07-09.

[2] Hervé Pierre (b. 1955, Fins, Doubs). CF j2007 s11.

[3] See 'Marina Hands: Le théâtre m'a sauvée', in *Le Parisien* (18 February 2015).

dated; and the continuance of the lease of the Studio-Théâtre was uncertain. At the very least, the Comédie needed a better second house to compliment the Salle Richelieu.

The most extraordinary episode of Mayette's directorship came in October 2008. Mayette had started to mount co-productions with theatres in the Paris suburbs, such as Pascal Rambert's Théâtre de Gennevilliers. Now, with the Sarkozy government, she formulated a plan for the Comédie-Française to take over the Maison de la Culture (MC93) in the northern suburb of Bobigny, a predominantly working-class area with a large immigrant population. Discontent and anger had erupted into riots in Bobigny and its neighbouring districts in 2005. The plan tied in with the Comédie's search for an additional theatre, and was an admirable attempt to put into action the Comédie's often expressed (since the turn of the century) goal of making its work available to all sections of society. Since young people from the banlieues wouldn't come to the Comédie-Française, the Comédie-Française would come to them.

The MC93 had been established, along with the other Maisons de la Culture, to serve a local community, but its critics believed that this important task had been neglected while the MC93 had developed into a powerhouse of European drama serving a largely white middle-class clientele, people who travelled in from the fashionable arrondissements. The government's desire to turn the MC93 into the kind of organisation originally envisaged, was sound, but the proposed solution to use the House of Molière for this purpose looked contradictory. How would the people of Bobigny respond to a troupe that was almost exclusively white? Would the people the minister and Mayette wanted to attract really come to see such a troupe? Mayette, who lived in Bobigny, believed that the Comédie-Française could be transformed so that outreach programmes and a more youth-orientated repertoire became central to its work.

When the plan was leaked it faced opposition from all sides. The director of the MC93, Patrick Sommier, hadn't been told and was understandably outraged. He denied the government's claim that his theatre had lost its way, citing the 2005 riots as the reason for a

decline in ticket sales. The theatre community was outraged on behalf of the MC93. Although Mayette had informed the actors on
the management committee in June that a plan was being considered, she hadn't fully consulted with the troupe, so when, in
October, the ministry announced that the plan had been finalised
it felt like a *fait accompli*. The fifty-six members of the troupe signed
a press release in which they rejected the scheme:

> We refuse to be a predatory company; we want to be differenti-
> ated and mutually respectful. [...] Because of the seriousness of
> the situation, we must decline the government's proposal at this
> time, so that we can consult with all the parties concerned and
> find a means of preventing the MC93, a theatre rich in history,
> from simply disappearing.[1]

The Minister of Culture, Christine Albanel, expressed her dismay that the actors had gone public. She had assumed that the
Administrator would have their backing. Sommier expressed his
gratitude to the actors. Mayette released her own statement. She
shared the feeling of the troupe, but wrote that the controversy
shouldn't be allowed to undermine the 'générosité d'une utopie artistique et historique', continuing: 'We must weigh the strengths
and weaknesses of the project and strive to allay any worries.' However, a month later, in November, she told *Le Monde* that because
of the controversy, the unhappiness of the profession, the Comédie-Française had decided to abandon the Bobigny scheme. The

---

[1] Quoted (in French) in Clarisse Fabre, 'La troupe de la Comédie-Française
refuse d'annexer la MC93', in *Le Monde* (11 October 2008). More of the press
release in French: 'Nous n'irons pas à Bobigny, sans une concertation préalable
de l'ensemble des directeurs de théâtre de la région parisienne, dans la mesure
où ces établissements sont liés les uns aux autres par la même mission de service
public. Nous refusons de nous installer dans un théâtre contre ceux qui le
dirigent et le font vivre. Nous refusons d'être des entreprises concurrentes et
prédatrices. [...] La situation est telle, aujourd'hui, qu'il nous paraît nécessaire
de décliner la proposition de l'Etat dans un premier temps, de nous concerter
dans un second temps, avec l'ensemble des personnes concernées [...] afin
d'étudier les moyens de ne pas laisser la MC 93, riche d'histoire, d'exigence et
de vie, de disparaître peu à peu, purement et simplement, comme il semblerait
programmé.'

Comédie-Française would still seek a new theatre, but it would not be the Bobigny. Mayette distanced herself from the decision-making, stating that the Bobigny plan had been instigated not by her but by the government. However, her real feelings were revealed when she said, 'Je continue à penser que la venue de la Comédie-Française à Bobigny était un projet magnifique'.[1]

The government was committed to the plan. The Minister of Culture remained determined, announcing that there would be further consultation but that the plan would not be abandoned. However, without the troupe's backing it was dead.

Mayette's greatest strength lay in the selection of actors. Her choices created the company we see today: Serge Bagdassarian, Hervé Pierre, Gilles David and Stéphane Varupenne joined in 2007; Christian Hecq in 2008; Suliane Brahim and Georgia Scalliet in 2009; Adeline d'Hermy, Jérémy Lopez and Nâzim Boudjenah in 2010; Danièle Lebrun, Jennifer Decker and Elliot Jenicot in 2011; Benjamin Lavernhe, Sébastien Pouderoux and Laurent Lafitte in 2012; Noam Morgensztern, Claire de La Rüe du Can and Didier Sandre in 2013; and Anna Cervinka and Christophe Montenez in 2014.

In 2009/10, Mayette added a play by Jean-Luc Lagarce to the repertoire of the Comédie – *Juste la fin du monde*, directed in the Salle Richelieu by Michel Raskine. Pierre Louis-Calixte played Louis.[2] Later in the season there was a fine *Three Sisters* from Alain Françon, meticulously faithful to Chekhov, in which an undercurrent of disquietude was present from the start. The sisters were poignantly played by Florence Viala, Elsa Lepoivre and the remarkable young player Georgia Scalliet,[3] who was making her debut with the troupe. In February 2011, Tennessee Williams's *A Streetcar Named Desire* (*Un Tramway nommé désir*) entered the repertoire. The American Lee Breuer directed a very strong cast led by Anne Kessler (Blanche), Éric Ruf (Stanley) and Françoise

[1] Clarisse Fabre and Brigitte Salino, 'L'administratrice générale abandonne le rapprochement avec la MC93', in *Le Monde* (13 November 2008), p.24.

[2] Pierre Louis-Calixte. CF j2006 s12.

[3] Georgia Scalliet (b. Dijon, 1986). CF j2009 s17 d20.

Gillard (Stella). Bauer's stylised Japanese-influenced concept (utilising painted screens and a silent chorus of Kabuki figures) was brilliantly achieved, but felt like an imposition given the power and poetry of Williams's text and the intimacy achieved by Kessler, Ruf and Gillard. The production divided opinion. Yves Beaunesne directed a new staging of Musset's *On ne badine pas avec l'amour* at the Vieux-Colombier in the same season, and in 2011/12 Jacques Lassalle returned to direct the troupe's first new production of Molière's *L'École des femmes* in over ten years: the pensionnaire Julie-Marie Parmentier[1] played Camille, opposite Loïc Corbery, in the Musset and Agnès, opposite the formidable Thierry Hancisse, in the Molière. 'What is so magnificent,' wrote Armelle Héliot in her review of *L'École des femmes*, 'is that, under Jacques Lassalle's luminous direction, her voice changes and she matures before our eyes. Soon she is no longer the innocent girl. However, and this is Lassalle's stroke of genius, in the end she is defeated. She can't stand Arnolphe's suffering, she can't stand the discovery that her union with Horace has been pre-arranged. She realises that she is a prisoner in every way.'[2]

Parmentier left the Comédie in 2012. Soon after her departure she told *Libération*:

> At the Comédie-Française it is beautiful to know that you are a link in a chain, between the plays, and in the troupe. For two years, I was a pensionnaire in the most reassuring and protective place in the world. I was on a staircase without knowing where it leads, and I especially didn't want to stop at a step. I was insensitive to fatigue, like a frog that doesn't feel pain when immersed in water, because the temperature rises imperceptibly. I played every night but eventually there was a play that was too much. I

[1] Julie-Marie Parmentier (b. 1981, Saint-Quentin, Aisne). CF j2010 pensionnaire 10-12.

[2] Armelle Héliot, 'L'Ecole des femmes, une grande leçon de théâtre à la Comédie-Française', in *Le Figaro* blog, 22 November 2011, at https://blog.lefigaro.fr/theatre/2011/11/lecole-des-femmes-une-grande-l.html (accessed 19/3/2020).

heard myself say a first 'no' and then a second.[1]

Another pensionnaire, Adeline d'Hermy,[2] took over the role of Agnès when *L'École des femmes* was revived in 2012.

With major repair work closing the Salle Richelieu in 2011, Mayette ensured that a full programme would continue by arranging for a temporary theatre to be constructed in the courtyard of the Palais-Royal. The Théâtre Éphémère's timber shell was slotted in the avenue of the Galerie d'Orléans between the courtyard and the garden. There was no proscenium and the seating was frontal to the stage and steeply raked (740 places).

Mayette chose to inaugurate the new space (in January 2012) with the Comédie's first production of Carlo Goldoni's exquisitely observed and constructed *La Trilogie de la villégiature* since Giorgio Strehler's legendary staging of 1978. The production was directed by Alain Françon. Françon discovered that Goldoni, in these late works, pre-dated Chekhov not only in the lyrical tone of his writing but also in the theme of an impoverished bourgeoisie living beyond its means. Without trying to compete with Strehler, Françon ensured that the production was handsome, with beautiful period costumes by Renato Bianchi and attractive décor by Jacques Gabel. Françon allowed his stage pictures to resonate: the soft light of an Italian dusk was magically evoked by lighting designer Joël Hourbeig. The show, four and a half hours long, took spectators on a journey from spring to winter, from laughter to tears. The evening belonged to the actors – Éric Ruf, Elsa Lepoivre, Georgia Scalliet, Anne Kessler, Bruno Raffaelli, Florence Viala, Jérôme Pouly, Laurent Stocker, Guillaume Gallienne, Michel Vuillermoz, Hervé Pierre, Adeline d'Hermy, Danièle Lebrun, and Adrien Gamba-Gontard. Later in the season, an inspired version of *Peer Gynt*, designed and directed by Ruf, was performed on a traverse stage at the Grand Palais by Hervé Pierre (masterly in the title role) and an ensemble drawn from all the generations of the troupe. Catherine

---

[1] Quoted (in French) in Anne Diatkine, 'Interview: Si j'ai un pic de peur, je le cache', in *Libération* (27 July 2012).

[2] Adeline d'Hermy (b. Bois-Bernard, Pas de Calais, 1987). CF j2010 s16.

Samie came out of retirement to play Ase.

The troupe performed in the Théâtre Éphémère until January 2013. The Comédie's first-ever production of Shakespeare's *Troilus and Cressida* reopened the Salle Richelieu. Jean-Yves Ruf directed. Stéphane Varupenne and Georgia Scalliet played the title roles; Éric Ruf, Michel Vuillermoz and Sébastien Pouderoux were Ulysses, Hector and Achilles. Concurrently, at the Vieux-Colombier, Nicolas Lormeau[1] directed Jérôme Pouly[2] and Jennifer Decker in a new staging of Hugo's *Hernani*. During the spring and summer, the troupe performed a new version of Georges Feydeau's *Un Fil à la patte*. Christian Hecq,[3] the Comédie's most singular interpreter of Feydeau, played Bouzin. The most intriguing production of the 2013/14 season was *Psyché* at the Salle Richelieu. Molière's five-hour-long comédie-ballet of 1671, a work rarely seen in modern times, was re-imagined by Véronique Vella as a contemporary musical comedy. In her review for the *Financial Times*, Laura Cappelle wrote: 'Jennifer Decker is cast against type as one of Psyche's envious sisters, but the double act she forms with Coraly Zahonero[4] provides hilarious comic relief throughout: their clumsy tap-dancing number is a witty nod to the play's original dance content. Françoise Gillard, meanwhile, is a diminutive Psyche with short, dishevelled hair, as charismatic as she is modern.'[5]

Clément Hervieu-Léger had been a member of the Comédie since 2005.[6] Mayette launched his career as a director by giving him the opportunity to stage Molière's *La Critique de l'École des femmes* in the Studio-Théâtre (2011) followed by a big prize – *Le Misanthrope* at the Salle Richelieu (2014). From its very first presentation by the troupe de Molière in 1666, *Le Misanthrope* was viewed as a new and different kind of comedy: a comedy centred on an enigmatic love affair, imbued with melancholy, its final meaning deeply

---

[1] Nicolas Lormeau (b. 1965). CF j1996 s2014.

[2] Jérôme Pouly. CF j1998 s2004.

[3] Christian Hecq (b. 1964, Nivelles, Belgium). CF j2008 s13.

[4] Coraly Zahonero (b. 1969, Montpellier). CF j1994 s2000.

[5] Laura Cappelle, 'Psyché, Comédie-Française, Paris – Review', in the *Financial Times* (11 December 2013).

[6] Clément Hervieu-Léger (b. 1977, Paris). CF j2005 s18.

ambiguous. The writer Jean Donneau de Visé commented, in his *Lettre écrite sur la comédie du Misanthrope*, published in 1667, that 'the verses are very beautiful to the feeling of everybody in the play.' The play's modernity lies in Célimène's independence, Alceste's refusal to pander to social norms, and in the fact that the characters are motivated by desire rather than by reason, convention or rules. 'Ma raison me le dit chaque jour,' remarks Alceste, 'mais la raison n'est pas ce qui règle l'amour.' The innovative nature of the contemporary Comédie-Française meant that its members were fully in support of a new approach. Loïc Corbery,[1] cast as Alceste, had played a number of Molière's leading characters, as well as Ajax in Shakespeare's *Troilus and Cressida* and Christian in Edmond Rostand's *Cyrano de Bergerac*, since joining the troupe in 2005.

Hervieu-Léger's decision to perform the play in modern dress released the actors physically. Éric Ruf, who also played Philinte in the initial run of performances, designed an 18th century room in light grey, and Caroline de Vivaise dressed Célimène in *robes de cocktail*. There was an upright piano that Alceste played as if to escape the world, and, in the second act, the characters sat down to a meal served by housemaids. As the play progressed, golden light faded into twilight. Reviewing the production in *Le Monde*, Brigitte Salino wrote

> What a pleasure to see the comedy of Molière played differently, in the spirit of today. We forget the grumpy old Alceste of tradition and discover a Molière who, as surprising as it may seem, has accents of Chekhov.[2]

Hervieu-Léger's approach paid dividends both in Georgia Scalliet's interpretation of Célimène and in the decision to present Alceste as a man in his prime. In this production, Célimène engaged in the mockery of absent acquaintances as a performance, a means of hiding her true self, and her behaviour towards Alceste was partly explained by fear; for Corbery's Alceste was hysterical

---

[1] Loïc Corbery (b. Avignon, 1976). CF j2005 s10.

[2] Brigitte Salino, 'Quand Molière rencontre Tchekhov', in *Le Monde* (25 April 2014).

and troubled from the start, and his jealousy broke into violence. Hervieu-Léger gave space to Philinte and Éliante (surely the loveliest young woman in all of Molière's work): the journey of their relationship was beautifully played by Ruf and Adeline d'Hermy and later by Éric Génovèse and Jennifer Decker.[1] The role of Célimène was shared by Georgia Scalliet and Adeline d'Hermy when the production was revived. Arguably, the most original performance was given by Christophe Montenez,[2] who used silences and body language to turn Acaste into a figure of real menace. In Hervieu-Léger's interpretation, Alceste and Célimène are not only apart at the end but also isolated, with Ruf's Philinte roughly pushing Alceste away from Éliante, and Éliante responding to his suggestion that they should follow after Alceste (to change his mind about abandoning society) by taking his hand and leading him in the opposite direction into her apartment.

Mayette was a passionate advocate of Shakespeare. She began the process that has seen Shakespeare become the most performed author at the Comédie after Molière. As well as the premiere of *Troilus and Cressida* in 2013, she programmed *The Taming of the Shrew* (*La Mégère apprivoisée*) in 2008, *The Merry Wives of Windsor* (*Les Joyeuses commères de Windsor*) in 2009, *Hamlet* in 2013, and, during the 2013/14 season, *Othello* at the Vieux-Colombier and *A Midsummer Night's Dream* (*Le Songe d'une nuit d'été*) at the Salle Richelieu. Andrés Lima's metaphorical interpretation of *The Merry Wives of Windsor* was intriguing, but, despite the splendid performances of Catherine Hiegel and Bruno Raffaelli[3] as Mistress Quickly and Falstaff, much of the comedy fell flat, as often happens with this play. Both Lima and Léonie Simaga[4] in her production of *Othello*, the troupe's first of this tragedy since 1950, made effective use of candle-light and darkness. Othello, Iago and Desdemona were played by Bakary Sangaré, Nâzim Boudjenah[5] and Elsa Lepoivre.

---

[1] Jennifer Decker (b. 1982). CF j2011.
[2] Christophe Montenez (b. 1988, Paris). CF j2014 s20.
[3] Bruno Raffaelli (b. 1959, Avignon). CF j1994 s98 d2019 sh20.
[4] Léonie Simaga (b. 1978). CF j2005 s10 d15.
[5] Nâzim Boudjenah (b. 1972, Paris). CF j2010.

Mayette's production of the *Dream* used modern dress, abstract settings (by Didier Monfajon) and superb ensemble acting in a realisation of the play's exploration of the subconscious mind which transcended the 19th century translation by François-Victor Hugo. For Armelle Héliot: 'La troupe alterne habilement grâce amoureuse et déchaînement sexuel. [...] Le spectacle est très original et met en lumière la cocasserie comme le désir effréné sans jamais renoncer à la poésie.'[1]

Muriel Mayette had become the Comédie's Administrator in controversial circumstances, and her own time in charge would end in controversy. Many of the influential members of the troupe had not been fully behind her since the Bobigny debacle and didn't want her to continue in post at the end of her second three-year term. In November 2013, eight months before the end of her contract, thirty-six members of the troupe sent a letter to the Minister of Culture (with Mayette copied in) in which they said that their Administrator did not have a real 'artistic policy'. The letter was made public. Denis Podalydès, one of the chief advocates of change along with Éric Ruf, told *Le Monde*: 'We have come to the end of a cycle that has seen some very beautiful things, but we want a new horizon, there is no war between us.'[2] When asked by *Le Figaro* to explain the case against Mayette, he said: 'A tendency to want to control and never to consult the representatives of the troupe.'[3] Although she had engaged good actors, she hadn't, he said, enlisted any of the great directors of the period. Éric Ruf had always been open with Mayette that he would put his name forward for the top job, and Podalydès backed Ruf.

Publicly, Mayette was philosophical about the actors' letter. Even though the troupe didn't support her, she let it be known that she wanted her contract to be renewed, a decision that surprised many. She wanted to complete her work by securing a new theatre.

---

[1] Armelle Héliot, 'Le Songe d'une nuit d'été, un rêve éveillé', in *Le Figaro* (18 February 2014).

[2] Quoted (in French) in Laurent Carpentier, 'A la Comédie-Française, la guerre de succession est déclarée', in *Le Monde* (19 December 2013), p.12.

[3] Quoted (in French) in Armelle Héliot, 'Comédie-Française, la guerre de succession', in *Le Figaro* (9 January 2014).

Excellent box figures across the three theatres backed up her claim that she had rejuvenated the troupe as far as the public was concerned. She let it be known that she had invited Deborah Warner and Christoph Marthaler to work at the Comédie, but that they had declined. Her decision to give opportunities to members of the troupe to direct was criticised, but it did, as we have noted, reveal two major talents – Éric Ruf and Clément Hervieu-Léger.

Mayette's political allies had been members of Sarkozy's regime. Aurélie Filippetti, Minister of Culture in the new socialist government, approached Stéphane Braunschweig. She thought it best to appoint someone from outside the company. The other leading candidates were Christian Schiaretti, director of the Théâtre national populaire de Villeurbanne, and Ruf, who had the support of his fellow sociétaires. Mayette wasn't considered. After interviews with Aurélie Filippetti, only Braunschweig and Ruf were invited to meet President Hollande at the Élysée. To the embarrassment of Filippetti, Hollande chose Ruf.

14

Éric Ruf

2014-2020

25. Rebecca Marder at the Salle Richelieu, 2015. Photograph by Manuel Lagos Cid.

1   A Clear Vision

By choosing Ruf over Braunschweig (a director with a European-wide reputation), the government opted for continuity and reflected the wishes of the troupe (Hollande and Podalydès were friends); but Ruf was a major talent in his own right, responsible (as director and designer) for a magnificent production of *Peer Gynt* (2012), as well as striking sets for Podalydès's *Cyrano de Bergerac* (2006) and Hervieu-Léger's *Le Misanthrope* (2014).

Éric Ruf was born in Belfort in north-eastern France in 1969. He has revealed that his Swiss father, a cardiologist and National Front supporter, was strict and sometimes violent; his mother was a teacher of English. The family's faith was an austere form of Protestantism on both sides.

Ruf and his brother were meant to follow their father into the medical profession, but found an outlet – a release from the stress of their family life – in acting in plays. Ruf is somewhat unusual in the theatre in that he is equally an actor, a designer and a director. In common with most members of the Comédie-Française, he trained for the stage at the Conservatoire, but, before that, he attended the École nationale supérieure des arts appliqués et des métiers d'art and then the Cours Florent. He joined the Comédie in 1993, while still at the Conservatoire, and emerged as one of the leaders of his generation during the 2000s.

As an actor, Ruf was most interested in the overall effect of a play, and had a strong sense of the primacy of the text and the secondary role of the actor, the feeling of being an 'impostor':

On stage, we utter words that are not ours, and whose power we hardly understand; we commune with great authors but we are ourselves nothing at all. I saw in magnificent sociétaires like Jean-Yves Dubois and Jean Dautremay a real sense of pain. We can never forget that we are just water carriers.[1]

His move into design and direction was, therefore, a natural progression. On becoming Administrator, he gave up his place as a sociétaire so that it could be released for another actor. He has indicated that at the end of his tenure, he will continue his life as an actor but not at the Comédie.

'I truly believe that to run this theatre,' Ruf said in an interview, 'it is necessary to understand all the cogs, to respect the structure and to know its intrinsic strengths.'[2] This had also been true of Mayette. Now that Mayette had been replaced, the newspapers acknowledged her achievements. Armelle Héliot wrote in *Le Figaro*: '[Mayette] renewed the troupe by 50%. She selected young people, such as Adeline d'Hermy, or established talents, such as Laurent Lafitte, Danièle Lebrun, Didier Sandre and Samuel Labarthe, without ever overshadowing those who were already there. A great job. Members of the troupe are stars, as they were in the days of Robert Hirsch and Jacques Charon.'[3] Ruf praised Mayette's achievements. He agreed with his predecessor that the Comédie should show its best work throughout France and abroad, and that an additional theatre, with state of the art machinery and a reconfigurable stage, was essential for its future development (this aim actually dates back to Dux). The Salle Richelieu was home, but conditions were cramped and the troupe needed breathing space. A production like Ruf's *Peer Gynt*, using a traverse stage, could not be presented at

---

[1] Quoted (in French) in Fabienne Pascaud, 'Je n'ai pas un physique de perdant: Éric Ruf, patron de la Comédie-Française', in *Télérama*, at https://www.telerama.fr/scenes/je-n-ai-pas-un-physique-de-perdant-eric-ruf-patron-de-la-comedie-francaise,120633.php (accessed 8/7/2019).

[2] Quoted (in French) in Mathilde Bergon, 'Éric Ruf: La Comédie-Française doit se tourner vers l'international', in *Le Figaro* (17 July 2014).

[3] Armelle Héliot, 'La Comédie-Française tourne la page', in *Le Figaro* (3 August 2014).

the Salle Richelieu. A new theatre would become urgent if, as expected, the troupe lost the Studio-Théâtre.

In his first statements and interviews, Ruf was highly articulate and spoke with authority: 'Je me vois plus comme un jardinier qu'un paysagiste. Je connais la terre, l'ensoleillement, les recoins.'[1] ('I see myself more as a gardener than a landscape artist. I know the land, where the sun shines, the nooks and crannies.') In summing up the challenge that lay ahead, he said:

> The big difficulty for the Administrator is that he must have one eye turned inwards and one turned outwards. This squint is complicated! I'm only at the beginning of my grimace. Looking inwards is indeed important. I have never been exclusively a theatre director, but my profile is unusual in that I have a technical knowledge of the theatre. As a scenographer, I often work at Sarcelles, where we construct our sets. This is not the case for most members. So I have the expertise to avoid some mistakes. This must be the duty of the Administrator, for he is the artistic director, responsible for a project from its beginning to its end.[2]

Ruf was in favour of members of the troupe being given opportunities to direct if they had the talent, for an in-house team of directors, dedicated to the troupe and comfortable with its working methods, was essential; but in recent times the balance had been too much in their favour. Ruf had benefitted from the experience of working with Vassiliev, and believed that it was important for members of the troupe to work with top directors who would introduce them to different methods and styles. The Comédie-Française cannot offer outside directors the rehearsal time they are used to, nor guarantee the exclusive attention of the actors cast (for they would also be working for other directors and performing in other plays). Ruf believed that the directors he wanted to bring to the Comédie would come if he formed relationships with them, explained the strengths of the troupe, and persevered. His initial

---

[1] Quoted in Etienne Sorin and Armelle Héliot, 'Éric Ruf: Je connais tous les recoins de la Comédie-Française', in *Le Figaro* (11 September 2014).

[2] Quoted (in French) in Etienne Sorin and Armelle Héliot, 'Éric Ruf: Je connais tous les recoins de la Comédie-Française'.

wish list included Thomas Ostermeier, Jean-Louis Martinelli, Rodolphe Dana and Sylvain Creuzevault. He intended to invite Stéphane Braunschweig and Christian Schiaretti, and to bring back Alain Françon and Jacques Lassalle. Overturning the pre-conceived ideas of directors would be key. 'The image of the troupe is not always positive,' Ruf said in an interview. 'Abroad, many of the artists I contact – Thomas Ostermeier, Katie Mitchell, Michael Thalheimer – imagine that the troupe is against artistic daring, when, in fact, the opposite is true.'[1]

As a designer-director, Ruf wanted to present 'total' theatre, productions in which spectacle was fully integrated into the *mise en scène*, while at the same time ensuring that the work was rooted in the present, in terms of its ideas and its stagecraft. And part of this, meant presenting new work by contemporary playwrights. These ambitions would only be fully realised if Ruf was successful in his search for a new, modular, theatre space. 'This will be my main project,' Ruf said. 'As long as this problem is not solved, the Comédie will not really be able to enter the modern world.'[2]

2   On the Stage

The 2014/15 season, programmed by Mayette, included Pinter's *Betrayal* (*Trahisons*), starring Denis Podalydès, Laurent Stocker[3] and Léonie Simaga (who decided to leave the troupe at the end of the season), Marivaux's *La Double inconstance* – Anne Kessler directed for the first time at the Salle Richelieu – and García Lorca's *La Maison de Bernarda Alba*, directed by Lilo Baur. The latter showed off the talent of many of the women of the Comédie – Claude Mathieu, Véronique Vella, Cécile Brune (as Bernarda), Sylvia Bergé, Florence Viala, Coraly Zahonero, Elsa Lepoivre, Adeline

---

[1] Quoted (in French) in Fabienne Pascaud, 'Je n'ai pas un physique de perdant: Éric Ruf, patron de la Comédie-Française', in *Télérama*.

[2] Quoted (in French) in Fabienne Darge, 'Éric Ruf: Redonner un lustre artistique au Français', in *Le Monde* (12 September 2014).

[3] Laurent Stocker (b. 1973, Saint-Dizier, Haute-Marne). CF j2001 s04.

d'Hermy, Jennifer Decker and Claire de La Rüe du Can.

Anne Kessler set *La Double inconstance* in a representation of the *foyer des artistes* of the Richelieu (designed by Jacques Gabel) and arranged her interpretation around the idea that a connection exists between the prince and Flaminia's manipulation of Silvia and Arlequin and the creation of a theatre production. Some scenes were performed in costume and others in normal dress. The concept added to the essential strangeness of Marivaux's play. Kessler acknowledged the issues of power and abuse raised by the play without delving deeply into a dark interpretation; instead, she concentrated on the playful elegance of Marivaux's game of seduction, adored by his contemporaries. During their pivotal scene, Loïc Corbery's prince and Adeline d'Hermy's Silvia performed an impromptu dance routine to an arrangement of George and Ira Gershwin's 'They Can't Take That Away from Me'. This allusion to the charm of old Hollywood was as essential to Kessler's concept as the enigmatic Flaminia created by Florence Viala.

Ruf only brought in a few new actors – Rebecca Marder, Pauline Clément, Julien Frison, and the great Dominique Blanc, joining the Comédie for the first time. In January 2015, the pensionnaire Pierre Niney, a member of the troupe since 2010, resigned to take up the opportunities created by his award-winning performance in the film *Yves Saint Laurent*. He expressed the hope, on Twitter, that one day the Comédie's management would find a means of accommodating those pensionnaires 'who have the deep desire to be part of the troupe but who also want to participate in major cinema projects in France and abroad'.

Ruf began the process of realising his vision for the Comédie in his first season, 2015/16. He engaged outside directors and took the company to Avignon for the first time in over twenty years. Three major directors with a history at the Comédie – Anatoli Vassiliev, Jean-Louis Benoit and Alain Françon – returned to direct, respectively, Marguerite Duras's *La Musica* (Vieux-Colombier), Goldoni's *Les Rustres* (Vieux-Colombier) and Edward Bond's *La Mer* (Salle Richelieu). Other highpoints included Arnaud Desplechin's production of Strindberg's *Père* and Stéphane Braunschweig's modern dress *Britannicus*. *Le Misanthrope, Cyrano de Bergerac* and *Lucrèce Borgia* were revived, and Ruf directed Jérémy Lopez[1] and Suliane Brahim[2] in a new version of *Roméo et Juliette*. Benoit's *Les Rustres* proved to be Gérard Giroudon's final appearance as a sociétaire: he retired from the troupe at the end of 2016, but remains in the family as a sociétaire honoraire.

The event of the season, perhaps of the decade at the Comédie, was Ivo van Hove's *Les Damnés*, adapted from Visconti's iconic film – the rise of the Nazis is played out, in microcosm, in the dysfunctional and depraved relationships of a family of industrialists. The arrival of Van Hove was significant, despite the fact that the Comédie was meeting him rather late, after his successes in New York and London, and after the world had become aware of his tropes. When Ruf received the offer from Olivier Py to headline the Avignon festival, he wrote to Ivo van Hove to invite him to create a production for both the Salle Richelieu and the Cour d'Honneur du Palais des Papes in Avignon. Van Hove was surprised to receive the offer, admitting that his prejudiced view of the Comédie was that it was old-fashioned and stuck in its ways. He suggested Shakespeare, but Ruf wanted something unique, that would showcase the versatility of the troupe – it was an opportunity to make a statement on the world stage. Van Hove offered a stage version of *Les Damnés* and Ruf was enthusiastic.

The actors – Éric Génovèse, Denis Podalydès, Alexandre Pavloff, Guillaume Gallienne, Elsa Lepoivre, Loïc Corbery, Adeline d'Hermy, Clément Hervieu-Léger, Jennifer Decker, Didier Sandre, Christophe Montenez and Sébastien Baulain – fully embraced Van Hove's trademark style, juxtaposing forensic minimalism with moments of baroque theatricality, and his use of music (referencing Bach, Strauss and Schoenberg) and live film (projecting close-ups of the actors' faces on screens) to achieve a psychological effect; they committed themselves totally to the demands of performing a play almost entirely made up of acts of political terror and personal depravity on a mostly bare stage (painted a sickly orange) under white

---

[1] Jérémy Lopez (b 1984, Lyon). CF j2010 s17.
[2] Suliane Brahim (b. 1978, Chartres, Eure-et-Loir). CF j2009 s16.

lights. The production was two hours and ten minutes of unrelenting tension, a disturbing 'celebration of evil' (Van Hove's own phrase) during which the six empty coffins waiting at the side of the stage were filled one by one.

The Comédie's presentation of *Les Damnés* in the courtyard of the Palais des Papes in July 2016 was a moment of rediscovery for people who had not taken much notice of the 'venerable' troupe in recent times. Reviewing the production for *The Guardian*, Andrew Todd called it a 'masterstroke':

> The production excels theatrically, technically, spatially and musically. […] A real, ear-splitting steam whistle signals deaths, which are also marked by blinding house lights and a ritual procession to the coffin. […] The synergy between Van Hove and la Troupe is evidently exceptional. The actors work together and individually to perfection, and are able to fill the vast space and focus on tiny details without it ever seeming forced. Among this wonderful ensemble, Christophe Montenez's psychopathic, paedophile, gender-fluid Nazi turncoat, Martin von Essenbeck, shines in some remarkable setpieces, including a final tableau in which – naked and covered in his victims' ashes – he turns his arms-dealing family's machine gun on the audience. People in my row jumped; the Bataclan is a painful recent memory. During the subsequent audience ovation, a man a few seats from me booed and snarled at his neighbours. He should have been on stage.[1]

The Comédie toured *Les Damnés* to New York in 2018 and to London in 2019. Van Hove returned to the Salle Richelieu in 2019 to stage Euripide's *Électre/Oreste*.

Braunschweig's *Britannicus* and Ruf's *Roméo et Juliette* were both contemporary in tone for all their classical elegance. *Les Damnés* occupied some of the same territory as Racine's Roman tragedy, in which Nero attempts to break free from the influence of his controlling mother Agrippine and schemes to murder his adopted brother Britannicus because of his desire for Britannicus's fiancé

---

[1] Andrew Todd, 'The Damned five-star review – Van Hove's chillingly prescient masterstroke', in *The Guardian* (10 July 2016).

Junie. The action was played out in the meeting rooms of a modern palace. Dominique Blanc played Agrippine, with Laurent Stocker as Néron, Georgia Scalliet as Junie and Stéphane Varupenne[1] as Britannicus.

Ruf's *Roméo et Juliette* was the Comédie's first production of this most iconic of plays since 1954. Ruf used the old translation by François-Victor Hugo, and one had to accept its deficiencies. He set the play in southern Italy between the wars, placing the action beneath high facades, off-white and shuttered, sun-kissed or drenched in moonlight. The setting was poetic, a metaphor for the faded grandeur of the old Mediterranean. The costumes were by Christian Lacroix, and evocative use was made of popular songs of the period. The balcony scene was staged traditionally. In Armelle Héliot's description:

> Juliet appears, barefoot, swamped in an overcoat. [...] Below, at the foot of the high gable, Jérémy Lopez's Romeo, barely out of adolescence, listens. We are afraid for her, this fine girl played wonderfully by Suliane Brahim. It is the most beautiful declaration of love in dramatic literature and the scene has never been so beautiful.[2]

Mercutio, Capulet, the Nurse and Friar Laurent were well played by Pierre Louis-Calixte, Didier Sandre,[3] Claude Mathieu and Serge Bagdassarian,[4] despite the fact that Hugo's translation reduced their complexity. Laurent Lafitte[5] was luxury casting in the role of Benvolio. Ruf's decision to set Romeo and Juliet's first exchange of words in a washroom may have seemed bizarre, but it had its purpose. Before beginning the sonnet about 'pilgrim's hands', Romeo blew on Juliet's wet fingers.

Leaving *Les Damnés* aside, the most striking statement of Ruf's first season came at the very beginning with the season's opening

[1] Stéphane Varupenne. CF j2007 s15.

[2] Armelle Héliot, 'Roméo et Juliette en plein soleil', in *Le Figaro* (19 December 2015).

[3] Didier Sandre (b. 1946, Paris). CF j2013 s20.

[4] Serge Bagdassarian. CF j2007 s11.

[5] Laurent Lafitte (b. 1973, Paris). CF j2012 pensionnaire 12

show, in the Studio-Théâtre – *Comme une pierre qui*, adapted from an episode in Greil Marcus's book *Like a Rolling Stone: Bob Dylan at the Crossroads*. The work was created and directed by Marie Rémond with Sébastien Pouderoux,[1] who also played Dylan. The Studio was transformed into Columbia Record's recording studio in New York, on 16 June 1965, the night Bob Dylan recorded his classic track 'Like a Rolling Stone'.

Pouderoux was supported by Stéphane Varupenne, as guitarist Mike Bloomfield, and Christophe Montenez, as Al Kooper, the young guitarist who, famously, was told to play the organ. Gilles David[2] played producer Tom Wilson. The cast was completed by two non-members of the Comédie, Gabriel Tur, as drummer Bobby Gregg, and Hugues Duchêne, as pianist Paul Griffin. Pouderoux's Dylan hardly communicated with the other musicians (Dylan only knew Bloomfield). All of them were going through a personal crisis of some kind. Their attempt to record the song was wrecked by mishaps and interruptions, until, suddenly, everything clicked, a mysterious alchemy happened, and the song was realised in all its electronic glory. These actor-musicians captured the excitement of rock music in a remarkable way. Fabienne Darge wrote in *Le Monde* that Pouderoux had not attempted to imitate Dylan but had created a character 'inhabited from within, in his doubts, his poetry, and his humour too'.[3]

The 2016/17 season didn't quite live up to Ruf's first year. He revived *Les Damnés*, *Père*, *Comme une pierre qui*, and *Roméo et Juliette*. An ambitious production based on Renoir's film *La Règle du jeu*, directed by Christiane Jatahy, combined theatre with recorded and live film. It was engaging in parts, but somehow misfired. The on-stage section was essentially an extended cabaret, boozy and chaotic, in which the players sang beautifully while remaining in character. The tragic dénouement, in the place Colette, was shown on film. The Comédie's first production of Alfred Musset's *Il faut qu'une porte soit ouverte ou fermée* since 1980 was directed in the

---

[1] Sébastien Pouderoux. CF j2012 s19.

[2] Gilles David (b. 1956, Paris). CF j2007 s14.

[3] Fabienne Darge, 'Un petit miracle Bob Dylan à la Comédie-Française', in *Le Monde* (22 September 2015).

Studio-Théâtre by Laurent Delvert (previously an assistant director at the Comédie). Musset's game of seduction between a young woman and an older man, was stylishly played by Jennifer Decker and Christian Gonon.[1] Jennifer Decker also shone in a new piece written and directed by Pascal Rambert, *Une Vie* (Vieux-Colombier). Written for six of the Comédie's actors, this meditation on a man's life and the nature of artistic creation was set in the mundane environment of a radio studio, where a self-important critic (Hervé Pierre) interviewed a troubled artist (Denis Podalydès). Both actors were on superb form. Memories became real as figures from the artist's life appeared to take their seats at the table, including his formidable mother (Cécile Brune), his estranged brother (Alexandre Pavloff[2]), and a former lover (Decker). 'Je n'écris pas sur la vie privée des acteurs,' Rambert said, 'j'écris pour leur voix, leur corps, leur énergie, précise-t-il, ce sont des êtres humains, pas des personnages de papier.'[3]

Ruf's invitation to the young director Julie Deliquet, founder of the actors' collectif In Vitro, to create a production for the Comédie resulted in an admired version of Chekhov's *Vania* at the Vieux-Colombier in September 2016. Following her usual method, Julie Deliquet set the play in the present to achieve a 'theatre of reality' and worked collaboratively with her cast. This approach was not new, for, internationally, there have been many 'deconstructions' of Chekhov's plays in the last two decades, but Julie Deliquet used it to create theatre that was intimate and thought-provoking rather than cold and iconoclastic. *Vania*, presented on a traverse stage, was performed by Laurent Stocker as Vania, Stéphane Varupenne as Astrov, Florence Viala as Elena, Anna Cervinka as Sonia, Hervé Pierre as Serebriakov, Noam Morgensztern as Tielieguine, and Dominique Blanc as Maria.

In February 2017, Jacques Lassalle, making a much-anticipated return to the Comédie to direct Heinrich von Kleist's *The Broken Jug* at the Vieux-Colombier, withdrew during rehearsals because of

---

[1] Christian Gonon (b. 1961, Toulouse). CF j1998 s2009.

[2] Alexandre Pavloff (b. 1974, Boulogne-Billancourt, Hauts-de-Seine). CF j1997 s2002.

[3] Quoted in the programme (2017), p.9.

the death of his wife. In place of the show, Ruf decided to create, in less than two months, a new production of Racine's *Bajazet*, with the actors assembled for *The Broken Jug* – Denis Podalydès, Clotilde de Bayser, Laurent Natrella,[1] Alain Lenglet,[2] Anna Cervinka, and Rebecca Marder. Racine's rarely performed play, with its convoluted plot, in which love and politics fatally clash, had not been staged by the Comédie in over twenty years. The seraglio, in Ruf's design, was a strange boudoir: the tall Norman cabinets were empty and women's shoes were lined in rows on the stage. Denis Podalydès was at his most disturbing as the malignant Acomat, but the evening belonged to the troupe's youngest pensionnaire, Rebecca Marder, who was playing her first leading role. She was still a student at the school of the théâtre national de Strasbourg when Ruf offered her a place at the Comédie. As Atalide, she compelled attention even in her scenes with Podalydès.

The highlight of the season was a surprise, Marivaux's comedy *Le Petit-maître corrigé*. This play was premiered at the Comédie-Française in 1734, withdrawn after two performances and then forgotten. So the first night of Clément Hervieu-Léger's revival was only the third performance of the play. Éric Ruf created a duneland setting of tall grasses below beautiful skies, while reminding the audience of the conceit by revealing the stage machinery that worked the set. This was classic Marivaux, deploying, in the words of Armelle Héliot, 'all of his most daring themes: money, marriage, love, sex, ambivalence, servants and masters, new men and aristocrats, town versus country, false oaths, adults and the young, language with double meaning, cruelty resolved, manoeuvres, arrogance, and manipulative women.'[3] *Le Petit-maître corrigé* was performed by Dominique Blanc, Didier Sandre, Claire de La Rüe du Can,[4] Loïc Corbery (le petit-maître), Pierre Hancisse, Florence Viala, Christophe Montenez and Adeline d'Hermy.

---

[1] Laurent Natrella (b. 1964, Marsailles). CF j1998 s2007 d18.

[2] Alain Lenglet (b. 1954, Suresnes, Hauts-de-Seine). CF j1993 s2000.

[3] Armelle Héliot, 'Un Marivaux passionnant et passionnément interprété à la Comédie-Française', in *Le Figaro* (18 December 2016).

[4] Claire de La Rüe du Can. CF j2013 pensionnaire 13.

2017/18 opened with a vibrant new production, by Denis Podalydès, of Molière's *Les Fourberies de Scapin* (Salle Richelieu), the Comédie's first since Jean-Louis Benoit's renowned staging of 1997. Éric Ruf designed. Podalydès exposed the meanness that underpins much of the comedy. Benjamin Lavernhe,[1] as Scapin, combined the spirit of commedia dell'arte with a modern sensibility. Laura Cappelle, reviewing the production for the *Financial Times*, wrote: 'The sack in which one of the fathers, Géronte, is trapped and beaten by Scapin, ends up suspended from a crane and thrown against a wall – a startling reinvention of a scene most French schoolchildren are familiar with.'[2] Podalydès was doffing his hat to Benoit, who also suspended the sack so that it could be swung across the stage like a pendulum. There was a rare Jean Genet in the Studio-Théâtre, *Haute surveillance*, directed by Cédric Gourmelon, and acted by Pierre Louis-Calixte, Jérémy Lopez, Sébastien Pouderoux and Christophe Montenez. A new work entered the official repertoire by being staged at the Salle Richelieu – Lars Norén's *Poussière* (*Dust*). Norén directed. This unremittingly bleak family drama by Sweden's most important contemporary playwright was complemented by a masterpiece for three actors by Sweden's greatest, August Strindberg's *Les Créanciers* (*Creditors*): Adeline d'Hermy, Sébastien Pouderoux and Didier Sandre were directed by Anne Kessler.

Ten years after its production of *Juste la fin du monde* at the Salle Richelieu, the Comédie returned to the theatre of Jean-Luc Lagarce by staging the second of his deliberations on family and death, *J'Étais dans ma maison et j'attendais que la pluie vienne*, in a staging by Chloé Dabert at the Vieux-Colombier. This play for five women, in which words combine and separate like lines of music, was performed by Cécile Brune, Clotilde de Bayser, Suliane Brahim, Jennifer Decker and Rebecca Marder, with echoes of Chekhov's *Three Sisters* and Greek tragedy. Dabert chose a semi-abstract setting, in white.

---

[1] Benjamin Lavernhe (b. 1984, Poitiers). CF j2012 s19.
[2] Laura Cappelle, 'Molière and Genet team up at the Comédie-Française', in the *Financial Times* (26 September 2017).

A major work from the end of the 19th century entered the repertoire, Wedekind's *L'Éveil du printemps* (*Spring Awakening*). This exploration of sexual awakening in the young still has the power to provoke and disturb. To explore the universality of Wedekind's theme, director Clément Hervieu-Léger took the play out of its period. The costumes were influenced by English school uniforms of the 1950s and 60s; and Patrice Chéreau's great designer Richard Peduzzi created an abstract setting of tall panels in deep blue, moved to form solid walls or narrow columns, and divided into shapes by the sculptural lighting of Bertrand Couderc. Georgia Scalliet, Sébastien Pouderoux and Christophe Montenez were wholly convincing as the teenagers.

Five years after his celebrated *La Trilogie de la villégiature*, Alain Françon revived one of Goldoni's best-known works – *La Locandiera*. This was Françon's ninth production for the troupe since 1986. Goldoni's comedy, in which the patroness of a little hotel, an independent woman of wit, charm and self-possession, uses her femininity to seduce and therefore get her own back on a misogynistic knight who has insulted her, provided a wonderful role for Florence Viala. Françon allowed the piece to speak for itself and did not impose an overtly feminist reading.

Ruf's policy of bringing the world's best directors to the Comédie continued with the arrival of Robert Carsen, who directed Shakespeare's *La Tempête* in the Salle Richelieu, and Thomas Ostermeier, who staged *La Nuit des rois* (*Twelfth Night*) at the beginning of the 2018/19 season. *La Tempête* featured a white set and video of a grey ocean churning beneath a grey sky, one of the poetic images deployed by Carsen and his designers to conjure Shakespeare's territory of the mind, his final meditation on life, death, love and redemption. Carsen's cast included Michel Vuillermoz as Prospero, Stéphane Varupenne as Caliban, Christophe Montenez as Ariel, Georgia Scalliet as Miranda, Loïc Corbery as Ferdinand, and Serge Bagdassarian as Antonio.

La Nuit des rois was archetypical Ostermeier, with additions to the text that referenced President Macron (a new translation by Olivier Cadiot was adapted by the director). The big idea was to see the play through a lens of 21st century gender politics. But

Shakespeare's interest in the play of the sexes was much more ambiguous and subtle than Ostermeier's. The costumes were hideous, but the actors performed valiantly. Ostermeier had a dream cast. Viola and Olivia were played by Georgia Scalliet and Adeline d'Hermy, Orsino by Denis Podalydès, Malvolio by Sébastien Pouderoux, Feste by Stéphane Varupenne, Sir Toby by Laurent Stocker, and Sir Andrew by Christophe Montenez. Ostermeier's non-Shakespearean additions were enjoyed in the auditorium and by some of the reviewers. In contrast, Emmanuel Daumas's new production of Marivaux's *L'Heureux stratagème*, at the Vieux-Colombier, used its white abstract setting and modern dress in a style that was mostly fresh and nuanced. Marivaux's bitter-sweet comedy was beautifully performed by the Comédiens-français.

In the summer of 2019, Ruf premiered a new play by Pauline Bureau, her first for the Comédie. *Hors la loi*, which Bureau directed at the Vieux-Colombier, was based on the Bobigny trial of 1972. Claire de La Rüe du Can played the young victim. This was her second big success of the season following her performance as the Comtesse in *L'Heureux stratagème*. Also that summer, Ruf directed a new production of Brecht's *La Vie de Galilée*, a work last staged at the Comédie by Antoine Vitez in 1991, and took Ivo van Hove's *Électre/Oreste* to the ancient theatre at Epidaurus in Greece. This was the Comédie's first visit to Epidaurus. Shortly afterwards, the success of Ruf's first five years was acknowledged by the Minister of Culture, Franck Riester, who renewed Ruf's contract for a second term.

The 2019/20 season was disrupted during its first months by the national strikes that followed the Macron government's decision to change the pensions system, and then, in March, closed down altogether as the government introduced measures to halt the spread of COVID-19. The revival of Ivo van Hove's *Électre/Oreste* was the production most affected by the strikes in November and December. The season opened at the Vieux-Colombier with the Comédie-Française's first-ever production of Shakespeare's *Julius Caesar*, directed by Rodolphe Dana, making his debut with the troupe. Dana adapted the play for five actors and five actresses and cast the women in the leading roles of Caesar (Martine Chevallier), Marc

Antony (Georgia Scalliet) and Cassius (Clotilde de Bayser). The thinking behind this decision formed part of Ruf's openness to new ideas, including controversial ideas, and was influenced by his desire to give the women in the troupe parity with the men when it came to the casting of major roles. He told *L'Express*: 'In Anglo-Saxon countries there is a greater desire for quotas than in France. Ten years ago, I would not have considered the question of parity. Today we have to think about it. Beyond parity, it can be theatrically very fertile. It reveals something else in actors and actresses. If the role is beautifully interpreted by a man or a woman, that is enough.'[1] The Comédie's *Julius Caesar* was an experiment motivated by artistic considerations. Marc Antony was Georgia Scalliet's fifth Shakespearean part in ten years, following Anne in the *Merry Wives of Windsor*, Cressida in *Troilus and Cressida*, Miranda in *The Tempest* and Viola in *Twelfth Night*. She decided to leave the Comédie at the end of the season, a major blow for the troupe.

The most newsworthy play in the Salle Richelieu was Tony Kushner's *Angels in America*, a work championed in England by the National Theatre in productions by Declan Donnellan (1993) and Marianne Elliott (2017). Arnaud Desplechin, who directed, condensed the two parts into a single play. His actors were Dominique Blanc, Jennifer Decker, Clément Hervieu-Léger, Gaël Kamilindi, Jérémy Lopez, Christophe Montenez, Florence Viala and Michel Vuillermoz.

Before the arrival of COVID-19, the plan had been to close the Salle Richelieu in April so that it could be modernised to improve access for people with reduced mobility and to lease the Théâtre Marigny (1,000 seats, so a little larger than the Salle Richelieu) and the Marigny's studio (300 seats) on the Champs-Élysées from April until the end of the season. At the Marigny, Ruf had planned to present a new production of Molière's *Le Bourgeois gentilhomme* alongside revivals of *Le Malade imaginaire*, Rostand's *Cyrano de Bergerac*, Marivaux's *Le Petit-maître corrigé*, Marie Rémond et Sébastien Pouderoux's *Comme une pierre qui* (in the studio), and

---

[1] Quoted (in French) in 'A la Comédie-Française, les femmes prennent le pouvoir', in *L'Express* (1 October 2019).

Paul Claudel's *Partage de Midi* – a revival of Yves Beaunesne's production of 2007 with its original cast, Éric Ruf, Hervé Pierre, Christian Gonon and Marina Hands.

During the surreal and sombre months of the lockdown, the Comédie-Française served its public by creating a daily programme of talks and readings, including readings for children, online. The troupe called the programme 'La Comédie Continue':

> The whole company and staff have mobilised, at a time when it is impossible to perform in our theatres in Paris or on tour. With 'La Comédie continue!' we offer a programme that is family-orientated and educational, poetic, diverting and always theatrical. Welcome to everyone![1]

Members of the company used their phones or computers to broadcast from their homes. The actors were calm and engaging in these difficult circumstances. Each evening the Comédie released a live recording from its archive, most of them for the first time. Anne Kessler's production of *La Double inconstance* (2015) was broadcast on the first evening, 30 March, followed, later in the week, by Alain Françon's *Three Sisters* (2011), Clément Hervieu-Léger's *Le Misanthrope* (2014), and Éric Ruf's *Peer Gynt*, filmed at the Grand Palais in 2012. During the second week, Christiane Jatahy's 2017 production of *La Règle du jeu* and Hervieu-Léger's 2018 production of *L'Éveil du printemps*, both yet to be revived on the stage, made their screen debuts, followed by a classic from the 1980s – Racine's *Bérénice*, directed by Klaus-Michaël Gruber and starring Ludmila Mikaël in the title role. The Comédie's response to the crisis was admirable.

---

[1] From the Comédie-Française's website (March 2020). 'Toute la Troupe et la Maison se mobilisent, à l'heure de l'impossibilité de jouer dans les différentes salles parisiennes et en tournée. Avec 'La Comédie continue!' nous vous proposons une programmation à la fois familiale et pédagogique, poétique, divertissante et toujours théâtrale. Bienvenue à tous!'

3   La Cité du Théâtre

While planning his seasons, Ruf was also working to achieve his primary goal of acquiring new theatres. With the support of President Hollande and the Ministry of Culture, Ruf worked with his colleagues at the Odéon, the Opéra and the Conservatoire (Stéphane Braunschweig, Stéphane Lissner, and Claire Lasne-Darcueil) to present a joint project that would bring together three of the national institutions at the location of the Ateliers Berthier (the Odéon's second theatre) at the Porte de Clichy in northern Paris, just inside the Périphérique, at a point where central Paris meets outer Paris. Ruf had acted in the Ateliers Berthier's inaugural production in 2003, Chéreau's *Phèdre*, created on a bifrontal stage, and the experience had, in part, led to his conviction that the Comédie needed a similar kind of theatre space. A proscenium theatre like the Salle Richelieu could only be configured in one way.

The warehouses beside the Ateliers Berthier housed the workshops of the Opéra. The Opéra would move these to the Bastille, allowing the warehouses to be redeveloped to create two theatres for the Comédie, enhanced facilities for the Odéon and a new home for the Conservatoire. Nothing less than a Cité du Théâtre would be created. The project would form part of the rejuvenation of the Clichy-Batignolles quarter.

The larger, modular, stage would have around six-hundred seats; the smaller would have around two-hundred-and-fifty. The Comédie would give up the Vieux-Colombier and the Studio-Théâtre. Ruf and his fellow artistic directors agreed that the shared, communal nature of the project was key. They would house their archives jointly and staff would share one canteen. The public facilities, including a restaurant, would serve patrons of both the Comédie and the Odéon. Crucially, all parties understood that the project had to have the credo of 'theatre for all' at its heart; it had to be inclusive, and aim to be, in its architecture and ethos, as welcoming as possible to people who lived on the other side of the Périphérique. Ruf even suggested that the new base could, over time, become more important than the Salle Richelieu:

> The Boulevards des Maréchaux form a symbolic barrier between a conquered public and an audience still to be conquered. We who are historically in the centre of Paris, will move to one of the districts of Greater Paris. Perhaps one day, the Cité du Théâtre will be the main home of the Comédie-Française. It is up to us to publicise this change as a great opportunity for the public.[1]

It seems that Ruf was the main driver of the scheme, for he had spoken to Hollande about his plans, in the abstract, at their very first meeting. The scheme was announced by the Ministry of Culture in October 2016. Approved by Hollande, it would fall to his successor to decide whether to allocate the estimated 150 million Euros required.

Emmanuel Macron had been a schoolboy actor. On the night of his election victory, 7 May 2017, he conceived a moment of personal theatre that would have won the admiration of both Louis XIV and Napoléon. To reach the platform that had been constructed in the place du Carrousel, Macron walked alone across the Cour Napoléon of the Louvre. The large square was empty and silent. A camera tracked Macron as he made his slow journey around the Pyramide du Louvre until he finally reached the platform and was greeted by the waiting crowd. Macron was not a president to undervalue the arts or to miss the kind of opportunity afforded by the Cité du Théâtre (even if it had been instigated by his predecessor).

Macron gave the green light in June 2017. There is a risk associated with a new development on this scale. Arts centres went out of fashion some time ago, and a new audience could be hard to attract, as the Royal Shakespeare Company discovered when it moved to the Barbican Centre in east London. The hope is that, with stylish architecture and attractive open spaces, the Porte de Clichy will become one of the most happening quarters of the city. The opening of the Cité du Théâtre, in (if all goes to plan) 2024,

---

[1] Quoted (in French) in Éric le Mitouard, 'Paris: la Cité du théâtre s'impose à Berthier', in *Le Parisien* (30 November 2017).

will be a landmark moment in the history of the Comédie-Française.[1] It will inevitably define Éric Ruf's second term as Administrator.

[1] At the time of writing, April 2020, there have been no recent updates on progress.

Previous double page:
26. *Le Petit-maître corrigé* by Marivaux, Richelieu, 2016. Clément Hervieu-Léger (mise en scène), Éric Ruf (décor), Caroline de Vivaise (costumes), Bertrand Couderc (lighting). L-R: Adeline d'Hermy (Marton), Loïc Corbery (Rosimond), Dominique Blanc (La Marquise), Claire de La Rüe du Can (Hortense), Didier Sandre (Le Comte). Photograph by Raphael Gaillarde.

15

La Maison de Shakespeare?

27. *Troilus et Cressida* by Shakespeare, Richelieu, 2013.
Jean-Yves Ruf (mise en scène), Éric Ruf (décor), Claudia Jenatsch
(costumes), Christian Dubet (lighting).

L-R: Laurent Cogez (Patrocle), Sébastien Pouderoux (Achille), Louis Arene (Diomede), Georgia Scalliet (Cressida), Éric Ruf (Ulysse), Laurent Natrella (Agamemnon). Photograph by Pascal Victor.

'French masterpieces have been performed before every court and in every academy of Italy. They are played everywhere from the borders of the Arctic Sea to the sea which separates Europe from Africa. It will be time to argue when the same honour has been done to a single piece by Shakespeare.'[1] – Voltaire

During the period 2007 to 2019, the Comédie-Française staged ten of Shakespeare's plays, four of them after Éric Ruf became Administrator in 2014.[2] Only Molière was performed more frequently. Five plays by Racine were produced, three by Corneille and none by Voltaire. For the first time in its history, the Comédie made producing Shakespeare one of the key priorities of its work.

To get to this point was a long process. During the first 325 years of the troupe's existence, 1680 to 2005, there were less than forty separate productions. The vogue for Shakespeare during the romantic era didn't immediately result in even the few plays that were widely known to the French being performed with any regularity. 'Shakespeare,' wrote Victor Hugo, 'est un esprit anglais. Il est très anglais – trop anglais. […] Mais en même temps […] ce poëte anglais est un génie humain.'[3] For many of Hugo's compatriots, Shakespeare's Englishness was a problem. The French acknowledged Shakespeare's genius, but still found much of his art alien.

The consensus view, in the period up until the Great War, was

---

[1] Quoted in John Pemble, *Shakespeare Goes to Paris*, p.4.

[2] See Notebook, section VI.

[3] Victor Hugo, *William Shakespeare* (Paris: Librairie Internationale, 1864), p.473.

that admiration for Shakespeare should not be allowed to challenge the superiority of Molière and Racine for the French. A narrowly nationalistic interpretation of the cultural meaning of both Shakespeare and Racine took hold, fuelled by clichés and stereotypes. Shakespeare was indelibly English; Racine was indelibly French. Shakespeare's unruly creativity posed a threat to Racine's logic and refinement.

Attitudes started to change during the first two decades of the 20th century. The longstanding view in France that Shakespeare's plays were too multi-faceted to be fully realised in the theatre, and were better read and studied, was dismissed by André Antoine and Jacques Copeau, who both placed interpretation and *mise en scène* above star actors and who were determined to stage the plays in translations that strove for authenticity. This meant commissioning new translations or translating the plays themselves. Antoine's production of *King Lear* (translated by Pierre Loti) at his Théâtre Antoine in the 10th arrondissement in 1904 was a landmark. It proved popular too. For the first time, French audiences were seeing a play by Shakespeare translated into French rather than a French play loosely based on Shakespeare. At the Odéon, between 1906 and 1912, Antoine staged *Julius Caesar*, *Romeo and Juliet*, *Coriolanus* and *Troilus and Cressida* (a work unseen in England since its premiere) in prose translations that were at least faithful to the plots and characters. The torch was passed to Copeau, who, as we have seen, mounted a revolutionary production of *Twelfth Night* at the Vieux-Colombier in 1914. Audiences embraced Copeau's sparse aesthetic. At the same time, the Comédie was performing *Macbeth* in an old translation by Jean Richepin. 'Its rhyming alexandrines and Romantic stage effects,' writes John Pemble in *Shakespeare Goes to Paris*, 'were made to seem even more old-fashioned by Copeau's Shakespeare.'[1]

After the Second World War, a new generation recast Shakespeare as European – his humanism and affinity to Montaigne were suddenly as important as his Englishness. While Barrault at the Marigny could proclaim that Shakespeare was more relevant than

---

[1] John Pemble, *Shakespeare Goes to Paris*, p.128.

Racine, and Jean Vilar could make Shakespeare's virtually unknown (in France) *Richard II* and *Henry IV* the centrepieces of the
first Avignon Festivals (1947-50), the Comédie-Française, as the
national theatre, shared responsibility with the education system to
proclaim and uphold the importance of Racine, Corneille and Molière, and this may be why the Comédie was slow to programme
Shakespeare's plays with any regularity. When, in the 1950s, the
presence of Racine's plays at the Comédie started to slip, it didn't
go unnoticed. De Gaulle's culture minister André Malraux raised
the issue with the Comédie, and demanded more Racine. In the
1990s, Jean-Pierre Miquel was so concerned about the neglect of
most of Racine's output that he instigated a cycle of his plays across
several seasons. In the meantime, Terry Hands's productions of
Richard III, *Pericles* and *Twelfth Night* (1972-76) transformed the
troupe's fortunes with Shakespeare, at least for a time. The departure of Pierre Dux ended this important chapter. It would be
almost ten years before the Comédie returned to Shakespeare with
a production of *Macbeth* in 1985.

Half of Shakespeare's thirty-eight plays remain unperformed by
the Comédie-Française. Of those performed, seven have been
staged only once; and four only twice. The most popular are *Hamlet* (seven productions – although the first two contained very little
of Shakespeare's play) and *Othello* (five productions – although the
first one contained little of Shakespeare's play), followed by *Twelfth
Night*, *The Merchant of Venice*, and *Romeo and Juliet* (four productions each). For the modern period (since 1945), *Twelfth Night* and
A Midsummer Night's Dream come out on top, with three productions each.

Some of the omissions are curious. Ducis's *King Lear* was staged
in 1783, but a faithful translation has never been produced at the
Comédie. The two parts of *Henry IV*, for many the pinnacle of
Shakespeare's art, have never been staged, despite the precedent of
Jean Vilar's production at Avignon in 1950. Perhaps the most sur-
prising omissions are the comedies *Love's Labour's Lost* and *The
Comedy of Errors*, plays that occupy the same territory explored a
hundred years later by Molière and Marivaux. It remains to be seen

whether the Comédie will continue to stage Shakespeare at the current rate of a production every season. Shakespeare's plays, with their long cast lists, linguistic complexity and reliance on intricate ensemble playing as well as dominant title roles, are best served by permanent theatre companies, and no such company exists today in England. The Comédie-Française is the last genuine company still standing and, if it wasn't for the knotty issues surrounding translation – is translated Shakespeare ever really Shakespeare? –, it could mischievously be argued that the troupe has a responsibility to Shakespeare. Voltaire, one hopes, would have enjoyed the irony if nothing else.

28. *Le Songe d'une nuit d'été* by Shakespeare, Richelieu, 2014. Muriel Mayette
(mise en scène), Didier Monfajon (décor), Sylvie Lombart (costumes), Pascal Noël
(lighting). L-R: Sébastien Pouderoux (Lysander), Suliane Brahim (Hermia), Laurent
Lafitte (Demetrius), Adeline d'Hermy (Helena).
Photograph by Christophe Raynaud de Lage.

Notebook

29. *Les Créanciers* by Strindberg, Studio, 2018. Anne Kessler (mise en scène),
Gilles Taschet (décor), Éric Dumas (lighting), Bernadette Villard (costumes).
Adeline d'Hermy (Tekla), Sébastien Pouderoux (Adolf).
Photograph by Brigitte Enguérand.

I The Troupe in 2019/20

ADMINISTRATEUR GÉNÉRAL
Éric Ruf

SOCIÉTAIRES
Claude Mathieu (1985)
Martine Chevallier (1988)
Véronique Vella (1989)
Michel Favory (1992)
Thierry Hancisse (1993)
Anne Kessler (1994)
Cécile Brune (1997)
Sylvia Bergé (1998)
Éric Génovèse (1998)
Bruno Raffaelli (1998)
Alain Lenglet (2000)
Florence Viala (2000)
Coraly Zahonero (2000)
Denis Podalydès (2000)
Alexandre Pavloff (2002)
Françoise Gillard (2002)
Clotilde de Bayser (2004)
Jérôme Pouly (2004)
Laurent Stocker (2004)
Guillaume Gallienne (2005)
Laurent Natrella (2007)
Michel Vuillermoz (2007)
Elsa Lepoivre (2007)
Christian Gonon (2009)
Julie Sicard (2009)
Loïc Corbery (2010)
Serge Bagdassarian (2011)
Hervé Pierre (2011)
Bakary Sangaré (2012)
Pierre Louis-Calixte (2012)

Christian Hecq (2012)
Nicolas Lormeau (2014)
Gilles David (2014)
Stéphane Varupenne (2015)
Suliane Brahim (2016)
Adeline d'Hermy (2016)
Georgia Scalliet (2017)
Jérémy Lopez (2017)
Clément Hervieu-Léger (2018)
Benjamin Lavernhe (2019)
Sébastien Pouderoux (2019)
Didier Sandre (2020)
Christophe Montenez (2020)

PENSIONNAIRES
Nâzim Boudjenah
Danièle Lebrun
Jennifer Decker
Laurent Lafitte
Noam Morgensztern
Claire de La Rüe du Can
Anna Cervinka
Rebecca Marder
Pauline Clément
Dominique Blanc
Julien Frison
Gaël Kamilindi
Yoann Gasiorowski
Jean Chevalier
Élise Lhomeau
Birane Ba
Élissa Alloula

Marina Hands
Clément Bresson

SOCIÉTAIRES HONORAIRES
Micheline Boudet
Ludmila Mikaël
Michel Aumont
Geneviève Casile
Jacques Sereys
François Beaulieu
Roland Bertin
Claire Vernet
Nicolas Silberg

Simon Eine
Alain Pralon
Catherine Salviat
Catherine Ferran
Catherine Samie
Catherine Hiegel
Pierre Vial
Andrzej Seweryn
Éric Ruf
Muriel Mayette-Holtz
Gérard Giroudon
Martine Chevallier
Michel Favory

II General Administrators since 1859

1859-1871	Édouard Thierry
1871-1885	Émile Perrin
1885-1913	Jules Claretie
1913-1915	Albert Carré
1915-1936	Émile Fabre
1936-1940	Édouard Bourdet
1940-1941	Jacques Copeau
1941-1944	Jean-Louis Vaudoyer
1944-1944	André Brunot
1944-1944	Jean Sarment
1944-1945	Pierre Dux
1945-1945	Joseph Denis
1945-1946	André Obey
1947-1953	Pierre-Aimé Touchard
1953-1959	Pierre Descaves
1959-1960	Claude Bréart de Boisanger
1960-1970	Maurice Escande
1970-1979	Pierre Dux
1979-1983	Jacques Toja
1983-1986	Jean-Pierre Vincent
1986-1988	Jean Le Poulain
1988-1988	Claude Winter
1988-1990	Antoine Vitez
1990-1993	Jacques Lassalle
1993-2001	Jean-Pierre Miquel
2001-2006	Marcel Bozonnet
2006-2014	Muriel Mayette
2014-	Éric Ruf

30. *La Double inconstance* by Marivaux, Richelieu, 2014. Anne Kessler (mise en scène), Jacques Gabel (décor), Renato Bianchi (costumes), Arnaud Jung (lighting). Adeline d'Hermy (Silvia), Florence Viala (Flaminia). Photograph by Raphael Gaillarde.

III Seasons 2002/03 to 2019/20

2002/03

Studio
QUATRE AVEC LE MORT
by François Bon
dir Charles Tordjman
From 2 October 2002

Richelieu
SAVANNAH BAY
by Marguerite Duras
dir Éric Vigner
From 12 October 2002

Vieux-Colombier
UNE VISITE INOPPORTUNE
by Copi
dir Lukas Hemleb
From 15 October 2002

Richelieu
DOM JUAN OU LE FESTIN DE
PIERRE
by Molière
dir Jacques Lassalle
From 16 October 2002

Richelieu
LE MARCHAND DE VENISE
by William Shakespeare
dir Andrei Serban
From 28 October 2002

Vieux-Colombier
L'EXTERMINATION DU
PEUPLE
by Werner Schwab
dir Philippe Adrien

From 6 November 2002

Richelieu
LE DINDON
by Georges Feydeau
dir Lukas Hemleb
From 16 November 2002

Studio
COURTELINE AU GRAND-
GUIGNOL
by André-Paul Antoine and
Georges Courteline
dir Nicolas Lormeau
From 20 November 2002

Richelieu
RUY BLAS
by Victor Hugo
dir Brigitte Jaques-Wajeman
From 11 December 2002

Richelieu
PRÉSENCES
by Yacine Kateb
dir Mohamed Kacimi
From 6 January 2003

Richelieu
LE MALADE IMAGINAIRE
by Molière
dir Claude Stratz
From 9 January 2003

Vieux-Colombier
LES PAPIERS D'ASPERN
by Jean Pavans
dir Jacques Lassalle

From 15 January 2003

Vieux-Colombier
LE THÉÂTRE DE NATALIE
DESSAY
Rencontre
From 22 January 2003

Studio
LA CANTATE À TROIS VOIX
by Paul Claudel
dir Madeleine Marion
From 29 January 2003

Richelieu
PAPA DOIT MANGER
by Marie NDiaye
dir André Engel
From 22 February 2003

Vieux-Colombier
QUATRE QUATUORS POUR
UN WEEK-END
by Gao Xingjian
dir Gao Xingjian
From 12 Mars 2003

Studio
AH, VOUS VOILÀ DUMAS!
by Alain Pralon after Alexandre
Dumas
dir Alain Pralon
From 2 April 2003

Richelieu
LA FORÊT
by Alexandre Ostrovski
dir Piotr Fomenko
From 14 April 2003

Vieux-Colombier
MONSIEUR DE
POURCEAUGNAC
by Molière
dir Philippe Adrien
From 7 May 2003

Richelieu
ESTHER

by Jean Racine
dir Alain Zaepffel
From 24 May 2003

Vieux-Colombier
NEDJMA
by Kateb Yacine
dir Ziani-Chérif Ayad
From 25 June 2003

2003/04

Vieux-Colombier
BRITANNICUS
by Jean Racine
dir Brigitte Jaques-Wajeman
From 21 January 2003

Vieux-Colombier
HOMEBODY / KABUL
by Tony Kushner
dir Jorge Lavelli
From 17 Septembre 2003

Richelieu
LA FORÊT
by Alexandre Ostrovski
dir Piotr Fomenko
From 18 Septembre 2003

Studio
CONVERSATIONS AVEC
ANTOINE VITEZ
by Émile Copfermann
dir Daniel Soulier
From 25 Septembre 2003

Richelieu
LE DINDON
by Georges Feydeau
dir Lukas Hemleb
From 29 Septembre 2003

Richelieu
LA NUIT DES ROIS
by William Shakespeare
dir Andrzej Seweryn
From 7 October 2003

Richelieu
LE MALADE IMAGINAIRE
by Molière
dir Claude Stratz
From 9 October 2003

Vieux-Colombier
LE JEU D'ADAM
by Adam de la Halle
dir Jacques Rebotier
From 9 November 2003

Richelieu
PLATONOV
by Anton Tchekhov
dir Jacques Lassalle
From 22 November 2003

Studio
BOULI MIRO
by Fabrice Melquiot
dir Christian Gonon
From 27 November 2003

Studio
LES EFFRACTEURS
by José Pliya
dir José Pliya
From 29 January 2004

Richelieu
FABLES DE LA FONTAINE
by Jean de La Fontaine
dir Robert Wilson
From 30 January 2004

Vieux-Colombier
L'HISTOIRE DU THÉÂTRE /
FRANÇOIS REGNAULT
From 10 February 2004

Vieux-Colombier
LE THÉÂTRE DE GISÈLE
CASADESUS
Rencontre
From 18 February 2004

Richelieu
LE GRAND THÉÂTRE DU
MONDE ET PROCÉS EN
SÉPARATION DE L'ÂME ET
DU CORPS
by Pedro Calderon de la Barca
dir Christian Schiaretti
From 13 Mars 2004

Vieux-Colombier
GENGIS CHEZ LES PYGMÉES
by Grégory Motton
dir Thierry de Peretti
From 24 Mars 2004

Studio
LE CONTE D'HIVER
by William Shakespeare
dir Muriel Mayette-Holtz
From 31 Mars 2004

Richelieu
PAPA DOIT MANGER
by Marie NDiaye
dir André Engel
From 1 April 2004

Vieux-Colombier
LES PAPIERS D'ASPERN
by Jean Pavans
dir Jacques Lassalle
From 18 May 2004

2004/05

Vieux-Colombier
FEU LE MUSIC-HALL
by Colette
dir Karine Saporta
From 22 September 2004

Studio
LE PRIVILÈGE DES CHEMINS
by Fernando Pessoa
dir Éric Génovèse
From 13 October 2004

Richelieu
LE MENTEUR
by Pierre Corneille
dir Jean-Louis Benoit
From 15 October 2004

Richelieu
LA NUIT DES ROIS
by William Shakespeare
dir Andrzej Seweryn
From 20 October 2004

Richelieu
LE GRAND THÉÂTRE DU
MONDE ET PROCÉS EN
SÉPARATION DE L'ÂME ET
DU CORPS
by Pedro Calderon de la Barca
dir Christian Schiaretti
From 28 October 2004

Richelieu
FABLES DE LA FONTAINE
by Jean de La Fontaine
dir Robert Wilson
From 12 November 2004

Vieux-Colombier
LE MYSTÈRE DE LA RUE
ROUSSELET
by Eugène Labiche
dir Thierry de Peretti
From 17 November 2004

Studio
BOULI MIRO
by Fabrice Melquiot
dir Christian Gonon
From 18 November 2004

Richelieu
PLACE DES HÉROS
by Thomas Bernhard
dir Arthur Nauzyciel
From 22 December 2004

Vieux-Colombier
LES GRELOTS DU FOU
by Luigi Pirandello

dir Claude Stratz
From 19 January 2005

Studio
LE DÉBUT DE L'A.
by Pascal Rambert
dir Pascal Rambert
From 27 January 2005

Studio
LABORATOIRE DES FORMES /
ROBERT GARNIER
Rencontre
From 10 February 2005

Richelieu
LES BACCHANTES
by Euripide
dir André Wilms
From 12 February 2005

Richelieu
PLATONOV
by Anton Chekhov
dir Jacques Lassalle
From 28 February 2005

Richelieu
JOURNÉE L'INTÉGRALE /
TEXTES D'ARTHUR
RIMBAUD
Lecture
From 10 March 2005

Vieux-Colombier
EMBRASSER LES OMBRES
by Lars Norén
dir Joël Jouanneau
From 16 March 2005

Richelieu
L'AMOUR MÉDECIN ET LE
SICILIEN OU L'AMOUR
PEINTRE
by Molière
dir Jean-Marie Villégier and
Jonathan Duverger
From 9 April 2005

Vieux-Colombier
BRITANNICUS
by Jean Racine
dir Brigitte Jaques-Wajeman
From 17 May 2005

Richelieu
TARTUFFE
by Molière
dir Marcel Bozonnet
From 21 May 2005

Richelieu
INTÉGRALE RIMBAUD
by Arthur Rimbaud
dir Bruno Raffaelli, Jean-Pierre
Jourdain, Christine Fersen, Michel
Favory
From 5 June 2005

Richelieu
LA FORÊT
by Alexandre Ostrovski
dir Piotr Fomenko
From 24 June 2005

Richelieu
LE MALADE IMAGINAIRE
by Molière
dir Claude Stratz
From 30 June 2005

2005/06

Richelieu
TARTUFFE
by Molière
dir Marcel Bozonnet
From 12 September 2005

Studio
DRAMUSCULES
by Thomas Bernhard
dir Muriel Mayette-Holtz
From 22 September 2005

Richelieu
FABLES DE LA FONTAINE

by Jean de La Fontaine
dir Robert Wilson
From 11 October 2005

Richelieu
LE MALADE IMAGINAIRE
by Molière
dir Claude Stratz
From 14 October 2005

Richelieu
LE CID
by Pierre Corneille
dir Brigitte Jaques-Wajeman
From 29 October 2005

Vieux-Colombier
OH LES BEAUX JOURS
by Samuel Beckett
dir Frederick Wiseman
From 22 November 2005

Studio
BOULI REDÉBOULE
by Fabrice Melquiot
dir Philippe Lagrue
From 24 November 2005

Richelieu
LES BACCHANTES
by Euripide
dir André Wilms
From 1 December 2005

Richelieu
L'ESPACE FURIEUX
by Valère Novarina
dir Valère Novarina
From 21 January 2006

Vieux-Colombier
LA MAISON DES MORTS
by Philippe Minyana
dir Robert Cantarella
From 1 February 2006

Richelieu
LE MENTEUR
by Pierre Corneille

dir Jean-Louis Benoit
From 10 February 2006

Studio
GRIEF[S]
by August Strindberg, Henrik
Ibsen and Ingmar Bergman
dir Anne Kessler
From 16 February 2006

Vieux-Colombier
TÊTE D'OR
by Paul Claudel
dir Anne Delbée
From 29 March 2006

Richelieu
L'AMOUR MÉDECIN ET LE
SICILIEN OU L'AMOUR
PEINTRE
by Molière
dir Jean-Marie Villégier and
Jonathan Duverger
From 10 April 2006

Studio
MON CORPS, MON GENTIL
CORPS, DIS-MOI
by Jan Fabre
dir Marcel Bozonnet
From 26 April 2006

Studio
SAINT-FRANÇOIS, LE DIVIN
JONGLEUR
by Dario Fo
dir Claude Mathieu
From 10 May 2006

Studio
L'INATTENDU
by Fabrice Melquiot
dir Thierry Hancisse
From 24 May 2006

Richelieu
CYRANO DE BERGERAC
by Edmond Rostand
dir Denis Podalydès

From 27 May 2006

Vieux-Colombier
LES GRELOTS DU FOU
by Luigi Pirandello
dir Claude Stratz
From 3 June 2006

Studio
MARYS' À MINUIT
by Serge Valletti
dir Laurent Stocker
From 7 June 2006

2006/07

Richelieu
IL CAMPIELLO
by Carlo Goldoni
dir Jacques Lassalle
From 16 September 2006

Vieux-Colombier
L'ÉLÉGANT PROFIL D'UNE
BUGATTI
by Jean Audureau
dir Serge Tranvouez
From 20 September 2006

Studio
CINQ DRAMATICULES
by Samuel Beckett
dir Jean Dautremay
From 21 September 2006

Richelieu
LE CID
by Pierre Corneille
dir Brigitte Jaques-Wajeman
From 22 September 2006

Vieux-Colombier
OH LES BEAUX JOURS
by Samuel Beckett
dir Frederick Wiseman
From 26 October 2006

Vieux-Colombier
LES TEMPS DIFFICILES
by Édouard Bourdet
dir Jean-Claude Berutti
From 22 November 2006

Studio
OPHÉLIE ET AUTRES
ANIMAUX
by Jacques Roubaud
dir Jean-Pierre Jourdain
From 30 November 2006

Richelieu
PEDRO ET LE
COMMANDEUR
by Felix Lope de Vega
dir Omar Porras
From 2 December 2006

Richelieu
LE MALADE IMAGINAIRE
by Molière
dir Claude Stratz
From 23 December 2006

Vieux-Colombier
ORGIE
by Pier Paolo Pasolini
dir Marcel Bozonnet
From 17 January 2007

Studio
SUR LA GRAND-ROUTE
d'Anton Chekhov
dir Guillaume Gallienne
From 1 February 2007

Richelieu
LE RETOUR AU DÉSERT
by Bernard-Marie Koltès
dir Muriel Mayette-Holtz
From 17 February 2007

Vieux-Colombier
LA FESTA
by Spiro Scimone
dir Galin Stoev
From 13 March 2007

Richelieu
PARTAGE DE MIDI
by Paul Claudel
dir Yves Beaunesne
From 31 March 2007

Studio
POUR UN OUI OU POUR UN
NON
by Nathalie Sarraute
dir Léonie Simaga
From 19 April 2007

Richelieu
LE MISANTHROPE
by Molière
dir Lukas Hemleb
From 26 May 2007

2007/08

Vieux-Colombier
UNE CONFRÉRIE DE
FARCEURS
by Bernard Faivre
dir François Chattot and Jean-
Louis Hourdin
From 17 September to 27 October
2007

Richelieu
LE MARIAGE DE FIGARO OU
LA FOLLE JOURNÉE
by Beaumarchais
dir Christophe Rauck
From 22 September 2007 to 27
February 2008

Studio
LES SINCÈRES
by Marivaux
dir Jean Liermier
From 27 September to 18
November 2007

Richelieu
PEDRO ET LE

COMMANDEUR
by Felix Lope de Vega
dir Omar Porras
From 27 September to 29
December 2007

Richelieu
LE MALADE IMAGINAIRE
by Molière
dir Claude Stratz
From 4 October to 26 December
2007

Richelieu
FABLES DE LA FONTAINE
by Jean de La Fontaine
dir Robert Wilson
From 17 October 2007 to 29
January 2008

Vieux-Colombier
LES PRÉCIEUSES RIDICULES
by Molière
dir Dan Jemmett
From 14 November to 29
December 2007

Studio
LA FIN DU
COMMENCEMENT
by Sean O'Casey
dir Célie Pauthe
From 8 December 2007 to 20
January 2008

Richelieu
LA MÉGÈRE APPRIVOISÉE
by William Shakespeare
dir Oskaras Koršunovas
trans François-Victor Hugo
From 8 December 2007 to 15 July
2008

Richelieu
PENTHÉSILÉE
by Heinrich von Kleist
dir Jean Liermier
From 26 January to I June 2008

Studio
SAINT-FRANÇOIS, LE DIVIN
JONGLEUR
by Dario Fo
dir Claude Mathieu
From 30 January to 24 February
2008

Vieux-Colombier
POUR UN OUI OU POUR UN
NON
by Nathalie Sarraute
dir Léonie Simaga
From 13 February to 2 March
2008

Richelieu
LE MISANTHROPE
by Molière
dir Lukas Hemleb
From 15 February to 27 April
2008

Richelieu
JUSTE LA FIN DU MONDE
by Jean-Luc Lagarce
dir Michel Raskine
From 1 March to 1 July 2008

Studio
DOUCE VENGEANCE ET
AUTRES SKETCHES
by Hanokh Levin
dir Galin Stoev
From 13 March to 20 April 2008

Vieux-Colombier
BONHEUR?
d'Emmanuel Darley
dir Andrés Lima
From 26 March to 27 April 2008

Richelieu
VIE DU GRAND DOM
QUICHOTTE
d'Antonio José da Silva
dir Émilie Valantin
trans Marie-Hélène Piwnik
From 19 April to 20 July 2008

Studio
TROIS HOMMES DANS UN
SALON
by François-René Cristiani
dir Anne Kessler
From 15 May to 29 June 2008

Vieux-Colombier
YERMA
by Federico García Lorca
dir Vicente Pradal
From 20 May to 29 June 2008

Richelieu
FIGARO DIVORCE
by Ödön von Horváth
dir Jacques Lassalle
From 31 May to 19 July 2008

Richelieu
CYRANO DE BERGERAC
d'Edmond Rostand
dir Denis Podalydès
From 20 June to 26 July 2008

2008/09

Richelieu
FANTASIO
by Alfred de Musset
dir Denis Podalydès
From 18 September 2008 to 15
March 2009

Studio
LES MÉTAMORPHOSES, LA
PETITE DANS LA FORÊT
PROFONDE
by Philippe Minyana
dir Marcial Di Fonzo Bo
From 19 September to 26 October
2008

Vieux-Colombier
FANNY
by Marcel Pagnol
dir Irène Bonnaud

From 24 September to 31 October
2008

Richelieu
LE MARIAGE DE FIGARO OU
LA FOLLE JOURNÉE
by Beaumarchais
dir Christophe Rauck
From 26 September 2008 to 25
January 2009

Richelieu
FIGARO DIVORCE
by Ödön von Horváth
dir Jacques Lassalle
From 3 October to 14 December
2008

Richelieu
LA MÉGÈRE APPRIVOISÉE
by William Shakespeare
dir Oskaras Koršunovas
Traduction Français Victor Hugo
From 13 October to 31 December
2008

Vieux-Colombier
LE VOYAGE DE MONSIEUR
PERRICHON
by Eugène Labiche
dir Julie Brochen
From 19 November 2008 to 11
January 2009

Studio
LE MARIAGE FORCÉ
by Molière
dir Pierre Pradinas
From 20 November 2008 to 8
January 2009

Richelieu
L'ILLUSION COMIQUE
by Pierre Corneille
dir Galin Stoev
From 6 December 2008 to 24 June
2009

Richelieu
CYRANO DE BERGERAC
by Edmond Rostand
dir Denis Podalydès
From 18 December 2008 to 22
March 2009

Vieux-Colombier
LA DISPUTE
by Marivaux
dir Muriel Mayette-Holtz
From 28 January to 15 March
2009

Studio
LES CHAISES
by Eugène Ionesco
dir Jean Dautremay
From 29 January to 8 March 2009

Richelieu
L'ORDINAIRE
by Michel Vinaver
dir Michel Vinaver and Gilone
Brun
From 7 to 8 February 2009

Studio
BÉRÉNICE
by Jean Racine
dir Faustin Linyekula
From 26 March to 7 May 2009

Richelieu
LA GRANDE MAGIE
by Eduardo De Filippo
dir Dan Jemmett
From 28 March to 19 July 2009

Richelieu
VIE DU GRAND DOM
QUICHOTTE ET DU GROS
by Antonio José da Silva
dir Émilie Valantin
Traduction Marie-Hélène Piwnik
From 8 April to 26 June 2009

Vieux-Colombier
PUR

by Lars Norén
dir Lars Norén
From 15 April to 17 May 2009

Richelieu
UBU ROI
by Alfred Jarry
dir Jean-Pierre Vincent
From 23 May to 21 July 2009

Vieux-Colombier
LES PRÉCIEUSES RIDICULES
by Molière
dir Dan Jemmett
From 27 May to 28 June 2009

Studio
VIVANT
by Annie Zadek
dir Pierre Meunier
From 28 May to 28 June 2009

Richelieu
IL CAMPIELLO
by Carlo Goldoni
dir Jacques Lassalle
From 12 June to 22 July 2009

Richelieu
LE MALADE IMAGINAIRE
by Molière
dir Claude Stratz
From 19 June to 23 July 2009

2009/10

Richelieu
L'AVARE
by Molière
dir Catherine Hiegel
From 19 September 2009 to 21
February 2010

Vieux-Colombier
QUATRE PIÈCES DE FEYDEAU
by Georges Feydeau
dir Gian Manuel Rau
From 23 September to 25 October

2009

Studio
COCTEAU-MARAIS
by Jacques Sereys
dir Jean-Luc Tardieu
From 24 September to 8
November 2009

Richelieu
FIGARO DIVORCE
by Ödön von Horváth
dir Jacques Lassalle
From 26 September 2009 to 7
February 2010

Richelieu
LA GRANDE MAGIE
by Eduardo De Filippo
dir Dan Jemmett
From 7 October 2009 to 17
January 2010

Richelieu
JUSTE LA FIN DU MONDE
by Jean-Luc Lagarce
dir Michel Raskine
From 26 October 2009 to 3
January 2010

Vieux-Colombier
LES AFFAIRES SONT LES
AFFAIRES
by Octave Mirbeau
dir Marc Paquien
From 18 November 2009 to 3
January 2010

Studio
LE LOUP / LES CONTES DU
CHAT PERCHÉ
by Marcel Aymé
dir Véronique Vella
From 26 November 2009 to 17
January 2010

Richelieu
LES JOYEUSES COMMÈRES
DE WINDSOR

by William Shakespeare
dir Andrés Lima
From 5 December 2009 to 2 May
2010

Vieux-Colombier
PAROLES, PAS DE RÔLES /
VAUDEVILLE
by De Schrijver, Van den Eede, de
Koning
dir TG STAN, DE KOE,
DISCORDIA
From 20 January to 28 February
2010

Studio
LE BRUIT DES OS QUI
CRAQUENT
by Suzanne Lebeau
dir Anne-Laure Liégeois
From 11 to 21 February 2010

Richelieu
MYSTÈRE BOUFFE ET
FABULAGES (VERSION 1)
by Dario Fo
dir Muriel Mayette-Holtz
From 13 February to 19 June 2010

Richelieu
MYSTÈRE BOUFFE ET
FABULAGES (VERSION 2)
by Dario Fo
dir Muriel Mayette-Holtz
From 14 February to 20 June 2010

Richelieu
FANTASIO
by Alfred de Musset
dir Denis Podalydès
From 19 February to 31 May 2010

Studio
BURN BABY BURN
by Carine Lacroix
dir Anne-Laure Liégeois
From 25 February to 7 March
2010

Richelieu
L'ILLUSION COMIQUE
by Pierre Corneille
dir Galin Stoev
From 2 March to 13 May 2010

Vieux-Colombier
LES NAUFRAGÉS
by Guy Zilberstein
dir Anne Kessler
From 24 March to 30 April 2010

Studio
LE BANQUET
by Platon
dir Jacques Vincey
From 25 March to 9 May 2010

Richelieu
LES OISEAUX
by Aristophane
dir Alfredo Arias
From 10 April to 18 July 2010

Vieux-Colombier
LA SEULE CERTITUDE QUE
J'AI
by Pierre Desproges
dir by Christian Gonon, Alain
Lenglet and Marc Fayet
From 5 to 19 May 2010

Richelieu
LES TROIS SŒURS
by Anton Chekhov
dir Alain Françon
From 22 May to 16 July 2010

Studio
LE MARIAGE FORCÉ
by Molière
dir Pierre Pradinas
From 27 May to 11 July 2010

Vieux-Colombier
LA FOLIE D'HÉRACLÈS
by Euripide
dir Christophe Perton
From 28 May to 30 June 2010

Richelieu
UBU ROI
by Alfred Jarry
dir Jean-Pierre Vincent
From 2 June to 15 July 2010

Richelieu
CYRANO DE BERGERAC
by Edmond Rostand
dir Denis Podalydès
From 17 June to 25 July 2010

Richelieu
LE MARIAGE DE FIGARO OU
LA FOLLE JOURNÉE
by Beaumarchais
dir Christophe Rauck
From 1 to 18 July 2010

2010/11

Richelieu
L'AVARE
by Molière
dir Catherine Hiegel
From 18 September to 2 January
2010

Richelieu
LA GRANDE MAGIE
by Eduardo De Filippo
dir Dan Jemmett
From 19 September to 28
November 2010

Richelieu
LES OISEAUX
by Aristophane
dir Alfredo Arias
From 20 September to 15
December 2010

Studio
CHANSONS DES JOURS
by Philippe Meyer
dir Philippe Meyer
From 23 September to 31 October

2010

Vieux-Colombier
LES FEMMES SAVANTES
by Molière
dir Bruno Bayen
From 23 September to 7
November 2010

Richelieu
ANDROMAQUE
by Jean Racine
dir Muriel Mayette-Holtz
From 16 October 2010 to 4
February 2011

Studio
LA CONFESSION D'UN
ENFANT DU SIÈCLE
by Alfred de Musset
dir Nicolas Lormeau
From 27 to 31 October 2010

Vieux-Colombier
LE MARIAGE
by Nikolaï Gogol
dir Lilo Baur
From 24 November 2010 to 2
January 2011

Studio
LES HABITS NEUFS DE
L'EMPEREUR
by Hans Christian Andersen
dir Jacques Allaire
From 25 November 2010 to 9
January 2011

Richelieu
UN FIL À LA PATTE
by Georges Feydeau
dir Jérôme Deschamps
From 4 December 2010 to 18 June
2011

Richelieu
LES TROIS SŒURS
by Anton Chekhov
dir Alain Françon

From 16 December 2010 to 28
March 2011

Vieux-Colombier
LA MALADIE DE LA FAMILLE
M.
by Fausto Paravidino
dir Fausto Paravidino
From 19 January to 20 February
2011

Studio
LA CRITIQUE DE L'ÉCOLE
DES FEMMES
by Molière
dir Clément Hervieu-Léger
From 27 January to 6 March 2011

Richelieu
UN TRAMWAY NOMMÉ
DÉSIR
by Tennessee Williams
dir Lee Breuer
From 5 February to 2 June 2011

Richelieu
LES JOYEUSES COMMÈRES
DE WINDSOR
by William Shakespeare
dir Andrés Lima
From 15 February to 22 May 2011

Vieux-Colombier
RENDEZ-VOUS
CONTEMPORAIN: LE DRAP
by Yves Ravey
dir Laurent Fréchuret
From 3 to 9 March 2011

Vieux-Colombier
LE BRUIT DES OS QUI
CRAQUENT
by Suzanne Lebeau
dir Anne-Laure Liégeois
From 11 to 18 March 2011

Vieux-Colombier
LA SEULE CERTITUDE QUE
J'AI

by Pierre Desproges
dir by Christian Gonon, Alain
Lenglet and Marc Fayet
From 13 to 20 March 2011

Studio
POIL DE CAROTTE
by Jules Renard
dir Philippe Lagrue
From 24 March to 8 May 2011

Vieux-Colombier
LES AFFAIRES SONT LES
AFFAIRES
by Octave Mirbeau
dir Marc Paquien
From 30 March to 24 April 2011

Richelieu
L'OPÉRA DE QUAT'SOUS
by Bertolt Brecht, musique by Kurt
Weill
dir Laurent Pelly
From 2 April to 19 July 2011

Vieux-Colombier
ON NE BADINE PAS AVEC
L'AMOUR
by Alfred de Musset
dir Yves Beaunesne
From 11 May to 26 June 2011

Studio
TROIS HOMMES DANS UN
SALON
by François-René Cristiani
dir Anne Kessler
From 19 May to 12 June 2011

Richelieu
AGAMEMNON
by Sénèque Le Jeune
dir Denis Marleau
From 21 May to 23 July 2011

Richelieu
UBU ROI
by Alfred Jarry
dir Jean-Pierre Vincent

From 3 June to 20 July 2011

Richelieu
LE MALADE IMAGINAIRE
by Molière
dir Claude Stratz
From 22 June to 24 July 2011

Studio
LE LOUP / LES CONTES DU
CHAT PERCHÉ
by Marcel Aymé
dir Véronique Vella
From 23 June to 10 July 2011

2011/12

Studio
CHANSONS DÉCONSEILLÉES
by Philippe Meyer
dir Philippe Meyer
From 15 September to 30 October
2011

Richelieu
L'AVARE
by Molière
dir Catherine Hiegel
From 19 September to 14 October
2011

Richelieu
BÉRÉNICE
by Jean Racine
dir Muriel Mayette-Holtz
From 22 September to 27
November 2011

Vieux-Colombier
LA PLUIE D'ÉTÉ
by Marguerite Duras
dir Emmanuel Daumas
From 28 September to 30 October
2011

Richelieu
ANDROMAQUE
by Jean Racine

dir Muriel Mayette-Holtz
From 7 October to 7 November
2011

Studio
NOTRE CHER ANTON
by Catherine Salviat
dir Catherine Salviat
From 7 to 9 October 2011

Richelieu
LE JEU DE L'AMOUR ET DU
HASARD
by Marivaux
dir Galin Stoev
From 11 October to 17 November
2011

Vieux-Colombier
LA NOCE
by Bertolt Brecht
dir Isabel Osthues
From 16 November 2011 1
January 2012

Richelieu
L'ÉCOLE DES FEMMES
by Molière
dir Jacques Lassalle
From 19 November 2011 to 6
January 2012

Studio
LE PETIT PRINCE
by Antoine de Saint-Exupéry
dir Aurélien Recoing
From 24 November 2011 to 8
January 2012

Studio
UN FIL À LA PATTE
by Georges Feydeau
dir Jérôme Deschamps
From 2 December 2011 to 22 July
2012

Studio
LE JUBILÉ D'AGATHE
by Pascal Lainé

dir Gisèle Casadesus
From 16 to 18 December 2011

Vieux-Colombier
DU CÔTÉ DE CHEZ PROUST
by Jacques Sereys
dir Jean-Luc Tardieu
From 6 to 11 January 2012

Vieux-Colombier
À LA RECHERCHE DU TEMPS
CHARLUS
by Jacques Sereys
dir Jean-Luc Tardieu
From 6 to 11 January 2012

Richelieu
LE MALADE IMAGINAIRE
by Molière
dir Claude Stratz
From 15 January to 24 April 2012

Théâtre Éphémère
LA TRILOGIE DE LA
VILLÉGIATURE
by Carlo Goldoni
dir Alain Françon
From 19 January to 12 March
2012

Vieux-Colombier
LE MARIAGE
by Nikolaï Gogol
dir Lilo Baur
From 19 January to 26 February
2012

Studio
POIL DE CAROTTE
by Jules Renard
dir Philippe Lagrue
From 26 January to 4 March 2012

Vieux-Colombier
SIGNATURE, SPECTACLE
DANSÉ
by Sidi Larbi Cherkaoui
dir Claire Richard
From 26 January to 12 February

2012

Studio
LA SEULE CERTITUDE QUE
J'AI
by Pierre Desproges
dir Alain Lenglet and Marc Fayet
From 12 February to 12 March
2012

Vieux-Colombier
ERZULI DAHOMEY, DÉESSE
DE L'AMOUR
by Jean-René Lemoine
dir Éric Génovèse
From 14 March to 15 April 2012

Studio
LE CERCLE DES
CASTAGNETTES
by Georges Feydeau
dir Alain Françon and Gilles David
From 22 March to 22 April 2012

Théâtre Éphémère
LE MARIAGE DE FIGARO OU
LA FOLLE JOURNÉE
by Beaumarchais
dir Christophe Rauck
From 23 March to 6 May 2012

Studio
LES CENDRES DU SOLEIL
by Vincent Bréal
Mise en espace Laurent Stocker
3 April 2012

Studio
CE QUE J'APPELLE OUBLI
by Laurent Mauvignier
dir Denis Podalydès
From 12 to 22 April 2012

Théâtre Éphémère
UNE PUCE, ÉPARGNEZ-LA
by Naomi Wallace
dir Anne-Laure Liégeois
From 26 April to 12 June 2012

Vieux-Colombier
AMPHITRYON
by Molière
dir Jacques Vincey
From 9 May to 24 June 2012

Théâtre Éphémère
ON NE BADINE PAS AVEC
L'AMOUR
by Alfred de Musset
dir Yves Beaunesne
From 9 May to 17 June 2012

Studio
LA VOIX HUMAINE,
PRÉCÉDÉE DE LA DAME DE
MONTE-CARLO
by Jean Cocteau
dir Marc Paquien
From 10 May to 3 June 2012

Grand Palais
PEER GYNT
by Henrik Ibsen
dir Éric Ruf
From 12 May to 14 June 2012

Théâtre Éphémère
UNE HISTOIRE DE LA
COMÉDIE-FRANÇAISE
by Muriel Mayette-Holtz
dir Muriel Mayette-Holtz
From 18 May to 25 June 2012

Studio
LE BANQUET
by Platon
dir Jacques Vincey
From 15 June to 1 July 2012

Studio
UN CHÂTEAU DE NUAGES
by Yves Gasc
dir Yves Gasc
From 22 to 24 June 2012

Théâtre Éphémère
NOS PLUS BELLES
CHANSONS / CABARET

by Philippe Meyer
dir Philippe Meyer
From 1 to 15 July 2012

Théâtre Éphémère
LES INESTIMABLES
CHRONIQUES
after François Rabelais
Musique by Jean Françaix
From 2 to 6 July 2012

2012/13

Vieux-Colombier
ANTIGONE
by Jean Anouilh
dir Marc Paquien
From 14 September to 25 October
2012

Théâtre Éphémère
DOM JUAN OU LE FESTIN DE
PIERRE
by Molière
dir Jean-Pierre Vincent
From 18 September to 11
November 2012

Studio
LA CRITIQUE DE L'ÉCOLE
DES FEMMES
by Molière
dir Clément Hervieu-Léger
From 22 September to 28 October
2012

Théâtre Éphémère
L'ÉCOLE DES FEMMES
by Molière
dir Jacques Lassalle
From 25 September 2012 to 22
July 2013

Vieux-Colombier
DU COTÉ DE CHEZ PROUST
by Jacques Sereys
dir Jean-Luc Tardieu
From 31 October to 11 November

2012

Théâtre Éphémère
UN CHAPEAU DE PAILLE
D'ITALIE
by Eugène Labiche and Marc-
Michel
dir Giorgio Barberio Corsetti
From 31 October 2012 to 7
January 2013

Vieux-Colombier
À LA RECHERCHE DU TEMPS
CHARLUS
by Jacques Sereys, after Marcel
Proust
dir Jean-Luc Tardieu
From 2 to 11 November 2012

Théâtre Éphémère
LE JEU DE L'AMOUR ET DU
HASARD
by Marivaux
dir Galin Stoev
From 13 November 2012 to 3
January 2013

Studio
LES TROIS PETITS COCHONS
by Thomas Quillardet
dir Thomas Quillardet
From 15 November to 30
December 2012

Vieux-Colombier
LA PLACE ROYALE
by Pierre Corneille
dir Anne-Laure Liégeois
From 28 November 2012 to 13
January 2013

Centquatre
LA MALADIE DE LA FAMILLE
M.
by Fausto Paravidino
dir Fausto Paravidino
From 8 to 13 January 2013

Théâtre Éphémère
LE MALADE IMAGINAIRE
by Molière
dir Claude Stratz
From 14 January to 25 February
2013

Studio
CANDIDE
by Voltaire
dir Emmanuel Daumas
From 17 January to 3 March 2013

Théâtre Éphémère
QUATRE FEMMES ET UN
PIANO
Spectacle sous la direction
artistique de Sylvia Bergé
From 19 to 26 January 2013

Richelieu
TROÏLUS ET CRESSIDA
by William Shakespeare
dir Jean-Yves Ruf
From 26 January to 5 May 2013

Richelieu
ANDROMAQUE
by Jean Racine
dir Muriel Mayette-Holtz
From 29 January to 26 February
2013

Vieux-Colombier
HERNANI
by Victor Hugo
dir Nicolas Lormeau
From 30 January to 18 February
2013

Richelieu
PHÈDRE
by Jean Racine
dir Michael Marmarinos
From 2 March to 26 June 2013

Vieux-Colombier
LA TÊTE DES AUTRES
by Marcel Aymé

dir Lilo Baur
From 8 March to 17 April 2013

Richelieu
L'AVARE
by Molière
dir Catherine Hiegel
From 8 March to 13 April 2013

Studio
EXISTENCE
by Edward Bond
dir Christian Benedetti
From 21 March to 28 April 2013

Richelieu
UN FIL À LA PATTE
by Georges Feydeau
dir Jérôme Deschamps
From 21 March to 9 June 2013

Studio
LAMPEDUSA BEACH
by Lina Prosa
dir Christian Benedetti
From 4 to 28 April 2013

Richelieu
LES TROIS SŒURS
by Anton Chekhov
dir Alain Françon
From 18 April to 20 May 2013

Vieux-Colombier
OBLOMOV
by Ivan Alexandrovitch
Gontcharov
dir Volodia Serre
From 7 May to 9 June 2013

Studio
CE QUE J'APPELLE OUBLI
by Laurent Mauvignier
dir Denis Podalydès
From 8 to 19 May 2013

Richelieu
RITUEL POUR UNE

MÉTAMORPHOSE
by Saadallah Wannous
dir Sulayman Al-Bassam
From 18 May to 11 July 2013

CABARET BORIS VIAN
by Boris Vian
dir Serge Bagdassarian
From 23 May to 30 June 2013

Jardin d'Acclimatation
POIL DE CAROTTE
by Jules Renard
dir Philippe Lagrue
From 11 to 26 June 2013

Vieux-Colombier
AMPHITRYON
by Molière
dir Jacques Vincey
From 19 June to 7 July 2013

Richelieu
CYRANO DE BERGERAC
by Edmond Rostand
dir Denis Podalydès
From 28 June to 28 July 2013

Vieux-Colombier
LES ÉLÈVES-COMÉDIENS
Pièces de guerre (extraits)
by Edward Bond
mise en scène Gilles David
11 July 2013

2013/14

Richelieu
LA TRILOGIE DE LA
VILLÉGIATURE
by Carlo Goldoni
dir Alain Françon
From 16 to 30 September 2013

Vieux-Colombier
L'ANNIVERSAIRE
by Harold Pinter
dir Claude Mouriéras

From 18 September to 24 October
2013

Richelieu
QUATRE FEMMES ET UN
PIANO
Cabaret dirigé par Sylvia Bergé
Direction musicale by Osvaldo
Caló
From 21 September to 13 October
2013

Studio
LA FLEUR À LA BOUCHE
by Luigi Pirandello
dir Louis Arene
From 26 September to 3
November 2013

Studio
LA SEULE CERTITUDE QUE
J'AI
by Pierre Desproges
dir Alain Lenglet and Marc Fayet
From 2 to 27 October 2013

Richelieu
LA TRAGÉDIE D'HAMLET
by William Shakespeare
dir Dan Jemmett
From 7 October 2013 to 12
January 2014

Richelieu
UN FIL À LA PATTE
by Georges Feydeau
dir Jérôme Deschamps
From 15 October to 22 December
2013

Richelieu
DOM JUAN OU LE FESTIN DE
PIERRE
by Molière
dir Jean-Pierre Vincent
From 28 October 2013 to 9
February 2014

Vieux-Colombier
LE SYSTÈME RIBADIER
by Georges Feydeau
dir Zabou Breitman
From 13 November 2013 to 5
January 2014

Studio
LA PRINCESSE AU PETIT POIS
by Hans Christian Andersen
dir Édouard Signolet
From 21 November 2013 to 5
January 2014

Richelieu
PSYCHÉ
by Molière
dir Véronique Vella
From 7 December 2013 to 4
March 2014

Richelieu
ANTIGONE
by Jean Anouilh
dir Marc Paquien
From 20 December 2013 to 2
March 2014

Vieux-Colombier
LA MALADIE DE LA MORT
by Marguerite Duras
dir Muriel Mayette-Holtz
From 15 to 29 January 2014

Studio
CANDIDE
by Voltaire
dir Emmanuel Daumas
From 16 January to 16 February
2014

Vieux-Colombier
COUPES SOMBRES
by Guy Zilberstein
dir Anne Kessler
30 January 2014

Vieux-Colombier
TRIPTYQUE DU NAUFRAGE:

LAMPEDUSA SNOW
by Lina Prosa
dir Lina Prosa
From 31 January to 4 February
2014

Studio
TRIPTYQUE DU NAUFRAGE:
LAMPEDUSA BEACH
by Lina Prosa
dir Lina Prosa
From 1 to 3 February 2014

Vieux-Colombier
TRIPTYQUE DU NAUFRAGE:
LAMPEDUSA WAY
by Lina Prosa
dir Lina Prosa
From 1 to 5 February 2014

Richelieu
LE SONGE D'UNE NUIT
D'ÉTÉ
by William Shakespeare
dir Muriel Mayette-Holtz
From 8 February to 15 June 2014

Vieux-Colombier
LA VISITE DE LA VIEILLE
DAME
by Friedrich Dürrenmatt
dir Christophe Lidon
From 19 February to 30 March
2014

Richelieu
UN CHAPEAU DE PAILLE
D'ITALIE
by Eugène Labiche
dir Giorgio Barberio Corsetti
From 21 February to 13 April
2014

Richelieu
ANDROMAQUE
by Jean Racine
dir Muriel Mayette-Holtz
From 28 February to 31 May 2014

Studio
L'ÎLE DES ESCLAVES
by Marivaux
dir Benjamin Jungers
From 6 March to 13 April 2014

Richelieu
LE MISANTHROPE
by Molière
dir Clément Hervieu-Léger
From 12 April to 17 July 2014

Vieux-Colombier
OTHELLO
by William Shakespeare
dir Léonie Simaga
From 23 April to 1 June 2014

Studio
CABARET GEORGES
BRASSENS
by Georges Brassens
dir Thierry Hancisse
From 3 May to 15 June 2014

Richelieu
LUCRÈCE BORGIA
by Victor Hugo
dir Denis Podalydès
From 24 May to 20 July 2014

Richelieu
LE MALADE IMAGINAIRE
by Molière
dir Claude Stratz
From 3 June to 20 July 2014

Vieux-Colombier
HERNANI
by Victor Hugo
dir Nicolas Lormeau
From 10 June 2014 to 6 July 2014

Richelieu
PHÈDRE
by Jean Racine
dir Michael Marmarinos
From 13 June to 15 July 2014

Studio
LES TROIS PETITS COCHONS
by Thomas Quillardet
dir Thomas Quillardet
From 26 June to 6 July 2014

Vieux-Colombier
ÉLÈVES-COMÉDIENS
Ce démon qui est en lui
by John Osborne
dir Hervé Pierre
From 10 to 12 July 2014

2014/15

Vieux-Colombier
TRAHISONS
by Harold Pinter
dir Frédéric Bélier-Garcia
From 17 September to 26 October
2014

Richelieu
TARTUFFE
by Molière
dir Galin Stoev
From 20 September 2014 to 16
February 2015

Richelieu
ANTIGONE
by Jean Anouilh
dir Marc Paquien
From 26 September to 2 December
2014

Studio
CABARET BARBARA
by Barbara
dir Béatrice Agenin
From 27 September to 2
November 2014

En tournée
OBLOMOV
by Ivan Alexandrovitch
Gontcharov
dir Volodia Serre

From 27 September to 19
December 2014

Studio
SI GUITRY M'ÉTAIT CONTÉ
by Sacha Guitry
dir Jean-Luc Tardieu
From 4 October to 2 November
2014

Richelieu
UN CHAPEAU DE PAILLE
D'ITALIE
by Eugène Labiche
dir Giorgio Barberio Corsetti
From 8 October 2014 to 14
January 2015

Richelieu
DOM JUAN OU LE FESTIN DE
PIERRE
by Molière
dir Jean-Pierre Vincent
From 17 October to 16 December
2014

Vieux-Colombier
GEORGE DANDIN
by Molière
dir Hervé Pierre
From 12 November 2014 to 1
January 2015

Studio
LA PETITE FILLE AUX
ALLUMETTES
by Hans Christian Andersen
dir Olivier Meyrou
From 20 November 2014 to 4
January 2015

Richelieu
LA DOUBLE INCONSTANCE
by Marivaux
dir Anne Kessler
From 29 November 2014 to 1
March 2015

Richelieu
LE MISANTHROPE
by Molière
dir Clément Hervieu-Léger
From 17 December 2014 to 23
March 2015

Vieux-Colombier
OBLOMOV
by Ivan Alexandrovitch
Gontcharov
dir Volodia Serre
From 9 to 25 January 2015

Studio
LA DAME AUX JAMBES
D'AZUR
by Eugène Labiche
dir Jean-Pierre Vincent
From 22 January to 8 March 2015

Vieux-Colombier
L'AUTRE
by Françoise Gillard and Claire
Richard
dir Françoise Gillard and Claire
Richard
From 5 to 22 February 2015

Richelieu
LES ESTIVANTS
by Maxime Gorki
dir Gérard Desarthe
From 7 February to 25 May 2015

Richelieu
LE SONGE D'UNE NUIT
D'ÉTÉ
by William Shakespeare
dir Muriel Mayette-Holtz
From 18 February to 25 May 2015

Vieux-Colombier
LA TÊTE DES AUTRES
by Marcel Aymé
dir Lilo Baur
From 6 to 29 March 2015

Studio
DANCEFLOOR MEMORIES
by Lucie Depauw
dir Hervé Van der Meulen
From 26 March to 10 May 2015

Richelieu
INNOCENCE
by Dea Loher
dir Denis Marleau
From 28 March to 29 June 2015

Vieux-Colombier
COUPES SOMBRES
by Guy Zilberstein
dir Anne Kessler
From 7 to 8 April 2015

Richelieu
LUCRÈCE BORGIA
by Victor Hugo
dir Denis Podalydès
From 14 April to 19 July 2015

Vieux-Colombier
LES ENFANTS DU SILENCE
by Mark Medoff
dir Anne-Marie Étienne
From 15 April to 17 May 2015

Richelieu
LA MAISON DE BERNARDA
ALBA
by Federico García Lorca
dir Lilo Baur
From 23 May to 25 July 2015

Studio
LA PRINCESSE AU PETIT POIS
by Hans Christian Andersen
dir Édouard Signolet
From 29 May to 28 June 2015

Vieux-Colombier
LE SYSTÈME RIBADIER
by Georges Feydeau
dir Zabou Breitman
From 29 May to 17 July 2015

Richelieu
LA TRAGÉDIE D'HAMLET
by William Shakespeare
dir Dan Jemmett
From 5 June to 26 July 2015

Richelieu
UN FIL À LA PATTE
by Georges Feydeau
dir Jérôme Deschamps
From 19 June to 26 July 2015

Studio
ÉLÈVES-COMÉDIENS
Kadoc
by Rémi De Vos
dir Michel Vuillermoz
From 8 to 10 July 2015

2015/16

Studio
COMME UNE PIERRE QUI...
by Greil Marcus (adaptation by
Marie Rémond and Sébastien
Pouderoux)
dir Marie Rémond and Sébastien
Pouderoux
From 15 September to 25 October
2015

Richelieu
PÈRE
by August Strindberg
dir Arnaud Desplechin
From 19 September 2015 to 4
January 2016

Richelieu
LE MISANTHROPE
by Molière
dir Clément Hervieu-Léger
From 24 September to 8 December
2015

Vieux-Colombier
20,000 LIEUES SOUS LES MERS
by Jules Verne

dir Christian Hecq and Valérie
Lesort
From 29 September to 8
November 2015

Richelieu
LA MAISON DE BERNARDA
ALBA
by Federico García Lorca
dir Lilo Baur
From 2 October 2015 to 6 January
2016

Richelieu
LA DOUBLE INCONSTANCE
by Marivaux
dir Anne Kessler
From 16 October 2015 to 14
February 2016

Studio
LE LOUP
by Marcel Aymé
dir Véronique Vella
From 19 November 2015 to 3
January 2016

Vieux-Colombier
LES RUSTRES
by Carlo Goldoni
dir Jean-Louis Benoit
From 25 November 2015 to 10
January 2016

Richelieu
ROMÉO ET JULIETTE
by William Shakespeare
dir Éric Ruf
From 5 December 2015 to 30 May
2016

Richelieu
CYRANO DE BERGERAC
by Edmond Rostand
dir Denis Podalydès
From 23 December 2015 to 28
March 2016

Studio
LE CHANT DU CYGNE /
L'OURS
by Anton Chekhov
dir Maëlle Poésy
From 21 January to 28 February
2016

Richelieu
LUCRÈCE BORGIA
by Victor Hugo
dir Denis Podalydès
From 22 January to 30 April 2016

Vieux-Colombier
LES DERNIERS JOURS DE
L'HUMANITÉ
by Karl Kraus
dir David Lescot
From 27 January to 28 February
2016

Richelieu
LA MER
by Edward Bond
dir Alain Françon
From 5 March to 15 June 2016

Vieux-Colombier
LA MUSICA, LA MUSICA
DEUXIÈME
by Marguerite Duras
dir Anatoli Vassiliev
From 16 March to 30 April 2016

Studio
CABARET LÉO FERRÉ
by Léo Ferré
dir Claude Mathieu
From 17 March to 8 May 2016

Richelieu
TARTUFFE
by Molière
dir Galin Stoev
From 21 March to 19 June 2016

Studio
SINGULIS / LES FOUS NE

SONT PLUS CE QU'ILS
ÉTAIENT
Textes by Raymond Devos par
Elliot Jenicot
From 30 March to 10 April 2016

Centquatre
NADIA C.
by Lola Lafon
dir Chloé Dabert
From 13 to 20 April 2016

Studio
SINGULIS / COMPAGNIE
by Samuel Beckett
dir Christian Gonon
From 13 to 24 April 2016

Richelieu
HOMMAGE À SHAKESPEARE
Hommage exceptionnel par la
Troupe
23 April 2016

Studio
SINGULIS / GRISÉLIDIS
by Grisélidis Réal
dir Coraly Zahonero
From 27 April to 8 May 2016

Richelieu
BRITANNICUS
by Jean Racine
dir Stéphane Braunschweig
From 7 May to 23 July 2016

Vieux-Colombier
GEORGE DANDIN / LA
JALOUSIE DU BARBOUILLÉ
by Molière
dir Hervé Pierre
From 8 May to 26 June 2016

Studio
LA DEMANDE D'EMPLOI
by Michel Vinaver
dir Gilles David
From 26 May to 3 July 2016

Richelieu
UN CHAPEAU DE PAILLE
D'ITALIE
by Eugène Labiche
dir Giorgio Barberio Corsetti
From 31 May to 24 July 2016

Richelieu
UN FIL À LA PATTE
by Georges Feydeau
dir Jérôme Deschamps
From 16 June to 24 July 2016

Avignon
LES DAMNÉS
after the film by Luchino Visconti
dir Ivo van Hove
From 6 to 16 July 2016

Studio
RHAPSODIES
by Sylvain Levey
dir Serge Bagdassarian
8 July 2016

2016/17

Studio
L'INTERLOPE (CABARET)
by Serge Bagdassarian
dir Serge Bagdassarian
From 17 September to 30 October
2016

Vieux-Colombier
VANIA
after Oncle Vania by Anton
Chekhov
dir Julie Deliquet
From 21 September to 6
November 2016

Richelieu
LES DAMNÉS
after the film by Luchino Visconti
dir Ivo van Hove
From 24 September 2016 to 13
January 2017

Richelieu
ROMÉO ET JULIETTE
by William Shakespeare
dir Éric Ruf
From 30 September 2016 to 1
February 2017

Richelieu
PÈRE
by August Strindberg
dir Arnaud Desplechin
From 7 October to 4 December
2016

Studio
LE CERF ET LE CHIEN
Les Contes du chat perché by
Marcel Aymé
dir Véronique Vella
From 17 November 2016 to 8
January 2017

Vieux-Colombier
LA RONDE
by Arthur Schnitzler
dir Anne Kessler
From 23 November 2016 to 8
January 2017

Richelieu
LE PETIT-MAÎTRE CORRIGÉ
by Marivaux
dir Clément Hervieu-Léger
From 3 December 2016 to 24
April 2017

Richelieu
LE MISANTHROPE
by Molière
dir Clément Hervieu-Léger
From 21 December 2016 to 26
March 2017

Théâtre Antoine
LES ENFANTS DU SILENCE
by Mark Medoff
dir Anne-Marie Étienne
From 17 January to 26 February

2017

Vieux-Colombier
20 000 LIEUES SOUS LES MERS
by Jules Verne (adaptation by
Christian Hecq and Valérie Lesort)
dir Christian Hecq and Valérie
Lesort
From 25 January to 19 March
2017

Studio
INTÉRIEUR
by Maurice Maeterlinck
dir Nâzim Boudjenah
From 26 January to 5 March 2017

Studio
SINGULIS / LE BRUITEUR
by Christine Montalbetti
dir Pierre Louis-Calixte
From 2 to 12 February 2017

Richelieu
LA RÈGLE DU JEU
after the film by Jean Renoir
dir Christiane Jatahy
From 4 February to 15 June 2017

Studio
SINGULIS / L'ENVERS DU
MUSIC-HALL
by Colette
dir Danièle Lebrun
From 22 February to 5 March
2017

Richelieu
LUCRÈCE BORGIA
by Victor Hugo
dir Denis Podalydès
From 22 February to 28 May 2017

Studio
IL FAUT QU'UNE PORTE
SOIT OUVERTE OU FERMÉE
by Alfred de Musset
dir Laurent Delvert
From 23 March to 7 May 2017

Studio
SINGULIS / AU PAYS DES
MENSONGES
by Etgar Keret
dir Noam Morgensztern
From 29 March to 9 April 2017

Richelieu
LA RÉSISTIBLE ASCENSION
D'ARTURO UI
by Bertolt Brecht
dir Katharina Thalbach
From 1 April to 30 June 2017

Vieux-Colombier
BAJAZET
by Jean Racine
dir Éric Ruf
From 5 April to 7 May 2017

Studio
SINGULIS / L'ÉVÉNEMENT
by Annie Ernaux
dir Françoise Gillard
From 19 to 30 April 2017

Odéon
LE TESTAMENT DE MARIE
by Colm Tóibín
dir Deborah Warner
From 5 May to 3 June 2017

Richelieu
L'HÔTEL DU LIBRE-
ÉCHANGE
by Georges Feydeau
dir Isabelle Nanty
From 20 May to 25 July 2017

Vieux-Colombier
UNE VIE
by Pascal Rambert
dir Pascal Rambert
From 24 May to 2 July 2017

Studio
COMME UNE PIERRE QUI...
after Greil Marcus

dir Marie Rémond and Sébastien
Pouderoux
From 25 May to 2 July 2017

Richelieu
CYRANO DE BERGERAC
by Edmond Rostand
dir Denis Podalydès
From 7 June to 20 July 2017

Richelieu
LA DOUBLE INCONSTANCE
by Marivaux
dir Anne Kessler
From 22 June to 24 July 2017

2017/18

Studio
HAUTE SURVEILLANCE
by Jean Genet
dir Cédric Gourmelon
From 16 September to 29 October
2017

Richelieu
LES FOURBERIES DE SCAPIN
by Molière
dir Denis Podalydès
From 20 September 2017 to 11
February 2018

Richelieu
LES DAMNÉS
after the film by Luchino Visconti
dir Ivo van Hove
From 29 September to 10
December 2017

Vieux-Colombier
VANIA
after Oncle Vania by Anton
Chekhov
dir Julie Deliquet
From 4 October to 12 November
2017

Richelieu
L'HÔTEL DU LIBRE-
ÉCHANGE
by Georges Feydeau
dir Isabelle Nanty
From 10 October 2017 to 1
January 2018

Richelieu
LA RÈGLE DU JEU
after the film by Jean Renoir
dir Christiane Jatahy
From 20 October 2017 to 8
January 2018

Studio
LE CERF ET LE CHIEN
Les Contes du chat perché by
Marcel Aymé
dir Véronique Vella
From 16 November 2017 to 7
January 2018

Vieux-Colombier
APRÈS LA PLUIE
by Sergi Belbel
dir Lilo Baur
From 29 November 2017 to 7
January 2018

Richelieu
LA TEMPÊTE
by William Shakespeare
trans Jean-Claude Carrière
dir Robert Carsen
From 9 December 2017 to 21 May
2018

Richelieu
LE PETIT-MAÎTRE CORRIGÉ
by Marivaux
dir Clément Hervieu-Léger
From 22 December 2017 to 12
April 2018

Richelieu
POUSSIÈRE
by Lars Norén
dir Lars Norén

From 10 February to 16 June 2018

Vieux-Colombier
J'ÉTAIS DANS MA MAISON
by Jean-Luc Lagarce
dir Chloé Dabert
From 20 February to 4 March
2018

Studio
L'INTERLOPE (CABARET)
by Serge Bagdassarian
dir Serge Bagdassarian
From 21 February to 11 March
2018

Studio
SINGULIS / LES FORÇATS DE
LA ROUTE
by Albert Londres
Conception Nicolas Lormeau
From 21 February to 11 March
2018

Richelieu
LA RÉSISTIBLE ASCENSION
D'ARTURO UI
by Bertolt Brecht
dir by Katharina Thalbach
From 27 February to 21 May 2018

Vieux-Colombier
FAUST
by Goethe
dir Valentine Losseau and Raphaël
Navarro
From 21 March to 6 May 2018

Studio
PHÈDRE
by Sénèque
dir Louise Vignaud
From 29 March to 13 May 2018

Richelieu
L'ÉVEIL DU PRINTEMPS
by Frank Wedekind
dir Clément Hervieu-Léger
From 14 April to 8 July 2018

Vieux-Colombier
LES ONDES MAGNÉTIQUES
by David Lescot
dir David Lescot
From 23 May to 1 July 2018

Richelieu
LA LOCANDIERA
by Carlo Goldoni
dir Alain Françon
From 26 May to 24 July 2018

Studio
LES CRÉANCIERS
by August Strindberg
dir Anne Kessler
From 31 May to 8 July 2018

Richelieu
BRITANNICUS
by Jean Racine
dir Stéphane Braunschweig
From 8 June to 20 July 2018

Richelieu
ROMÉO ET JULIETTE
by William Shakespeare
dir Éric Ruf
From 22 June to 25 July 2018

2018/19

Studio
CONSTRUIRE UN FEU
by Jack London
dir Marc Lainé
From 15 September to 21 October
2018

Vieux-Colombier
L'HEUREUX STRATAGÈME
by Marivaux
dir Emmanuel Daumas
From 19 September to 4
November 2018

Richelieu
LA NUIT DES ROIS
by William Shakespeare
dir Thomas Ostermeier
From 22 September 2018 to 28
February 2019

Richelieu
LUCRÈCE BORGIA
by Victor Hugo
dir Denis Podalydès
From 1 October 2018 to 1 April
2019

Richelieu
BRITANNICUS
by Jean Racine
dir Stéphane Braunschweig
From 8 October 2018 to 1 January
2019

Richelieu
LA LOCANDIERA
by Carlo Goldoni
dir Alain Françon
From 27 October 2018 to 10
February 2019

Studio
LA PETITE SIRÈNE
after Hans Christian Andersen
dir Géraldine Martineau
From 15 November 2018 to 6
January 2019

Vieux-Colombier
20,000 LIEUES SOUS LES MERS
after Jules Verne
dir Christian Hecq and Valérie
Lesort
From 17 November 2018 to 6
January 2019

Richelieu
LES FOURBERIES DE SCAPIN
by Molière
dir Denis Podalydès
From 21 December 2018 to 19
March 2019

Studio
IL FAUT QU'UNE PORTE
SOIT OUVERTE OU FERMÉE
by Alfred de Musset
dir Laurent Delvert
From 16 January to 24 February
2019

Studio
SINGULIS / LA SEULE
CERTITUDE QUE J'AI, C'EST
D'ÊTRE DANS LE DOUTE
by Pierre Desproges
dir Marc Fayet and Alain Lenglet
Conception Christian Gonon
From 16 January to 3 February
2019

Vieux-Colombier
LES OUBLIÉS (ALGER-PARIS)
dir Julie Bertin and Jade Herbulot
From 24 January to 10 March
2019

Studio
SINGULIS / (HAMLET, À
PART)
after William Shakespeare
Conception Loïc Corbery
From 6 to 24 February 2019

Richelieu
FANNY ET ALEXANDRE
by Ingmar Bergman
dir Julie Deliquet
From 9 February to 16 June 2019

Studio
CHANSON DOUCE
after Leïla Slimani
dir Pauline Bayle
From 14 March to 28 April 2019

Richelieu
LES DAMNÉS
after the film by Luchino Visconti
dir Ivo van Hove
From 20 March to 2 June 2019

[Barbican Centre, London: 19-25
June 2019]

Vieux-Colombier
LE VOYAGE DE G.
MASTORNA
after Federico Fellini
dir Marie Rémond
From 28 March to 5 May 2019

Richelieu
L'HÔTEL DU LIBRE-
ÉCHANGE
by Georges Feydeau
dir Isabelle Nanty
From 2 April to 24 July 2019

Richelieu
ÉLECTRE / ORESTE
by Euripide
dir Ivo van Hove
From 27 April to 3 July 2019

Studio
LES SERGE (GAINSBOURG
POINT BARRE)
Conception Stéphane Varupenne
and Sébastien Pouderoux
From 16 May to 30 June 2019

Vieux-Colombier
HORS LA LOI
by Pauline Bureau
dir Pauline Bureau
From 24 May to 7 July 2019

Richelieu
LA VIE DE GALILÉE
by Bertolt Brecht
dir Éric Ruf
From 1 June to 25 July 2019

Richelieu
LE MISANTHROPE
by Molière
dir Clément Hervieu-Léger
From 14 June to 20 July 2019

2019/20 [* cancelled, ‡ delayed, Covid-19]

Vieux-Colombier
JULES CÉSAR
by William Shakespeare
dir Rodolphe Dana
From 20 September to 3 November 2019

Richelieu
LA PUCE À L'OREILLE
by Georges Feydeau
dir Lilo Baur
From 21 September 2019 to 23 February 2020

Studio
LA PETITE SIRÈNE
after Hans Christian Andersen
dir Géraldine Martineau
From 26 September to 10 November 2019

Richelieu
LA VIE DE GALILÉE
by Bertolt Brecht
dir Éric Ruf
From 30 September 2019 to 19 January 2020

Richelieu
LES FOURBERIES DE SCAPIN
by Molière
dir Denis Podalydès
From 9 October 2019 to 2 February 2020

Richelieu
ÉLECTRE/ORESTE
by Euripide
Version scénique and mise en scène Ivo van Hove
From 25 October 2019 to 16 February 2020

Vieux-Colombier
L'HEUREUX STRATAGÈME
by Marivaux

dir Emmanuel Daumas
From 15 November to 31 December 2019

Studio
LA CONFÉRENCE DES OBJETS
by Christine Montalbetti
dir Christine Montalbetti
From 28 November 2019 to 5 January 2020

Richelieu
ANGELS IN AMERICA
by Tony Kurshner
dir Arnaud Desplechin
From 18 January to 22 March 2020

Vieux-Colombier
FORUMS
by Patrick Goujon, Hélène Grémillon, Maël Piriou
dir Jeanne Herry
From 22 January to 1 March 2020

Studio
MASSACRE
by Lluïsa Cunillé
dir Tommy Milliot
From 23 January to 8 March 2020

Richelieu
LA NUIT DES ROIS
by William Shakespeare
dir Thomas Ostermeier
From 4 February to 22 March 2020

Vieux-Colombier
7 MINUTES
by Stefano Massini
dir Maëlle Poésy
From March to April 2020

Studio
JUSTINE OU LES MALHEURS DE LA VERTU
by Sade * or ‡

Conception Anne Kessler
From April to October 2020

Théâtre Marigny
LE MALADE IMAGINAIRE
by Molière *
dir Claude Stratz
From April to May 2020

Théâtre Marigny
LE CÔTÉ DE GUERMANTES
after Marcel Proust *
dir Christophe Honoré
From April to June 2020

Studio Marigny
COMME UNE PIERRE QUI...
after Greil Marcus *
dir Marie Rémond and Sébastien
Pouderoux
From April to May 2020

Studio
L'ÉVÉNEMENT
by Annie Ernaux *
Conception Françoise Gillard
From April to October 2020

Studio
SAINT FRANÇOIS, LE DIVIN
JONGLEUR
by Dario Fo *
dir Claude Mathieu
Conception Guillaume Gallienne
From April to October 2020

Studio
LA PENSÉE, LA POÉSIE ET LE
POLITIQUE, DIALOGUE
AVEC JACK RALITE
by Karelle Ménine *
Conception Christian Gonon
From April to October 2020

Studio
(HAMLET, À PART)
Shakespeare and others * or ‡
Conception Loïc Corbery
From April to October 2020

Studio
LES FORÇATS DE LA ROUTE
by Albert Londres * or ‡
Conception Nicolas Lormeau
From April to October 2020

Studio
L'ENVERS DU MUSIC-HALL
by Colette * or ‡
Conception Danièle Lebrun
From April to October 2020

Studio
LA MESSE LÀ-BAS
by Paul Claudel * or ‡
Conception Didier Sandre
From April to October 2020

Théâtre Marigny
LE PETIT-MAÎTRE CORRIGÉ
by Marivaux *
dir Clément Hervieu-Léger
From May to June 2020

Vieux-Colombier
BAJAZET
by Jean Racine *
dir Éric Ruf
From May to June 2020

Studio Marigny
PATAMUSIC-HALL
after Boris Vian *
dir Serge Bagdassarian
From June to July 2020

Vieux-Colombier
BUREAU DES LECTEURS
Lectures d'auteurs contemporains *
3rd cycle
From 13 to 15 June 2020

Théâtre Marigny
PARTAGE DE MIDI
by Paul Claudel ‡
dir Yves Beaunesne
From 1 June to 25 October 2020

Théâtre Marigny
CYRANO DE BERGERAC
by Edmond Rostand
dir Denis Podalydès
July 2020

Théâtre Marigny
LE BOURGEOIS
GENTILHOMME
by Molière
dir Valérie Lesort and Christian
Hecq
From September to October 2020

Studio Marigny
LES SERGE (GAINSBOURG
POINT BARRE)
dir Stéphane Varupenne and
Sébastien Pouderoux
From September to October 2020

Vieux-Colombier
À VIF
by Lars Norén
dir Lars Norén
From September to October 2020

31. *Une Vie* by Pascal Rambert, Vieux-Colombier, 2017. Pascal Rambert (mise en scène and décor), Anaïs Romand (costumes), Yves Godin (lighting). Jennifer Decker (Iris), Denis Podalydès (Invité). Photograph by Christophe Raynaud de Lage.

IV Authors and Plays 2000/01 to 2019/20

Marcel Aymé
LE LOUP / LES CONTES DU CHAT
    PERCHÉ 2009
LA TÊTE DES AUTRES 2013, 2015
LE LOUP 2015
LE CERF ET LE CHIEN 2016, 2017

Hans Christian Andersen
LES HABITS NEUFS DE
    L'EMPEREUR 2010
LA PRINCESSE AU PETIT POIS 2013,
    2015
LA PETITE FILLE AUX
    ALLUMETTES 2015
LA PETITE SIRÈNE 2018, 2019

Jean Anouilh
ANTIGONE 2012, 2013, 2014

André-Paul Antoine, Georges Courteline
COURTELINE AU GRAND-
    GUIGNOL 2002

Aristophane
LES OISEAUX 2010

Jacques Audiberti
LE MAL COURT 2000, 2002

Serge Bagdassarian
L'INTERLOPE (CABARET) 2016, 2018

Barbara
CABARET BARBARA 2014

Beaumarchais
LE MARIAGE DE FIGARO 2007,
    2008, 2010, 2012

Samuel Beckett
OH LES BEAUX JOURS 2005, 2006
CINQ DRAMATICULES 2006
SINGULIS / COMPAGNIE 2016

Sergi Belbel
APRÈS LA PLUIE 2017

Sylvia Bergé
QUATRE FEMMES ET UN PIANO
    2013

Ingmar Bergman
GRIEF[S] 2006
FANNY ET ALEXANDRE 2019

Thomas Bernhard
PLACE DES HÉROS 2004
DRAMUSCULES 2005

Julie Bertin and Jade Herbulot
LES OUBLIÉS (ALGER-PARIS) 2019

François Bon
QUATRE AVEC LE MORT 2002

Edward Bond
EXISTENCE 2013
LES ÉLÈVES-COMÉDIENS: Pièces de
    guerre (extraits) 2013
LA MER 2016

Édouard Bourdet
LES TEMPS DIFFICILES 2006

Georges Brassens
CABARET GEORGES BRASSENS
    2014

Bertolt Brecht
L'OPÉRA DE QUAT'SOUS 2011
LA NOCE 2011
LA RÉSISTIBLE ASCENSION
  D'ARTURO UI 2017, 2018
LA VIE DE GALILÉE 2019

Vincent Bréal
LES CENDRES DU SOLEIL 2012

Georg Büchner
LENZ, LÉONCE ET LÉNA CHEZ
  GEORG BÜCHNER 2002

Pauline Bureau
HORS LA LOI 2019

Pedro Calderon de la Barca
LE GRAND THÉÂTRE DU MONDE
  ET PROCÉS EN SÉPARATION DE
  L'ÂME ET DU CORPS 2004

Anton Chekhov
PLATONOV 2003, 2005
SUR LA GRAND-ROUTE 2007
LES TROIS SŒURS 2010, 2011, 2013
LE CHANT DU CYGNE / L'OURS
  2016
VANIA 2016, 2017

Sidi Larbi Cherkaoui
SIGNATURE, SPECTACLE DANSÉ
  2012

Paul Claudel
LA CANTATE À TROIS VOIX 2003
TÊTE D'OR 2006
LA MESSE LÀ-BAS 2020
PARTAGE DE MIDI 2006, 2020

Jean Cocteau
LA VOIX HUMAINE, PRÉCÉDÉE DE
  LA DAME DE MONTE-CARLO
  2012

Colette
FEU LE MUSIC-HALL 2004
SINGULIS / L'ENVERS DU MUSIC-
  HALL 2017

L'ENVERS DU MUSIC-HALL 2020

Émile Copfermann
CONVERSATIONS AVEC ANTOINE
  VITEZ 2003

Copi
UNE VISITE INOPPORTUNE 2001,
  2002

Pierre Corneille
CINNA OU LA CLÉMENCE
  D'AUGUSTE 2000
LE MENTEUR 2004, 2006
LE CID 2005, 2006
L'ILLUSION COMIQUE 2008, 2010
LA PLACE ROYALE 2012

François-René Cristiani
TROIS HOMMES DANS UN SALON
  2008, 2011

Lluïsa Cunillé
MASSACRE 2020

Daniel Danis
LE LANGUE-À-LANGUE DES
  CHIENS DE ROCHE 2001

Emmanuel Darley
BONHEUR? 2008

Eduardo De Filippo
LA GRANDE MAGIE 2009, 2010

Lucie Depauw
DANCEFLOOR MEMORIES 2015

Pierre Desproges
LA SEULE CERTITUDE QUE J'AI
  2010, 2012, 2013, 2019

Raymond Devos par Elliot Jenicot
SINGULIS / LES FOUS NE SONT
  PLUS CE QU'ILS ÉTAIENT 2016

Marguerite Duras
SAVANNAH BAY 2002
LA PLUIE D'ÉTÉ 2011

LA MALADIE DE LA MORT 2014
LA MUSICA, LA MUSICA
 DEUXIÈME 2016

Friedrich Dürrenmatt
LA VISITE DE LA VIEILLE DAME
 2014

Xavier Durringer
LA NUIT À L'ENVERS 2000

Annie Ernaux
SINGULIS / L'ÉVÉNEMENT 2017
L'ÉVÉNEMENT 2020

Euripide
LES BACCHANTES 2005
LA FOLIE D'HÉRACLÈS 2010
ÉLECTRE / ORESTE 2019

Jan Fabre
MON CORPS, MON GENTIL
 CORPS, DIS-MOI 2006

Bernard Faivre
UNE CONFRÉRIE DE FARCEURS
 2007

Federico Fellini
LE VOYAGE DE G. MASTORNA 2019

Léo Ferré
CABARET LÉO FERRÉ 2016

Geroges Feydeau
LE DINDON 2002, 2003
QUATRE PIÈCES DE FEYDEAU 2009
UN FIL À LA PATTE 2010, 2011, 2013,
 2015, 2016
LE CERCLE DES CASTAGNETTES
 2012
LE SYSTÈME RIBADIER 2013, 2015
L'HÔTEL DU LIBRE-ÉCHANGE
 2017, 2019
LA PUCE À L'OREILLE 2019

Dario Fo
SAINT FRANÇOIS, LE DIVIN
 JONGLEUR 2006, 2008, 2020

MYSTÈRE BOUFFE ET FABULAGES
 (VERSION 1) 2010
MYSTÈRE BOUFFE ET FABULAGES
 (VERSION 2) 2010

Yves Gasc
UN CHÂTEAU DE NUAGES 2012

Laurent Gaudé
PLUIE DE CENDRES 2001

Jean Genet
LES BONNES 2000
HAUTE SURVEILLANCE 2017

Françoise Gillard and Claire Richard
L'AUTRE 2015

Goethe
FAUST 2018

Nikolaï Gogol
LE RÉVIZOR 2001
LE MARIAGE 2010, 2012

Carlo Goldoni
IL CAMPIELLO 2006, 2009
LA TRILOGIE DE LA
 VILLÉGIATURE 2012, 2013
LES RUSTRES 2015
LA LOCANDIERA 2018

Witold Gombrowicz
LE MARIAGE 2001

Ivan Alexandrovitch Gontcharov
OBLOMOV 2013

Maxime Gorki
LES ESTIVANTS 2015

Vassili Grossman
LA DERNIÈRE LETTRE 2000

Sacha Guitry
SI GUITRY M'ÉTAIT CONTÉ 2014

Patrick Goujon, Hélène Grémillon, Maël

Piriou
FORUMS 2020

Adam de la Halle
LE JEU D'ADAM 2003

Ödön von Horváth
FIGARO DIVORCE 2008, 2010

Victor Hugo
RUY BLAS 2001, 2002
HERNANI 2013, 2014
LUCRÈCE BORGIA 2014, 2015, 2016,
    2017, 2018

Henrik Ibsen
HEDDA GABLER 2002
GRIEF[S] 2006
PEER GYNT 2012

Eugène Ionesco
LES CHAISES 2009

Alfred Jarry
UBU ROI 2009, 2010, 2011

Yacine Kateb
PRÉSENCES 2003

Etgar Keret
SINGULIS / AU PAYS DES
    MENSONGES 2017

Heinrich von Kleist
PENTHÉSILÉE 2008

Bernard-Marie Koltès
LE RETOUR AU DÉSERT 2007

Karl Kraus
LES DERNIERS JOURS DE
    L'HUMANITÉ 2016

Tony Kurshner
HOMEBODY / KABUL 2003
ANGELS IN AMERICA 2020

Marie Laberge
OUBLIER 2000

Pascal Lainé
LE JUBILÉ D'AGATHE 2011

Carine Lacroix
BURN BABY BURN 2010

Eugène Labiche
LE MYSTÈRE DE LA RUE
    ROUSSELET 2004
LE VOYAGE DE MONSIEUR
    PERRICHON 2008
UN CHAPEAU DE PAILLE D'ITALIE
    2012, 2014, 2015
LA DAME AUX JAMBES D'AZUR
    2015

Jean de La Fontaine
FABLES DE LA FONTAINE 2004,
    2005, 2007

Jean-Luc Lagarce
JUSTE LA FIN DU MONDE 2008,
    2009
J'ÉTAIS DANS MA MAISON 2018

Lola Lafon
NADIA C. 2016

Suzanne Lebeau
LE BRUIT DES OS QUI CRAQUENT
    2010

Jean-René Lemoine
ERZULI DAHOMEY, DÉESSE DE
    L'AMOUR 2012

David Lescot
LES ONDES MAGNÉTIQUES 2018

Sylvain Levey
RHAPSODIES 2016

Hanokh Levin
DOUCE VENGEANCE ET AUTRES
    SKETCHES 2008

Dea Loher
INNOCENCE 2015

Jack London
CONSTRUIRE UN FEU 2018

Albert Londres
SINGULIS / LES FORÇATS DE LA
    ROUTE 2018
LES FORÇATS DE LA ROUTE 2020

Felix Lope de Vega
PEDRO ET LE COMMANDEUR
    2006, 2007

Federico García Lorca
YERMA 2008
LA MAISON DE BERNARDA ALBA
    2015

Pierre-Henri Loÿs
LE GNA 2001

Maurice Maeterlinck
INTÉRIEUR 2017

Jean-Daniel Magnin
OPÉRA SAVON 2002

Karin Mainwaring
LES DANSEURS DE LA PLUIE 2001

Greil Marcus (adaptation)
COMME UNE PIERRE QUI... 2015,
    2017, 2020

Pierre de Marivaux
LA MÈRE CONFIDENTE 2001
LES SINCÈRES 2007
LA DISPUTE 2009
LE JEU DE L'AMOUR ET DU
    HASARD 2011, 2012
L'ÎLE DES ESCLAVES 2014
LA DOUBLE INCONSTANCE 2014,
    2015, 2017
LE PETIT-MAÎTRE CORRIGÉ 2016,
    2017, 2020
L'HEUREUX STRATAGÈME 2018,
    2019

Stefano Massini
7 MINUTES 2020

Laurent Mauvignier
CE QUE J'APPELLE OUBLI 2012,
    2013

Mark Medoff
LES ENFANTS DU SILENCE 2015,
    2016

Fabrice Melquiot
BOULI MIRO 2003, 2004
BOULI REDÉBOULE 2005
L'INATTENDU 2006

Karelle Ménine
LA PENSÉE, LA POÉSIE ET LE
    POLITIQUE, DIALOGUE AVEC
    JACK RALITE 2020

Philippe Meyer
CHANSONS DÉCONSEILLÉES 2011
NOS PLUS BELLES CHANSONS /
    CABARET 2012

Philippe Minyana
LA MAISON DES MORTS 2006
LES MÉTAMORPHOSES, LA PETITE
    2008

Octave Mirbeau
LES AFFAIRES SONT LES AFFAIRES
    2009, 2011
ON NE BADINE PAS AVEC
    L'AMOUR 2011

Molière
L'AVARE [a] 2000; [b] 2009, 2010,
    2011, 2013
LE BOURGEOIS GENTILHOMME [a]
    2000; [b] 2020
SGANARELLE OU LE COCU
    IMAGINAIRE 2001
MONSIEUR DE POURCEAUGNAC
    2001, 2003
LE MALADE IMAGINAIRE 2001,
    2003, 2005, 2006, 2007, 2009, 2011,
    2012, 2013, 2014, 2020

LE MISANTHROPE [a] 2001; [b] 2006, 2008; [c] 2014, 2015, 2016, 2019
AMPHITRYON [a] 2002; [b] 2012, 2013
DOM JUAN OU LE FESTIN DE PIERRE [a] 2002; [b] 2012, 2013, 2014
TARTUFFE [a] 2005; [b] 2014, 2016
L'AMOUR MÉDECIN ET LE SICILIEN 2005, 2006
LES PRÉCIEUSES RIDICULES 2007, 2009
LE MARIAGE FORCÉ 2008, 2010
LES FEMMES SAVANTES 2010
LA CRITIQUE DE L'ÉCOLE DES FEMMES 2011, 2012
L'ÉCOLE DES FEMMES 2011, 2012
PSYCHÉ 2013
GEORGE DANDIN 2014
GEORGE DANDIN / LA JALOUSIE DU BARBOUILLÉ 2016
LES FOURBERIES DE SCAPIN 2017, 2018, 2019

Christine Montalbetti
SINGULIS / LE BRUITEUR 2017
LA CONFÉRENCE DES OBJETS 2019

Grégory Motton
GENGIS CHEZ LES PYGMÉES 2004

Alfred de Musset
L'ÂNE ET LE RUISSEAU 2001
FANTASIO 2008, 2010
LA CONFESSION D'UN ENFANT DU SIÈCLE 2010
ON NE BADINE PAS AVEC L'AMOUR 2012
IL FAUT QU'UNE PORTE SOIT OUVERTE OU FERMÉ 2017, 2019

Marie Ndiaye
PAPA DOIT MANGER 2003, 2004

Lars Norén
EMBRASSER LES OMBRES 2005
PUR 2009
POUSSIÈRE 2018
À VIF 2020

Valère Novarina
L'ESPACE FURIEUX 2006

Sean O'Casey
LA FIN DU COMMENCEMENT 2007

John Osborne
ÉLÈVES-COMÉDIENS: Ce démon qui est en lui 2014

Alexandre Ostrovski
LA FORÊT 2003, 2005

Marcel Pagnol
FANNY 2008

Fausto Paravidino
LA MALADIE DE LA FAMILLE M. 2011, 2012

Pier Paolo Pasolini
ORGIE 2007

Jean Pavans
LES PAPIERS D'ASPERN 2003, 2004

Fernando Pessoa
LE PRIVILÈGE DES CHEMINS 2004

Harold Pinter
LE RETOUR 2000
L'ANNIVERSAIRE 2013
TRAHISONS 2014

Luigi Pirandello
LES GRELOTS DU FOU 2005, 2006
LA FLEUR À LA BOUCHE 2013

Platon
LE BANQUET 2010, 2012

José Pliya
LES EFFRACTEURS 2004

Lina Prosa
TRIPTYQUE DU NAUFRAGE: LAMPEDUSA BEACH 2013, 2014
TRIPTYQUE DU NAUFRAGE:

LAMPEDUSA SNOW, 2014
TRIPTYQUE DU NAUFRAGE:
   LAMPEDUSA WAY, 2014

Marcel Proust
LE CÔTÉ DE GUERMANTES 2020

Thomas Quillardet
LES TROIS PETITS COCHONS 2012,
   2014

François Rabelais
LES INESTIMABLES CHRONIQUES
   2012

Jean Racine
ANDROMAQUE [a] 2001; [b] 2010,
   2011, 2013, 2014
ESTHER 2003
BRITANNICUS [a] 2003, 2005; [b]
   2016, 2018
BÉRÉNICE 2009, 2011
PHÈDRE 2013, 2014
BAJAZET 2017, 2020

Pascal Rambert
LE DÉBUT DE L'A 2005
UNE VIE 2017

Yves Ravey
RENDEZ-VOUS CONTEMPORAIN:
   LE DRAP 2011

Grisélidis Réal
SINGULIS / GRISÉLIDIS 2016

Jules Renard
POIL DE CAROTTE 2011, 2012, 2013

Jean Renoir (adaptation)
LA RÈGLE DU JEU 2017

Edmond Rostand
CYRANO DE BERGERAC 2006, 2008,
   2010, 2013, 2015, 2017, 2020

Jacques Roubaud
OPHÉLIE ET AUTRES ANIMAUX
   2006

Marquis de Sade
JUSTINE OU LES MALHEURS DE LA
   VERTU 2020

Antoine de Saint-Exupéry
LE PETIT PRINCE 2011

Catherine Salviat
NOTRE CHER ANTON 2011

Nathalie Sarraute
POUR UN OUI OU POUR UN NON
   2007, 2008

Werner Schwab
L'EXTERMINATION DU PEUPLE
   2002

Spiro Scimone
LA FESTA 2007

Sénèque
PHÈDRE 2018

Sénèque Le Jeune
AGAMEMNON 2011

Jacques Sereys
COCTEAU-MARAIS 2009
À LA RECHERCHE DU TEMPS
   CHARLUS 2012
DU COTÉ DE CHEZ PROUST 2012

Arthur Schnitzler
LA RONDE 2016

William Shakespeare
LE MARCHAND DE VENISE 2001,
   2002
LA NUIT DES ROIS [a] 2003, 2004; [b]
   2018, 2020
LE CONTE D'HIVER 2004
LA MÉGÈRE APPRIVOISÉE 2007,
   2008
LES JOYEUSES COMMÈRES DE
   WINDSOR 2009, 2011
TROÏLUS ET CRESSIDA 2013
HAMLET 2013, 2015

LE SONGE D'UNE NUIT D'ÉTÉ
  2014, 2015
OTHELLO 2014
ROMÉO ET JULIETTE 2015, 2016,
  2018
LA TEMPÊTE 2017
SINGULIS / (HAMLET, À PART)
  2019, 2020
JULES CÉSAR 2019

Leïla Slimani
CHANSON DOUCE 2019

Antonio José da Silva
VIE DU GRAND DOM QUICHOTTE
  2008, 2009

August Strindberg
GRIEF[S] 2006
PÈRE 2015, 2016
LES CRÉANCIERS 2018

George Tabori
WEISMAN ET COPPERFACE 2002

Colm Tóibín
LE TESTAMENT DE MARIE 2017

Serge Valletti
MARYS' À MINUIT 2006

Stéphane Varupenne and Sébastien
  Pouderoux
LES SERGE (GAINSBOURG POINT
  BARRE) 2019

Jules Verne
20,000 LIEUES SOUS LES MERS 2015,
  2017, 2018

Boris Vian
CABARET BORIS VIAN 2013

PATAMUSIC-HALL 2020

Michel Vinaver
L'ORDINAIRE 2009
LA DEMANDE D'EMPLOI 2016

Luchino Visconti (adaptation)
LES DAMNÉS 2016, 2017, 2019

Voltaire
CANDIDE 2013, 2014

Rémi De Vos
ÉLÈVES-COMÉDIENS: Kadoc 2015

Naomi Wallace
UNE PUCE, ÉPARGNEZ-LA 2012

Saadallah Wannous
RITUEL POUR UNE
  MÉTAMORPHOSE 2013

Frank Wedekind
L'ÉVEIL DU PRINTEMPS 2018

Tennessee Williams
UN TRAMWAY NOMMÉ DÉSIR 2011

Gao Xingjian
QUATRE QUATUORS POUR UN
  WEEK-END 2003

Kateb Yacine
NEDJMA 2003

Annie Zadek
VIVANT 2009

Guy Zilberstein
LES NAUFRAGÉS 2010
COUPES SOMBRES 2014, 2015

32. *J'Étais dans ma maison et j'attendais que la pluie vienne* by Jean-Luc Lagarce, Vieux-Colombier, 2018. Chloé Dabert (mise en scène), Pierre Nouvel (décor), Marie La Rocca (costumes), Kelig Le Bars (lighting). L-R: Suliane Brahim (L'Aînée), Rebecca Marder (La Plus Jeune), Jennifer Decker (Le Seconde), Clotilde de Bayser (La Mère). Photograph by Pascal Victor.

V Prominent Directors 2000/01 to 2019/20

Philippe Adrien
LES BONNES by Jean Genet -
    Richelieu 2000.
MONSIEUR DE POURCEAUGNAC
    by Molière -
    Vieux-Colombier 2001.
L'EXTERMINATION DU PEUPLE by
    Werner Schwab -
    Vieux-Colombier 2002.

Lilo Baur
LE MARIAGE by Nikolaï Gogol -
    Vieux-Colombier 2011.
LA TÊTE DES AUTRES by Marcel
    Aymé -
    Vieux-Colombier 2013.
LA MAISON DE BERNARDA ALBA by
    Federico García Lorca -
    Richelieu 2015.
APRÈS LA PLUIE by Sergi Belbel -
    Vieux-Colombier 2017.
LA PUCE À L'OREILLE by Georges
    Feydeau -
    Richelieu 2019.

Yves Beaunesne
PARTAGE DE MIDI by Paul Claudel -
    Richelieu 2007.
ON NE BADINE PAS AVEC
    L'AMOUR by Alfred de Musset -
    Vieux-Colombier 2011.

Jean-Louis Benoit
LE BOURGEOIS GENTILHOMME by
    Molière -
    Richelieu 2000.
LE RÉVIZOR by Nikolaï Gogol -
    Richelieu 2001.

LE MENTEUR by Pierre Corneille -
    Richelieu 2004.
LES RUSTRES by Carlo Goldoni -
    Vieux-Colombier 2016.

Marcel Bozonnet
TARTUFFE by Molière -
    Richelieu 2005.
MON CORPS, MON GENTIL CORPS
    by Jan Fabre -
    Studio 2006.
ORGIE by Pier Paolo Pasolini -
    Vieux-Colombier 2007.

Stéphane Braunschweig
BRITANNICUS by Jean Racine -
    Richelieu 2016.

Robert Carsen
LA TEMPÊTE by William Shakespeare -
    Richelieu 2017.

Emmanuel Daumas
LA PLUIE D'ÉTÉ by Marguerite Duras -
    Vieux-Colombier 2011.
CANDIDE by Voltaire -
    Studio 2013.
L'HEUREUX STRATAGÈME by
    Marivaux -
    Vieux-Colombier 2018.

Julie Deliquet
VANIA by Anton Chekhov -
    Vieux-Colombier 2017.
FANNY ET ALEXANDRE by Ingmar
    Bergman -
    Richelieu 2019.

Arnaud Desplechin
PÈRE by August Strindberg -
  Richelieu 2015.
ANGELS IN AMERICA by Tony
  Kurshner -
  Richelieu 2020.

Alain Françon
LES TROIS SŒURS by Anton Chekhov
  Richelieu 2010.
LA TRILOGIE DE LA
  VILLÉGIATURE by Carlo Goldoni -
  Théâtre Éphémère 2012.
LE CERCLE DES CASTAGNETTES by
  Georges Feydeau -
  Co-dir with Gilles David -
  Studio 2012.
LA MER by Edward Bond -
  Richelieu 2016.
LA LOCANDIERA by Carlo Goldoni -
  Richelieu 2018.

Lukas Hemleb
UNE VISITE INOPPORTUNE by Copi
  Vieux-Colombier 2002.
LE DINDON by Georges Feydeau -
  Richelieu 2002.

Clément Hervieu-Léger
LA CRITIQUE DE L'ÉCOLE DES
  FEMMES by Molière -
  Studio 2011.
LE MISANTHROPE by Molière -
  Richelieu 2014.
LE PETIT-MAÎTRE CORRIGÉ by
  Marivaux -
  Richelieu 2016.
L'ÉVEIL DU PRINTEMPS by Frank
  Wedekind -
  Richelieu 2018.

Catherine Hiegel
LE RETOUR by Harold Pinter -
  Richelieu 2000.
L'AVARE by Molière -
  Richelieu 2009.

Brigitte Jaques-Wajeman
RUY BLAS by Victor Hugo -
  Richelieu 2001.
BRITANNICUS by Jean Racine -
  Vieux-Colombier 2003.

Dan Jemmett
LES PRÉCIEUSES RIDICULES by
  Molière -
  Vieux-Colombier 2007.
LA GRANDE MAGIE by Eduardo De
  Filippo -
  Richelieu 2009.
HAMLET by William Shakespeare -
  Richelieu 2014.

Anne Kessler
GRIEF[S] by August Strindberg, Ibsen,
  Ingmar Bergman -
  Studio 2006.
TROIS HOMMES DANS UN SALON
  by François-René Cristiani -
  Studio 2008.
LES NAUFRAGÉS by Guy Zilberstein -
  Vieux-Colombier 2010.
COUPES SOMBRES by Guy
  Zilberstein -
  Vieux-Colombier 2014.
LA DOUBLE INCONSTANCE by
  Marivaux -
  Richelieu 2014.
LA RONDE by Arthur Schnitzler -
  Vieux-Colombier 2016.
LES CRÉANCIERS by August
  Strindberg -
  Studio 2018.
JUSTINE by Sade -
  Studio 2020.

Jacques Lassalle
DOM JUAN by Molière -
  Richelieu 2002.
LES PAPIERS D'ASPERN by Jean
  Pavans -
  Vieux-Colombier 2003.
PLATONOV by Anton Chekhov -
  Richelieu 2003.
IL CAMPIELLO by Carlo Goldoni -
  Richelieu 2006.
FIGARO DIVORCE by Ödön von
  Horváth -

Richelieu 2008.
L'ÉCOLE DES FEMMES by Molière -
Richelieu 2011.

Andrés Lima
BONHEUR? d'Emmanuel Darley -
Vieux-Colombier 2008.
LES JOYEUSES COMMÈRES DE
WINDSOR by William Shakespeare -
Richelieu 2009.

Muriel Mayette-Holtz
LES DANSEURS DE LA PLUIE by
Karin Mainwaring -
Vieux-Colombier 2001.
LE CONTE D'HIVER by William
Shakespeare -
Studio 2004.
DRAMUSCULES by Thomas Bernhard -
Studio 2005.
LE RETOUR AU DÉSERT by Bernard-
Marie Koltès -
Richelieu 2007.
LA DISPUTE by Marivaux -
Vieux-Colombier 2009.
MYSTÈRE BOUFFE ET FABULAGES
by Dario Fo -
Richelieu 2010.
ANDROMAQUE by Jean Racine -
Richelieu 2010.
BÉRÉNICE by Jean Racine -
Richelieu 2011.
UNE HISTOIRE DE LA COMÉDIE by
Muriel Mayette-Holtz -
Théâtre Éphémère 2012.
LA MALADIE DE LA MORT by
Marguerite Duras -
Vieux-Colombier 2014.
LE SONGE D'UNE NUIT D'ÉTÉ by
William Shakespeare -
Richelieu 2014.

Thomas Ostermeier
LA NUIT DES ROIS by William
Shakespeare -
Richelieu 2018.

Daniel Mesguich
ANDROMAQUE by Jean Racine -

Richelieu 2001.

Jean-Pierre Miquel
LE MISANTHROPE by Molière -
Vieux-Colombier 2001.
HEDDA GABLER by Henrik Ibsen -
Vieux-Colombier 2002.

Laurent Pelly
L'OPÉRA DE QUAT'SOUS by Bertolt
Brecht and Kurt Weill -
Richelieu 2011.

Denis Podalydès
CYRANO DE BERGERAC d'Edmond
Rostand -
Richelieu 2008.
FANTASIO by Alfred de Musset -
Richelieu 2008.
CE QUE J'APPELLE OUBLI by Laurent
Mauvignier -
Studio 2012.
LUCRÈCE BORGIA by Victor Hugo -
Richelieu 2014.
LES FOURBERIES DE SCAPIN by
Molière -
Richelieu 2017.

Pascal Rambert
LE DÉBUT DE L'A by Pascal Rambert -
Studio 2005.
UNE VIE by Pascal Rambert -
Vieux-Colombier 2017.

Éric Ruf
PEER GYNT by Henrik Ibsen -
Grand Palais 2012.
ROMÉO ET JULIETTE by William
Shakespeare -
Richelieu 2015.
BAJAZET by Jean Racine -
Vieux-Colombier 2017.
LA VIE DE GALILÉE by Bertolt Brecht -
Richelieu 2019.

Andrei Serban
L'AVARE by Molière -
Richelieu 2000.
LE MARCHAND DE VENISE by

William Shakespeare -
Richelieu 2001.

Andrzej Seweryn
LE MAL COURT by Jacques Audiberti -
Vieux-Colombier 2000.
LA NUIT DES ROIS by William
Shakespeare -
Richelieu 2003.

Léonie Simaga
POUR UN OUI OU POUR UN NON
by Nathalie Sarraute -
Studio 2007.
OTHELLO by William Shakespeare -
Vieux-Colombier 2014.

Galin Stoev
LA FESTA by Spiro Scimone -
Vieux-Colombier 2007.
DOUCE VENGEANCE ET AUTRES
SKETCHES by Hanokh Levin -
Studio 2008.
L'ILLUSION COMIQUE by Pierre
Corneille -
Richelieu 2008.
LE JEU DE L'AMOUR ET DU
HASARD by Marivaux -
Richelieu 2011.
TARTUFFE by Molière -
Richelieu 2014.

Claude Stratz
LE MALADE IMAGINAIRE by Molière
Richelieu 2001.
LES GRELOTS DU FOU by Luigi
Pirandello -
Vieux-Colombier 2005.

Ivo van Hove
LES DAMNÉS by Luchino Visconti -
Avignon 2016.
ÉLECTRE / ORESTE by Euripide -
Richelieu 2019.

Anatoli Vassiliev
AMPHITRYON by Molière -
Richelieu 2002.
LA MUSICA by Marguerite Duras -

Vieux-Colombier 2016.

Véronique Vella
LE LOUP by Marcel Aymé -
Studio 2009.
PSYCHÉ by Molière -
Richelieu 2013.
LE CERF ET LE CHIEN by Marcel
Aymé -
Studio 2016.

Jean-Pierre Vincent
UBU ROI by Alfred Jarry -
Richelieu 2009.
DOM JUAN by Molière -
Théâtre Éphémère 2012.
LA DAME AUX JAMBES D'AZUR by
Eugène Labiche -
Studio 2015.

Robert Wilson
FABLES DE LA FONTAINE by Jean de
La Fontaine -
Richelieu 2004.

33. *La Tempête* by Shakespeare, Richelieu, 2017. Robert Carsen (mise en scène),
Radu Boruzescu (décor), Petra Reinhardt (costumes), Robert Carsen and Peter Van Praet
(lighting). L-R: Christophe Montenez (Ariel), Loïc Corbery (Ferdinand), Michel Vuillermoz
(Prospero), Georgia Scalliet (Miranda). Photograph by Pascal Victor.

VI Shakespeare at the Comédie-Française

7 productions:
HAMLET 1769, 1803, 1886, 1932,
1942, 1994, 2013

5 productions:
OTHELLO 1792, 1829, 1899, 1950,
2014

4 productions:
TWELFTH NIGHT 1940, 1976,
2004, 2018
THE MERCHANT OF VENICE
1829, 1905, 1987, 2001
ROMEO AND JULIET 1772, 1920,
1952, 2015

3 productions:
AS YOU LIKE IT 1856, 1951, 1989
MACBETH 1784, 1914, 1985
A MIDSUMMER NIGHT'S
DREAM 1966, 1986, 2014

2 productions:
CORIOLANUS 1933, 1956
THE TAMING OF THE SHREW
1891, 2007
THE TEMPEST 1998, 2017
THE WINTER'S TALE 1950, 2004

1 production:
ANTONY AND CLEOPATRA 1945
JULIUS CAESAR 2019
KING LEAR 1783
THE MERRY WIVES OF
WINDSOR 2009
PERICLES 1974
RICHARD III 1972
TROILUS AND CRESSIDA 2013

Chronology

1700-1799 (5 productions):

HAMLET (1769)
tr Jean-François Ducis
22 performances, 12 during the initial run (1769/70 season): revived
1787/88, 89/90

ROMEO AND JULIET (1772)
tr Jean-François Ducis
41 performances up until 1793, 19
during the initial run (1772/73 season): revived 1776/77, 77/78,
82/83, 85/86, 88/89, 92/93

KING LEAR (1783)
tr Jean-François Ducis
27 performances, 18 during the initial run (1782/83 season): revived
83/84, 84/85, 85/86

MACBETH (1784)
tr Jean-François Ducis
12 performances, 7 during the initial run (1783/84 season): revived
1790/91

OTHELLO (1792)
tr Jean-François Ducis

1800-1899 (7 productions):

HAMLET (1803)
tr Jean-François Ducis

THE MERCHANT OF VENICE
(1829)
tr Alfred de Vigny

OTHELLO (1829)
tr Alfred de Vigny

AS YOU LIKE IT (Comme il vous
plaira) (1856)
tr George Sand

HAMLET (1886)
tr Alexandre Dumas and Paul
Meurice

THE TAMING OF THE
SHREW (La Mégère apprivoisée)
(1891)
tr Paul Delair

OTHELLO (1899)
tr Jean Aicard; dir Jules Claretie

1900-1945 (8 productions):

THE MERCHANT OF VENICE
(1905)
tr Alfred de Vigny

MACBETH (1914)
tr Jean Richepin; dir Albert Carré

JULIETTE ET ROMÉO (1920)
tr André Rivoire; dir Émile Fabre

HAMLET (1932)
tr Morand-Schwob; dir Charles
Granval

CORIOLANUS (1933)
tr René-Louis Piachaud; dir Émile
Fabre

TWELFTH NIGHT (La Nuit des
rois) (1940)
tr Théodore Lascaris; dir Jacques
Copeau

HAMLET (1942)
tr Guy de Pourtalès; dir Charles
Granval

ANTONY AND CLEOPATRA
(1945)
tr André Gide; dir Jean-Louis Barrault

1946-1999 (15 productions):

OTHELLO (1950)
tr Georges Neveux; dir Jean Meyer

THE WINTER'S TALE (Un
Conte d'hiver) (1950)
tr Claude-André Puget; dir Julien
Bertheau

AS YOU LIKE IT (Comme il vous
plaira) (1951) Odéon
tr Jules Supervielle; Jacques Charon

ROMEO AND JULIET (1952)
Odéon
tr Jean Sarment; dir Julien
Bertheau

CORIOLANUS (1956)
tr René-Louis Piachaud; dir Jean
Meyer

A MIDSUMMER NIGHT'S
DREAM (Le Songe d'une nuit
d'été) (1966)
tr Charles Charras; dir Jacques Fabbri

RICHARD III (1972)
tr Jean-Louis Curtis; dir Terry
Hands

PERICLES (1974)
tr Jean-Louis Curtis; dir Terry
Hands

TWELFTH NIGHT (La Nuit des
rois) (1976) Odéon
tr Jean-Louis Curtis; dir Terry

Hands

MACBETH (1985)
tr Jean-Michel Déprats; dir Jean-
Pierre Vincent

A MIDSUMMER NIGHT'S
DREAM (Le Songe d'une nuit
d'été) (1986)
tr Stuart Seide; dir Jorge Lavelli

THE MERCHANT OF VENICE
(1987) Odéon
tr Jean Michel Déprats; dir Luca
Ronconi

AS YOU LIKE IT (Comme il vous
plaira) (1989)
tr Raymond Lepoutre; dir Lluis
Pasqual

HAMLET (1994)
tr Yves Bonnefoy; dir Georges
Lavaudant

THE TEMPEST (La Tempête)
(1998)
tr Daniel Mesguich, Xavier Maurel;
dir Daniel Mesguich

2000-2020 (13 productions):

THE MERCHANT OF VENICE
(2001)
tr Jean-Michel Déprats; dir Andrei
Serban

THE WINTER'S TALE (Un
Conte d'hiver) (2004) Studio
tr Claude-André Puget; dir Muriel
Mayette

TWELFTH NIGHT (La Nuit des
rois) (2004)
tr Jean-Michel Déprats; dir Andrzej
Seweryn

THE TAMING OF THE

SHREW (La Mégère apprivoisée)
(2007)
tr François-Victor Hugo; dir
Oskaras Korsunovas

THE MERRY WIVES OF
WINDSOR (Les Joyeuses
commères de Windsor) (2009)
tr Jean-Michel Déprats and Jean-
Pierre Richard; dir Andrés Lima

HAMLET (2013)
tr Yves Bonnefoy; dir Dan Jemmett

TROILUS AND CRESSIDA
(2013)
tr André Markowicz; dir Jean-Yves
Ruf

OTHELLO (2014) Vieux-
Colombier
tr Norman Chaurette; dir Léonie
Simaga

A MIDSUMMER NIGHT'S
DREAM (Le Songe d'une nuit
d'été) (2014)
tr François-Victor Hugo; dir
Muriel Mayette

ROMEO AND JULIET (2015)
tr François-Victor Hugo; dir Éric
Ruf

THE TEMPEST (La Tempête)
(2017)
tr Jean-Claude Carrière; dir Robert
Carsen

TWELFTH NIGHT (La Nuit des
rois) (2018)
tr Olivier Cadiot; dir Thomas Ostermeier

JULIUS CAESAR (Jules César)
(2019) Vieux-Colombier
tr François-Victor Hugo; dir
Rodolphe Dana

34. *Les Fourberies de Scapin* by Molière, Richelieu, 2018. Denis Podalydès (mise en scène), Éric Ruf (décor), Christian Lacroix (costumes), Stéphanie Daniel (lighting). L-R: Maïka Louakairim (Carle), Benjamin Lavernhe (Scapin), Adeline d'Hermy (Zerbinette), Gilles David (Argante), Julien Frison (Octave), Didier Sandre (Géronte), Pauline Clément (Hyacinte), Bakary Sangaré (Silvestre), Gaël Kamilindi (Léandre), Aude Rouanet (Nérine). Photograph by Christophe Raynaud de Lage.

VII Performances in Great Britain

1871 (2 May-8 Jun)
London: Opera Comique
TARTUFFE by Molière
LE MISANTHROPE by Molière
L'AVARE by Molière
LE MENTEUR by Corneille
LE BARBIER DE SEVILLE by
Beaumarchais
LES PLAIDEURS by Racine
LE JEU DE L'AMOUR ET DU
HASARD by Marivaux
LES FOLIES AMOUREUSES by
Jean-François Regnard
LES FOURBERIES DE SCAPIN
by Molière
LE MEDICIN MALGRE by
Molière
LE MALADE IMAGINAIRE by
Molière
L'ECOLE DES MARIS by Molière
LE DEPIT AMOUREUX by
Molière
L'HONNEUR ET L'ARGENT by
François Ponsard
LE DUC JOB by Léon Laya
MADEMOISELLE DE BELLE-
ISLE by Dumas
L'AVENTURIÈRE by Émile
Augier
LE GENDRE DE M. POIRIER
by Émile Augier and Jules
Sandeau
IL NE FAUT JURER DE RIEN
by Musset
LE JEUNE MARI by Édouard
Mazères
MERCADET by Balzac
VALÉRIE by Eugène Scribe

ON NE BADINE PAS AVEC
L'AMOUR by Musset
LE BONHOMME JADIS by
Henri Murger
LE DERNIER QUARTIER by
Édouard Pailleron
LES CAPRICES DE MARIANNE
by Musset
UNE TEMPETE DANS UN
VERRE D'EAU by Léon
Gozlan
LA NUIT D'OCTOBRE by
Musset
AU PRINTEMPS by Léopold
Laluyé
IL FAUT QU'UNE PORTE
SOIT OUVERTE OU
FERMÉE by Musset
UN CAS DE CONSCIENCE by
Octave Feuillet
UNE CAPRICE by Musse

1879 (2 Jun-12 Jul)
London: Gaiety Theatre
Plays by: Molière, Racine, Dumas
fils (L'ÉTRANGÈRE, LE FILS
NATUREL, LE DEMI-
MONDE), Musset, Emile de
Girardin, Corneille, George
Sand, Hugo (HERNANI),
Dumas, Émile Augier, Henri
Meilhac, François Coppée,
Octave Feuillet, Émile
Erckmann and Alexandre
Chatrian, Voltaire (ZAÏRE),
Marivaux, Théodore de
Banville, Jules Sandeau,
Édouard Pailleron, Balzac,

Emile de Girardin, Jean Aicard

1893 (ca.12 Jun-11 Jul)
London: Drury Lane Theatre
Plays by: Émile Augier, Théodore
de Banville, Jean Richepin,
Hugo (HERNANI), Dumas
(HENRI III ET SA COUR),
Henri Meilhac, Shakespeare
(HAMLET), Molière, Jules
Sanseau, Guy de Maupassant,
Édouard Pailleron, Émile de
Girardin, Sophocles (OEDIPE
ROI), Alexandre Parodi

1921 (31 May)
London: New Oxford Theatre
UNE CAPRICE by Musset

1922 (28-29 May)
London: His Majesty's Theatre
IL ETAIT UNE BERGÈRE by
André Rivoire
L'AVARE by Molière
LE MISANTHROPE by Molière
UN AMI DE JEUNESSE by
Edmond See

1922 (Nov, four-week season)
London: Coliseum
HAMLET by Shakespeare
(extracts)
GRINGOIRE by Théodore de
Banville
TARTUFFE by Molière (extracts)

1923
London: Lyric Theatre
AIMER by Paul Géraldy

1934 (May, two-week season)
London: Cambridge Theatre
RUY BLAS by Hugo
OEDIPUS REX by Sophocles
LE CID by Corneille
LE MISANTHROPE by Molière
l'INSOUMISE by Pierre Frondaie

1939 (28 Feb-4 Mar)

London: Savoy Theatre
L'ÉCOLE DES MARIS by Molière
LE CHANDELIER by Musset
A QUOI RÊVENT LES JEUNES
FILLES by Musset
LE LÉGATAIRE UNIVERSEL by
Regnard

1945 (2-14 Jul)
London: New Theatre
TARTUFFE by Molière
L'IMPROMPTU DU
VERSAILLES by Molière
PHÈDRE by Racine
LE BARBIER DE SEVILLE by
Beaumarchais
RUY BLAS by Hugo
LE BOULINGRIN by Courteline

1948 (11-30 Oct)
London: Cambridge Theatre
LE MISTHANTROPE by Molière
LE MALADE IMAGINAIRE by
Molière
ANDROMAQUE by Racine
UNE CAPRICE by Musset
LA NAVETTE by Becque
LE BOUQUET by Meilhac

1953 (4-23 May)
London: St James's Theatre
TARTUFFE by Molière
BRITANNICUS by Racine
LE JEU DE L'AMOUR ET DU
HASARD by Marivaux
ON NE SAURAIT PENSER A
TOUT by Musset

1954
Edinburgh Festival
LE BOURGEOIS
GENTILHOMME by Molière

1959 (16 Mar-4 Apr)
London: Princess Theatre
LE DINDON by Feydeau
LES FEMMES SAVANTES by
Molière
LES FOURBERIES DE SCAPIN

by Molière
UN CAPRICE by Musset

1963 (18-23 Mar)
London: Piccadilly Theatre
LE MARIAGE DE FIGARO by
Beaumarchais

1964 (Mar)
London: RSC Aldwych Theatre
TARTUFFE by Molière
UN FIL À LA PATTE by Feydeau

1967 (Apr)
London: RSC Aldwych Theatre
LE CID by Corneille
LE JEU DE L'AMOUR ET DU
HASARD by Marivaux
FEU LA MÈRE DE MADAME by
Feydeau

1970 (Apr)
London: RSC Aldwych Theatre
AMPHITRYON by Molière
DOM JUAN by Molière
LA NAVETTE by Becque

1973 (16-28 Apr)
London: RSC Aldwych Theatre
LE MALADE IMAGINAIRE by
Molière: dir Jean-Laurent
Cochet
LE MÉDECIN VOLANT by
Molière: dir Francis Perrin
RICHARD III by Shakespeare: dir
Terry Hands

1997 (30 Sep-4 Oct)
London: National Theatre
LES FAUSSES CONFIDENCES
by Marivaux: dir Jean-Pierre
Miquel

2000 (Jun)
London: RSC Barbican Theatre
LES FOURBERIES DE SCAPIN
by Molière: dir Jean-Louis
Benoit

2019 (19-25 Jun)
London: Barbican Theatre
LES DAMNÉS after Visconti: dir
Ivo van Hove

VIII Sociétaires 1680 to 2020

1 Mlle de Brie (1680)
2 Du Croisy (1680)
3 La Grange (1680)
4 Armande Béjart (1680)
5 André Hubert (1680)
6 Mlle La Grange (1680)
7 Rosimond (1680)
8 Mlle Du Croisy (1680)
9 Dauvilliers (1680)
10 Guérin (1680)
11 Verneuil (1680)
12 Mlle Dupin (1680)
13 Mlle Guiot (1680)
14 Champmeslé (1680)
15 Mlle Champmeslé (1680)
16 Michel Baron (1680)
17 Beauval (1680)
18 Mlle Beauval (1680)
19 Mlle Baron (1680)
20 Belleroche (1680)
21 La Thuillerie (1680)
22 Mlle Le Comte (1680)
23 Mlle Dennebault (1680)
24 Jean-Baptiste Raisin (1680)
25 Mlle Raisin (1680)
26 Deschamps de Villiers (1680)
27 Hauteroche (1680)
28 Le Comte (1680)
29 Brécourt (1682)
30 Jacques Raisin (1684)
31 La Thorillière (1684)
32 Mlle Dancourt 1685)
33 Mlle des Brosses (1685)
34 Mlle Du Rieu (1685)
35 Mlle Beaubour (1685)
36 Nicolas Desmares (1685)
37 Dancourt (1685)
38 Rochemore (1685)

39 Du Périer (1686)
40 Paul Poisson (1686)
41 Rosélis (1688)
42 Sévigny (1688)
43 Mlle Du Feÿ (1691)
44 Mlle de Villiers (1691)
45 Beaubour (1692)
46 Mlle Duclos (1693)
47 Mlle Godefroy (1693)
48 De Villiers (1694)
49 Baron fils (1695)
50 Lavoy (1695)
51 Du Feÿ (1695)
52 Jean Quinault (1695)
53 Mlle Fonpré (1695)
54 Mlle Champvallon (1697)
55 Charlotte Desmares (1699)
56 Manon Dancourt (1699)
57 Mimi Dancourt (1699)

58 Mlle Dangeville tante (1700)
59 Sallé (1701)
60 Ponteuil (1701)
61 Marc-Antoine Legrand (1702)
62 Dangeville (1702)
63 Fonpré (1702)
64 Du Boccage (1704)
65 Philippe Poisson (1704)
66 Mlle Sallé (1706)
67 Mlle de Nesle (1706)
68 Catherine Dangeville (1708)
69 Durant (1712)
70 Quinault l'aîné (1712)
71 Fontenay (1712)
72 Clavareau (1712)
73 Quinault-Dufresne (1712)
74 Mlle de Morancour (1712)
75 Dumirail (1712)

76 Moligny (1713)
77 Mlle Lachaise (1713)
78 Mlle Quinault l'aînée (1714)
79 Marie-Jeanne Gautier (1716)
80 Adrienne Lecouvreur (1717)
81 Duchemin (1718)
82 Mlle Quinault cadette (1718)
83 Duclos (1719)
84 Le Grand (1720)
85 Mlle Duchemin (1720)
86 Mlle Aubert (1721)
87 Mlle Jouvenot (1721)
88 Champvallon (1722)
89 Mlle Livry (1722)
90 La Thorillière fils (1722)
91 Mlle Du Breuil (1722)
92 Mlle Labatte (1722)
93 Mlle La Motte (1722)
94 Mlle Du Boccage (1723)
95 Armand (1724)
96 Mlle de Seine (1725)
97 Poisson de Roinville (1725)
98 Du Breuil (1725)
99 Charlotte Le Grand (1725)
100 Duchemin fils (1726)
101 Mlle de Balicourt (1728)
102 Montmény (1728)
103 Mlle de Clèves (1728)
104 Bercy (1729)
105 Grandval (1729)
106 Sarrazin (1729)
107 Mlle Baron petite-fille (1729)
108 Mlle Dangeville (1730)
109 Dangeville cadet (1730)
110 Mlle de La Traverse (1731)
111 Mlle Gaussin (1731)
112 François Liard Fleury (1733)
113 Fierville (1734)
114 Mlle Grandval (1734)
115 Mlle Connell (1736)
116 Mlle Poisson (1736)
117 Dubois (1736)
118 Mlle Dumesnil (1738)
119 Mlle Lavoy (1740)
120 Baron petit-fils (1741)
121 Jean-Baptiste Bonneval (1742)
122 La Noue (1742)
123 Louis-François Paulin (1742)
124 Mme Drouin (1742)

125 Deschamps (1742)
126 Rosely (1742)
127 Mlle Clairon (1743)
128 Drouin (1745)
129 Mlle Laballe (1746)
130 De Vos (1746)
131 Ribou (1748)
132 Mlle Bellecour (1749)
133 Marie-Jeanne Brillant (1750)
134 Lekain (1751)
135 Bellecour (1752)
136 Mlle Hus (1753)
137 Préville (1753)
138 Mlle Guéant (1754)
139 Mme Préville (1757)
140 Brizard (1758)
141 Dalainville (1758)
142 Blainville (1758)
143 Bernaut (1760)
144 François-René Molé (1761)
145 Mlle Lekain (1761)
146 Mlle Camouche (1761)
147 Mlle Dubois (1761)
148 Dauberval (1762)
149 Mme Molé (1763)
150 Augé (1763)
151 Antoine Claude Bouret (1764)
152 Mlle Doligny (1764)
153 Mlle Luzy (1764)
154 Aufresne (1765)
155 Alexandrine Fanier (1766)
156 Louis Henri Feulie (1766)
157 Mlle Saint-Val aînée (1767)
158 Mlle Durancy (1767)
159 Mlle Dugazon 1768)
160 Mme Vestris (1769)
161 Mlle Lachassaigne (1769)
162 Dalainval (1769)
163 Vellenne (1769)
164 Monvel (1772)
165 Dugazon (1772)
166 Mlle Raucourt (1773)
167 Des Essarts (1773)
168 Larive (1775)
169 Mme Suin (1776)
170 Mlle Saint-Val cadette (1776)
171 Louise Contat (1777)
172 Dazincourt (1778)
173 Fleury (1778)

174 Bellemont (1778)
175 Courville (1779)
176 Vanhove (1779)
177 Dorival (1779)
178 Florence (1779)
179 Ponteuil (1779)
180 Mme Thenard (1781)
181 Jeanne Olivier (1782)
182 Marie-Élisabeth Joly (1783)
183 Saint-Prix (1784)
184 Saint-Fal (1784)
185 Mlle Devienne (1785)
186 Émilie Contat (1785)
187 Charlotte Vanhove (1785)
188 Charlotte Laurent (1785)
189 Julie Candeille (1785)
190 Jean-Baptiste Naudet (1785)
191 Dunant (1787)
192 Grammont de Roselly (1787)
193 Larochelle (1787)
194 Louise Desgarcins (1789)
195 Talma (1789)
196 Mlle Fleury (1791)
197 Mlle Masson (1791)
198 Champville (1791)
199 Grandmesnil (1792)
201 Mlle Lange (1793)
202 Mlle Mézeray (1799)
203 Duval (1799)
204 Michot (1799)
205 Baptiste cadet (1799)
206 Damas (1799)
207 Baptiste aîné (1799)
208 Caumont (1799)
209 Mlle Desbrosses (1799)
210 Mlle Mars (1799)
211 Armand (Roussel) (1799)

212 Pierre Lafon (1800)
213 Mlle Bourgoin (1802)
214 Mlle Volnais (1802)
215 Desprez (1802)
216 Mlle Duchesnois (1804)
217 Mlle George (1804)
218 Louis-Claude Lacave (1804)
219 Mlle Desroziers (1804)
220 Amalric Contat (1805)
221 Émilie Leverd (1809)
222 Thénard aîné (1810)

223 De Vigny (1811)
224 Michelot (1811)
225 Rose Dupuis (1812)
226 Anne Demerson (1813)
227 Cartigny (1814)
228 Mlle Dupont (1815)
229 Monrose (1817)
230 Baudrier (1817)
231 Firmin (1817)
232 Desmousseaux (1817)
233 Saint-Eugène (1817)
234 Mme Tousez (1819)
235 Grandville (1822)
236 Paradol (1823)
237 Mme Mante (1823)
238 Mme Desmousseaux (1824)
239 Menjaud (1825)
240 Saint-Aulaire (1826)
241 Joseph Samson (1827)
242 Mme Menjaud (1828)
243 Suzanne Brocard (1828)
244 Édouard David (1828)
245 Mlle Hervey (1828)
246 Perrier (1828)
247 Joanny (1828)
248 Mlle Valmonzey (1828)
249 Pierre-Mathieu Ligier (1831)
250 Armand-Dailly (1831)
251 Beauvallet (1832)
252 Mlle Anaïs (1832)
253 Guiaud (1832)
254 Edmond Geffroy (1835)
255 Regnier (1835)
256 Mlle Plessy (1836)
257 Alexandrine Noblet (1837)
258 Jean-Baptiste Provost (1839)
259 Georges Guyon (1840)
260 Mlle Rachel (1842)
261 Augustine Brohan (1843)
262 Mme Mélingue (1843)
263 Édouard Brindeau (1843)
264 Mlle Denain (1846)
265 Paul-Louis Leroux (1846)
266 Adolphe Maillart (1847)
267 Rébecca Félix (1850)
268 Edmond Got (1850)
269 Louis-Arsène Delaunay (1850)
270 Maubant (1852)
271 Clarisse Bonval (1852)

272 Mlle Nathalie (1852)
273 Madeleine Brohan (1850)
274 Mlle Judith (1852)
275 Monrose (1852)
276 Prosper Bressant (1854)
277 Delphine Fix (1854)
278 Mlle Favart (1854)
279 Émilie Dubois (1855)
280 Anselme (1856)
281 Émilie Guyon (1858)
282 Talbot (1859)
283 Augustine Figeac (1860)
284 Henri Lafontaine (1863)
285 Victoria Lafontaine (1863)
286 Clémentine Jouassain (1863)
287 Coquelin aîné (1864)
288 Édile Riquer (1864)
289 Eugène Provost (1865)
290 Zélia Ponsin (1866)
291 Frédéric Febvre (1867)
292 Dinah Félix (1871)
293 Charles Thiron (1872)
294 Suzanne Reichenberg (1872)
295 Marie Royer (1873)
296 Sophie Croizette (1873)
297 Mounet-Sully (1874)
298 Jules Laroche (1875)
299 Sarah Bernhardt (1875)
300 Léopold Barré (1876)
301 Blanche Barretta (1876)
302 Émilie Broisat (1877)
303 Worms (1878)
304 Coquelin cadet (1879)
305 Jeanne Samary (1879)
306 Mlle Lloyd (1881)
307 Julia Bartet (1881)
308 Charles Prud'hon (1883)
309 Mlle Granger (1883)
310 Eugène Silvain (1883)
311 Mlle Dudlay (1883)
312 Gabrielle Tholer (1883)
313 Blanche Pierson (1886)
314 Georges Baillet (1887)
315 Charles Le Bargy (1887)
316 Maurice de Féraudy (1887)
317 Mlle Müller (1887)
318 Jules Boucher (1888)
319 Jules Truffier (1888)
320 Céline Montaland (1888)

321 Louis-Eugène Garraud (1889)
322 Louis Leloir (1889)
323 Albert Lambert (1891)
324 Paul Mounet (1891)
325 Mlle Marsy (1891)
326 Georges Berr (1893)
327 Jeanne Ludwig (1893)
328 Pierre Laugier (1894)
329 Mary Kalb (1894)
330 Leitner (1896)
331 Raphaël Duflos (1896)
332 Renée du Minil (1896)
333 Marthe Brandès (1896)
334 Louise Lara (1899)

335 Eugénie Segond-Weber (1902)
336 Émile Dehelly (1903)
337 Marie Leconte (1903)
338 Marie-Thérèse Kolb (1904)
339 Cécile Sorel (1904)
340 Louis Delaunay (1905)
341 Henry Mayer (1905)
342 Marie-Thérèse Piérat (1905)
343 Jacques Fenoux (1906)
344 Georges Grand (1908)
345 Charles Siblot (1909)
346 Berthe Cerny (1909)
347 Marcel Dessonnes (1910)
348 Marcelle Géniat (1910)
349 Jeanne Delvair (1910)
350 Louise Silvain (1910)
351 André Brunot (1910)
352 Madeleine Roch (1912)
353 Jean Croué (1914)
354 Léon Bernard (1914)
355 Édouard de Max (1918)
356 Georges Le Roy (1919)
357 Suzanne Devoyod (1920)
358 Émilienne Dux (1920)
359 Berthe Bovy (1920)
360 René Alexandre (1920)
361 Denis d'Inès (1920)
362 Maxime Desjardins (1921)
363 Béatrix Dussane (1922)
364 Charles Granval (1922)
365 Mlle Valpreux (1922)
366 Marie Ventura (1922)
367 Roger Monteaux (1923)
368 Pierre Fresnay (1924)

369 Gabrielle Robinne (1924)
370 Huguette Duflos (1924)
371 Jean Hervé (1925)
372 G Colonna-Romano (1926)
373 André Luguet (1927)
374 Madeleine Renaud (1928)
375 Marie Bell (1928)
376 Mary Marquet (1928)
377 Jacques Guilhène (1929)
378 Jean Yonnel (1929)
379 Andrée de Chauveron (1929)
380 Béatrice Bretty (1929)
381 Georges Lafon (1930)
382 Catherine Fonteney (1930)
383 Fernand Ledoux (1931)
384 Pierre Bertin (1931)
385 Jean Weber (1932)
386 Élisabeth Nizan (1932)
387 André Bacqué (1934)
388 Lucien Dubosq (1935)
389 Pierre Dux (1935)
390 Maurice Escande (1936)
391 Maurice Donneaud (1936)
392 Véra Korène (1936)
393 Germaine Rouer (1936)
394 Jeanne Sully (1937)
395 Maurice Chambreuil (1937)
396 Jean Martinelli (1937)
397 Henriette Barreau (1937)
398 Aimé Clariond (1937)
399 Jean Debucourt (1937)
400 Gisèle Casadesus (1939)
401 Irène Brillant (1942)
402 Antoine Balpêtré (1942)
403 Julien Bertheau (1942)
404 Jean Meyer (1942)
405 Mony Dalmès (1942)
406 Renée Faure (1942)
407 Louis Seigner (1943)
408 Jean-Louis Barrault (1943)
409 Jean Chevrier (1945)
410 Jacques Charon (1947)
411 Robert Manuel (1948)
412 Louise Conte (1948)
413 Annie Ducaux (1948)
414 Micheline Boudet (1950)
415 Georges Chamarat (1950)
416 Yvonne Gaudeau (1950)
417 André Falcon (1950)

418 Jean Davy (1950)
419 Lise Delamare (1951)
420 Robert Hirsch (1952)
421 Denise Noël (1953)
422 Marie Sabouret (1953)
423 Jean Piat (1953)
424 Paul-Émile Deiber (1954)
425 Jacques Eyser (1954)
426 Hélène Perdrière (1954)
427 Jean Marchat (1954)
428 Thérèse Marney (1956)
429 Denise Gence (1958)
430 Georges Descrières (1958)
431 Jacques Sereys (1959)
432 Jean-Paul Roussillon (1960)
433 Claude Winter (1960)
434 Henri Rollan (1960)
435 François Chaumette (1960)
436 Jacques Toja (1960)
437 Bernard Dhéran (1961)
438 Catherine Samie (1962)
439 Michel Etcheverry (1964)
440 Michel Aumont (1965)
441 Geneviève Casile (1965)
442 René Camoin (1966)
443 Michel Duchaussoy (1967)
444 Jean-Claude Arnaud (1968)
445 Jacques Destoop (1968)
446 Françoise Seigner (1968)
447 René Arrieu (1970)
448 Paule Noëlle (1970)
449 Simon Eine (1972)
450 Bérengère Dautun (1972)
451 Alain Pralon (1972)
452 François Beaulieu (1973)
453 Claire Vernet (1975)
454 Ludmila Mikaël (1975)
455 Jean-Luc Boutté (1975)
456 Christine Fersen (1976)
457 Tania Torrens (1976)
458 Catherine Hiegel (1976)
459 Nicolas Silberg (1976)
460 Claude Giraud (1976)
461 Catherine Salviat (1977)
462 Dominique Rozan (1977)
463 Francis Huster (1977)
464 Patrice Kerbrat (1977)
465 Dominique Constanza (1977)
466 Béatrice Agenin (1979)

467 Jean Le Poulain (1980)
468 Catherine Ferran (1981)
469 Gérard Giroudon (1981)
470 Yves Gasc (1982)
471 Christine Murillo (1983)
472 Richard Fontana (1983)
473 Roland Bertin (1983)
474 Claude Mathieu (1985)
475 Guy Michel (1986)
476 Marcel Bozonnet (1986)
477 Muriel Mayette (1988)
478 Martine Chevallier (1988)
479 Véronique Vella (1989)
480 Alberte Aveline (1989)
481 Jean-Paul Moulinot (1989)
482 Jean-Yves Dubois (1990)
483 Catherine Sauval (1990)
484 Jean-Luc Bideau (1991)
485 Michel Favory (1992)
486 Thierry Hancisse (1993)
487 Jean Dautremay (1993)
488 Anne Kessler (1994)
489 Philippe Torreton (1994)
490 Jean-Pierre Michaël (1994)
491 Isabelle Gardien (1995)
492 Igor Tyczka (1995)
493 Andrzej Seweryn (1995)
494 Cécile Brune (1997)
495 Michel Robin (1997)
496 Sylvia Bergé (1998)
497 Jean-Baptiste Malartre (1998)
498 Éric Ruf (1998)
499 Éric Génovèse (1998)
500 Bruno Raffaelli (1998)

501 Christian Blanc (2000)

502 Alain Lenglet (2000)
503 Florence Viala (2000)
504 Coraly Zahonero (2000)
505 Denis Podalydès (2000)
506 Alexandre Pavloff (2002)
507 Françoise Gillard (2002)
508 Céline Samie (2004)
509 Clotilde de Bayser (2004)
510 Jérôme Pouly (2004)
511 Laurent Stocker (2004)
512 Pierre Vial (2005)
513 Guillaume Gallienne (2005)
514 Laurent Natrella (2007)
515 Michel Vuillermoz (2007)
516 Elsa Lepoivre (2007)
517 Christian Gonon (2009)
518 Julie Sicard (2009)
519 Loïc Corbery (2010)
520 Léonie Simaga (2010)
521 Serge Bagdassarian (2011)
522 Hervé Pierre (2011)
523 Bakary Sangaré (2012)
524 Pierre Louis-Calixte (2012)
525 Christian Hecq (2012)
526 Nicolas Lormeau (2014)
527 Gilles David (2014)
528 Stéphane Varupenne (2015)
529 Suliane Brahim (2016)
530 Adeline d'Hermy (2016)
531 Georgia Scalliet (2017)
532 Jérémy Lopez (2017)
533 Clément Hervieu-Léger (2018)
534 Benjamin Lavernhe (2019)
535 Sébastien Pouderoux (2019)
536 Didier Sandre (2020)
537 Christophe Montenez (2020)

Works Cited

Jean le Rond d'Alembert, *Éloge de Marivaux* (Paris: Seuil, 1967)

Archibald Alison, *Travels in France, During the Years 1814-15*, 2nd ed., vol.1 (Edinburgh: Macredie, Skelly and Muckersy, 1816)

Les Archives du Spectacle, at https://www.lesarchivesduspectacle.net

Archives parlementaires de 1787 à 1860, t.22 (Paris: Paul Dupont, 1885)

Archives parlementaires de 1787 à 1860, t.70 (Paris: Paul Dupont, 1906)

Matthew Arnold, 'The French Play in London', in *The Nineteenth Century: a Monthly Review*, vol.6, no.30 (August 1879)

Assemblée Nationale website, at http://www2.assemblee-nationale.fr/

Julian Barnes, *The Man in the Red Coat* (London: Jonathan Cape, 2019)

Pierre-Augustin Caron de Beaumarchais (trans. David Coward), *The Figaro Trilogy* (Oxford: OUP, 2003)

Pierre-Augustin Caron de Beaumarchais, 'Pierre-Augustin Caron de Beaumarchais aux Auteurs du Journal', in *Journal de Paris*, n.66 (7 March 1785)

Antony Beevor and Artemis Cooper, *Paris After the Liberation* (London: Hamish Hamilton, 1994)

Paul Benchettrit, 'Hamlet at the Comédie Française: 1769-1896', in *Shakespeare Survey*, vol.9 (January 1956)

Adam Benedick, 'Obituary: Pierre Dux', in *The Independent* (28 December 1990)

Mathilde Bergon, 'Éric Ruf: La Comédie-Française doit se tourner vers l'international', in *Le Figaro* (17 July 2014)

Hector Berlioz (trans. Rachel Holmes and Eleanor Holmes), *The Autobiography of Hector Berlioz, from 1803 to 1865*, vol.1 (London: Macmillan and Co., 1884)

Nicole Bernard-Duquenet, *La Comédie-Française en tourne ou Le Théâtre des cinq continents 1868-2011* (Paris: L'Harmattan, 2013)

Sarah Bernhardt, *My Double Life* (London: Heinemann, 1907)

Yifen Beus, 'Alfred de Musset's Romantic Irony', in *Nineteenth-Century French Studies*, vol.31, no.3/4 (University of Nebraska Press, 2003)

Bibliothèque nationale de France, *Gallica*, at https://gallica.bnf.fr

Michael Billington, 'Richard III at the Aldwych', in *The Guardian* (24 April 1973)

Michael Billington, 'Michael Billington on the lessons we can learn from the richness of French theatre', in *The Guardian* (31 December 1991)

Michael Billington, 'Class Act', in *The Guardian* (10 June 2000)

Edward Boothroyd, *The Parisian Stage During the Occupation, 1940-1944: a Theatre of Resistance?* PhD Thesis, University of Birmingham (2009)

Victor de Broglie, *Sur Othello traduit en vers français par M. Alfred de Vigny et sur l'état de l'art dramatique en France en 1830* (Paris: Didier, 1852)

Peter Brook, *Threads of Time: a Memoir* (London: Methuen, 1998)

Albert Camus, 'Copeau, seul maître', in *Théâtre, Récits, Nouvelles* (Paris: Éditions de la Pléiade, 1962)

Albert Camus, *Théâtre, Récits, Nouvelles* (Paris: Éditions de la Pléiade, 1962)

Laurent Carpentier, 'A la Comédie-Française, la guerre de succession est déclarée', in *Le Monde* (19 December 2013)

Giacomo Casanova (trans. Willard R. Trask), *History of My Life*, vol.3 (Baltimore: Johns Hopkins University Press, 1997)

Laura Cappelle, 'Molière and Genet team up at the Comédie-Française', in the *Financial Times* (26 September 2017)

Laura Cappelle, 'Psyché, Comédie-Française, Paris – Review', in the *Financial Times* (11 December 2013)

Marie-Joseph de Chénier, *Charles IX, ou L'Ecole des rois, tragédie* (Paris: De l'imprimerie de P. Fr. Didot jeune, 1790)

[Harold Hannyngton Child], 'Comédie-Française in Provence', in *The Times* (28 July 1922)

Rupert Christiansen, *Paris Babylon: Grandeur, Decadence and Revolution, 1869-1875* (London: Pimlico, 2003)

Mlle Clairon, *Mémoires de Mlle Clairon, actrice du Théâtre-Français, écrits par elle-même*, Nouvelle ed. (Paris, 1822)

Jules Claretie, *Paris assiégé: journal, 1870-1871* (Paris: Armand Colin, 1992)

Paul Claudel, *Théâtre*, t.1-2 (Bibliothèque de la Pléiade, 2011)

'Georges Clemenceau (29 janvier 1891)', Assemblée Nationale website, at http://www2.assemblee-nationale.fr/decouvrir-l-assemblee/histoire/grands-moments-d-eloquence/georges-clemenceau-29-janvier-1891

Comédie-Française, *The Comédie-Française website*, at https://www.comedie-francaise.fr

Comédie-Française, *The Comédie-Française Registers Project*, at https://www.cfregisters.org

Comité de salut public (ed. F.-A. Aulard), *Recueil des actes du Comité de salut public*, t.6, entry for [2 sept. 1793] (Paris: Impr. Nationale, 1893)

Jacques Copeau, 'Un Essai de rénovation dramatique: le théâtre du Vieux-Colombier', in *La Nouvelle Revue Française*, no.57 (1 September 1913)

Jacques Copeau (ed. Claude Sicard), *Journal, 1901-1948* (Paris: Seghers, 1991)

Croix-Rouge Française, at https://www.croix-rouge.fr/La-Croix-Rouge/La-Croix-Rouge-francaise/Historique/Seconde-Guerre-mondiale/Aout-1944-liberation-de-Paris-le-poste-de-secours-de-la-Comedie-francaise-1791

Fabienne Darge, 'Éric Ruf: Redonner un lustre artistique au Français', in *Le*

Monde (12 September 2014)

Fabienne Darge, 'Un petit miracle Bob Dylan à la Comédie-Française', in *Le Monde* (22 September 2015)

Fabienne Darge and Michel Guerrin, 'La Comédie-Française doit reprendre un peu de panache', in *Le Monde* (8 September 2006)

Ian Davidson, *Voltaire: A Life* (London: Profile Books, 2010)

Alain Decaux (ed.), *L'Histoire pour tous*, n.96 (1968)

Anne Delbée, 'La crise à la Comédie-Française: Les "suicidés" du Français', in *Le Figaro* (1 March 1999)

Anne Diatkine, 'Interview [avec Julie-Marie Parmentier]: Si j'ai un pic de peur, je le cache', in *Libération* (27 July 2012)

Denis Diderot, *Paradoxe sur le comédien* (Paris: Société française d'imprimerie et de librairie, 1902)

Denis Diderot, *Œuvres complètes de Diderot: revues sur les éditions originales*, t.7 (Paris: Garnier, 1875)

Denis Diderot and Jean le Rond d'Alembert (eds.), *Encyclopédie, ou Dictionnaire raisonné des sciences, des arts et des métiers*, 17 t. (Paris: Chez Briasson [and others], 1751-1765)

Jean Donneau de Visé, *Mercure galant* (14 June 1673)

Jean Donneau de Visé, *Les Nouvelles nouvelles*, t.2 (February 1663)

Jean-François Ducis, *Hamlet: tragédie, imitée de l'anglois* (Pars, 1770)

Jean-François Ducis, *Othello, ou Le more de Venise, tragédie* (Paris: chez André, imprimeur-libraire, rue de la Harpe, 1799)

Ashley Dukes, 'Theatre and Life', in *The Observer* (8 July 1945)

Alexandre Dumas, *Hamlet, Prince de Danemark* in Paul Meurice, *Théâtre (études et copies)* (Paris: Pagnerre, 1864)

Alexandre Dumas, *Henri III et sa cour: drame historique en cinq actes et en prose* (Paris: Vezard, 1829)

Alexandre Dumas (trans. E.M. Waller), *My Memoirs*, vol.3 (New York: Macmillan Company, 1908)

Alexandre Dumas fils, *L'Etrangère: comédie en cinq actes* (Paris: Calmann Lévy, 1879)

Béatrix Dussane, *La Comédie française* (Paris: Renaissance du livre, 1928)

Electronic Enlightenment Scholarly Edition of Correspondence, ed. Robert McNamee et al. Vers. 3.0. University of Oxford. 2018

L'Express [Magazine Paris]:
   'A la Comédie-Française, les femmes prennent le pouvoir', in *L'Express* (1 October 2019)

Richard Eyre, *National Service: Diary of a Decade* (London: Bloomsbury, 2003)

Clarisse Fabre, 'La troupe de la Comédie-Française refuse d'annexer la MC93', in *Le Monde* (11 October 2008)

Clarisse Fabre and Brigitte Salino, 'L'administratrice générale abandonne le rapprochement avec la MC93', in *Le Monde* (13 November 2008)

La Fameuse comédienne, ou histoire de la Guérin (1688)

Le Figaro [Newspaper, Paris]

Financial Times [Newspaper, London]

Fleury (ed. Theodore Hook), *The French Stage and the French People as Illustrated in the Memoirs of M. Fleury*, vol.1-2 (London: Henry Colburn, 1841)

John E. Flower, 'An Armchair Dispute: François Mauriac, Jean-Louis Vaudoyer, the Académie Française and the Occupation', in *Journal of War and Culture Studies*, vol.2, no.1 (2009)

Angelica Garnett, *The Unspoken Truth* (London: Chatto & Windus, 2010)

Théophile Gautier, *Tableaux du siege* (Paris, 1886)

Colette Godard, 'Strehler at the Odéon: a French institution for Europe', in *The Guardian* (20 March 1983)

Jean-Léonor Le Gallois de Grimarest, *La Vie de M. de Molière* (Paris: Jacques le Febvre, 1705)

Olympe de Gouges, *L'Esclavage des noirs, ou L'Heureux naufrage: drame en trois actes, en prose* (Paris: chez la veuve Duchesne, 1792)

Olympe de Gouges, *Mémoire pour madame de Gouges, contre la Comédie-françoise* (1790)

Friedrich Melchior Grimm, *Correspondance litteraire, philosophique et critique*, vol.4 (Paris: Garnier, 1878)

The Guardian [Newspaper, London]:

'Mr Charles Laughton at the Comédie Française', in *The Guardian* (8 May 1936)

'Mr Laughton in Molière: Ovation at the Comédie', in *The Guardian* (10 May 1936)

Terry Hands, 'Hands Across the Sea', in *The Guardian* (23 April 1973)

Terry Hands et al (ed. Michael Billington), *RSC Directors' Shakespeare: Approaches to Twelfth Night* (London: Nick Hern Books, 1990)

Julie Hankey (ed.), *Othello* (Cambridge: Cambridge University Press, 2005)

Armelle Héliot, 'Comédie-Française, la guerre de succession', in *Le Figaro* (9 January 2014)

Armelle Héliot, 'La Comédie-Française tourne la page', in *Le Figaro* (3 August 2014)

Armelle Héliot, '*L'Ecole des femmes*, une grande leçon de théâtre à la Comédie-Française', in *Le Figaro* blog, 22 November 2011, at https://blog.lefigaro.fr/theatre/2011/11/lecole-des-femmes-une-grande-l.html

Armelle Héliot, 'Un Marivaux passionnant et passionnément interprété à la Comédie-Française', in *Le Figaro* (18 December 2016)

Armelle Héliot, 'Roméo et Juliette en plein soleil', in *Le Figaro* (19 December 2015)

Armelle Héliot, 'Le Songe d'une nuit d'été, un rêve éveillé', in *Le Figaro* (18 February 2014)

F.W.J. Hemmings, *Culture and Society in France 1789-1848* (Bloomsbury

Reader, 2011)

George d'Heylli, *La Comédie-française à Londres (1871-1879): journal inédit* de E. Got; *Journal* de F. Sarcey (Paris: Paul Ollendorff, 1880)

Histoire de la vie et mœurs de Mlle Cronel, dite Frétillon, écrite par elle-même, actrice de la Comédie de Rouen (La Haye 1739)

Ton Hoenselaars, 'Great War Shakespeare: Somewhere in France, 1914-1919', *Actes des congrès de la Société française Shakespeare* [online], 33, 2015

William D. Howarth (ed.), *French Theatre in the Neo-classical Era, 1550-1789* (Cambridge: Cambridge University Press, 2008)

Victor Hugo, *Les Rayons et les ombres* (1840)

Victor Hugo, 'Preface to Cromwell', in Charles W. Eliot (ed.), *Prefaces and Prologues*. Vol.39. *The Harvard Classics*. (New York: P.F. Collier and Son, 1909-14)

Victor Hugo, *William Shakespeare* (Paris: Librairie Internationale, 1864)

Victor Hugo, *Théâtre complet*, t.1-2 (Bibliothèque de la Pléiade, 1964)

Henry James, *French Poets and Novelists* (London: Macmillan, 1878)

Jean Knauf, *La Comédie-Française: 1944*, at https://www.lesarchivesduspectacle.net/Documents/P/P85857_8.pdf

La Grange, *Registre de La Grange (1658-1685): précédé d'une notice biographique*. Publié par les soins de la Comédie-Française. (Paris: J. Claye, 1876)

Jean-François de La Harpe, *Adresse des auteurs dramatiques à l'Assemblée nationale prononcée par M. de La Harpe, dans la séance du mardi soir 24 août* [1790] (1795)

Libération [Newspaper, Paris]

Louis XV, *Lettres patentes... pour la construction des bâtimens devant servir à la Comédie françoise, sur les terreins de l'ancien hôtel de Condé... Registrées en Parlement le 19 août [1773]* (Paris, 1773)

Émile Mas, *Comoediana: journal d'Émile Mas*, no.1, 7 octobre 1917 (Paris, 1917)

Pierre de Marivaux, *Théâtre complet*, t.1-2 (Bibliothèque de la Pléiade, 1993-94)

Patrick Marsh, *The Theatre in Paris During the German Occupation, 1939-1944*. PhD Thesis, University of Warwick (1973)

Patrick Marsh, 'Censorship in France During the German Occupation', in *Theatre Research International*, vol.4, no.1 (1978)

Mercure de France (March 1730)

Didier Mereuze, 'Nomination surprise de Muriel Mayette à la tête de la Comédie-Française', *La Croix* (21 July 2006)

Éric le Mitouard, 'Paris: la Cité du théâtre s'impose à Berthier', in *Le Parisien* (30 November 2017)

Molière, *Œuvres complètes*, t.1-2 (Bibliothèque de la Pléiade, 2010)

Molière, *Le Tartuffe, ou L'imposteur* (Paris: Imprimé aux despens de l'autheur, 1669)

Le Monde [Newspaper, Paris]:

'Entretien avec Jacques Lassalle', in *Le Monde* (21 March 1991)

Henri de Montherlant, *Théâtre* (Bibliothèque de la Pléiade, 1954)

Lucy Moore, *Liberty* (London: Harper Press, 2006)

Alfred de Musset, *Théâtre complet* (Bibliothèque de la Pléiade, 1990)

Benedict Nightingale, 'Chill comedy in this bleak French house', in *The Times* (2 October 1997)

La Nouvelle Revue Française [Journal, Paris]

Opéra (16 October 1945)

John Palmer, 'Jacques Copeau', in *The Times* (28 November 1928)

Le Parisien [Magazine, Paris]:

'Marina Hands: Le théâtre m'a sauvée', in *Le Parisien* (18 February 2015)

John Pemble, *Shakespeare Goes to Paris: How the Bard Conquered France* (London: Hambledon and London, 2005)

Fabienne Pascaud, 'Je n'ai pas un physique de perdant: Éric Ruf, patron de la Comédie-Française', in *Télérama*, at https://www.telerama.fr/scenes/je-n-ai-pas-un-physique-de-perdant-eric-ruf-patron-de-la-comedie-francaise,120633.php

Le Point [Magazine, Paris]

Ignacio Ramos Gay, 'The Comédie-Française in London (1879) and the Call for an English National Theatre', in the *Revue de littérature comparée*, vol.345 (January-March 2013)

Jacqueline Razgonnikoff, 'La Comédie-Française au Théâtre aux armées', in *Mission Centenaire 14-18*, at http://centenaire.org/fr/espace-scientifique/arts/la-comedie-francaise-au-theatre-aux-armees-souvenirs-du-front

Jean Renoir, *La Règle du jeu* (Paris: Gallimard, 1998)

Graham Robb, *Victor Hugo* (London: Picador, 1998)

Jean-Jacques Rousseau, *Lettre à M. d'Alembert sur les spectacles* (1758)

John Rudlin, *Jacques Copeau* (Cambridge: CUP, 1986)

Brigitte Salino, 'Quand Molière rencontre Tchekhov', in *Le Monde* (25 April 2014)

Brigitte Salino, 'Philippe Torreton et Jean-Luc Bideau claquent la porte de la Comédie-Française', in *Le Monde* (23 January 1999)

San Francisco Call, vol.87, no.99 (9 March 1900)

Agathe Sanjuan, Martial Poirson, *Comédie Française: une histoire du théâtre* (Paris: Seuil, 2018)

Simon Schama, *Citizens: a Chronicle of the French Revolution* (London: Penguin Books, 1989)

Virginia Scott, *Molière: a Theatrical Life* (Cambridge: Cambridge University Press, 2000)

Virginia Scott, *Women on the Stage in Early Modern France, 1540-1750* (Cambridge: Cambridge University Press, 2010)

William Shakespeare (trans. François-Victor Hugo), *Œuvres complètes de W.*

Shakespeare (Paris: Alphonse Lemerre, 1875)

William Shakespeare (trans. Pierre Letourneur), *Œuvres complètes de Shakespeare*, Nouvelle éd. (Paris, 1821)

William Shakespeare (trans. Alfred de Vigny), *Le More de Venise, Othello* (Paris: Levavasseur, 1830)

Etienne Sorin and Armelle Héliot, 'Éric Ruf: Je connais tous les recoins de la Comédie-Française', in *Le Figaro* (11 September 2014)

François-Joseph Talma (ed. Alexandre Dumas), *Mémoires de J.-F. Talma: écrits par lui-même*, t.1-4 (Paris: H. Souverain, 1850)

Philippe Tesson, 'Bourdet, l'anti-Brecht', in *Le Figaro Magazine* (1 December 2006)

Édouard Thierry, *La Comédie française pendant les deux siéges (1870-1871): journal de l'Administrateur Générale* (Paris: Tresse et Stock, 1887)

Hélène Tierchant and Gérard Watelet, *La Grande histoire de la Comédie-Française* (Paris: Éditions SW Télémaque, 2011)

The Times [Newspaper, London]:

'John Hollingshead to the editor', in *The Times* (9 May 1879)

'La Comédie Française at the Gaiety', in *The Times* (3 June 1879)

'The Comédie Française at the Gaiety', in *The Times* (4 June 1879)

'The Comédie Française at the Gaiety', in *The Times* (6 June 1879)

'The Comédie Française at the Gaiety', in *The Times* (11 June 1879)

'Hamlet in Paris', in *The Times* (30 September 1886)

'Drury Lane Theatre', in *The Times* (4 July 1893)

'Comédie Française: M. de Max in Hamlet', *The Times* (31 October 1922)

'A Comédie-Française Dispute', in *The Times* (14 December 1927)

'French Dramatists to Fight Duel', in *The Times* (19 May 1938)

'House of Molière Rides a Storm', in *The Times* (18 June 1960)

'Comédie Adapts its Style to Chekhov', in *The Times* (3 April 1961)

Andrew Todd, '*The Damned* five-star review – Van Hove's chillingly prescient masterstroke', in *The Guardian* (10 July 2016)

Alfred de Vigny, 'Lettre à Lord *** Earl of *** sur la soirée de 24 octobre 1829' in William Shakespeare (trans. Alfred de Vigny), *Le More de Venise, Othello* (Paris: Levavasseur, 1830)

Luchino Visconti, *Les Damnés* in *L'Avant-scène théâtre*, no.1404 (2016)

Voltaire, *Œuvres complètes de Voltaire* (Oxford: Voltaire Foundation, 1968-2020)

Voltaire, *Appel à toutes les nations* (1761)

Voltaire (trans. Leonard Tancock), *Letters on England* (Penguin, 1980)

Mary Ann Frese Witt, *The Search for Modern Tragedy: Aesthetic Fascism in Italy and France* (Ithaca: Cornell University Press, 2001)

Tomasz Wysłobocki, 'Olympe de Gouges à la Comédie-Française: un naufrage dramatique', in *Fabula / Les colloques, Théâtre et scandale*, at http://www.fabula.org/colloques/document5884.php

Arthur Young, *Travels During the Years 1787, 1788 and 1789* (Dublin, 1793)

List of Illustrations

1. *L'École des femmes* by Molière, Richelieu, 1973. Photo: © Patrice Picot / Gamma-Rapho via Getty Images.
2. *La Nuit des rois* by Shakespeare, Richelieu, 1980. Photo: © Manuel Litran / Paris Match via Getty Images.
3. *Le Misanthrope* by Molière, Richelieu, 2014. Photo: © Alain Richard.
4. *L'Heureux stratagème* by Marivaux, Vieux-Colombier, 2018. Photo: © Christophe Raynaud de Lage.
5. *Le Barbier de Séville* by Beaumarchais. Dazincourt as Figaro. Print. Martinet (Paris), 1786. Bibliothèque nationale de France.
6. *Hamlet* by Jean-François Ducis. Talma (Hamlet) and Joséphine Duchesnois (Gertrude). Print. Martinet (Paris), 1807. Bibliothèque nationale de France.
7. *Roméo et Juliette* by Shakespeare, Richelieu, 2015. Photo: © Alain Richard.
8. Sarah Bernhardt by Nadar, ca.1864. © Ian Dagnall Computing / Alamy Stock Photo.
9. *Les Trois Sœurs* by Chekhov, Richelieu, 2010. Photo: © Raphael Gaillarde / Gamma-Rapho via Getty Images.
10. Edmond Got by Nadar (published 1900). Bibliothèque nationale de France.
11. *Ruy Blas* by Hugo, 1879. Sarah Bernhardt and Mounet-Sully. Artist unknown. Bibliothèque nationale de France.
12. Béatrix Dussane, 1910. Agence de presse Meurisse / Bibliothèque nationale de France.
13. *L'Éveil du printemps* by Wedekind, Richelieu, 2018. Photo: © Brigitte Enguérand / Divergence.
14. *Asmodée* by Mauriac, 1937. Photo: © Lipnitzki / Roger Viollet via Getty Images.
15. *Les Damnés*, Palais des Papes, Avignon, 2016. Photo: © Anne-Christine Poujoulat / AFP via Getty Images.
16. *The Liberation of Paris*, August 1944. Granger Historical Picture Archive / Alamy Stock Photo.
17. *La Machine à écrire* by Jean Cocteau, Odéon, 1956. Photo: © Keystone Pictures USA / ZUMAPRESS.
18. *Les Espagnols au Danemark* by Prosper Mérimée. Jeanne Moreau,

backstage, 1948. Photographer unknown.

19. Michel Aumont, Isabelle Adjani and Pierre Dux, 1973. Photo: © Patrice Picot / Gamma-Rapho via Getty Images.

20. *Dom Juan* by Molière, Polish tour, January 2004. Photo: © Mariusz Grzelak / Agencja Forum / Alamy Stock Photo.

21. *Les Fourberies de Scapin* by Molière, RSC Barbican, 2000. Photo: © Geraint Lewis / Alamy Stock Photo.

22. *Tartuffe* by Molière, Richelieu, 2005. Photo: © Raphael Gaillarde / Gamma-Rapho via Getty Images.

23. *L'École des femmes* by Molière, Richelieu, 2011. Photo: © Raphael Gaillarde / Gamma-Rapho via Getty Images.

24. *Le Misanthrope* by Molière, Richelieu, 2014. Photo: © Brigitte Enguérand / Divergence.

25. Rebecca Marder at the Salle Richelieu, 2015. Photo: © Manuel Lagos Cid / Paris Match via Getty Images.

26. *Le Petit-maître corrigé* by Marivaux, Richelieu, 2016. Photo: © Raphael Gaillarde / Gamma-Rapho via Getty Images.

27. *Troilus et Cressida* by William Shakespeare, Richelieu, 2013. Photo: © Pascal Victor/ArtComPress / Bridgeman Images.

28. *Le Songe d'une nuit d'été* by Shakespeare, Richelieu, 2014. Photo: © Christophe Raynaud de Lage.

29. *Les Créanciers* by Strindberg, Studio, 2018. Photo: © Brigitte Enguérand / Divergence.

30. *La Double inconstance* by Marivaux, Richelieu, 2014. Photo: © Raphael Gaillarde / Gamma-Rapho via Getty Images.

31. *Une Vie* by Pascal Rambert, Vieux-Colombier, 2017. Photo: © Christophe Raynaud de Lage.

32. *J'Étais dans ma maison et j'attendais que la pluie vienne* by Jean-Luc Lagarce, Vieux-Colombier, 2018. Photo: © Pascal Victor/ArtComPress / Bridgeman Images.

33. *La Tempête* by William Shakespeare, Richelieu, 2017. Photo: © Pascal Victor/ArtComPress / Bridgeman Images.

34. *Les Fourberies de Scapin* by Molière, Richelieu, 2018. Photo: © Christophe Raynaud de Lage.

Index

À quoi rêvent les jeunes filles
  (Musset), 205, 215
Abbott, William, 112
Abetz, Otto, 231
Académie des sciences, 78
Académie Française, 65, 69, 231, 244
Académie Royale de Musique, 40, 45
Adjani, Isabelle, 33, 282
Adrien, Philippe, 296, 300, 301
Agan, 28
Aicard, Jean, 164
Aiglon, L'
  (Rostand), 180
Aix-la-Chapelle, 38
Albanel, Christine, 317
Albouy, Joseph Jean-Baptiste
  (Dazincourt), 81, 100, 103, 426
Aldwych
  (London), 146, 162, 269, 274, 277
Alembert, Jean le Rond d', 38, 56, 65,
  69, 70
Alexander I
  (Russia), 107
Alexandre le Grand
  (Racine), 42
Alexandre, René, 202, 214, 227, 242,
  244, 428
Algeria, 237, 264
Alison, Archibald, 107
Allan-Despréaux, Louise Rosalie
  (Louise Despréaux), 119, 122, 132
Alziari de Roquefort, Blanche
  (Mlle Saint-Val cadette), 73, 81
Alziari de Roquefort, Pauline
  (Mlle Saint-Val aînée), 72, 426
Alzire
  (Voltaire), 91

Amants, Les
  (Malle), 258
Ambigu-Comique
  (Paris), 105, 175
Amédée et les messieurs en rang
  (Romains), 258
Ami des Lois, L'
  (Laya), 99
Amour médecin, L'
  (Molière), 40
Amours de Chérubin, Les
  (Gouges), 93
Amphitryon
  (Molière), 308
Andromaque
  (Racine), 42, 106, 127, 157, 180,
  268, 272
Angelo, tyran de Padoue
  (Hugo), 126
Angels in America
  (Kushner), 345
Annibal
  (Marivaux), 54
Annonce faite à Marie, L'
  (Claudel), 237, 256
Anouilh, Jean, 203, 268, 384, 387,
  388, 402
Antigone
  (Sophocles), 157, 292
Antoine, André, 187, 204, 357
Antony and Cleopatra
  (Shakespeare), 204, 245
Apres Moi
  (Bernstein), 189
Aquitaine, 28
Arcadia
  (Stoppard), 296, 300
Archer, William, 174

Arlequin poli par l'amour
  (Marivaux), 54
Arms and the Man
  (Shaw), 246, 259
Arnold, Matthew, 127, 158, 170
Arnould, Sophie, 74
As You Like It
  (Shakespeare), 290
Ascenseur pour l'échafaud
  (Malle), 258
Ashcroft, Peggy, 202
Asmodée
  (Mauriac), 216
Assommoir, L'
  (Zola), 175
Ateliers Berthier, 347
Athalie
  (Racine), 137, 257, 295
Atrée et Thyeste
  (Crébillon), 65
Auger, Geneviève, 244
Augier, Émile, 179
Aumont, Louis-Marie-Victor d', 47
Aumont, Michel, 256, 268, 278, 290,
  364, 429
Auvergne, 53
Avare, L'
  (Molière), 51, 147, 203, 209, 278
Aventurière, L'
  (Augier), 170
Avignon Festival, 238, 256, 257, 269,
  277, 278, 293, 335, 336, 358, 392

Bacqué, André, 237, 429
Bagdassarian, Serge, 34, 36, 37, 318,
  338, 343, 363, 386, 392, 395,
  399, 402, 430
Bajazet
  (Racine), 42, 89, 127, 216, 295,
  296, 341
Bal masqué, Le
  (Lermontov), 293
Balcony, The
  (Genet), 274, 289
Balibar, Jeanne, 293
Balletti, Silvia, 54
Balpétré, Antoine, 244
Banu, Georges, 312
Barbican Centre

(London), 397
Barbier de Séville, Le
  (Beaumarchais), 78, 79, 147, 246,
  260, 282
Barbieri, Niccolò, 29
Baron, Michel, 39, 41, 47, 48, 57,
  425, 426
Barrault, Jean-Louis, 229, 231, 232,
  233, 235, 237, 238, 239, 240,
  245, 251, 253, 256, 265, 270,
  271, 272, 281, 282, 357, 429
Barton, John, 60
Bastille
  (Paris), 83, 90, 94, 347
Baulain, Sébastien, 336
Baur, Lilo, 334, 380, 382, 385, 389,
  390, 391, 395, 398
Bayser, Clotilde de, 295, 308, 341,
  342, 363, 430
BBC, 245
Beaton, Cecil, 267
Beauchamps, Pierre, 34
Beaulieu, François, 278, 279, 280,
  293, 296, 364, 429
Beaumarchais, Pierre-Augustin Caron
  de, 77, 78, 79, 80, 81, 82, 83, 93,
  103, 117, 134, 147, 158, 188,
  190, 246, 290, 383, 402
Beaunesne, Yves, 315, 319, 346, 381,
  383
Beauvais, 192
Becket
  (Anouilh), 268, 280
Beckett, Samuel, 267, 278, 283, 296,
  309, 392, 402
Becque, Henry, 175
Becquerelle, J.-B. François
  (Firmin), 118, 122, 427
Béjart, Armande, 33, 34, 37, 40, 47,
  425
Béjart, Madeleine, 25, 30, 31, 36, 40
Belfort, 331
Bell, Marie, 22, 37, 128, 205, 206,
  216, 233, 236, 239, 240, 241,
  245, 247, 251, 253, 429
Belloy, Pierre-Laurent de, 66
Belmondo, Jean-Paul, 256
Bénard, Abraham Joseph
  (Fleury), 59, 64, 65, 73, 74, 75,

89, 91, 92, 95, 96, 101, 103, 426, 427

Benoit, Jean-Louis, 297, 301, 309, 335, 342, 391

Bérard, Christian, 252

Bérénice
 (Racine), 180, 268, 289, 295

Bergé, Sylvia, 295, 334, 363, 385, 386, 402, 430

Bergman, Ingmar, 280, 397, 402

Berlin, 213, 231, 291

Berlioz, Hector, 111, 114, 115

Bernard, Jean-Jacques, 201

Bernhardt, Sarah, 65, 128, 136, 137, 138, 157, 158, 159, 160, 163, 164, 165, 166, 167, 168, 169, 170, 178, 180, 195, 204, 428

Bernstein, Henry, 189, 218, 219

Berry, Richard, 282

Bertheau, Julien, 240, 429

Bertin, Pierre, 229, 244, 429

Bertin, Roland, 291, 297, 364, 430

Besnard, Albert, 182

Bianchi, Renato, 320

Bianchini, Charles, 177

Bideau, Jean-Luc, 290, 293, 300, 430

Billington, Michael, 277, 292, 298

Bing, Suzanne, 209

Blake, William, 356

Blanc, Christian, 292, 430

Blanc, Dominique, 335, 338, 340, 341, 345, 363

Blin, Roger, 278

Bobigny, 316, 317, 324

Boissy, Gabriel, 210

Bond, Edward, 307, 335, 385, 386, 391, 402

Bonifas, Paul, 245

Bonnard, Abel, 240

Bonnefoy, Yves, 299

Bonnet, Audrey, 310

Bordeaux, 28, 102, 144, 225

Boucher, Jules, 143, 428

Boudet, Micheline, 252

Boudjenah, Nâzim, 36, 318, 323, 363, 393

Bouffes du Nord
 (Paris), 19

Boulez, Pierre, 251, 272

Bourbier, Virginie, 119

Bourdet, Edouard, 210, 212, 213, 217, 218, 219, 225, 226, 255, 257, 272, 365

Bourgeois gentilhomme, Le
 (Molière), 35, 38, 241, 255, 259, 281, 282, 297, 345

Boursault, Edmé, 34

Bourseiller, Antoine, 37

Boutet, Anne-Françoise-Hippolyte
 (Mlle Mars), 105, 106, 118, 119, 121, 122, 126, 427

Boutté, Jean-Luc, 36, 37, 294, 295, 429

Bovy, Berthe, 207, 210, 214, 428

Bozonnet, Marcel, 36, 292, 301, 307, 308, 309, 310, 311, 312, 365, 430

Brahim, Suliane, 37, 134, 318, 336, 338, 342, 363, 430

Brakni, Rachida, 308

Brasillach, Robert, 231

Braunschweig, Stéphane, 325, 331, 334, 335, 337, 347, 392, 396

Bréart de Boisanger, Claude, 265, 365

Bressant, Jean Baptiste Prosper, 146, 148, 428

Bretty, Béatrice, 227, 244, 259, 260, 429

Breuer, Lee, 318

Bridges-Adams, William, 201

Brie, Catherine de, 30, 31, 34, 36, 37, 47, 425

Brieux, Eugène, 193

Brindeau, Édouard, 135, 427

Britannicus
 (Racine), 20, 42, 81, 108, 158, 191, 254, 295, 335, 337, 338

Britten, Benjamin, 252

Brocéliande
 (Montherlant), 256

Brohan, Madeleine, 135, 143, 167, 177, 427, 428

Broken Jug, The
 (Kleist), 340, 341

Brook, Peter, 19, 178, 208, 210, 252, 253, 257, 266, 270, 271, 293

Brune, Cécile, 36, 295, 334, 340, 342, 363, 430

Brunot, André, 229, 239, 241, 244,

365, 428
Brutus
  (Voltaire), 58, 96, 97, 101
Bureau, Pauline, 344
Burgraves, Les
  (Hugo), 127
Burgundy, 210, 225
Byron, George Gordon, 111, 112

C'est la guerre M. Gruber
  (Sternberg), 282
Cain, Henri
  (Le Kain), 50, 58, 59, 60, 61, 62,
    66, 68
Caïus Gracchus
  (Chénier), 97, 101
Caligula
  (Camus), 292
  (Dumas), 126
Camus, Albert, 210, 229, 266, 267,
  292
Canada, 269
Candeille, Julie, 99, 427
Candide
  (Voltaire), 65
Capitant, René, 243
Caprice, Une
  (Musset), 132, 259
Caprices de Marianne, Les
  (Musset), 133, 134, 147, 166
Carcassonne, 177
Carné, Marcel, 240
Carré, Albert, 187, 201, 365
Carré, Marguerite, 193
Carsen, Robert, 343, 395
Casablanca, 225
Casadesus, Gisèle, 216, 252, 382, 429
Casanova, Giacomo, 51, 52
Casile, Geneviève, 268, 279, 290, 292,
  364, 429
Cat on a Hot Tin Roof
  (Williams), 257
Cathédrals, Les
  (Morand), 195
Catherine ou la belle fermière
  (Candeille), 99
Caves du Vatican, Les
  (Gide), 255, 257
Célibataires, Les

  (Montherlant), 233
Cerisaie, La
  (Chekhov), 297
Cervinka, Anna, 36, 318, 340, 341,
  363
Chacun sa vérité
  (Pirandello), 203
Chahine, Youssef, 291
Chambon, Alain, 309
Champmeslé, Marie, 47
Chandelier, Le
  (Musset), 133, 215
Charles IX
  (Chénier), 90, 91
Charles X, 120, 124, 125
Charon, Jacques, 37, 268, 269, 275,
  332, 429
Château de Chambord, 38
Château de Vincennes, 31
Châteaubriant, Alphonse de, 227
Chateauneuf, Marie-Anne de
  (Mlle Duclos), 50, 425
Châtiments, Les
  (Hugo), 141, 142
Chatterton
  (Vigny), 112, 126
Chaumette, Pierre Gaspard, 100
Chautemps, Camille, 212
Chekhov, Anton, 202, 203, 267, 268,
  278, 297, 318, 322, 340
Chemla, Judith, 315
Chénier, Marie-Joseph, 88, 90, 97
Chéreau, Patrice, 19, 289, 293, 309,
  343, 347
Chevallier, Martine, 296, 344, 363,
  364, 430
Chevillet, Charles, 47
Chevrier, Jean, 242
Chez les Titch
  (Calaferte), 282
Chiappe, Jean, 212
China, 237, 315
Christiansen, Rupert, 142, 143
Christine
  (Dumas), 117, 118, 134, 393, 398,
    407, 429, 430
Churchill, Winston, 237
Cibber, Susannah Maria, 58
Cid, Le

(Corneille), 69, 90, 104, 259, 268, 269, 280

Cinna
(Corneille), 31, 106, 108, 127

Cité du Théâtre, 347, 348

Claretie, Jules, 140, 176, 177, 178, 180, 183, 187, 189, 365

Clariond, Aimé, 37, 216, 229, 240, 429

Claudel, Camille, 238

Claudel, Paul, 209, 210, 236, 237, 238, 239, 256, 267, 278, 281, 293, 295, 309, 315, 346, 399, 403

Claveau, Marie
(Mlle du Croisy), 47

Clemenceau, Georges, 175, 176

Clément, Pauline, 335, 363

Clichy-Batignolles, 347

CNSAD. *See* Conservatoire (Paris)

Cocteau, Jean, 204, 207, 211, 231, 236, 237, 241, 254, 255, 258, 383, 403

Cœur à deux
(Foissy), 282

Colette Baudoche
(Frondaie), 188

Coliseum
(London), 203

Collège de Clermont. *See* Louis-le-Grand

Collot d'Herbois, Jean-Marie, 102

Comédie Continue, La, 346

Comédiens du roi, 27, 34, 42, 45

Comédiens-Italiens. *See* Théâtre-Italien (Paris)

Comedy of Errors, The
(Shakespeare), 358

Comme il vous plaira. See As You Like It

Comme une pierre qui
(Marcus), 339, 345

Commedia dell'arte, 29, 30, 78

Committee of Public Safety, 99, 100, 101, 102, 103

Comœdia, 210

Compagnie des Quinze, 210, 252

Compagnie du Saint-Sacrement, 35

Comte, Catherine-Caroline
(Mlle Valmonzey), 118, 427

Comtesse d'Escarbagnas, La
(Molière), 293

Confession d'un enfant du siècle, La
(Musset), 131

Confessions of an English Opium-Eater
(Da Quincey), 132

Conservatoire
(Paris), 21, 137, 192, 256, 258, 272, 273, 282, 290, 294, 307, 308, 312, 331, 347

Contat, Louise, 81, 96, 106

Conte d'hiver. See Winter's Tale, The

Contes d'Espagne et d'Italie
(Musset), 131

Conti, Prince de, 28, 29, 35

Copeau, Jacques, 21, 37, 133, 207, 208, 209, 210, 213, 214, 216, 217, 225, 226, 227, 228, 229, 230, 232, 233, 237, 252, 279, 294, 309, 357, 365

Coquelin, Constant
(Coquelin Aîné), 145, 149, 165, 180, 182, 428

Coquelin, Ernest, 143

Corbeaux, Les
(Becque), 175

Corbery, Loïc, 34, 37, 309, 319, 322, 335, 336, 341, 343, 363, 397, 399, 430

Cordeliers Club, 91

Coriolanus
(Shakespeare), 211, 212, 255, 357

Corneille, Pierre, 27, 29, 52, 56, 58, 62, 68, 69, 104, 105, 106, 108, 116, 120, 122, 126, 127, 147, 171, 190, 213, 231, 259, 264, 268, 269, 280, 356, 358, 384, 403

Couderc, Bertrand, 343

Cours Florent
(Paris), 331

Courteline, Georges, 192, 193, 246

Coutaud, Lucien, 239

Couthon, Georges, 100

Covent Garden
(London), 181

COVID-19, closure of theatres
(2020), 344, 345

Créanciers, Les
(Strindberg), 20, 342

Crébillon, Claude Prosper Jolyot de, 56

Crébillon, Prosper Jolyot de, 52, 53, 65, 66, 76

Creuzevault, Sylvain, 334

Crèvecœur-le-Grand, 192

Crime et Châtiment (Dostoevsky), 267

Critique de l'école des femmes, La (Molière), 34, 321

Croizette, Sophie, 144, 159, 160, 164, 166, 167, 168, 428

Cromwell (Hugo), 116, 117, 121, 132

Crystal Palace (London), 150

Curtis, Jean-Louis, 275, 279

Cyrano de Bergerac (Rostand), 180, 268, 310, 322, 331, 336, 345

D'Annunzio, Gabriele, 203

Dabert, Chloé, 342, 392, 395

Dacquemine, Jacques, 236

Daladier, Édouard, 212

Damnés, Les (Visconti), 336, 337, 338, 339

Dana, Rodolphe, 334, 344, 398

Dangeville, Marie-Anne (Mlle Dangeville), 50, 426

Danton, Georges, 91

Daubeny, Peter, 274, 281

Daudet, Leon, 189

Daumas, Emmanuel, 344

Dautremay, Jean, 36, 300, 332, 430

Dave au bord de mer (Kalisky), 282

David, Gilles, 318, 339, 363, 383, 386, 392, 430

David, Jacques-Louis, 96, 97

Dax, Jean, 193

Debucourt, Jean, 37, 244, 251, 255, 429

Debut de l'A, Le (Rambert), 310

Decker, Jennifer, 37, 128, 318, 321, 323, 335, 336, 340, 342, 345, 363

Déclaration des droits de la femme et de la citoyenne

(Gouges), 95

Décret de Moscou, 108

Deiber, Paul-Émile, 268, 269, 429

Déjazet, Virginie, 146

Delacroix, Eugène, 111

Delamare, Lise, 229, 242, 269, 429

Delaunay, Louis-Arsène, 135, 164, 427

Delbée, Anne, 296, 300, 301, 309

Deliquet, Julie, 340, 392, 394, 397

Delvert, Laurent, 340, 393, 397

Demerson, Anne, 118, 427

Demi-monde, Le (Dumas fils), 163, 164, 171

Dénouement imprévu, Le (Marivaux), 55

Dépit amoureux, Le (Molière), 148

Des Garcins, Magdelaine-Marie (Louise Desgarcins), 89, 97, 98, 427

Descaves, Pierre, 255, 365

Descrières, Georges, 37, 429

Desfontaines, Nicolas, 27

Desgarcins, Louise. *See* Des Garcins, Magdelaine-Marie

Desmares, Charlotte, 49, 52, 425

Desmoulins, Louis Camille, 91

Desplechin, Arnaud, 335, 345, 390, 393, 398

Destouches, Philippe Néricault, 52

Deux amis, Les (Beaumarchais), 78

Devan, Armantine Émile (Mme Menjaud), 119, 427

Diderot, Denis, 26, 50, 51, 57, 58, 61, 62, 63, 70, 77, 78

Dijon, 29, 59, 65, 147

Dindon, Le (Feydeau), 257, 258

Disraeli, Benjamin, 147, 150

Dissertation sur la tragédie ancienne et moderne (Voltaire), 76

Dom Garcie de Navarre (Molière), 32

Dom Juan (Molière), 37, 278, 293, 308

Donneau de Visé, Jean, 33, 41, 322

Donneaud, Maurice, 244, 429
Donnedieu de Vabres, Renaud, 310, 312
Donnellan, Declan, 314, 345
Dorval, Marie, 124, 126, 131
Double inconstance, La
  (Marivaux), 54, 257, 334, 335, 346
Doumergue, Gaston, 212
Drame romantique, 111, 119, 121, 177
Dréville, Valérie, 290, 292, 294
Dreyfus, Abraham, 193
Drieu La Rochelle, Pierre, 190
Drury Lane Theatre
  (London), 58, 82, 148, 173, 179, 181
Du Bus, Pierre-Louis
  (Préville), 50, 72, 78, 81, 82, 426
Dubois, Émilie, 146, 428
Dubois, Jean-Yves, 296, 332, 430
Dubuisson, Simon-Henri, 55
Ducaux, Annie, 256, 269, 429
Duchaussoy, Michel, 275, 429
Ducis, Jean-François, 68, 69, 97, 106
Duflos, Huguette, 203, 206, 429
Dufresne, Charles, 28, 52, 57, 61, 62, 425
Dugazon. *See* Gourgaud, Jean-Henri
Duhamel, Jacques, 273
Dulait, Adeline-Elie-Françoise
  (Mlle Dudlay), 181, 428
Dullin, Charles, 209, 213, 217, 225, 226, 227, 229, 232
Dumas *fils*, 160, 163, 165, 190, 276
Dumas, Alexandre, 111, 112, 113, 115, 117, 118, 119, 120, 121, 122, 126, 137, 138, 177, 178, 180, 190
Dumoulin, Évariste, 118
Dunkirk, 245
Duquesnel, Felix, 137, 138
Duras, Marguerite, 296, 308, 335, 381, 387, 391, 403, 414
Durfort, Emmanuel-Félicité de, duc de Duras, 72
Dussane, Béatrix, 192, 193, 194, 195, 214, 230, 428
Dux, Pierre, 33, 37, 235, 239, 240, 243, 244, 245, 246, 247, 251, 257, 261, 272, 273, 274, 275, 276, 277, 279, 280, 281, 282, 283, 288, 289, 290, 291, 294, 307, 332, 358, 365, 428, 429, 431
Dylan, Bob, 339

Échange, L'
  (Claudel), 209, 237
École des femmes, L'
  (Molière), 33, 34, 78, 81, 105, 202, 282, 319
École des maris, L'
  (Molière), 32, 104, 132, 147, 215
École des pères, L'
  (Piron), 76
École nationale supérieure des arts appliqués et des métiers d'art
  (Paris), 331
Effets surprenants de la sympathie, Les
  (Marivaux), 54
Églantine, Fabre d', 106
Eine, Simon, 37, 300, 364, 429
Électre
  (Crébillon), 53
  (Euripides), 337, 344
  (Giraudoux), 272
Élévation, L'
  (Bernstein), 189, 190
Elliott, Marianne, 345
En attendant Godot
  (Beckett), 278
Encyclopédie, L', 57, 69, 77, 78
Enfants du paradis, Les
  (Carné), 240
England, 22, 57, 66, 69, 89, 112, 114, 133, 145, 146, 147, 148, 160, 163, 202, 205, 210, 237, 240, 245, 254, 275
Ennemi du peuple, Un
  (Ibsen), 203
Entrée de Dumouriez à Bruxelles, L'
  (Gouges), 95
Épernon, Duc d', 28
Épreuve, L'
  (Marivaux), 55, 257
Erfurt, 107, 147
Escande, Maurice, 236, 244, 251, 264, 265, 266, 267, 269, 272,

288, 365, 429
Esclavage des Noirs
(Gouges), 94
États Généraux de Languedoc, 28
Étourdi ou les contretemps, L'
(Molière), 29, 30
Étrangère, L'
(Dumas fils), 160, 163, 164, 165,
168
Eugénie
(Beaumarchais), 78, 428
Éveil du printemps
(Wedekind), 20, 343, 346
Eyre, Richard, 299
Eyser, Jacques, 279, 429

Fabbri, Jacques, 267
Fables de La Fontaine
(La Fontaine), 315
Fabre, Emile, 106, 128, 187, 188,
190, 191, 201, 203, 205, 210,
211, 212, 231, 237, 365
Fâcheux, Les
(Molière), 34, 203
Fagan, Barthélemy-Christophe, 52
Fantasio
(Musset), 133
Farrah, 274, 275
Faure, Renée, 216, 229, 251, 255,
256, 268, 429
Fausse suivante, La
(Marivaux), 54, 292
Fausses confidences, Les
(Marivaux), 54, 192, 282, 298
Faust
(Goethe), 296
Favart, Charles-Simon, 191
Favart, Marie, 146, 149, 428
Favory, Michel, 296, 308, 363, 364,
430
Febvre, Frédéric, 146, 428
Félix, Elisabeth
(Mlle Rachel), 126, 127, 132, 148,
158, 171, 427
Féraudy, Maurice de, 188, 203, 428
Ferdane, Marie-Sophie, 314
Ferran, Catherine, 36, 297, 364, 430
Fersen, Christine, 295, 299, 429
Festa, La

(Scimone), 315
Feu qui reprend mal, Le
(Bernard), 201
Feydeau, Georges, 257, 258, 266, 269,
295, 321, 380, 382, 383, 385,
386, 387, 390, 392, 394, 395,
397, 398, 404, 412
Fil à la patte, Un
(Feydeau), 269, 321
Filippetti, Aurélie, 325
Fils naturel, Le
(Diderot), 77
Finney, Albert, 281
Fiorillo, Tiberio, 30, 31, 49
Fleuron, Lise, 194
Fleury. *See* Bénard, Abraham Joseph
Florence, 35, 177, 318, 341, 363, 427,
430
Floridor, 27
Fo, Dario, 292, 293, 399, 404
Folies Bergère
(Paris), 241
Fontana, Richard, 290, 292, 294, 430
Fontenelle, Bernard Le Bovier de, 54
Fonteney, Catherine, 203, 251, 429
Fouquet, Nicolas, 34
Fouquier-Tinville, Antoine Quentin,
103
Fourberies de Scapin, Les
(Molière), 147, 297, 342
François-Poncet, André, 211
Françon, Alain, 297, 318, 320, 334,
335, 343, 346, 380, 382, 383,
385, 386, 391, 396
Free French, 237, 245
French Poets and Novelists
(James), 145, 162
Fresnay, Pierre, 206, 210, 428
Fric-Frac
(Bourdet), 213
Frison, Julien, 335, 363
Frondaie, Pierre, 188
Furet, Yves, 244

Gabel, Jacques, 320, 335
Gaiety Theatre
(London), 160, 162, 171
Galasso, Michael, 309
Gallienne, Guillaume, 295, 296, 320,

336, 363, 399, 430
Gamba-Gontard, Adrien, 320
Gamiani ou deux nuits d'excès
   (Musset), 131
Gardien, Isabelle, 292, 293, 299, 309,
   430
Garrick Theatre
   (London), 181
Garrick, David, 58, 59, 63, 66, 67,
   68, 75, 78, 89, 209
Gascogne, 28
Gate Theatre
   (London), 202
Gaulle, Charles de, 237, 243, 264,
   268, 269, 270, 273, 288
Gaussin, Jeanne-Catherine
   (Mlle Gaussin), 50, 57, 58, 60,
   426
Gautier, Théophile, 127, 132, 142,
   177
Gence, Denise, 275, 429
Genet, Jean, 267, 272, 274, 289, 342,
   394, 404
Geneva, 65
Génovèse, Éric, 36, 295, 296, 308,
   311, 323, 336, 363, 383, 430
George Dandin
   (Molière), 38, 53, 293
Gérardin, Jeanne-Adélaïde
   (Mlle Olivier), 81
Gerbe, La, 227, 233, 239, 244
Gershwin, George, 335
Gide, André, 204, 208, 210, 245, 251,
   255, 257
Gielgud, John, 162
Gillard, Françoise, 295, 297, 308,
   310, 319, 321, 363, 389, 394,
   399, 404, 430
Gilles
   (Drieu La Rochelle), 190
Girardot, Annie, 256, 257, 258, 282
Giraudoux, Jean, 211, 216, 230, 272,
   282
Giroudon, Gérard, 292, 336, 364,
   430
Goethe, Johann Wolfgang von, 107,
   120, 296, 395, 404
Gogol, Nikolai, 297, 380, 382, 404
Goldoni, Carlo, 20, 280, 320, 343,

382, 386, 391, 396, 404, 412
Gonon, Christian, 340, 346, 363,
   381, 392, 397, 399, 430
Got, Edmond, 145, 149, 150, 164,
   169, 178, 427
Gouges, Olympe de, 92, 93, 94
Gourgaud, Françoise-Rose
   (Mme Vestris), 50, 72, 97, 426
Gourgaud, Jean-Henri
   (Dugazon), 89, 96, 97, 426
Gourmelon, Cédric, 342, 394
Grand Palais
   (Paris), 320
Grande Catherine, La
   (Shaw), 267
Grandval, Charles-François Racot de,
   51, 57, 426
Grant, Duncan, 209, 217
Granval, Charles, 203, 232, 428
Granville-Barker, Harley, 170, 174
Grasse, 234
Grenier des Augustins studio
   (Paris), 233
Gresset, Jean-Baptiste-Louis, 52
Grétry, André, 98
Grimm, Friedrich Melchior, Baron
   von, 51, 56
Grüber, Klaus-Michaël, 289
Guadet, Julien, 182
Guette, Georges, 274
Guilhène, Jacques, 203, 214, 429
Guillaume Tell
   (Lemierre), 101
Guitry, Sacha, 187, 192, 389, 404
Guthrie, Tyrone, 246
Guyenne, 28

Halévy, Léon, 121
Hall, Peter, 147, 202, 210, 265, 274
Halles, Les
   (Paris), 25, 282
Hamlet
   (Shakespeare), 68, 69, 106, 113,
   114, 116, 157, 176, 177, 178,
   179, 180, 190, 204, 232, 251,
   294, 296, 299, 323, 358
Hancisse, Pierre, 38
Hancisse, Thierry, 32, 33, 297, 308,
   314, 319, 341, 363, 388, 430

Handke, Peter, 310, 311, 312, 313
Hands, Marina, 309, 314, 315, 346
Hands, Terry, 274, 275, 276, 277,
    278, 279, 280, 281, 289, 309, 358
Hardy, Alexandre, 27
Hauptmann, Gerhart, 230
Haute surveillance
    (Genet), 342
Hecq, Christian, 318, 321, 363, 391,
    393, 396, 400, 430
Hedda Gabler
    (Ibsen), 203
Hemleb, Lukas, 37, 314
Henri III et sa cour
    (Dumas), 112, 118, 119
Henri VIII
    (Chénier), 97
Henriot, Jane, 181, 182
Henriot, Philippe, 182, 225, 244
Henry IV
    (Shakespeare), 358
Henry V
    (Shakespeare), 190, 279, 281
Hermy, Adeline d', 37, 318, 320, 323,
    332, 335, 336, 341, 342, 363, 430
Hernani
    (Hugo), 112, 120, 121, 122, 123,
        124, 126, 127, 128, 141, 159,
        164, 167, 171, 181, 321
Hervé, Jean, 237, 429
Hervieu-Léger, Clément, 34, 37, 321,
    322, 323, 325, 331, 336, 341,
    343, 345, 346, 363, 380, 384,
    388, 389, 390, 393, 395, 397,
    399, 430
Heureux stratagème, L'
    (Marivaux), 344
Hiegel, Catherine, 37, 268, 280, 292,
    297, 300, 308, 323, 364, 379,
    381, 385, 429
Hirsch, Robert, 256, 258, 267, 269,
    274, 275, 276, 332, 429
His Majesty's Theatre
    (London), 203
Hitchcock, Alfred, 206, 245
Hollande, François, 325, 331, 347,
    348
Hollingshead, John, 160, 163, 164,
    168, 169

Homecoming, The
    (Pinter), 297
Honegger, Arthur, 239
Horace
    (Corneille), 67, 126, 141
Hors la loi
    (Pauline Bureau), 344
Hossein, Robert, 128, 281, 282
Hôtel de Bourgogne
    (Paris), 27, 42, 45, 46, 47, 49, 50
Hôtel du Petit-Bourbon
    (Paris), 30
Houdar de la Motte, Antoine, 54
Hourbeig, Joël, 320
Hugo, Victor, 111, 112, 113, 116,
    117, 119, 120, 121, 122, 123,
    124, 125, 126, 127, 128, 131,
    132, 133, 138, 139, 140, 141,
    142, 147, 157, 159, 164, 167,
    171, 180, 190, 246, 278, 294,
    295, 308, 338, 356, 385, 388,
    390, 391, 393, 396, 405
Huis-clos
    (Sartre), 290
Huster, Francis, 37, 280, 301, 429

Ibsen, Henrik, 180, 202, 203, 383,
    405
Idoménée
    (Crébillon), 65
*Il faut qu'une porte soit ouverte ou
    fermée*
    (Musset), 132, 133, 147, 339
Il ne faut jurer de rien
    (Musset), 132, 147, 202
Île de la raison, L'
    (Marivaux), 55
Illustre Théâtre
    (Paris), 26, 27
Impromptu de Versailles, L'
    (Molière), 34
Inavvertito, L'
    (Barbieri), 29
Inès de Castro
    (Houdar de la Motte), 50
Inès, Denis d', 203, 229, 256, 428
Intrigue et amour
    (Schiller), 296
Ionesco, Eugène, 295

Iphigénie
   (Racine), 42, 106, 127, 137, 292,
   295
Irène
   (Voltaire), 65, 429
Irving, Henry, 173
Israel, 269
Ivernel, Daniel, 268

*J'Étais dans ma maison et j'attendais
   que la pluie vienne*
   (Lagarce), 342
Jacobins club, 101
Jalousie du Barbouillé, La
   (Molière), 209
James, Henry, 157, 161, 162
Jane Shore
   (Rowe), 112
Japan, 269
Jarrett, Edward, 163
Jatahy, Christiane, 134, 393, 395
Jaucourt, Louis, 69
Je suis partout, 231, 235, 241, 254
Jelinek, Elfriede, 310
Jemmett, Dan, 31, 315, 379, 386, 390
Jenicot, Elliot, 318
Jeu de l'amour et du hasard, Le
   (Marivaux), 54, 105, 144, 147,
   181, 258, 269
Jeunes filles, Les
   (Montherlant), 233
Jodelet, 27, 30
Jouassain, Clémentine, 146, 428
Jouvet, Louis, 209, 213, 217, 225,
   226, 256, 309
Judith
   (Bernstein), 218
Jugement dernier des rois, Le
   (Maréchal), 99
Julius Caesar
   (Shakespeare), 344, 357
Juste la fin du monde
   (Lagarce), 318, 342

Kalisky, René, 282
Kamilindi, Gaël, 345
Kane, Sarah, 307
Kean
   (Dumas), 137, 138

Kean, Edmund, 113
Kemble, Charles, 113, 114, 115
Kessler, Anne, 295, 296, 311, 318,
   320, 334, 335, 342, 346, 363,
   381, 387, 389, 390, 391, 393,
   394, 396, 399, 430
King Lear
   (Shakespeare), 70, 116, 204, 275,
   357, 358
Klephte, Le
   (Dreyfus), 193
Kokkos, Yannis, 281, 290, 296, 300
Kolb, Thérèse, 193, 428
Koltès, Bernard-Marie, 307, 314
Korder, Alexander, 241
Korène, Véra, 227, 244, 256, 260,
   429
Krejča, Otomar, 292
Kushner, Tony, 345

La Bussière, Charles de, 103
La Chapelle, 47
La Ferté, Denis-Pierre-Jean Papillon
   de, 73
La Fontaine, Jean de, 308
La Grange, 30, 31, 32, 33, 36, 37, 38,
   45, 47, 48, 49, 425
La Harpe, Jean-François de, 87
La Rose, Claude de, 47
La Rüe du Can, Claire de, 38, 318,
   335, 341, 344, 363
La Thorillière, 45
Labarthe, Samuel, 332
Lacroix, Christian, 338
Lafferre, Louis, 205, 206
Lafitte, Laurent, 134, 318, 332, 338,
   363
Lafontaine, Henri, 144
Lagarce, Jean-Luc, 318, 342, 375,
   378, 395, 405
Lamartine, Alphonse de, 112
Lang, Alexander, 296
Lang, Jack, 288, 289, 290, 294
Lange, Elisabeth, 91, 101, 103
Languedoc, 28
Laroche, Jules, 143, 428
Lasne-Darcueil, Claire, 347
Lassalle, Jacques, 20, 33, 37, 288, 291,
   292, 293, 294, 295, 307, 319,

334, 340, 365, 382, 384
Latin Quarter
  (Paris), 25, 137
Laubreaux, Alain, 235, 241, 254
Laughton, Charles, 214, 215, 241
Lavastre, Jean-Baptiste, 177
Lavaudant, Georges, 290, 299
Lavelli, Jorge, 289, 300
Lavernhe, Benjamin, 318, 342, 363,
  430
Law, John, 54
Le Kain. *See* Cain, Henri
Le Poulain, Jean, 36, 289, 365, 430
Lebreton, Noël, 47
Lebrun, Danièle, 318, 320, 332, 363,
  393, 399
Leconte, Marie, 188, 428
Lecouvreur, Adrienne, 52, 54, 426
Ledoux, Fernand, 237, 429
Légataire universel, Le
  (Regnard), 215
Legs, Le
  (Marivaux), 55
Lemaître, Frédérick, 125
Lenglet, Alain, 295, 341, 363, 381,
  383, 386, 397, 430
Lepoivre, Elsa, 36, 309, 318, 320,
  323, 334, 336, 363, 430
Leris, Clair Josèphe Hippolyte
  (Mlle Clairon), 50, 58, 59, 62, 63,
  426
Lermontov, Mikhaïl, 293
Lescot, David, 20, 391, 396, 405
Letourneur, Pierre, 70
Lettre à l'Académie Française
  (Voltaire), 70
Lettre aux littérateurs français
  (Gouges), 95
*Lettre écrite sur la comédie du
  Misanthrope*
  (Donneau), 322
Lettres françaises clandestines, 235, 240
Lettres philosophiques
  (Voltaire), 66
Limoges, 53
Lincoln Center
  (New York), 315
Lissagaray, Prosper-Olivier, 175, 176
Lissner, Stéphane, 347

Locandiera, La
  (Goldoni), 20, 343
Lois de Minos, Les
  (Voltaire), 73, 74
London, 89, 93, 112, 113, 114, 123,
  127, 138, 146, 147, 150, 160,
  163, 166, 168, 169, 179, 180,
  181, 202, 203, 206, 210, 215,
  217, 231, 237, 245, 246, 247,
  252, 260, 272, 274, 277, 280,
  281, 298, 299, 307, 336, 337,
  396, 397, 406, 422
Lopez, Jérémy, 134, 318, 336, 342,
  345, 363, 430
Lorenzaccio
  (Musset), 133, 280, 290
Lormeau, Nicolas, 128, 308, 321,
  363, 380, 385, 388, 395, 399, 430
Louis XIV, 19, 45, 49, 104, 148, 348
Louis XV, 75
Louis XVI, 79, 80, 100
Louis, Victor, 97, 182
Louis-Calixte, Pierre, 318, 338, 342,
  363, 393, 430
Louis-le-Grand
  (Paris), 25
Louvre
  (Paris), 21, 30, 97, 182, 295, 348
Love's Labour's Lost
  (Shakespeare), 358
Lucrèce Borgia
  (Hugo), 124, 125, 295, 296, 336
Lully, Jean-Baptiste, 34, 39, 45
Lune pour les desherites, Une
  (O'Neill), 282
Lyceum Theatre
  (London), 180
Lyon, 28, 29, 59, 102, 147

Macbeth
  (Shakespeare), 59, 115, 116, 190,
  357, 358
Machine à écrire, La
  (Cocteau), 258
Macready, William, 113, 150
Macron, Emmanuel, 348
Madame Butterfly
  (Puccini), 187
Mademoiselle

(Deval), 258
Mahomet
  (Voltaire), 58, 89, 97
Maintenon, Mme de, 49
Maison de Bernarda, La
  (Garcia Lorca), 282, 334
Maisons de Culture, 271
Maître de Santiago, Le
  (Montherlant), 256, 278
Maître Puntila et son valet Matti
  (Brecht), 278
Malade imaginaire, Le
  (Molière), 40, 147, 243, 245, 293,
  315, 345
Mal-aimés, Les
  (Mauriac), 245
Malle, Louis, 258
Malraux, André, 264, 265, 266, 269,
  270, 273, 288, 358
Mandel, Georges, 227
Manet, Édouard, 111
Manuel, Robert, 227, 244, 267, 429
Marais, Jean, 236, 254, 257, 258, 260
Marat, Jean-Paul, 99
Marchand, Marie-Françoise
  (Mlle Dumesnil), 51, 59, 62, 426
Marchant, Jean, 268
Marder, Rebecca, 38, 335, 341, 342,
  363
Mari, Un
  (Svevo), 292
Mariage de Figaro, Le
  (Beaumarchais), 79, 82, 93, 106,
  257
Marie-Anne de Bavière, Mme la
  Dauphine, 47
Marie-Antoinette, 74, 79, 81, 93
Marigny Theatre
  (Paris), 251, 253, 272, 273, 281,
  345, 357, 399, 400
Marion Delorme
  (Dumas), 120, 124
Marius
  (Pagnol), 241
Marivaux, Pierre de, 53, 54, 55, 56,
  105, 118, 131, 134, 147, 164,
  181, 190, 192, 202, 217, 257,
  258, 269, 282, 292, 298, 341,
  358, 382, 384, 388, 389, 391,

393, 394, 395, 396, 398, 399, 406
Marmontel, Jean-François, 38, 52, 56,
  82
Marquet, Mary, 208, 236, 429
Marrault, Pierre, 211
Marseilles, 147
Marthaler, Christoph, 325
Martin du Gard, Roger, 217
Martine
  (Bernard), 201, 202, 258, 363,
  430
Martinelli, Jean-Louis, 334, 429
Mas, Émile, 189, 213
Mathieu, Claude, 290, 334, 338, 363,
  391, 399, 430
Matinée d'une jolie femme
  (Vigée), 100
Mauclair, Jacques, 267
Maurey, Max, 192
Mauriac, François, 191, 216, 230,
  231, 243, 244, 245
Max, Édouard de, 204, 428
Mayette, Muriel, 292, 293, 297, 300,
  309, 311, 312, 313, 314, 315,
  316, 317, 318, 320, 321, 324,
  325, 332, 334, 364, 365, 380,
  381, 382, 383, 385, 387, 389,
  414, 430
Mazarin, 28
Mazerolle, Alexis-Joseph, 181, 182
MC-93
  (Bobigny), 316, 317
McKellen, Ian, 62
Médecin malgré lui, Le
  (Molière), 40, 49, 214, 292
Médecin volant, Le
  (Molière), 292
Mégère apprivoisée, La. See Taming of
  the Shrew
*Mémoire pour Mme de Gouges contre la
  Comédie-Française*
  (Gouges), 94
Menteur, Le
  (Corneille), 309
Menzel, Jiri, 292
Merchant of Venice
  (Shakespeare), 115, 190, 274, 307,
  358
Mère coupable, La

(Beaumarchais), 82

Mérimée, Prosper, 255, 257

Mérope
(Voltaire), 60, 64

Merry Wives of Windsor
(Shakespeare), 323, 345

Mesguich, Daniel, 296, 301

Meurice, Paul, 177, 178, 180

Meurisse, Paul, 255

Meurtre dans la cathédrale
(Eliot), 280

Mexico, 269

Meyer, Jean, 37, 244, 255, 256, 257,
258, 260, 265, 267, 278, 379,
381, 384, 406, 429

Michaël, Jean-Pierre, 297, 430

Michelot, Pierre-Marie-Nicolas, 119,
122, 427

Midsummer Night's Dream
(Shakespeare), 267, 289, 323, 358

Mikaël, Ludmila, 133, 268, 275, 278,
279, 280, 281, 309, 364, 429

Miles, Bernard, 245

Miquel, Jean-Pierre, 37, 273, 282,
294, 295, 296, 297, 298, 299,
300, 301, 307, 358, 365

Mirbeau, Octave, 175, 381, 406

Misanthrope, Le
(Molière), 37, 51, 106, 141, 144,
147, 160, 163, 164, 203, 216,
314, 321, 331, 335, 346

Misérables, Les
(Hugo), 258

Mitchell, Katie, 209, 334

Mithridate
(Racine), 42, 127, 295, 296

Mitrovitsa, Redjep, 290, 299

Mlle Bartet. *See* Regnault, Julia

Mlle Clairon. *See* Leris, Clair Josèphe
Hippolyte

Mlle du Croisy. *See* Claveau, Marie

Mlle du Parc. *See* Parc, Mlle du

Mlle Duchesnois. *See* Rafuin,
Catherine-Joséphine

Mlle Duclos. *See* Chateauneuf, Marie-
Anne de

Mlle Dudlay. *See* Dulait, Adeline-Elie-
Françoise

Mlle Dumesnil. *See* Marchand, Marie-
Françoise

Mlle Gaussin. *See* Gaussin, Jeanne-
Catherine

Mlle George. *See* Weimer, Marguerite-
Joséphine

Mlle Mars. *See* Boutet, Anne-
Françoise-Hippolyte

Mlle Rachel. *See* Félix, Elisabeth

Mlle Raucourt. *See* Saucerotte,
Françoise-Marie-Antoinette

Mlle Saint-Val aînée. *See* Alziari de
Roquefort, Pauline

Mlle Saint-Val cadette. *See* Alziari de
Roquefort, Blanche

Mlle Valmonzey. *See* Comte,
Catherine-Caroline

Mme Vestris. *See* Gourgaud,
Françoise-Rose

Mnouchkine, Ariane, 19, 309

Mois à la campagne, Un
(Turgenev), 297

Molé, François-René, 50, 69, 73, 80,
82, 89, 94, 97, 104, 106, 426

Molière, 23, 25, 27, 28, 29, 30, 31,
32, 33, 34, 35, 36, 37, 38, 39, 40,
41, 42, 45, 46, 47, 49, 53, 54, 56,
58, 78, 81, 104, 105, 107, 115,
116, 118, 120, 122, 132, 135,
147, 148, 149, 151, 164, 165,
171, 181, 188, 190, 192, 202,
203, 208, 209, 214, 227, 232,
241, 245, 246, 255, 259, 267,
273, 276, 278, 283, 292, 293,
308, 315, 316, 319, 321, 322,
323, 342, 356, 358, 379, 380,
381, 382, 383, 384, 385, 386,
387, 388, 389, 390, 391, 392,
393, 394, 396, 397, 398, 399,
400, 406, 414

Molière à Shakespeare
(Aicard), 164

Montaigne, Michel de, 357

Montalant, Denis-Stanislas
(Talbot), 146, 149, 428

Montauban, 92

Montenez, Christophe, 36, 318, 323,
336, 337, 339, 341, 342, 343,
345, 363

Montesquieu, 51, 54

Montfleury, 34
Montherlant, Henry de, 233, 234,
    235, 236, 255, 256, 267, 295
Monval, Georges, 169
Morand, Eugène, 195
Moreau, Jeanne, 256, 257, 260, 282
Morgensztern, Noam, 318, 340, 363,
    394
Mort de César, La
    (Voltaire), 97
Mort de Pompée, La
    (Corneille), 105, 268
Moscow, 259, 268
Mounet, Jean-Sully
    (Mounet-Sully), 128, 157, 158,
        159, 164, 165, 174, 177, 178,
        179, 190, 428
Mounet, Paul, 190, 428
Mrs Warren's Profession
    (Shaw), 259
Musica, La
    (Duras), 335
Musique aux Tuileries, La
    (Manet), 111
Musset, Alfred de, 112, 127, 131,
    132, 133, 134, 135, 147, 160,
    164, 166, 180, 190, 202, 205,
    209, 215, 232, 257, 259, 280,
    290, 319, 339, 340, 380, 381,
    383, 393, 397, 407

Nantes, 28
Napier, John, 279
Napoléon, 104, 105, 106, 107, 108,
    121, 147, 205, 264, 269, 348
Napoléon III, 135, 136
Nathan le sage
    (Lessing), 296
National Theatre
    (London), 133, 170, 202, 274,
        298, 345
National Theatre, Scheme and
    Estimates, A
    (Archer and Granville-Barker), 174
Natrella, Laurent, 295, 341, 363, 430
Naturalism, 175
Naturalisme au théâtre, La
    (Zola), 175
Naudet, Jean-Baptiste, 89, 91, 92, 94,

102, 104, 427
Nerval, Gérard de, 112
Neufchâteau, François de, 101, 103,
    104
New Theatre
    (London), 246
New York, 112, 117, 180, 209, 213,
    315, 336, 337, 339
Newton, Isaac, 53, 69
Nicomède
    (Corneille), 29
Niney, Pierre, 335
Nizan, Elisabeth, 193
Noble, Adrian, 292
Nodier, Charles, 111, 112, 117, 118,
    131
Noé
    (Obey), 252
Noel, Denise, 268
Norén, Lars, 20, 342, 395, 400, 407
Nouvelle littéraires, Les, 211
Nouvelle Revue Française, 208, 209
Nouvelle Vague, 256, 257
Nuit d'octobre, La
    (Musset), 147
Nuit de l'iguane, La
    (Williams), 292
Nuit des rois, La. See Twelfth Night
Nuit vénitienne, La
    (Musset), 131
Nunn, Trevor, 274

O'Casey, Sean, 203
Oberle, Jean, 259
Obey, André, 251, 365
Occasion, L'
    (Mérimée), 257
Occupe-toi d'Amélie
    (Feydeau), 295
Odéon
    (Paris), 76, 80, 89, 90, 102, 104,
        112, 113, 114, 131, 137, 157,
        158, 169, 181, 191, 203, 204,
        229, 252, 255, 258, 259, 265,
        270, 271, 272, 273, 278, 280,
        282, 288, 309, 315, 347, 357,
        394
Œdipe
    (Voltaire), 52, 56, 57, 65, 108

Œdipe roi
    (Sophocles), 174, 204
Oh les beaux jours
    (Beckett), 309
Old Vic Company, 246
Oldfield, Anne, 53
Olivier, Jeanne. *See* Gérardin, Jeanne-
    Adélaïde
Olivier, Laurence, 246
On ne badine pas avec l'amour
    (Musset), 132, 133, 147, 160, 180,
    257, 319
Oncle Vania
    (Chekhov), 267, 268, 340, 392,
    394
Ondes magnétiques, Les
    (Lescot), 20
Ondine
    (Giraudoux), 282
Opéra
    (Paris), 90, 99, 105, 135, 157,
    174, 181, 187, 191, 193, 295,
    347
Opera Comique
    (London), 146
Opéra-Buffa, 105
Opéra-Comique
    (Paris), 105, 181, 187, 191, 193,
    201, 295
Orbay, François d', 48
Oreste
    (Voltaire), 60
Orphelin de la Chine, L'
    (Voltaire), 65
Ostermeier, Thomas, 334, 343, 396,
    398
Otage, L'
    (Claudel), 237
Othello
    (Shakespeare), 57, 62, 71, 97, 115,
    122, 157, 255, 257, 294, 323,
    358
Oudot, Roland, 235
Ours, L'
    (Chekhov), 267

Pagnol, Marcel, 241, 407
Pailleron, Édouard, 179
Pain dur, Le

    (Claudel), 278
Palais des Tuileries
    (Paris), 75
Palais du Luxembourg
    (Paris), 75
Palais-Royal
    (Paris), 21, 32, 42, 45, 49, 97,
    104, 113, 181, 236, 320
Pamela
    (Richardson), 101
Paradoxe sur le comédien
    (Diderot), 50, 58, 61, 62
Paravents, Les
    (Genet), 272
Parc, Mlle du, 28, 30, 34, 37, 42
Parents terribles, Les
    (Cocteau), 236
Paris, 25, 27, 28, 29, 42, 49, 50, 53,
    56, 57, 59, 65, 66, 75, 76, 77, 89,
    93, 94, 97, 104, 107, 112, 120,
    124, 131, 132, 134, 135, 136,
    137, 138, 145, 147, 149, 150,
    166, 168, 169, 170, 174, 176,
    179, 181, 187, 188, 189, 190,
    191, 192, 203, 204, 205, 207,
    209, 210, 212, 215, 217, 225,
    226, 230, 231, 232, 233, 234,
    236, 239, 241, 244, 251, 252,
    254, 257, 258, 260, 266, 274,
    280, 281, 293, 295, 299, 316,
    347, 348
Paris Commune, 145
Parmentier, Julie-Marie, 33, 319
Parodi, Alexandre, 179
Parry, Sefton, 146
Partage de Midi
    (Claudel), 237, 278, 281, 315, 346
Pasiphaé
    (Montherlant), 256
Pasqual, Lluis, 290, 420
Passant, Le
    (Coppée), 137
Pavloff, Alexandre, 295, 296, 310,
    336, 340, 363, 430
Paysan magistrat, Le
    (Collot), 102
Peduzzi, Richard, 343
Peer Gynt
    (Ibsen), 246, 293, 320, 331, 332,

346
Péguy, Charles, 228
Pelléas et Mélisande
  (Debussy), 187
Pellegrin, Simon-Joseph, 52
Perdrière, Hélène, 259, 429
Père
  (Strindberg), 290, 335
Père de famille, Le
  (Diderot), 77, 78
*Père prudent et équitable ou Crispin
  l'heureux fourbe, Le*
  (Marivaux), 53
Pericles
  (Shakespeare), 274, 278, 358
Pernand-Vergelesses, 210
Perrin, Émile, 157, 365
Perrin, Pierre, 40
Persian Letters
  (Montesquieu), 51
Petit Odéon, 273
Petit-maître corrigé, Le
  (Marivaux), 55, 341, 345
Peyre, Marie-Joseph, 76
Pézenas, 28
Phèdre
  (Racine), 42, 47, 49, 60, 106, 108,
    127, 158, 163, 164, 165, 233,
    246, 247, 295, 296, 309, 347
Philinte de Molière, Le
  (Églantine), 106
Philippe I, duc d'Orléans, 29
Philippe II, Duke of Orléans
  (Regent of France), 49
Piat, Jean, 256, 268, 429
Picard, Louis-Benoît, 118
Picardy, 42
Piérat, Marie Thérèse, 203
Pierre, Hervé, 38, 315, 318, 320, 340,
  346, 363, 388, 389, 392, 430
Pingaud, Maria
  (Marie Favart), 141, 142, 144
Pinter, Harold, 297, 334, 386, 388,
  407
Pintilié, Lucian, 292
Pirandello, Luigi, 203, 216, 267, 386,
  407
Piron, Alexis, 52
Pitoiset, Dominique, 36

Plaideurs, Les
  (Racine), 132, 147
Planchon, Roger, 19, 269, 295
Podalydès, Denis, 295, 297, 309, 310,
  311, 315, 324, 331, 334, 336,
  340, 341, 342, 363, 383, 385,
  386, 388, 390, 391, 393, 394,
  396, 398, 400, 430
Poil de carotte
  (Renard), 259
Poisson, Jeanne Antoinette
  Mme de Pompadour, 65
Polyeucte
  (Corneille), 62
Ponsin, Zélia, 146, 428
Portrait de peintre
  (Boursault), 34
Port-Royal
  (Montherlant), 256, 278, 282
Pouderoux, Sébastien, 318, 339, 342,
  343, 345, 363, 390, 394, 397,
  399, 400, 409, 430
Pouly, Jérôme, 38, 128, 295, 308,
  320, 321, 363, 430
Poussière
  (Norén), 20, 342
Pralon, Alain, 268, 293, 297, 364,
  429
Précieuses ridicules, Les
  (Molière), 31, 163, 165
Préface de Cromwell
  (Hugo), 117
Préjugé vaincu, Le
  (Marivaux), 55
Préville. *See* Du Bus, Pierre-Louis
Prince de Hombourg, Le
  (Kleist), 295, 296
Princesse d'Elide, La
  (Molière), 203
Princesse lointaine, La
  (Rostand), 180
Prisonnière, La
  (Bourdet), 213
Provost, Jean-Baptiste, 69, 135, 427
Prud'hon, Charles, 143, 428
Psyché
  (Molière), 39, 40, 321
Putzulu, Bruno, 297
Py, Olivier, 307, 336

Pygmalion
(Shaw), 257

Querelle des Anciens et des Modernes, 54
Quinault, Philippe, 39, 52, 57, 61, 62, 425

Racine, Jean, 20, 42, 46, 47, 49, 56, 60, 68, 106, 108, 113, 120, 127, 132, 137, 147, 157, 158, 164, 171, 180, 190, 191, 213, 216, 233, 236, 246, 254, 257, 264, 266, 268, 272, 273, 283, 289, 292, 295, 296, 337, 341, 356, 357, 358, 380, 381, 385, 387, 388, 392, 394, 396, 399, 408, 414
Raffaelli, Bruno, 128, 295, 309, 320, 323, 363, 430
Rafuin, Catherine-Joséphine (Mlle Duchesnois), 106, 120, 427
Raimu, 241, 243, 255
Rambert, Pascal, 310, 316, 340, 394, 408
Rameau, Jean-Philippe, 90
Raskine, Michel, 318, 375, 378
Ratabon, Antoine de, 31
Raynal, Paul, 201
Règle du jeu, La
(Renoir), 134, 339, 346
Regnard, Jean-François, 193, 215
Regnault, Julia
(Mlle Bartet), 180, 193, 428
Reichenberg, Suzanne, 178, 428
Reine morte, La
(Montherlant), 233, 234, 235, 243, 256
Reinhardt, Max, 213
Rémi, Jean-François, 290, 390, 409
Rémond, Marie, 339, 390, 394, 397, 399
Renaud et Armide
(Cocteau), 236
Renaud, Madeleine, 22, 202, 203, 205, 206, 207, 214, 233, 235, 239, 251, 267, 429
Renoir, Jean, 134, 393, 395, 408
Renoir, Pierre-Auguste, 182, 206
Retour au désert, Le

(Koltès), 314
Réunion des amours, La
(Marivaux), 55
Révizor, Le
(Gogol), 297
Revue d'Art Dramatique, 182
Revue des Deux Mondes, 131
Reynal, Raymond, 188
Riccoboni, Luigi, 49, 54
Riccoboni, Marie-Jeanne, 63
Richard II
(Shakespeare), 358
Richard III
(Shakespeare), 115, 246, 274, 275, 278, 358
Richardson, Ralph, 246
Richepin, Jean, 179, 357
Rigoletto
(Verdi), 124
Rigoult, Pierre de, 240, 244
Riom, 53
Rist, Christian, 296
Robb, Graham, 113, 124, 139
Roberto Zucco
(Koltès), 314
Robespierre, Maximilien, 93, 99, 101, 103, 104, 175, 293
Rocco et ses frères
(Visconti), 258
Roi s'amuse, Le
(Hugo), 124, 180
Roi se meurt, Le
(Ionesco), 278
Rollan, Henri, 128, 256, 429
Rolland, Romain, 182, 216
Romains, Jules, 258
Roman Arena, Orange, 157
Romanesques, Les
(Rostand), 180
Romanticism, 111, 112, 131
Roméo et Juliette
(Shakespeare), 114, 336, 337, 338, 339, 357, 358
Rosner, Jacques, 281, 282
Rostand, Edmond, 180, 232, 268, 322, 386, 391, 394, 400, 408
Rouen, 29
Rouer, Germaine, 247, 429
Roundhouse

(London), 272

Rousseau, Jean-Jacques, 26, 38

Roussillon, Jean-Paul, 36, 256, 269, 278, 429

Royal Shakespeare Company, 22, 62, 133, 147, 209, 210, 266, 269, 270, 273, 274, 275, 277, 278, 279, 292, 297, 298, 348

Rozan, Dominique, 279

RSC. *See* Royal Shakespeare Company

Ruf, Éric, 20, 39, 293, 295, 308, 311, 315, 318, 320, 322, 324, 325, 329, 331, 332, 333, 334, 335, 336, 337, 338, 339, 341, 342, 343, 346, 347, 348, 349, 356, 363, 364, 365, 383, 385, 391, 393, 394, 396, 397, 398, 399, 430

Ruf, Jean-Yves, 321

Russia, 107, 108, 259, 269, 291

Rustres, Les
(Goldoni), 335

Ruy Blas
(Hugo), 157, 246, 278, 308

Saint-Denis, Michel, 210, 245, 246, 252, 265

Saint-Germain
(Paris), 21, 27, 48, 50, 75, 80, 99, 208, 294

Saint-Germain fair, 50

Saint-Laurent fair, 50

Saint-Val affair, 72

Salle Richelieu, 19, 21, 32, 56, 97, 104, 112, 118, 119, 126, 132, 134, 135, 141, 142, 143, 145, 146, 149, 157, 158, 160, 169, 175, 181, 188, 191, 214, 227, 231, 233, 242, 246, 252, 255, 258, 260, 267, 271, 273, 276, 280, 281, 291, 294, 297, 301, 308, 310, 314, 315, 318, 320, 321, 323, 332, 334, 335, 336, 337, 342, 343, 345, 347, 439

Salviat, Catherine, 268, 364, 382, 408, 429

Samaritaine, La
(Rostand), 180

Samie, Catherine, 259, 268, 275, 290, 291, 292, 296, 308, 309, 321,

364, 429

Samie, Céline, 292, 296, 430

Sand, George, 131

Sandeau, Jules, 179

Sandre, Didier, 36, 318, 332, 336, 338, 341, 342, 363, 399

Sangaré, Bakary, 36, 312, 323, 363, 430

Sarcey, Francisque, 150, 167, 168, 175, 179

Sardou, Victorien, 175

Sarrazin, Pierre-Claude, 51, 57

Sartre, Jean-Paul, 240, 266, 267, 290

Saucerotte, Françoise-Marie-Antoinette
(Mlle Raucourt), 73, 74, 103, 426

Sauval, Catherine, 293

Savannah Bay
(Duras), 308

Savoy Theatre
(London), 215

Scalliet, Georgia, 34, 37, 318, 320, 322, 338, 343, 345, 363, 430

Schama, Simon, 90

Schiaretti, Christian, 325, 334

Schiller, Johann Christoph Friedrich von, 111, 120, 296

Schillertheater
(Berlin), 231

Schlegelmilch, Kuno, 309

School for Scandal
(Sheridan), 266, 267

Scott, Walter, 111, 112

Sea, The
(Bond), 335

Seagull, The
(Chekhov), 278

Seconde surprise de l'amour, La
(Marivaux), 53, 55

Seigner, Françoise, 268, 280, 429

Seigner, Louis, 247

Seigner, Yves, 244, 269, 429

Sémiramis
(Voltaire), 59, 62, 66, 97

Serban, Andrei, 307

Sereys, Jacques, 256, 299, 364, 382, 384, 408, 429

Serments indiscrets, Les
(Marivaux), 55

Seven Years War, 66
Seveste, Jules-Didier, 143
Seweryn, Andrzej, 37, 293, 299, 301,
    307, 308, 309, 364, 430
Sexe faible, La
    (Bourdet), 213
Sganarelle
    (Molière), 31
Shaga, Le
    (Duras), 296
Shakespeare Memorial National
    Theatre Committee, 174
Shakespeare, William, 22, 59, 66, 67,
    68, 69, 70, 89, 97, 106, 111, 112,
    113, 114, 115, 116, 117, 118,
    120, 121, 122, 131, 148, 151,
    157, 164, 167, 169, 171, 176,
    177, 178, 179, 190, 209, 211,
    216, 229, 232, 245, 255, 257,
    266, 267, 273, 274, 275, 276,
    278, 289, 294, 298, 299, 307,
    309, 321, 322, 323, 336, 343,
    344, 356, 357, 358, 359, 380,
    385, 386, 387, 388, 389, 390,
    391, 393, 395, 396, 397, 398,
    399, 408, 413, 414
Shaw, Bernard, 170, 174, 203, 259,
    267
Siblot, Charles, 193, 428
Sicard, Julie, 295, 363, 430
Siège de Calais, Le
    (Belloy), 66
Silberg, Nicolas, 297, 364, 429
Simaga, Léonie, 323, 334, 388, 430
Smithson, Harriet, 114, 115
Société des auteurs dramatiques, 82
Soif et la faim, Le
    (Ionesco), 267
Sommier, Patrick, 316
Sophocles, 52, 204, 292
Sorbonne
    (Paris), 57, 271
Sorel, Cécile, 203, 207, 428
Soulier de satin, Le
    (Claudel), 236, 237, 238, 239,
    240, 256
Spring Awakening
    (Strindberg). See Éveil du
        printemps

Square, Le
    (Duras), 296
Stavisky Scandal, 212
Stern, Laurence, 112
Stocker, Laurent, 295, 320, 334, 338,
    340, 363, 383, 430
Stoev, Galin, 36, 315, 382, 384, 388,
    391
Stoppard, Tom, 296, 297, 300
Stratford, 147, 201, 265, 266, 279,
    281, 298
Stratz, Claude, 315, 381, 382, 385,
    388, 399
Streetcar Named Desire, A
    (Williams), 318
Strehler, Giorgio, 229, 273, 280, 288,
    320
Strindberg, August, 20, 180, 203, 290,
    335, 342, 390, 393, 396, 409
Studio-Théâtre
    (Carrousel du Louvre, Paris), 21,
        133, 295, 301, 309, 310, 314,
        316, 321, 333, 339, 340, 342,
        347
Sully, Jeanne, 229, 429
Surprise de l'amour, La
    (Marivaux), 54, 217
Symphonie fantastique
    (Berlioz), 114

Tableaux du siege
    (Gautier), 142
Talma, François-Joseph, 69, 71, 87,
    89, 90, 91, 92, 96, 97, 98, 99,
    103, 104, 105, 106, 108, 111,
    112, 113, 121, 157, 171, 427
Taming of the Shrew
    (Shakespeare), 190, 323
Tardieu, André, 208, 211
Tartuffe
    (Molière), 35, 36, 106, 147, 148,
        149, 192, 204, 246, 247, 259,
        269
Tasca, Catherine, 301
Taylor, Isidore, 111, 117, 118, 121
Teatre Lliure
    (Barcelona), 290
Tempest, The
    (Shakespeare), 270, 272, 299, 343,

345

Temps difficiles, Les
(Bourdet), 213, 257, 272

Tennyson, Alfred, 150

Testement du Père Leleu, Le
(Martin du Gard), 217

Thalheimer, Michael, 334

Théâtre Antoine
(Paris), 357

Théâtre aux Armées, 191, 192, 194,
195

Théâtre de Gennevilliers, 316

Théâtre de Guénégaud, 45, 46, 48, 49

Théâtre de l'Athénée
(Paris), 256

Théâtre de l'Œuvre
(Paris), 180, 237

Théâtre de la Chimère
(Paris), 201

Théâtre de la Cité de Villeurbanne,
269

Théâtre de la Michodière
(Paris), 213

Théâtre de la Nation. *See* Odéon

Théâtre de la Porte-Saint-Martin
(Paris), 125, 141, 142, 178, 180

Théâtre de la République. *See* Salle
Richelieu

Théâtre de Paris, 272

Théâtre des Amandiers
(Nanterre), 19

Théâtre des Bouffes Parisiens, 257,
260

Théâtre des Nations Festival, 270

Théâtre des Quartiers d'Ivry, 281

Théâtre du Gymnase
(Paris), 137, 236, 253

Théâtre du Marais, 45
(Paris), 27, 30

Théâtre du Soleil, 19

Théâtre Éphémère, 320, 321

Théâtre Historique
(Paris), 177

Théâtre Montparnasse
(Paris), 268

Théâtre national de Strasbourg, 289,
291

Théâtre national populaire, 19, 133,
257, 265, 268, 271, 274, 290, 325

Théâtre Populaire de Reims, 282

Théâtre-Italien, 54, 55
(Paris), 49, 50, 60, 78

Théâtre-Libre
(Paris), 180, 187

Thébaïde, La
(Racine), 42, 295, 296

Thermidor
(Sardou), 174, 175, 176

Thiébaut, Marcel, 232

Thierry, Édouard, 136, 137, 139, 140,
141, 143, 144, 149, 157, 188, 365

Thiers, Adolphe, 144

Thomé, Georges, 212

Three Sisters
(Chekhov), 318, 346

Titus Andronicus
(Shakespeare), 266

TNP. *See* Théâtre national populaire

Toja, Jacques, 256, 268, 269, 283,
365, 429

Torche sous le boisseau, La
(D'Annunzio), 203

Torreton, Philippe, 36, 292, 297, 299,
300, 430

Tosca
(Puccini), 187

Touchard, Pierre-Aimé, 253, 365

Toulon, 147

Toulouse, 28, 93

Tragédie du roi Christophe, La
(Cesaire), 290

Trancrède
(Voltaire), 127

Trautmann, Catherine, 301

Trilogie de la villégiature, La
(Goldoni), 280, 320

Trochu, Louis-Jules, 139

Troilus and Cressida
(Shakespeare), 321, 322, 345, 357

Truffaut, François, 282

Turgenev, Ivan, 297

Twelfth Night
(Shakespeare), 209, 229, 232, 278,
279, 309, 343, 345, 357, 358

Two Fathers
(Asquith), 245

USA, 269

Uzès, 42

Vaillant, Édouard, 149
Valéry, Paul, 190
Valleran le Conte, 27
Van Hove, Ivo, 336, 337, 392, 394, 397, 398
Vania
    (Chekhov). *See* Oncle Vania
Varupenne, Stéphane, 318, 338, 339, 340, 343, 363, 397, 400, 409, 430
Vassiliev, Anatoli, 291, 293, 308, 309, 333, 335, 391
Vaudoyer, Jean-Louis, 230, 231, 232, 233, 234, 236, 239, 240, 241, 244, 365
Vaux-le-Vicomte, 34
Vella, Véronique, 40, 334, 363, 381, 387, 391, 393, 395, 430
Ventura, Marie, 226, 237, 428
Venture Malgache
    (Hitchcock), 245
Verdun, 188, 194, 195
Vergier, Jean-Pierre, 299
Vernet, Claire, 297
Versailles, 34, 45, 59, 66, 159, 203, 246
Viala, Florence, 36, 295, 297, 308, 318, 320, 334, 340, 341, 343, 345, 363, 430
Vichy, 225, 226, 230, 231, 232, 235, 237, 238, 240, 245
Vie de Galilée, La
    (Brecht), 291, 344
Vie de Marianne, La
    (Marivaux), 56
Vie, Une
    (Rambert), 340
Vienna, 82, 307
Vient de paraître
    (Bourdet), 213
Vieux-Colombier
    (Paris), 21, 207, 208, 209, 210, 213, 230, 237, 294, 296, 297, 309, 310, 314, 315, 340, 342, 347, 357
Vigner, Éric, 296, 300
Vignerot du Plessis, Louis François Armand de

(Duc de Richelieu), 59, 73
Vignet, Éric, 308
Vigny, Alfred de, 111, 112, 119, 122, 126, 427
Vilar, Jean, 19, 133, 256, 265, 269, 281, 358
Villepin, Dominique de, 310
Vincent, Jean-Pierre, 37, 289, 291, 300, 365, 381, 383, 384, 386, 389, 403
Vitez, Antoine, 281, 282, 288, 289, 290, 293, 294, 307, 312, 344, 365
Vitold, Michel, 267
Vivaise, Caroline de, 322
Voix humaine, La
    (Cocteau), 207, 236
Voltaire, 26, 27, 49, 51, 52, 53, 54, 55, 56, 57, 58, 59, 60, 61, 62, 64, 65, 66, 67, 68, 69, 70, 71, 73, 74, 75, 76, 77, 82, 89, 91, 96, 97, 99, 100, 101, 108, 113, 114, 116, 127, 135, 158, 171, 177, 181, 218, 276, 356, 359, 385, 387, 409
Volupté de l'honneur
    (Pirandello), 267
Vuillermoz, Michel, 36, 310, 320, 343, 345, 363, 390, 430

Wailly, Charles de, 76
Walpole, Horace, 58, 67, 100
Warner, Deborah, 293, 314, 325, 394
Watteau, Antoine, 49
Weber, Jean, 34, 214, 255, 428, 429
Wedekind, Frank, 20, 203, 343, 395, 409
Weimer, Marguerite-Joséphine
    (Mlle George), 106, 125, 427
Wieland, Christoph Martin, 107
Williams, Tennessee, 318
Wilson, Georges, 281
Wilson, Robert, 308, 312, 315
Winter, Claude, 259, 269, 289, 365, 429
Winter's Tale, The
    (Shakespeare), 209, 257, 309
Wion, Emmauelle, 308
Woman Killed With Kindness, A
    (Heywood), 209
Woolfenden, Guy, 275

Yonnel, Jean, 227, 247, 260, 429
Young, Arthur, 76
Younge, Elizabeth, 58

Zahonero, Coraly, 295, 321, 334,
  363, 392, 430
Zaïre

(Voltaire), 56, 57, 58, 59, 65, 90,
  158
Zamacoïs, Miguel, 194
Zamore et Mirza. See Esclavage des
  noirs, L'
Zay, Jean, 212, 225
Zeffirelli, Franco, 133, 280
Zola, Emile, 175